Musa Dagh Girl:

Daughter of Armenian Genocide Survivors

by

Virginia Matosian Apelian

xulon
PRESS

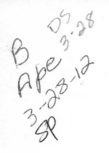

Copyright © 2011 by Virginia (Matosian) Apelian

Musa Dagh Girl: Daughter of Armenian Genocide Survivors
by Virginia (Matosian) Apelian

Printed in the United States of America

ISBN 9781612155517

To contact the author, write to Virginia Apelian,
15 Bromley Drive, Parsippany, NJ 07054.

Unless otherwise indicated, Bible quotations are taken from the *King James Version* of the Bible.

Artwork © 2011 by author Virginia (Matosian) Apelian.

Nickel Artistic Services LLC, Rockaway, NJ, provided graphics composition for the covers and spine.

www.xulonpress.com

A Brief Review

In this most compelling and inspirational memoir, **Musa Dagh Girl: Daughter of Armenian Genocide Survivors**, Virginia Matosian Apelian tells of her loving upbringing against a dark historical background.

The narrative takes the reader, step by step, as a young girl arrives in America full of dreams, but experiences culture shock. Eventually, her dreams are realized through hard work, loving parents, and, especially, faith in God. The author appeals to the very young and old with loving fervor as she tells her story of deportation, refugee camps, and the historical background of her people—the Armenians.

The author recounts the First Genocide of the 20th century with all its ugly ramifications, one which was waged by the Ottoman Turkish Empire against Armenians. The event shocked the world in 1915 and continues to impact foreign relations policies today.

It is highly educational for readers of all ages to understand the historical struggles of Armenians. Yet, how engaged the young Vergine Matosian became to climb the ladder to success despite the obstacles facing her. Her American patriotism is glowing and unyielding. Having been told by her parents and having studied other governments, including those in the Middle East, she acknowledges that the United States is the best country in the world—not perfect, but the best.

The author is a positive person who enjoys life fully. Her childhood was one of great memories and learned lessons. The emergence of Apelian's American life shows a dignified level of growth, respect for human beings, and love of country. Most importantly, she praises Almighty God for all of His blessings.

This book is dedicated to my beloved parents,
Christina and Hagop (James) Matosian,
who gave their unconditional love abundantly
and instilled the faith of God in me.

Their super exemplary life lessons of courage, dedication,
hard work, integrity and endurance
will remain with me forever.

4-19-11
In Celebration of Life
& 'Human Rights', I donate
this book to the Clark Library.
Best wishes to you all!

Virginia
Apelian

Contents

Foreword

Written with passion and vision, *Musa Dagh Girl: Daughter of Armenian Genocide Survivors* makes a compelling read. Virginia Apelian, the Turkish-born author, outlines how the lessons of Armenian history are relevant today.

Despite its focus on gut-wrenching suffering and mass killings, the memoir ends on a note of optimism: through hardship, people become resilient. By being content with what they have, people gain happiness.

As a Morris County Freeholder, I met the author in the 1970s when she was a Councilperson in Clark, N.J. We served together on the Board of the N.J. Association For Elected Women Officials (NJAFEWO). The purpose of the organization was to raise the visibility of women officials and to encourage more to enter the political arena, worthy goals we continue to pursue.

Virginia proudly touts her Armenian heritage, one of the world's oldest, going back over 3,000 years in an area known as "the cradle of civilization." Over the centuries, foreign empires, including Persia, Babylon and Rome, ruled the Armenians. In 301 A.D. the Kingdom of Armenia was the first government to declare Christianity as its state religion.

Turkey, Russia and Iran border the mountainous, landlocked Republic of Armenia with a population of over 3 million. Fleeing from persecution and/or seeking a better life, approximately 8 million Armenians live abroad, many in the U.S. Armenian-Americans make substantial contributions in diverse fields from politics and real estate to science and sports.

The author came to New Jersey from Ainjar, Lebanon as a girl of 12. She struggled to learn English by studying late at night to bring 15-20 new words into her vocabulary each day. She met her Armenian husband right after high school graduation at an event commemorating the 40th anniversary of the battle of Musa Dagh in 1915.

At that battle the Armenians bravely held their ground against the Turks, losing only 18 brave men. Buttressed by their faith and bravery, the Armenians survived on a mountaintop (including Virginia's mom and both sets of grandparents) until rescued by a French battleship, which took them to Port Said, Egypt. As part of the Ottoman Empire, the Turks continued their effort to wipe out the Armenians until after World War I.

Virginia rightly reveals her honors and accomplishments. After graduating with high honors from Union County College in 1973, while being a full-time mother to her four beautiful children, she immediately transferred to Douglass College of Rutgers University.

As an educator and a politician, she continues to remind her people of their heritage. People who do not remember history are bound to repeat it. For years in New Jersey she served on the Governor's Ethnic Advisory Council, delivering proclamations about Armenian Genocide to many Armenian organizations and churches and participating in cultural festivals.

Widely traveled, Virginia appreciates the freedoms provided by the U.S. Constitution. A strong patriot, she passionately advocates for human rights.

As part of her legacy to her children and grandchildren, she wrote this book. It is rich in history, human struggles and triumphs all in one, and will be an inspiration to many old and young.

Leanna Brown
CEO, Brown Global Enterprises, LLC
Member, NJ Advisory Committee to the
U.S. Commission on Civil Rights
NJ State Senator, 1984–1993

PART ONE:

Genocide

The First Genocide of the 20ᵗʰ Century

"I should like to see any power in this world destroy this race, this small tribe of unimportant people whose history is ended, whose wars have been fought and lost, whose structures have crumbled, whose literature is unread, whose music is unheard, and whose prayers are no more answered. Go ahead, destroy this race! Destroy Armenia! See if you can do it. Send them from their homes into the desert. Let them have neither bread nor water. Burn their homes and churches. Then, see if they will not laugh again, see if they will not sing and pray again. For, when two of them meet anywhere in the world, see if they will not create a New Armenia."

William Saroyan
(From a poster by Zaven Khanjian)

The word "genocide" is an ugly one. It is even uglier when one reads about it. Most importantly, it is ugliest of all when people are victims of it and the slaughter of human blood flows.

Major dictionaries define "genocide" as: *The American College Dictionary*— "the extermination of a national or racial group as a planned move"; *New*

Webster's Dictionary—"race murder"; *Random House Webster's Dictionary*—"planned extermination of a national or racial group"; and *The American Heritage Dictionary of the English Language*—"the systematic annihilation of a racial group." The word "genocide" was coined by Raphael Lemkin in 1944 from the root words *genos* (Greek for "race") and *cide* (Latin for "killing").

Who was Raphael Lemkin? He was a Polish lawyer of Jewish descent (1900–1959). Close to his heart was the Jewish Holocaust, which had claimed the lives of forty-nine members of his family. During his research, he came across the Armenian nation's extermination by the Ottoman Turkish Empire. These were the Armenian massacres of 1915–1923, a quarter of a century before the Jewish Holocaust. Lemkin, after reading about the planned killings and suffering of the Armenians, believed that these were definitely genocide committed by the Turks. As a matter of fact, prior to that, Winston Churchill called this event a "crime without a name," so writes Tanya Elder in the *Journal of Genocide Research* (2005). Until his death in 1959, Lemkin worked tirelessly for ratification of the International Convention on the Prevention and Punishment of the Crime of Genocide.

Prelude to the Genocide

There were a total of thirty-five Sultans at the House of Osman. The first ten were empire builders; the last twenty-five were the cause of the decline and demise of the Ottoman Empire. They were all despots who ruled the Empire with iron fists. Most of them were totalitarian terrorists, ruling their Empire with violence and oppression. The last Sultan was Abdul Hamid II, who ended the Empire by his incompetence and severe cruelty. Thus, the Ottoman Empire, the Osman's dynasty, was concluded.

Hamid's thirty-five year reign was filled with conspiracy and ruthless brutality. He was obsessed about his personal safety and did not trust anyone. He built maximum security around his palace and called his political ministers "parasites." He was a man filled with fear and hatred. He had established a big network of spies to check on everyone who came in contact with him. He fixed his domestic and foreign policies on the basis of Islamic fundamentalism. His main aim was to propagate the Islamic supremacy throughout the Empire.

Until the start of the 19th century, Armenians were considered the most faithful subjects of the Ottoman Empire. Turks looked up to the Armenians as their leaders, economists, and as advisers to the Sultan. This relationship helped both sides by making Armenians rich and the Turks well-informed. The economic growth continued through the non-Turkish merchant class. For example, the Armenians, the Greeks, and the Jews all had the business savvy to prosper with the economic and financial structures that the Sultan depended on. However, of these three groups, the Armenians were the most trustworthy towards the state. Although the Jews were also good merchants, they were discriminated against in Europe and, thus, received less favoritism from the European merchant houses. They gradually migrated to other countries for better opportunities, causing their communities to decline in Turkey. On the other hand, the Greeks were skilled in maritime commerce. But they began to lose their special privileges due to their resistance to Ottoman rule during the first quarter of 19th century. This gave an opportunity for the Armenians to move into areas which were previously held by Jews and Greeks.

Thus, the Armenians became central players in Turkish industrial development during the Ottoman Empire. At times of financial fallout and other difficulties, the Armenian bankers in Constantinople (Istanbul) often rescued the Empire from enormous economic collapse. This ability may have appeared as a great success for the Armenians, but the future implications frightened the Turkish Empire. They were depending too much on the Armenians' knowledge. Resentment soon was building rapidly and the repercussions began to be felt soon after.

The Turkish Empire was awakening to several obvious facts. The Armenians were Christian; they would never leave their Christian heritage. Also, the Armenians living in the Ottoman Empire held on to their traditional national identity and culture. All this made the Turks deeply concerned. Resentment grew more and more among the Turkish leaders, who wanted to propagate their Islamic faith and to crush all non-Islamic presence within the Empire. The leaders began their machinations to get rid of all these Armenians, no matter how loyal they had been thus far to the Ottoman Empire.

During 1894–1896, Sultan Abdul Hamid II's killings began, moving from one province to another. In Trabizond, the Turks attacked the Armenians and murdered over 1,000 people within a few days. The killings in Erzirjan came next, where 1,200 Armenians were butchered. The Turks move on to Bitlis, where the same fate was visited on the shop owners, who were all killed with bayonets. The town of Arapgir was set on fire. Young Armenian boys were covered by brush weed, which toasted them to death. Thousands of young Armenian soldiers who had served in the Ottoman Empire's army were taken to jail, had their guns seized, and were hung, one by one. The young maidens were carried off to the Turkish harems of the Moslem pashas (lords). Some of them were raped by the Turkish troops in a crowded church while the mullahs were reading verses from the *Koran*. In Sivas, 5,000 Armenian men, women, and children were slaughtered. In many other villages, thousands of Armenian bodies were cut in half at their waist and thrown by the roadsides.

The Sultan's principal adviser was Shakir Pasha, whose *modus operandi* was to gather all uneducated Moslems, young and old, in a big mosque and tell them that the Armenians wanted to destroy the Islamic faith. He ordered them to get out and kill the Armenians in the name of Mohammed, their prophet. After this meeting, a bugle call ordered the troops to get out and begin attacking. Followed by the Kurds, who were very brutal, the Moslems looted Armenian houses and shops and chased the victims to the mountains where they finished them off. As if that was not bad enough, they stripped the dead of their clothes and left them naked where wild animals could come and feed themselves.

One of the worst scenes happened in Urfa. The Turkish officer in charge of the extermination program ordered the Moslem mob to go to the Armenian quarter, ransack the houses and shops, and kill all the Armenian men above a certain age. Then he told them to bring the children in front of the mosque. The mob tied their hands and feet and forced them to lie down on their backs. Then, the Turkish officer in a routine way cut the throats of the children, one by one, while he was reciting verses from the *Koran*. The parents, witnessing this, ran sobbing into a church to pray. The Turkish mob followed them, broke down the door and started the slaughter. Right after that, they poured kerosene around the church and burned the people alive. Historian Douglas recounts more horrific acts by the Turks on the Armenians, but I must confess that I do not have the heart to continue listing those monstrous acts.

These massacres caused outrage all over the world. The European press reported all the gory details through the eyes of witnesses—foreign reporters and missionaries—who were able to smuggle photos also. The Diaspora Armenians made crucial appeals for help. The great powers urged the Sultan to stop the bloodshed. The Sultan finally listened because the Western powers were encouraged by their presses to send troops to topple the Sultan. Even the Turkish and the entire public opinion were against him.

The Armenian revolutionaries at this point, who were called the Tashnag party, were very angry and frustrated because the Western powers did not put a stop to all this from the very start. In 1896, the Tashnags seized the Ottoman Central Bank in Constantinople. They thought this action should capture the attention of the world. It did. The idea was not to rob the bank, but to seize it to show their anger and frustration in order to protect the Armenians. They demanded the cessation of the Turkish terror and killings in all of the Armenian provinces. They were determined to blow up the bank, they said. Hence, the foreign ambassadors intervened and the Tashnags released the hostages with no damage to the bank. The Turks sought revenge immediately. They butchered another 6,000 Armenians, spreading their bodies on the streets for wild dogs to feed on.

Finally, this massacre was over. Western Armenia was in ruins and over a quarter million Armenians were butchered. In total, 13 towns, 1,000 villages, and 20 districts were in ruin. At this point, an estimated 300,000 Armenians were dead. Many thousands of Armenians had fled to Europe and America, and 1,000 were left homeless. At a speech to his people, British Prime Minister William Gladstone branded the Ottoman Empire as a "disgrace to civilization" and continued, saying that the "Turks were the curse of mankind," and "the Sultan Hamid is the assassin."

The French press called Hamid the "Red Sultan" because of his bloodshed. And their minister referred to him as the "scum of the earth." However, sad to say, all these remarks came after all the killings were over. No foreign power cared enough or dared come forward and stop the carnage at its very beginning.

These horrific scenes and killings were only a prelude to the "first genocide of the 20th century" upon the Armenians by the Ottoman Empire.

The Rise of the Young Turks

Way back in 1840, another group was brewing in the Ottoman Empire—called the Young Turks. Their purpose was to reform the failing Turkish state by trying to adopt western methods of government. Some Armenians got excited that their burdens might be relieved from the yoke of Abdul Hamid. Even the Hamidians were in fear that the Young Turks might be lenient toward the Armenians. So, Sultan Hamid fought the new nationalists, the Young Turks, being afraid that they would change his strict reign. In the beginning, little did Hamid, or even the Armenians, know that this new group, the Young Turks, would be as bad and more organized to plan bigger and worse brutality upon the Armenians.

"We are Moslems," said one high Young Turk official, "and we can have nothing in common with unbelievers. The Empire of Islam is our heritage; it will be vast enough to enable us to break off all contact with Christians." The Young Turks were not talking about Pan-Islamism, but Pan-Turkism. This was a kind of Moslem nationalism—even more severe than Abdul Hamid's doctrine, which he thought was superior to Arabs, Persians, Egyptians and Indians. The Armenians were initially fooled by the Young Turks' agenda. They called their organization the Committee of Union and Progress (CUP). Originally, this was a secret society made up of many army officers. They were in opposition to Sultan Hamid. They threatened to march on the capital and depose him. Hamid was shaken by all this; he stepped down from power as Armenians, Greeks, Arabs, Bulgarians and Turks alike were happy for his dethronement.

Thus, the 1908 Young Turk revolution had taken place. However, a countercoup took place on April 13, 1909. Some Ottoman military forces were joined by Islam's theological students, hoping to return control of the country to the Sultan and the rule of Islamic law. Fighting and riots broke out between the CUP and the reactionary forces, until the CUP put down the uprising and tried the opposition leaders by court-martial.

On June 28, 1914, the murder of the Austrian Archduke Franz Ferdinand and his wife at Sarajevo sparked WWI. In November 1914, the Ottoman Empire joined the war on the side of the Central Powers. Turkish public opinion was that they would like to be neutral in the world conflict. Since the coup, the Young Turks wanted to secure their objective: to provide an opportunity for themselves to carry out their plan for getting rid of the Armenians. This plan was to their advantage during this specific wartime. Thus, a plan for the massacres of the Armenian genocide was secretly adopted by CUP and implemented under the cover of war.

Not knowing the Young Turks' intent, Turkish-Armenians behaved as loyal Turkish citizens. In August of 1914, the Tashnag party had their eighth party conference in Erzerum. They asked their Armenian people to carry out their patriotic duties as Turkish subjects in the event of war breaking out between Turkey and Russia. Nearly 250,000 Armenians were called to the Turkish armed forces, where they performed admirable service during the first battles of the war.

As time went on, army supplies of all kinds were loaded on Armenian soldiers' backs. They were whipped with bayonets without mercy. The Armenian soldiers' weary bodies carried heavy loads through the mountains of the Caucasus, and sometimes they slept on the bare ground. They were given only scraps of food and if they felt sick and dropped, they were left behind. Worse yet, as they fell, the Turks took the Armenian soldiers' clothes off their backs. As their number decreased, the Turks shot them in cold blood. Sometimes, the soldiers were forced to dig their own graves. After they were shot, they would be kicked into the ditches they had dug. At this point, the senseless slaughter of such loyal and useful workers provoked anger and great frustration among Turkey and Germany's allies.

The CUP, the new junta of the Young Turks, prohibited the formation of political parties and they sent opposition leaders into exile. The Young Turks' philosophy was that the non-Moslem minorities should be "Turkicized," religiously and culturally. Thus, the junta began to formulate a policy of Turkification of non-Moslem elements with renewed ruthlessness, which was more ferocious than Hamid's policies. To the Young Turks, the Armenian Christians were aliens, pollutants in the community of Islam. For them, a fellow Moslem was a brother anointed by the teachings of the prophet Mohammed. The CUP steered the Ottoman Empire towards closer diplomatic and military relations with Imperial Germany. The Turks also formed part of the Triple Alliance with the other Central Powers: Germany, Austria, and Hungary, and declared war on Russia and its Western Allies, Great Britain and France.

April 24, 1915

April 24, 1915 was the date of the initial massacres, beginning the first genocide of the Armenians in the 20th century by the Ottoman Empire. About 300 Armenian scholars, leaders, bankers, and clergy were gathered in Constantinople, tortured in public, and then were exiled and killed.

The junta of three pashas was formed, the big three of the planners of this genocide. They were as follows:

Talaat Pasha: a civilian and a former post office clerk, and a fanatic nationalist who became the Minister of the Interior. He outlined the acts of exterminations and ordered all the massacres.

Jemal Pasha: a competent military man who had a very bad and unpleasant disposition became the Military Governor of Constantinople, the capital, and the Minister of the Marine.

Enver Pasha: The youngest of the three was the son of a porter. He became the Minister of War and reported the Party's armed strength. He relied on the governors.

These three pashas were the butchers of Armenians. Additionally, the financial genius for the threesome was Javid, a former Jew who was a converted Moslem. He was appointed Minister of Finance, but he was not part of the big three.

Measures of the Armenian genocide were secretly adopted by the CUP and implemented under the cover of war. Initially, that was a big cover-up. The Young Turks' plan was to eradicate the Armenians from Turkish neighboring countries. Thus, the spring and summer of 1915, the Armenian population everywhere was ordered to be deported from their original homeland of 3,000 years. The Ottoman Empire heavily depended on the deportation agenda to get rid of the Armenians, because of two major reasons, both economic: 1) to save money and 2) to save ammunition.

They gathered all the men 45 years old and under and put them in prison. At night, the captors took them out—shot some and hung others to save ammunition. And the elderly, women, and children were marched on foot to a destination in the Syrian Der-Zor Desert. They were exhausted in the sizzling heat. With starvation and thirst came death. Some who were still alive, but so weak they could not walk any longer, were pushed into ditches and buried alive. The young girls were picked by the gendarmes and brought to the nearby Turkish villages to be sold as wives or brought to the pashas' harems.

All these deportations were initially disguised as resettlements elsewhere for these innocent deportees. But in reality, there was no real destination for them. These deportations really were *death marches*.

During August of 1991, my husband Henry and I visited Syria. My husband was born in Kessab, Syria, and later on, his family moved to Beirut, Lebanon, where he grew up from the age of seven. We wanted to go to Syria to visit Henry's mom who was not feeling well. We got an air-conditioned taxi from Damascus and headed to Latakia, another Syrian city, where my husband's cousin was to pick us up and head to Kessab. This was some journey! It brought tears to my eyes all the way to Latakia, what we had to ride through. Even though we had an air-conditioned car to ride in, it felt extremely hot through the Syrian Desert. And now, I was visualizing all those poor elderly and mothers, some with babies in their arms and with other children by their sides, walking with bare feet. The thoughts broke my heart and I started crying uncontrollably. How did they do it? What were they thinking when they took their last gasp of breath? My husband looked at me gently, and said somberly,

"You know, my father lost his mother and sister here, too."

Henry's eyes were filled with tears. The rest of the ride, we both were very quiet thinking about our sad Armenian history. Can any human being imagine such pain—to go to their death with such anguish, uncertainty, whippings and physical deprivation? It was, and is, beyond me to digest all this. How did they keep their sanity? But, of course, some did not.

We were greeted by Steve, Henry's cousin in Latakia. Henry and Steve hugged and greeted each other warmly and caught up with some interesting news of Steve's family and Henry's family. I adoringly watched the two, and I was introduced to Steve as Henry's wife.

Henry was very happy to see his mom. We found her in good spirits, but somewhat weak. It was a very sweet scene, kind of bittersweet, since Henry had not seen his mom for thirty-seven years. He had come to study in America in 1954 and attended Columbia University. After graduation, he never had a chance to go back to Syria. I was very happy for them, and soon all of Henry's other relatives arrived to see us. It was a *big* and joyous party.

So, during 1915 and the deportations and mass killings, the Turkish Nationalists prospered by taking all of the financial power of the Armenians in their own hands to promote Turkish control of Armenians' belongings and bank accounts. Also, U.S. Ambassador Henry Morgenthau tells in the memoirs of his ambassadorship in Turkey (1913–1916) that when he protested against the torturous killings of the Armenians, Talaat boasted saying, "What I have accomplished in three months, Sultan Hamid could not do in thirty years." Ambassador Morgenthau was angered and kept protesting about the massacres, and Talaat answered: "The massacres! What of them! They merely amuse me!" Then, Talaat tried to persuade Mr. Morgenthau to furnish him with a register of life insurance policies taken by American companies on rich Armenians now dead through the massacres, that they could put aside the total proceeds from the policies. Morgenthau vehemently refused the disgusting offer.

In Angora (Ankara), the *vali* (governor) was a humane man and refused to carry out the vicious orders of the Young Turks from the central government to deport the Armenians from Angora; they said the Armenians were law-abiding citizens. Also, the military commanders in that city agreed with the *vali*, not to deport the Armenians. There were about 20,000 Armenians in Angora, who were the leaders in commerce and other professions. The Armenian businesses and houses were often searched, and again in July of 1915, no weapons or any incriminating documents were ever found. None of these reports mattered; soon the *vali* and his colleagues were dismissed from their jobs. A new set of officers were placed in Angora and they exterminated all those Armenians immediately. It has been told that after this horrible carnage, flocks of vultures were perched upon the mounds of slaughtered Armenians, pecking at the eyes of the dead and the dying while still alive. As I write about these horrors and unspeakable acts, I feel the agony and the sadness of what my ancestors went through.

The deportations continued in the open-air concentration camps by starving and killing the Armenians. The expression, "the starving Armenians," circulated around the world. I remember a colleague of mine telling me that when her mother would not eat her vegetables, her grandmother would insist that she should eat them, "after all those poor Armenians were starving and dying," she would remind her mom.

Talaat would tell Ambassador Morgenthau, time after time, that the "Armenian question will be done soon," meaning the decimation of all Armenians from the face of the earth. Who, personally, did all the killings? Ordinary gendarmes, common criminals released from the Turkish prisons, uneducated Turkish mobs, and other disparate groups, such as Kurds, were instructed by Talaat to kill, burn, deport, and ransack houses and businesses. According to Ambassador Morgenthau, the real purpose of the deportations of the Armenian people was as follows:

"When the Turkish authorities gave the orders for these deportations, they were merely giving the death warrant to a whole race, they understood this well, and in their communication with me, and they made no particular attempt to conceal the fact."

Talaat had instructed that "All the rights of the Armenians to live and work on Turkish soil have been completely cancelled, and with regard to this the Government takes all the responsibility on itself, and has commanded that even babies in the cradle are not to be spared.... These general orders have been communicated from the War Office to all the commanders of the army that they are not to interfere in the work of deportation...Please send all reports of the results of your activities every week."

Before 1914, there were over 3 million Armenians living in ethnic Turkey. After the war and genocide, the figure hardly reached 100,000. The safe estimate for the number of Armenians dead was 1.5 to 1.8 million. The remaining number of Armenians became refugees spread around the world.

The Hi Tad (Armenian Question) is unfinished business. World leaders should possess a good stock in integrity in order to not allow a distortion of history for their own gain. I humbly make this remark that you, the reader, and each one of us, can be vigilant and fight for the truth to the end, for the love of peace, and peace of mind.

2

Denials

Distorting facts and avoiding the truth do not exonerate denial of genocide.

Overwhelming evidence exists to prove that the Armenian Genocide took place, including numerous photos taken by journalists, missionaries, foreign officers and U.S. ambassadors. Also, there are signed documents authorizing the killings and many eyewitness accounts by missionaries, genocide survivors, and foreign officials serving in Turkey during 1915.

For example, the U.S. ambassador to the Ottoman Empire, Henry Morgenthau, writes in 1915, "I am confident that the whole history of the human race contains no such horrible episode as this. The great massacres and persecutions of the past seem almost insignificant when compared to the suffering of the Armenian race in 1915."

The *New York Times International*, on April 25, 2010, reported that the Armenians in Yerevan solemnly observed the 95th anniversary of the start of the Armenian Genocide under the Ottoman Turkish government. There were thousands of people with banners and crosses to commemorate this very important day in Armenian history, April 24. Reporter Peter Baker also noted President Obama's words about the Armenian tragedy of April 24 did not include the word "genocide." President Obama had promised as a candidate to use the word "genocide" in describing the Ottoman mass slaughter of Armenians almost a century ago, but he declined to do so on Saturday, April 24, 2010. The reporter pointed out that when President Obama was running for president and was seeking the votes of the U.S. Armenians, he had emphatically promised that he would use the term "genocide." Obama had also criticized the Bush administration for recalling the ambassador from Armenia who had used the term "genocide." Here, I must remind my readers that, on both sides of the aisle, Republicans and Democrats must come to the realization that they should not succumb to Turkish threats. Let the truth be told once and for all. Mr. Ken Hachikian, chairman of the Armenian National Committee of America (ANCA) said that President

Obama's failure to follow through on his campaign pledge was "allowing Turkey to tighten its gag rule on American genocide resolution policies."

Thus far, U.S. administrations have opposed the passage of the Armenian Genocide resolution in Congress. They always have the vote, but at the last minute the order comes from the President, and it is canceled. The same thing happened, when Bill Clinton was in office. As the House was ready to vote on this resolution, President Clinton sent a note to House Speaker Hastert to halt the vote for passing it. How long will Turkey play this game: intimidating the most powerful country in the world? Some say that it is the fear of offending Turkey as an ally. However, if an ally has gone against human rights, and has conducted such an enormous monstrosity, is it right to excuse such actions? That is against the rule of any civilized nation to tolerate such acts. How could anyone, or any country, ignore such a great amount of archival data? There are plentiful data in the following countries' archives: Russia, Switzerland, Italy, the Vatican, France, England, Sweden, Jerusalem, at Etchmiadzin in Armenia, Germany and many more in the United States at the Holocaust and Genocide Museum in Washington, D.C. And at the U.S. National Archives, there are over 40,000 pages of history depicting the "systematic extermination" of the Armenian race—all written during the time when it was happening.

When the genocide was occurring in 1915, the *New York Times* covered the massacres 145 times, to the rate of every second day of its publication. All of these articles had details of the Armenians being slaughtered with photos and all. In recent years, Turkey has been pouring millions of dollars to lobbyists and professors at leading universities to make inaccurate comments on their behalf to derail the passage of a genocide resolution. For fifty years, the Turkish government sources have combed through and destroyed damaging, valid records in their possession. In fact, the Turkish government has not opened all the archives pertinent to the Armenian Genocide, such as the War Ministry, Interior Ministry, and the CUP. The Turkish government has used delaying tactics for years aimed at not revealing their atrocities.

In 1935, the Turkish government influenced and forced the U.S. Department of State to stop the Hollywood's MGM from making the film of Franz Werfel's classic historical novel, *The Forty Days of Musa Dagh*. This book tells the story of my own people's resistance on Mt. Musa (Mount Moses) during the massacres. My uncles fought in that battle of Musa Dagh, and my mother was a young lady. The Turkish government's guilt is so great that they do not want to admit their inhumane acts to the world. However, the more nations cover-up for them, the more this evil will occur over and over as has already happened. Let us not forget the more recent 20th century genocides that followed the Armenian one in 1915.

- 1941–45 Nazi Germany tried to destroy all the Jews, and massacred other groups of people, too.

"I have given orders to my Death Units to exterminate without mercy men women and children belonging to the Polish-speaking people. It is only in this manner that we can acquire the vital territory which we need. *Who, after all, speaks today of the annihilation of the Armenians?*" [Italics added]
Adolf Hitler, August 22, 1939

I always thought if the Ottoman Empire had been halted during the Armenian Genocide or if they had been punished severely, might the Nazi Holocaust never have happened? Otherwise, Hitler would not have been able to boast and dismiss the Armenian Genocide.

- 1932–33, The USSR starved Ukrainians to death
- 1950–59, China killed Buddhists in Tibet
- 1965, Indonesians killed people labeled "Communists"
- 1966, Nigeria massacred Ibo tribes
- 1971, Pakistan killed Bengalis
- 1972–73, Paraguay enslaved and killed Achi Indians
- 1978, Cambodian genocide
- 1980, Iran tortures and kills Bahas
- 1989, Beijing massacres
- 1992–95, Bosnian massacres
- 1994, Rwanda Genocide
- 2003, Darfur in Sudan genocide

The crime of genocide will continue unless it is completely eradicated from the face of humanity. The guilty parties should be immediately stopped before it escalates to great human loss. When nations sit by and watch without intervening, the crime will continue. Massacres and genocides persist if they are allowed to continue. There should be harsh repercussions for the evil-doers.

History books have not emphasized the Armenian Genocide. I was very sad when I mentioned the fact to my history professor at college in the 1970s; he knew nothing about it. That wasn't just sad, but also wrong to have no education pertaining to this huge human catastrophe included in history books. Thank goodness, now that trend is changing and moving towards the right direction, slowly but surely. Decent people are grateful for that. For example, the book, *Facing History and Ourselves: The Genocide of the Armenians*, was published in 2004. This is available in our schools, and could be utilized well by students and those uninformed teachers or professors.

The preparation is very lucid and it takes the student from beginning to end of the whole genocide story. I am so delighted that this type of book is available now and, hopefully, more will follow about other nations' human catastrophes, printed and made available. Education and clarification is an absolute necessity. We must all be vigilant always, whether we are Armenians or any other nationality. This type of human degradation and mass killings should never happen again.

However, there are those who still try to see if they can get away with it by employing with the "denial game." Some university scholars are being bought by millions of dollars' worth of bribes to chant the mantra of the Turkish government that "the genocide of the Armenians did not happen." Such a person is Heath Lowry of Princeton University in New Jersey. He gave shoddy, untrue accounts relating to the Armenian Genocide. Lowry had worked in Turkey in the 1970s. In the 1980s, he became director of the Turkish-funded Institute of Turkish Studies, Georgetown University, Washington, D.C. However, he was exposed in 1990 as having worked with the Turkish government. This chair at Princeton was funded by a wealthy Turkish-American called Ahmet Ertegun, the son of the Turkish ambassador who was instrumental in stopping the film version of *The Forty Days of Musa Dagh* in 1935. The Lowry scandal was covered by the *New York Times*, the *Boston Globe*, *The Chronicle of Higher Education* and many other prominent publications. This whole issue has reflected very badly on Princeton.

Professor, poet, and author Peter Balakian states that in the fall of 1997, major scholars in the U.S. once more signed a petition protesting the Turkish studies of seven American universities: Princeton, Harvard, Indiana, Chicago, Portland State, UCLA, and Georgetown. Thank goodness, for all those advocates standing for human rights.

Taner Akcam

Taner Akcam is a Turkish historian, sociologist, and he is the first Turkish academic that I know of that comes out and speaks the truth freely regarding the Armenian Genocide of 1915. He was born in the Ardahan Province of Turkey in 1953. He was granted political asylum in Germany after receiving a nine-year prison sentence in Turkey for speaking about the Turkish government's atrocities upon the Armenians. Formerly, a visiting professor at the Center for Holocaust and Genocide Studies at the University of Minnesota, he presently teaches at Clark University, Worcester, Mass. While doing extensive research on the Armenian Genocide in many European archives, such as those in Germany and Austria, he found hidden

18

Turkish documents that he fearlessly wrote about. In those German and Austrian records, he discovered quite revealing documents that confirmed the centrally planned decimation of the Armenians. A very significant part of his research findings was that Germany and Austria were military and political allies of the Ottoman Empire.

However, after the Armenian Genocide, Germany became very cautious not to be judged for their part; thus, it tried to ensure a more favorable result at the Paris Peace Conference. Akcam, having done his research very carefully, concluded in his findings that the Ottoman Empire's plan was "ethnic cleansing," and to get rid of the Armenians. He thought that the impetus for the rushed plan of extermination was that the Ottoman Empire was weakened in the Balkan War of 1912–13, losing more than 60 percent of their European territory. After that, they were afraid to live, surrounded by an empire of a Christian population. So, the Young Turks saw the Ottoman Christian Armenians as a big threat for their empire's survival. Greeks were also expelled. The quick-fix solution was the deportations with the intent of annihilation of the Armenians—period. We need more Turkish scholars to come out and expose the Turkish government's falsifications.

Dr. Akcam's most recent book, *A Shameful Act: the Armenian Genocide and the Question of Turkish Responsibility* was published in 2007. As a result, he has come under tremendous attacks by the Turkish government and their followers. He was charged under Article 301 of Turkey's penal code, which is used often against writers, and journalists. Amnesty International states that this charge "poses a direct threat to the fundamental right to freedom of expression."

Also, there are other misleading problems. The Armenian National Committee of America (ANCA) often informs us about important issues regarding the Armenian Genocide through fliers. We have learned that Turkey is bribing and paying millions of dollars to lobbyists who are former U.S. Congressmen, such as Gephardt, Livingston and Solarz. These money-hungry men have put aside any sense of integrity and have worked hard to derail the Armenian Genocide resolution to be passed by the U.S. government.

Also, Turkey's denial actions are still festering, because they are destroying Armenian monuments and traces of Armenian past—churches and cultural edifices.

The Assassination of Hrant Dink

Through many Armenian newspapers, and especially reports by the Armenian Diocese of New York City, we learned that Hrant Dink was assassinated on January 19, 2007. An eyewitness saw a man of about 20 years old shoot him three times, call out, "I shot the infidel," and run away. Hrant Dink was editor-in-chief of the bilingual Turkish-Armenian newspaper, *Agos*. Dink was a prominent member of the Armenian minority in Istanbul. He was known for advocating Turkish-Armenian reconciliation, and was a firm advocate for minority rights in Turkey. He had received many death threats from Turkish nationalists. Dink had founded the weekly Turkish-Armenian paper in 1996, and the circulation was growing quite fast. He always spoke on issues faced by Armenians, and he became a well-known public figure in Turkey. He was applauded by some for his viewpoints and criticized by others. He often talked about human rights, and the treatment of Armenians in Turkey. However, he felt if there was open discussion about the Armenian Question, there could be peace and reconciliation. As much as he wanted to make peace, his activism did not get rid of prejudices and unjust actions against the Armenians.

No matter how hard he tried to be a fair journalist, "Turkishness" was still the main agenda for those refusing to listen to him. The end result was, of course, his death. This is the country that U.S. considers an American ally? They are supposed to be a democratic republic? So, the denial continues in many facets and incidents to the present. One hundred thousand mourners marched at Dink's funeral, in protest of his assassination.

Yair Auron

Yair Auron is senior lecturer of The Open University of Israel and the Kibbutz College of Education. He is an expert on genocide and on contemporary Judaism. On December 2, 1997, I had the pleasure of meeting him at Rutgers University, by the invitation of the Rutgers Armenian Club. He was the speaker of that evening, which was very interesting. He autographed his book, *The Banality of Denial, Israel and the Armenian Genocide*, in which he gives a detailed account of the Armenian Genocide. Auron shares the statement of the Concerned Scholars and Writers made on April 24, 1998, honoring the 50th Anniversary of the United Nations Convention on the Prevention and Punishment of the Crime of Genocide.

"We commemorate the Armenian Genocide of 1915 and condemn the Turkish government's denial of this crime against humanity."

Auron emphasized in his comments: "We condemn Turkey's manipulation of the American government and American institutions for the purpose of denying the Armenian Genocide. We urge our government officials, scholars, and the media to refrain from using erroneous or euphemistic terminology to appease the Turkish government; we ask them to refer to the 1915 annihilation of the Armenians as 'genocide.'"

This statement has been signed by more than 150 renowned writers and scholars. Some of the signers are as follows:

- Michael Arlen—*writer*
- James Axtell—*history professor, College of William and Mary*
- Ben Bagdikian—*dean emeritus, University of California, Berkeley Graduate School of Journalism*
- Houston Baker—*professor of English at University of Pennsylvania*
- Peter Balakian—*writer and professor of English, Colgate University*
- Yehuda Bauer—*professor of Holocaust Studies, Hebrew University, Jerusalem*
- Israel Charny—*Director, Institute on the Holocaust and Genocide, Jerusalem*
- Rev. William Sloane Coffin—*pastor emeritus, Riverside Church, NYC*
- Vahakn Dadrian—*Director, Genocide Study Project, H.F. Guggenheim Foundation*
- David Brion Davis—*Sterling Professor of History, Yale University*
- James Der Derian—*professor of political science, University of Massachusetts Amherst*
- Marjorie Hovsepian Dobkin—*writer*
- Craig Etcheson—*acting director, Cambodian Genocide Program, Yale University*
- Helen Fein—*executive director, Institute for the Study of Genocide, John Jay College of Criminal Justice, CUNY*
- Lawrence J. Friedman—*professor of history, Indiana University*
- Henry Louis Gates, Jr.—*professor of Afro-American Studies, Harvard University*
- Sandor Goodhart—*director of Jewish studies, Purdue University*
- Vigen Guroian—*professor of theology and ethics, Loyola College*
- Richard G. Hovannisian—*professor of Armenian and Near Eastern history, UCLA*
- Robert Jay Lifton—*distinguished professor of Psychiatry and Psychology, John Jay College of Criminal Justice and the Graduate School, CUNY*
- Norman Mailer—*writer*
- Saul Medlowitz—*Dag Hammarskjold professor of law, Rutgers University*

- Arthur Miller—*writer*
- Henry Morgenthau III—*writer*
- Joyce Carol Oates—*writer*
- Kurt Vonnegut—*writer*
- Howard Zinn—*professor emeritus of history, Boston University*

This declarative statement was again published in November 1999 to honor the 51ˢᵗ Anniversary of the UN Genocide Convention, with more than 150 distinguished scholars and writers.

Association of Genocide Scholars

The Association of Genocide Scholars (AGS) unanimously passed the Armenian Genocide Resolution at the AGS conference in Montreal, Canada on June 13, 1997. It read as follows:

"That this assembly of the Association of Genocide Scholars in its conference held in Montreal, June 11-13, 1997, reaffirms that the mass murders of over a million Armenians in Turkey in 1915 is a case of genocide which conforms to the statutes of the United Nations Convention on the Prevention and Punishment of Genocide. It further condemns the denial of the Armenian Genocide by the Turkish government and its official and unofficial agents and supporters."

The following persons were among the supporting scholars:

- Israel Charny—*Hebrew University of Jerusalem, Israel*
- Frank Chalk—*Concordia University, Montreal, QC, Canada*
- Helen Fein, *past president of AGS*
- Michael Freeman—*University of Essex, Colchester, UK*
- Gunnar Heinsohn—*University of Bremen, Bremen, Germany*
- Rhoda Howard—*McMaster University, Hamilton, ON, Canada*
- Ben Kiernan—*Yale University of New Haven, CT*
- Mark Levene—*University of Warwick, Coventry, UK*
- Andrew Oberschall—*University of North Carolina, Chapel Hill*
- Roger W. Smith—*College of William and Mary; president of AGS*

Kudos goes to all these scholars and writers for their tireless efforts fighting for human rights. Bystanders who witness atrocities and know of them, but do not do anything to stop them, are part of the crime. And if not stopped, crimes against humanity will continue forever for gain of power or land. Neither is acceptable in civilized society.

New Jersey Ethnic Advisory Council and Ethnic Festivals

I was appointed to the New Jersey Ethnic Advisory Council on February 14, 1992, by the invitation of then Governor Jim Florio. The oath of office was administered to me on this day with many other ethnic leaders of New Jersey. A week before, Maria Efstratiades, the Director of the Council, had called me and asked me, having read on my resume that I was a lecturer, if I would please be the keynote speaker for that day with a speech of five to ten minutes. I did accept. This was such an honor for me. The ceremonies took place in the State House rotunda. All the Ethnic Advisory Council members had designated seats with their names on each seat according to their representative country of origin. Also, there was a section for family members and friends, plus dignitaries from the New Jersey Assembly and Senate, and Speaker of the N.J. State Assembly Chuck Haytaian.

The ceremonies began at 10:00 a.m. sharp with the Pledge of Allegiance. The master of ceremonies was Daniel Dalton, Secretary of State of N.J., who greeted everyone, then introduced me as the keynote speaker and as the representative of the Armenian community. I started by saying, "Good morning to you all: honorable Governor Florio, honorable Secretary of State, and all the honorable legislators here this morning, and guests and family members."

"Thank you, Governor Florio, for making this Ethnic Council a possibility, which is a most-needed body to cultivate unity and harmony amongst all ethnic groups. I am very happy to represent the Armenian community of New Jersey. It is very important for all of us here to know about our roots even though we are all devoted American citizens. Speaking of roots and history, do you believe in miracles?"

Here, I paused a few seconds to get a response, which I did get. The pause was well worth it. The audience nodded and verbally echoed, "Yes, yes." Then I continued saying,

"Yes, my friends, there is no more Berlin Wall, or a Soviet Armenia. Both of these areas are free of *fear* that caused much agony and tribulation for Germans and Armenians. Yes, it did take a long time, but it did happen.

23

No longer do these people have to live in continuous fear. You see, my dear ethnic friends, here in this country, we have freedoms unlike any country in the world. Let us not take that for granted. Let us be thankful and keep striving to make our communities a safe and harmonious place to live in without any consequence of fear. We should respect each other's differences with reverence, so this world will be a better place to live in. If we see prejudices occurring, we should put a stop to it. Courage will be the main ingredient in a situation like that.

"A friend of mine, Dr. Rev. Donald Lewis, minister of Fanwood Presbyterian Church once said, 'Courage is not the absence of fear, but it is the conquest of fear.' No one can say it better than that.

"So, in conclusion, thank you again Governor Florio for this unique opportunity for all of us. Let us hope and pray that we accomplish the task given to us in peacemaking projects. Thank you and God bless you all, and God bless this great country of ours."

After the applause, I humbly received Master of Ceremonies Dalton's commendations. He introduced the Governor who also thanked me with gracious remarks and then he began to speak. He emphasized that this Council would preserve the diverse cultures of all citizens of the State. He thanked everyone for giving their time to be a part of this Council, and wished each one of us a successful year ahead.

Here are the names and ethnicities of this diverse group, as of the end of the year, from twenty-six to thirty-five members.

Names	*Communities*
Toyoko Allen	Japanese
Virginia Apelian	Armenian
Juris Blodnicks	Latvian
Roberto Bustamante	Peruvian
Manuela da Luz Chaplin	Portuguese
Ved Chaudhary, Ph.D.	Asian-Indian
William Derbyshire	*Member-at-Large*
Esperanza Porras-Field	Colombian
Sam Fumosa	Italian
Ted Hierl	German
Chief Roy Crazy Horse	American-Indian

Norberto LaGuardia	Cuban
Yong Chin Lim	Korean
Margaret Ko Ma	Chinese
Peter MacKenzie	Scottish
Ariit Singh Mahal	Sikh
Rosalinda Mayo	Filipino
Luz P. Menza	Puerto Rican
Luu-Phuong Nguyen	Vietnamese
Bozhena Olshaniwsky	Ukranian
Ernest Olibrice	Haitian
Phillip Podell	*Member-at-Large*
Paul Pulitzer	Hungarian
Gregg Rackin	Jewish
Stephen Richer	*Member-at-Large*
Laura Sabater	Mexican
Loretta Stukas	Lithuanian
Leonid Surak	Belarus
George Szetela	Polish
Joseph Talafous	Slovak
Doris J. Taylor	African-American
Luinis Tejada	Dominican
Savis Tsivicos	Greek
Ada Vila	Argentine
John Walsh	Irish
Contact Person:	Maria Efstratiades. Director, Office of Ethnic Affairs

Ex-officio Members, Ethnic Advisory Council

Janet Baldaures	N.J. Dept. of Higher Education
Stephanie R. Bush	N.J. Dept. of Community Affairs
Daniel J. Dalton	Secretary of State
Marylee Fitzgerald	N.J. Dept. of Education
Edward D. Goldberg	Chancellor, N.J. Dept. of Higher Education
Douglas Greenberg	N.J. Historical Commission
Sharon Harrington	N.J. State Council on the Arts
C. Gregory Stewart	Director, Division of Civil Rights

25

Governor Florio administered the oath to the new members of the N.J. Ethnic Advisory Council by having them raise their right hands and repeat the oath after him. After he finished, there followed a robust applause by everyone.

Gov. Florio, the author, and N.J. Secretary of State Daniel Dalton.

Thereafter, we met every other month to keep abreast of all the activities, and committee formations. We all submitted reports of our community activities to the Governor's office via Maria Efstratiades.

There was a special Ethnic Festival in Atlantic City, June 6–7, 1992, at Brighton Park by Indiana Ave. and the famous Boardwalk. Members and friends were invited. There were fifty ethnic craft stations with artists, and entertainment by genuine ethnic performers. Stephen Richer, an at-large member and the president of the Greater Atlantic City Convention and Visitors Bureau had done a fantastic job informing us and having such a big event underway. We all celebrated this happy atmosphere with our friends and families.

Also, one of our responsibilities was to let the Governor know of any concerns we might have about our ethnic groups. We were asked to bring our concerns to him, and he would try to solve the troublesome issues. In the long run, there were some unpleasant, unjust rumors about Chinese restaurants; they were all taken care of by the Council.

In my case, since the Armenian community always reveres April 24, 1915, I requested to have special "proclamations" issued to me, at least twelve of them, so that I could deliver them personally to leading Armenian organizations and churches. My wish was granted and I thankfully delivered all of them either on April 24th or a few days earlier. It was a big task to run from one end of New Jersey to the other, but I was happy to do it, and all of the recipients, too, for honoring our martyrs by calling April 24th Armenian Martyrs Day. Many friendships were started with this unique Council. We encouraged each other's cultural programs during the year and thereafter. There was such interaction and warmth to propagate unity and goodwill.

Also, the Council members were invited to other functions at Drumthwacket, the Governor's official residence in Princeton. One special occasion was a breakfast reception in March 1993, honoring Women's Month. The First Lady of New Jersey, Lucinda Florio, and the Governor were so cordial with the guests that it made a beautiful memory for us all. Too bad Governor Florio did not make it for a second term, because of his tax-hike agenda. Otherwise, this was a handsome couple occupying Drumthwacket.

Chuck Haytaian, Speaker of the N.J. State Assembly and the author.

First Lady of N.J., Lucinda and Governor Florio and the author.

More About Drumthwacket

Drumthwacket has a long connection with New Jersey history. The first governor to live in the stately central portico was Charles Smith Olden. He built the structure in 1835, modeled after the architecture of New Orleans, where he had been in business for nine years before returning to New Jersey in 1834. This mansion was one of the most elegant in Princeton. Olden's vision resulted in the colossal portico that extends the full height and width of the six massive pillars. He became New Jersey's twenty-eighth chief executive in 1860. He died at home in 1876 at the age of 77. During his life, he was a state senator, a judge and a member of the commission that planned the State House. He also was State Treasurer and a Trustee of the original College of New Jersey, which became Princeton University in 1896. He was also the president of the Electoral College that reelected Ulysses S. Grant in 1872.

Drumthwacket was bought by the State in 1966 with money from the Green Acres Fund. The mansion was used occasionally for benefit fund-raisers and similar events. Thus, in 1981, Drumthwacket was designated the official residence of the Governor. This information is available by the State Historical Society to all who visit the Drumthwacket.

Gov. Whitman and the 1995 Ethnic Festival

The new Governor (1994), Christine Todd Whitman, was very well-organized. She immediately got started with plans for the Ethnic Advisory Council work. The former members were asked to renew their resumes and send them to the Secretary of State. After our backgrounds were checked, we were sent letters from then Secretary of State Lonna Hooks that we would be installed again as members. We were notified that our first meeting would be in March, which was the organizational meeting. Everyone was introduced with their ethnic background. We now had forty-two members. At this meeting, rules and regulations were explained by the Governor's aides. Our meetings were to take place at the Raritan Center, off the Garden State Parkway at exit 129. This was a centrally located State building convenient for members to travel from all parts of New Jersey.

Our second meeting took place May 1, 1995, and this meeting was led by Robert Currie, one of the Governor's aides. He first had the roll call; it was very important that we be at all meetings unless there was an important reason that we could not be there; then we needed to let them know we would be absent.

After the roll call, the mission statement was explained. Then the goals and obligations, and the code of ethics were explained. Lastly, the date of the Ethnic and Diversity Festival was announced as September 23, 1995, and the Festival would start at 11 a.m. and end at 6 p.m.

At the end of the second meeting, time was given to ask questions and comment. We discovered that the festival would take place at the Raritan Exposition and Convention Center in Edison. This Center could accommodate about 7,000 persons and had adequate space for stages to be placed for different activities and entertainment.

At our next meeting, we were presented with flyers with a special logo for us to pass around in our neighborhoods, libraries, any organizations that we knew of, schools, public buildings and supermarkets.

This logo represented "New Jersey. Many Faces – One Family." It depicted a dove in the center for peace and harmony, surrounded by four faces with different colors for diversity. It was very impressive; we all liked it. Different committees were formed:

Education Committee: planning the educational agenda and the ethnic groups' talent programs

Entertainment Committee: music, Newark Boys Choir, N.J. Symphony Orchestra, and other celebrities

Food/Hospitality Committee: to encourage merchants to provide ethnic foods

I volunteered for the Education Committee. This committee decided to have a children's educational center for arts and crafts, plus a stage for continuous poetry readings all day long. All entrants had to be pre-registered and the person's name would be on a list. They were introduced and a timeslot given to each to present their work, one or two poems each. This procedure worked very well. I decided to submit one of my eldest son's poems, which he wrote especially for this Diversity Festival, and he personally read it aloud.

"JOY TO THE WORLD"
By Gregory Apelian

"May every spirit hear and rejoice
A miracle has come
And continues to arrive
In each and every one of us
As love and the power of cooperation,
Every texture every hue
Of this living rainbow
Woven together by
Almighty Hands

As we in direct partnership
Arrange ourselves
To become the comforting
Work of all
We were always intended to be,
A blanket of light
Quenching every need
With glorious healing deeds.

"And deep in the far off distances
The children huddle and wait
For freedom. . .
Blessed freedom
That we drink now so deeply
Is singing our lives
In this universal prayer—
All children, all colors, all faiths,
All songs joyously planted in
The fertile soil of hope and vision
Indomitable seeds of truth
Bursting with a harvest of glory
For all to behold—
This song
This life we share
Drawing the same breath
Calling from the same merciful bounty
To be properly charged
For the harvest of harvests
Which even now is calling us
With sweet insistent intensity.

"And as I gaze out upon
This wondrous living mosaic
Of gathering hope,
I can't see the problems anymore,
Only answers waiting to be born.

"The great soul
We are all called to share
Goes on ringing
In our bones

'Build the one true home,
Build the one true home.'
And I am visited by the day
When mothers, fathers, artists, and
Lawyers, doctors, churches, temples, and
Mosques, universities, grade schools, graduates and
Teachers, all cultures, all blessings, all talents
Gathered together in a wondrous festival of life and
Love, generating a harvest of resources to house the
Homeless, to share self-respect with the
Esteemless, to provide daycare for the
Fatherless, job training and continuing education
For the resourceless a place where college
Students receive credits for tutoring kids who
Have no place to go, a place where church, temple,
And mosque volunteers can shine love unto the
Loveless, a place where every talent can sing
Appreciation to God by embracing those
Who have not until we awaken in a country where
Peace is celebrated and spreads through the
Fulfilling and fulfilled lives of each individual
Until every heart is bathed in the peace and
Prosperity of spirit this promised land,
This America is so ideally suited to achieve a
Partnership of wonder and of birth.
The ideal rescued from imagination
And made real.
This is what beats indelibly to my humbled breast,
This is what breathes us all as light and life.

"America...beacon of freedom,
Truth and dreams shine now as a new sun.
Warm all the world with your universal
Song of triumph
Invisibly received and transmitted now as love,
Sung by our humbly united lives,
As we all perpetually strive to protect
The blessed peace which glows so deeply
In our precious children's
Trusting eyes.

"Live long!

"Live strong!

"We all belong
in this glorious song!"

I had also invited the Shushi Cultural Dance Group of the St. Thomas Armenian Church of Tenafly under the direction of Ms. Seta Kantardjian. They did a superb job. Governor Whitman congratulated them, shaking everyone's hand and signing autographs for each performer.

I had another Armenian dance group of young boys and girls from the Hovnanian Armenian School of New Milford, N.J. They were so adorable and cheerful in demonstrating their ethnic dances. They also enjoyed the children's "Kids' Room" featuring storytelling, puppet shows and poster painting.

People walked around amazed by all the interesting talents and celebrities to meet. One celebrity was the anchorman of Channel 5, Ernie Anastos. I had a pleasant chat with him, and thanked him for taking the time to visit us. He graciously agreed to have a photo with me and my two granddaughters, Christee and Holly Curran.

Anchorman Ernie Anastos, the author and her granddaughters Christee and Holly.

The final highlight of the day was a jubilant one of 140 men and women becoming United States citizens. After they received the oath for becoming a faithful citizen, they joyfully clapped and many of them started dancing. That was a grand sight to see as the beautiful day ended at 6:00 p.m.

The Council members soon after received letters of congratulations and appreciation for having done a fantastic job for this beautiful event, separately from Governor Whitman, and Secretary of State Lonna Hooks.

NJ Ethnic Festival, September 28, 1996

I had borrowed one of the Armenian Cultural Dance group's Armenian folk dance attire from the St. Vartanantz Armenian Apostolic Church of Ridgefield Park. Yes, I was ready to go to the festival with full attire. Many other Council members came with their ethnic costumes, too.

This time, the Council worked even harder to make this festival an enormous success. Many meetings took place. By now, we were all experienced from last year's festival. Even though we had many additional duties this year, they were a little easier to cope with. Experience did help, and gave us confidence to do the job well. Having been on the Education Committee last year, I worked with the committee to expand the crafts for children and adults, which was amazingly successful. Long tables stretched from one end to a distance of 20-25 feet long, with council members on hand to supervise. This year, we had the festival at the Garden State Arts Center (now called the "PNC Bank Arts Center"), off of Exit 116 on the Garden State Parkway. It is a beautiful area where many professional artists perform in all seasons.

My dear Japanese friend, Toyoko Allen, wrote a note to me in Japanese, and translated it for me. I still have the note with very nice memories.

This time, I invited the, Armenian General Benevolent Union (AGBU) famous Antranig Dance Ensemble. This is the foremost Armenian dance group in the U.S. That year, they were celebrating their twenty-seventh anniversary. It was a pleasure to behold their exquisite talents and performance. They had performed all over the U.S. and in Canada, Europe and Armenia. They have performed in Carnegie Hall and Lincoln Center. It was truly an honor to have them as a part of our festival. Their dances included the full spectrum of the Armenian art form, with a repertoire from historic folk dance to contemporary ballet. Their artistic director at this time was Joyce Tamesian-Shenloogian, who had expertly mastered the techniques of "telling a story" through the medium of dance. My contact person was Armenine Sapah-Gulian who was the group's adviser. She was a sweet and gentle person to work with.

The author, Gov. Whitman, Armenine, and two dancers.

Gov. Whitman and the author.

Two other important events of the festival are essential to mention. First, it was Governor Whitman's 50th birthday. The whole group sang happy birthday to her, and a big decorative cake was enjoyed by everyone. Second, the Governor performed the naturalization ceremony for about 200 people. This scene is always very emotional and exhilarating to see.

The Governor thanked everyone for attending. She read the names of all the Ethnic Advisory Council members and made them rise to receive the recognition, and thanked them all.

Everyone left with happy feelings. I had my husband, brother, niece and her children, and our two granddaughters. Our other children were in college.

The *New Jersey Star Ledger* had a special supplement featuring this festival from September 28-October 5, 1996, where our logo was emphasized again. In addition, many photos of the festival filled the pages. One headline read, "Celebration of Many Faces. One Family Week." Also, Chief Roy Crazy Horse, our American Indian Council member, was quoted as saying, "Respect for diversity has always been a central feature of the culture of the Original Peoples of the Americas. We live diversity, we support diversity, and we encourage diversity. If anyone knows the American way, it is the Original People. And we know 'That Way' is respect for humanity." Roy Crazy Horse was Chief of the Powhatan Lenape Nation (1972–2004) in Rankokus Indian Reservation of South Jersey where there is an Indian Heritage Museum and an Educational Center.

Another Reception

Drumthwacket was the scene again for a reception held by Governor Whitman and Secretary of State Lonna Hooks for the members of the Ethnic Advisory Council. This was on March 15, 1996, in honor of Martin Luther King, Jr. Federal Holiday Commission. Again, we had a marvelous tour with the members of the Council. One never gets tired of visiting this magnificent mansion, especially with good friends from all walks of life. This whole involvement of our group with the festivals has been such an educational, interesting, challenging and inspirational experience for us all. And I will always cherish the memories of this.

These ethnic festivals brought all the people together celebrating life, and each nation's culture. What a beautiful world when people from all backgrounds and cultures come together to enjoy each other's heritage. As human beings, celebrating each other's existence in harmony makes life worthwhile and makes a better world for us all to live in.

The author standing next to Gov. Whitman cutting her birthday cake.

N.J. Sec. of State Lonna Hooks and the author with the group.

Very Special Events

The following special events were so meaningful to me and to the attendees that even nowadays people still make pleasant comments about them.

Onward to Rutgers

April 24, 1997, was a cloudy day and threatening to rain. I did not want rain for that day since the first Armenian rally was going to take place at the University, at Brower Commons, which was going to be outdoors from 12 p.m. to 2 p.m., commemorating the Armenian Genocide. My husband Henry, my brother Mike and I got in the car and started our trip at 10:30 a.m. to make sure we made it there on time. Routes 1 & 9 (same road) is always crowded with cars and trucks. As we drove through Menlo Park, the clouds were getting more pregnant with moisture and darker. I was in good spirits but those clouds were interfering with my thoughts. My brother, who was sitting on the backseat, gently touched my shoulder and said,

"Virginia, aren't you worried to be talking about Turkey's atrocities to all these people?"

I replied, "*Inchoo che?*" ("Why not?") He continued saying,

"There may be a radical person there who may do some harm to...." he did not finish his sentence, but I knew what he was referring to.

"No, I am not afraid to tell the truth," I replied calmly. He said nothing after that. My husband was the driver; he broke the silence saying,

"Look, look the clouds are disappearing, isn't that great?"

"Oh, that's wonderful so it won't be cancelled," I rang in.

When we got there, the crowd already was gathering, and we made good time getting there before 12 noon. We parked the car and walked through the crowd to the podium, where the president of the Armenian Club of Rutgers greeted me. Her name was Joy Hevsepian, a beautiful young lady from Paramus, New Jersey, who was a sophomore. She introduced me to historian Aram Arkun of the Armenian Diocese of NYC, the Director of the Krekor and Clara Zohrab Center. Soon, after the Pledge of Allegiance, Joy introduced Dr. Aram Arkun, who gave a summary of Armenia's past and dwelt on the genocide portion also. I was the second speaker. I first read a special proclamation by Governor Whitman, which declared this day Armenian Martyrs Day in New Jersey. I represented the Governor's office as a member of the Ethnic Advisory Council. Then, I handed the proclamation over to Ms. Hovsepian to keep for the Club. My speech covered the part when my mom and dad escaped the Turkish tyranny. My father's parents sent him to America to save his life, as other Armenian parents had, too. However, that made my mother very sad since she was engaged to my father at the time. The whole seven villages of Musa Dagh people had moved to the top of Musa Dagh (Mt. Moses) to resist the large Turkish army with up-to-date ammunition to attack my people. Read the famous classical novel of *Forty Days of Musa Dagh* by Franz Werfel to learn what hardships my people went through to fight courageously and not be slaughtered. It was not an easy task to relocate the population of seven villages, 5,000 people, to the top of that mountain, with children, pregnant women, elderly and babies, with many of their belongings, too. But they did it. With faith in God and confidence in their leaders, they sacrificed a lot to make it off of the mountain and safely rescued by the French warships. Thanks be to God that they survived and here I am able to tell you this story of courage and faith through my mother's witnessing it all.

Then, calmly, I made an appeal to the audience saying,

"If any one of you is of Turkish descent, please tell your government once and for all to recognize the Ottoman Empire's atrocities. Denial is a fraudulent game your government is playing to change true historical facts. You need to know the truth. As we know, 'the truth shall make you free.' I don't blame you personally. You have been kept from the truth; your history books delete the part concerning the Armenian Genocide. Other publications had been influenced not to include it. That is simply a shameful deed. May we all live harmoniously, and try not to change history. Thank you all for listening."

Father, Rev. Vahan Hovannesian, pastor of St. Leon Armenian Church of Fairlawn, N.J. gave the closing prayer.

Joy asked the Rutgers Armenian Club members to have a group photo taken with their adviser Professor Asbed Vassilian and the guest speakers.

Dr. Asbed Vassilian is professor of chemistry; however, he has succeeded the late Dr. Albert Wolohojian as the Rutgers Armenian Club adviser. He is the inspirational leader of the Armenian community at Rutgers. My husband Henry and I have had many opportunities to be at social events with Dr. Vassilian.

Dr. Albert Wolohojian was the founder of the Armenian Club at Rutgers. He came to Rutgers in 1962 and was an outstanding teacher, and he taught Armenian on a voluntary basis. He was a graduate of Harvard and Columbia universities, having majored in Greek, Latin, and French languages and literatures. He was the adviser to the Armenian Club until his death in December of 1990. In honor of him, a special fund was established to support an Armenian Studies Program at Rutgers.

Group picture of Rutgers Armenian Club: the author front row center with hat, Fr. Hovhannisian, to her right; Aram Arkun, on her left; and Dr. Vassilian, second from right.

This rally was the first Armenian one on the Rutgers campus, and it was covered by many local newspapers. The *Daily Targum*, the Rutgers newspaper covered it with the title, "Armenians Live." Other newspaper headlines read as follows: "Community Activist Virginia Apelian Busy with Armenian Martyrs Commemoration," the *Armenian Reporter International* wrote; Clark Eagle, *Rahway Progress* newspaper covered the rally with the headline, "Church, Community Leader Teaches History of Armenian Genocide." The Union County College newspaper, *UCC Network* called it, "Apelian Speaks on Armenian Genocide at Rutgers Rally." Other newspapers covered the story, too. What was important in all this was that people finally were getting acquainted with the real history as to what happened to the Armenians in 1915–1923.

April 22, 1998

Again, I was invited by the Rutgers Armenian Club, to the Brower Commons in the afternoon. I briefly went over some important historical events, and then again, I brought best wishes from Governor Christine Whitman conveyed by a new Proclamation for 1998, which declared April 24, 1998, Armenian Martyrs Day. The complete Proclamation was read by me; the audience applauded enthusiastically.

Rutgers Armenian Club

Many more activities took place on behalf of the Armenian Club, such as performances of traditional Armenian music, displays of art and culture, and reading of classic poetry. An Armenian-style buffet was available for all who attended. Everyone enjoyed these festivities. This event was held at the Rutgers Student Center on Sun., April 17, 1994, starting at 2 p.m.

Peter Balakian—September 22, 1999

Winants Hall, Old Queen's Campus, at Rutgers, The State University of New Jersey, New Brunswick, was the scene at 7:30 p.m. of a sumptuous dinner, lecture and book signing. A special group of this program's supporters, the Armenian Studies were invited. Also, dignitaries from Rutgers such as, Dr. Richard Foley, Executive Dean of Arts and Sciences, and the Dean of Graduate School; Richard A. Levao, chairman of The Board of Governors of Rutgers; and Dr. Barry V. Qualls, Dean of Humanities were all on hand.

Dr. Peter Balakian spoke about his new book, *Black Dog of Fate*, which was very dear to my heart, because of its contents. I purchased half a dozen books as gifts, which Dr. Balakian graciously autographed for me.

This evening's affair was sponsored by the Armenian Studies Program. At the time, its chairperson was James Sahagian.

Peter Balakian and the author.

Tenth Anniversary

The 10th Anniversary of the Armenian Students of Rutgers was celebrated on April 29, 2001 at 3 p.m. in the Kirkpatrick Chapel of Rutgers. The program was called "A Lyrical Legacy: Music of the Mayrenik (Motherland)." Three accomplished Armenian artists and one Russian artist performed magnificently, pieces of Sayat Nova (1717–1795), Komitas (1869–1935), and Aram Khachaturian (1903–1978). The artists were pianist violinist Sergei Panov; Cynthia Khachadurian; soprano Sarah Khatcherian; Armenian pianist Mariam Nazarian (Marie Nazar). Ms. Khachadurian had given solo concerts in the Middle East and had appeared with the N.J. Symphony Orchestra, Trenton Symphony, and Chicago Symphony. We all enjoyed this glorious musical, and afterwards we were invited to a reception at the Winants Hall with many Armenian pastries and other delicacies. Everyone socialized with one another and met the artists personally. This was a very good day.

Over the past decade, the Armenian Studies Program has continued to offer Armenian language and history courses to Rutgers University students. Also, they have sponsored lectures and cultural events for the general public. Through the dedication and hard work of alumni and friends, the rich culture and history of Armenia have become an integral part of academic studies at the University. As we celebrate past accomplishments, we look forward to the future.

The Rutgers Annual Fund Drive made all the activities possible, such as the ones that the Armenian Club sponsors routinely through the generous gifts to the Albert Wolohojian Memorial Fund for Armenian Studies. All such donations by anyone are eligible for charitable deductions.

Kudos to Drew University

On April 28, 1997 at Drew University, Madison, N.J., there was a very special conference of scholars, historians, community leaders, clergy and graduate students from different states focused on studying the Armenian Genocide. The day's programs were sponsored by Drew's Graduate School and co-sponsored by the Center for Holocaust Study. The main topic was "Political and Historical Controversies, and Academic Responsibility," since Heath W. Lowry, a professor at Princeton University, had made untrue remarks about the Armenian Genocide. Lowry was well-funded by the Turkish government.

The day's rich agenda began with Dr. James Pain, the Dean of the Graduate School at Drew. Also, greetings were given by former Governor Thomas Kean, then current president of Drew University. President Kean spoke emphatically that such atrocities as the Armenian Genocide should never, never occur again.

The first keynote speaker was Dr. Richard Hovannisian, the world renowned 20th century historian from UCLA. I think he is a giant among many well-known historians. I was delighted and honored to meet him. He has written numerous books on Armenian history and is eloquent in addressing an audience. He has a human encyclopedic knowledge. He concluded his talk with the challenge that we should not only concentrate on the Turkish denial, but also emphasize our victimization. He added: "Let's not call our heroes 'martyrs,' but 'victims,' because martyrs go to their death willingly, but our people were forced to die." I thought this was a very poignant observation, one which we had not heard before.

The second keynote speaker was Dr. Robert J. Lifton, a psychiatrist at City University of N.Y. He is also a writer and a historian, author of the

Nazi Doctors, depicting Nazi medical killings and the psychology of genocide. He opened his speech by saying,

"Where do we go from here? We should concentrate on *love* rather than destruction. There are identifiable truth, and identifiable falsehood. The ultimate humiliation is *denial*, and that was the Turkish government's last resort! This, of course, brings out anger in people, falsification of the truth. Heath W. Lowry of Princeton University was the Turkish consultant to deny the Armenian Genocide, because he was paid well. This scholarly failure in academia should not be allowed, and we must influence conscientiousness in human beings that this type of atrocity should never occur. The Turks cannot win out of denial, because, the types of scholars such as Lowry will invite new genocides."

Those words were so strong and meaningfully uttered. Dr. Lifton is a stately gentleman, and one can see his strong language fits his demeanor.

Another keynote speaker was to be Dr. Israel Charny of the Institute on the Holocaust and Genocide. I would have liked to have met him also, but he was unable to attend due to sickness in the family. Thus, Dr. Peter Ochs, Drew University professor of Jewish Studies, started by saying, "Jews and Armenians are both children of God, and they both have suffered Genocides." Then, he began reading Dr. Charny's paper (in part) "…The Turkish government coming from Ankara tries very hard to contaminate the truths and facts because they are being paid by grants by the Turkish government."

There was a panel of scholars on the following topics:

Panel I: "The Armenian Genocide: The Evidence of the Missionaries." I attended this one. Very factual, eyewitness diaries of people working in Turkey at the time of the Genocide were fully disclosed. The panel members were: Suzanne Moranian, Dale Patterson, Barbara Merguerian, and Susan Billington Harper. After the panel members spoke, there was a question and answer period.

Following the first panel we were served lunch at the Baldwin Gym. Again, my husband and I were honored to have Dr. Richard Hovannisian sit at our luncheon table with friends of ours, Mr. & Mrs. Onnik Marashian; Rev. Ara Heghinian of the Paramus Armenian Presbyterian Church; and Rev. Bakalian of the Armenian Evangelical Church of New York City. Following lunch, the panels continued.

Panel II: "The Role of Memory in the Meaning of the Genocide." The panel members were: Vigen Guroian, Loyola University Maryland; Peter Balakian, Colgate University; and Paul Boghossian, NYU.

Panel III: "Comparison of Genocide in the 20th Century," with Dr. Helen Fein, CUNY; Dr. Ervin Staub, University of Mass. Amherst; Robert

Melson, Purdue University; and Sybil Milton, senior historian of the U.S. Holocaust Museum.

Panel IV: "Contemporary Reaction to the Armenian Genocide." Panel members were: Henry Morgenthau III, grandson of U.S. Ambassador to Turkey from 1913–16; David Eisenberg of UCLA, another Morgenthau family member; Dr. Ara Sarafian of Columbia University; and Moderator Dr. David Cowell, Drew University.

Panel V: "Impact of Lewis Civil Trial in France on the Armenian Genocide Controversy." The panelists were: Dr. Rouben Adalian from the Armenian National Institute of Washington, D.C. (Dr. Adalian had been very helpful, having sent videos to me when I needed them for lectures to junior high students all over Union County and at Raritan Valley Community College) and Dr. Paul Boghossian of NY University.

Dr. Richard Hovannisian and the author.

Gov. Kean, the author, and Dr. Adalian.

Henry Morgenthau III and the author.

At the closing reception, Drew President Thomas Kean gave final remarks. It was truly a very fruitful, informative, and scholarly day. One can see how much care and preparation were given to such a big task. Kudos goes to Thomas Kean and Drew University's Graduate School.

A Few Words About Thomas Kean

I had worked with Thomas Kean at the NJ Assembly when I was an administrative aide to Assemblyman William J. Maguire of the 22nd District. After that time Tom Kean ran for Governor. He was a very well-liked person, and among many other candidates, he was the victor. He was also a great advocate for women's rights.

The author congratulates the Hon. Marie Garibaldi, first woman justice on the Supreme Court of N.J., upon her installation in 1982.

The Women's Political Caucus of NJ honored Justice Marie Garibaldi on March 11, 1983 at the Hyatt Regency Hotel in New Brunswick, NJ. Honorable Marie L. Garibaldi of Weehawken was the first woman to sit on the Supreme Court of New Jersey. Over 250 joined in saluting Justice Garibaldi. Three members of Union County from the Caucus served on the special committee to make the preparations for this affair. They were from the GOP Task Force: Sally Minshall, Elizabeth Cox, and the author. I was the main registrar of the whole event. Governor Kean took time from his busy schedule to preside at this celebration. At that time, he was one of 16 chief executives across the country who had appointed women to their state's highest court. I received a letter from First Lady Nancy Reagan that she was sorry not to be able to attend, but she sent her best wishes to Honorable Judge Garibaldi and congratulated her upon her outstanding achievements. Also, Honorable Sandra Day O'Connor, the first woman to sit in the U.S. Supreme Court, congratulated Justice Garibaldi as "a fine justice on your state's highest court, and I know all the citizens of New Jersey are delighted with her selection." The Governor praised Justice Garibaldi, and told us that he was honored to make this historic nomination.

After the two-hour festivities, Justice Garibaldi enjoyed dinner with all her friends.

The author dines with Justice Garibaldi.

Here I would like to mention happily that my family and I were invited to Governor Kean's inauguration. We attended the ceremony on Tuesday, Jan. 19, 1982, at the State House in Trenton. The prelude was at 11 a.m. to 12 noon with organist Robert McDonald and the Livingston High School Band.

Inauguration Ceremony Program

"The Star Spangled Banner"
Joint Session of the Senate and General Assembly called to
order by the Honorable Carmen A. Orecchio,
President of the Senate

Invocation by Rabbi Gershon B. Chertoff of Temple B'nai
Israel, Elizabeth, NJ (I served on the Board of Governors of
Union County College with Judge Chertoff)

Reading of the Certificate of Election of the Honorable
Thomas H. Kean, Governor of the State of New Jersey,
by the Honorable Donald Lan, Secretary of State

Administration of the Oath of Office of Governor to
the Honorable Thomas H. Kean
by Chief Justice Robert N. Wilentz

Salute of Nineteen Guns
"Hail to the Chief" by the
Livingston High School Band

Prayer by Reverend Otto L.M. Lolk of
St. Peter's Episcopal Church, Livingston, NJ

Delivery of the Great Seal of the State of New Jersey to
Governor Thomas H. Kean by the Honorable Donald Lan

Introduction of Governor Thomas H. Kean to the Members
of the Senate and General Assembly by
the Honorable Carmen Orrechio,
President of the Senate

Address by Governor H. Kean

Benediction by the Reverend Monsignor Harold A. Murray
of St. Rose of Lima Church, Short Hills, NJ

"Wow," I never thought that I would see this kind of ceremony as I stepped out of the *Nea Hellas* ship, a Greek Line, when I entered the USA as a preteen with my family. It was such an honor to be invited to a governor's inauguration about thirty years later.

Governor Kean did not have an Ethnic Advisory Council, but he never forgot the Armenians. Every year, during the April 24 anniversary, he would issue a Proclamation, plus, he would invite the Armenian community leaders and clergy on or around the date to have a ceremonial reception in Trenton honoring that day with all of us.

Raritan Valley Community College

Dr. Tulsi R. Maharjan, director of the Institute for Holocaust and Genocide, invited me with a formal letter, then a personal call, to be a speaker on March 16, 2000, at Raritan Valley Community College (RVCC). My name had been submitted to them by Governor Whitman's office and he had read some newspaper articles about my genocide speeches.

This was the 19th Annual Holocaust and Genocide Program: "Learning Through Experience." The day was well-organized, with transportation for junior high students from different localities. Topics covered were prejudice and bias. The RVCC Campus lies at the crossroads of central New Jersey, with Routes 22, 202 and 206 and Interstates 287 and 78 just minutes away. The College is situated on the north side of Route 28 in North Branch, N.J.

Agenda

9:15 a.m.	*Introduction*—Dr. Tulsi R. Maharjan, director, Institute for Holocaust and Genocide Studies
9:20 a.m.	*Welcoming Remarks*—Dr. G. Jeremiah Ryan, President, RVCC
	Greetings—Lawrence Zeller, Jewish Federation of Somerset, Hunterdon and Warren counties
9:25 a.m.	*Opening Keynote Speaker*—Floyd Cochran, director, Education and Vigilance Network

Floyd Cochran had a background that we would not want to be associated with. However, let's learn about his past activities. Until 1992, he was the chief recruiter and national spokesperson for the Church of Jesus Christ-Christian/Aryan Nations, which was a white supremacist group

51

that believed in Nazi ideas with a racist brand of fundamentalism known as "Christian identity." He was also a proud reader of Ku Klux Klan and Nazi literature for almost 25 of his 34 years of life.

In his role as recruiter, Cochran used music videos to carry the message of white supremacy to the nation's children. According to him, he said, "We (the Aryan Nations) used to send people into the cities to pick up homeless kids and bring them back to the compound. This was easy: you give these kids food and shelter, and tell them that you love them, you can do just about anything with those kids."

In the spring of 1992, Cochran denounced his membership in the Aryan Nations and began to travel in the U.S. speaking against racism. Thus, he had no job and no money and lived in a tent. Numerous community-minded people helped him. Today, as director of Education and Vigilance Network, he is very concerned about 25,000 activists in this cause, and 150,000 sympathizers in American hate groups. He said, he speaks mainly in high schools, colleges, universities and other communities around the nation as to how we can counter the message of racist indoctrination.

This was such an eye-opener, for this age and generation, that such hatred is cultivated by people filled with hate. I think it was worse yet to hate in the name of our Lord, Jesus Christ. Those people have no shame or conscience. That is not what our Lord teaches us.

10:15 a.m.	*Workshop A*
11:15 a.m.	*Workshop B*
12:15 p.m.	*Closing Session*, College Theater, Maude Dahme, Member N.J. Commission on Holocaust

My timeslots were both Workshops A and B in room N-329. I had busloads of students coming from different parts of New Jersey, from various junior high schools. I presented the same agenda to both groups, focusing on how one of the oldest established civilized Christian Armenian people in Western Asia became a Christian island in a Moslem state, and succumbed to the hands of Turkish Ottoman Empire and annihilation.

There were many questions asked after the workshops. The young people were hearing for the first time of the tragedy that befell the Armenian nation, and they knew nothing of the First Genocide of the 20th Century. I felt relieved by educating these young people of such atrocities of the past so they can learn and be vigilant in their future years to stop such acts and condemn those who do them. I was elated to learn that now academia is concerned and, therefore, education is being introduced in schools to propagate decency and human rights.

The author and the students at RVCC.

The author and Dr. Tulsi Maharjan.

In addition to thanking me in person, Dr. Tulsi R. Maharjan sent a gracious letter saying:

"Thank you for sharing your knowledge with our students. We appreciate the skill with which you engaged students in a dialogue on pressing matters affecting our community and the world.

"In such a huge understanding, we need the cooperation of many people. Your contribution to this program is greatly appreciated."

Soon after, in April of 2000, I received another invitation from RVCC, this time from Professor Angela Bodino, who said she learned through the evaluation sheets that everyone had learned a lot and appreciated such an educational presentation. She asked me to be the main speaker on April 4, 2000, to adults of the community, faculty members and college students. I sacrificed the day, because that was our wedding anniversary, but my husband was sweet for not making an issue of it. We celebrated with a nice dinner on the 5th of April.

The emphasis of my speech this time was a detailed historical background of Armenia and its people, whose history goes back thousands of years. Then I spoke of our kings and dynasties. Also, Armenians were the first government nationally to have accepted Christianity in 301 A.D. I explained how we were surrounded by many enemies, how we succumbed to the Turkish rule, and finally the Armenian Genocide in 1915.

There was a question and answer period that took longer than I expected, but I did not want to cut people off, because they were so interested to learn—especially the faculty members and the college students. I thought this mission on my part was worth the time. To my surprise, a few former neighbors of mine attended, which was very nice to see. When they read my name in the newspaper notice for the lecture, they wanted to come and see me, and stayed for the lecture. It was great seeing them; ten years had passed since their move from Clark. This was another productive day, and I was happy to do it.

All these programs at RVCC were sponsored by the Bridgewater Human Relations Committee, Somerset County Cultural Diversity Coalition, and the Institute for Holocaust and Genocide Studies, Raritan Valley Community College.

Following the program, a luncheon was prepared for the Holocaust survivors who were present and the faculty members at the Welpe Theater.

Finally, I thought, the Armenian Genocide will be remembered, and hoped it will not be called the "Forgotten Genocide" anymore.

A Gem of a Program at Union County College

Union County College in Cranford hosted "Overcoming Hatred/ Creating Community" events, February 26–March 1, 2001. The week was a series of different events open to the community, which were dedicated to creating a more civil society through understanding of the roots of hatred. All events were free, but donations were accepted. The events were made possible by a grant from the New Jersey Council for the Humanities, a state program of the National Endowment for the Humanities. Additional support was provided by Chase Manhattan Bank, the Karma Foundation, the Haremza Foundation, Union County Board of Chosen Freeholders, and the N.J. Division of Cultural and Heritage Affairs, and Cultural and Educational Affairs Committee (CEPAC), and Union County College Student Government.

An art exhibit was on display in the Tomasulo Art Gallery in the Kenneth Mackay Library. The works on exhibit were on loan from the New Jersey State Museum in Trenton and the Haremza Foundation Collection. Various pieces depicted the Holocaust and other examples of persecutions. On Monday, February 26, 2001, UCC Professor Emeritus Oscar Fishtein read from his book, *I'll Sell You a Million Jews*, at 6:00 p.m. in the Tomasulo Art Gallery. Then the Theater Project performed dramatic readings in a presentation called "It Can't Happen Here—The Rise of Nazi-ism in the 20th Century," in the Roy Smith Theater.

Tuesday, February 27, 2001, was my presentation: "Who Remembers the Armenians?" My role as a member of the Board of Governors, Foundation Trustee, and president of the UCC Alumni Association was to be in charge of this evening's program. I designed the invitations for the program with Mt. Ararat, a sunrise scene with birds flying in the air. Those invitations were sent to all faculty members, judges in Union County, school principals, board of education members, freeholders, N.J. and Federal elected officials, Governor Whitman, and other select personnel. I personally had invited District Attorney of New York County Robert Morgenthau to be present as a part of the program. His grandfather was Ambassador to Turkey, 1913–16, during the Armenian Genocide. His family had been very close to the Armenians, and they have supported the Armenian cause throughout these years. Furthermore, Ambassador Morgenthau had witnessed the Turkish atrocities and wrote about them in *Murder of a Nation* accusing the Turkish Ottoman Empire of slaughtering innocent Armenians. He kept the U.S. State Department informed about these horrendous acts throughout his tenure as the ambassador. He finally left his post in 1916 feeling helpless.

He was not able to help the Armenians, because the U.S. government was in an isolationist mode.

Since District Attorney Morgenthau was busy on February 27th, he was not able to attend, but sent me a very cordial letter and wished us all success.

Furthermore, it was announced in all local papers to have the evening open to the general public. However, in the invitations, there were reply cards for reserve seats for people who registered in advance. Everything was handled in a very well-organized way. My deepest thanks go to Bonnie Sirower, who was the director of Annual Giving at Union County College. She worked amicably and ably with me to the end of this program.

Prior to the evening of this big event, there were many chores to complete. I had to prepare the content, the procedure, and get the entertainment set appropriate to the program.

The Committee's last meeting before our week's events took place on Thursday, February 22. At this meeting, everyone was informed of their tasks, of all the programs, speakers, and special readings. For my part, I had my materials all ready. Since I was going to have a large group of Armenian dancers, I had to obtain an insurance certificate to be able to sign their performance contract. There was much to be done on everyone's part, but I took it to be my responsibility to have a successful evening presenting a totality of the Armenian history in an hour or two to complement the entertainment and other activities. The hard work paid off. It was a full house in the Roy Smith Theater. I was sorry to hear later on that some people came but could not get in; both the auditorium and the parking lot were full. At 7:30 p.m. everything was set to go!

Bonnie Sirower, the events chair, greeted everyone, then introduced me as the mistress of ceremony, and the person in charge of the evening's program. I greeted everyone cheerfully and enthusiastically and thanked them for traveling a long distance to be there. Although some were from local towns, I knew of others had traveled from New York State, Pennsylvania, and even Maryland to be with us. I thanked especially Bonnie Sirower, our committee had held meetings for six months to prepare the week's programs. All this was volunteer work on our part. Also, I thanked all the sponsors for making this opportunity a possibility with their generosity.

Then I began my planned work for the evening. I wanted the audience to be able to connect to the historical events that I was to talk about, especially those who were not familiar with the Armenian history. I began with a PowerPoint presentation outlining over 3,000 years of history. Fifteen sections were summarized, from the beginning times to the present.

The first slide was titled, "Who Remembers the Armenians?" Under it, I had chosen three important photos: one was a photo of the city of Yerevan; the second photo was the Sardarabad Monument, and the third photo was the carved monument of Karabagh, the grandma and grandpa figures. I explained each picture and clicked to the next set.

Author addressing the audience.

The title of second section was "Major Periods of Armenian History."
- Haiassa, Nairi: 13th–9th centuries B.C.
- Urartian Kingdom 810–600 B.C.
- Autonomous Satrapy of Persia: 600–344 B.C.
- Hellenistic Rule: 334–190 B.C.
- Dynasties of Ardashessians, Arshagoonies, Mamigonians: 190 B.C.–7th century
- Arab Rule: 7th–9th centuries

I briefly explained these periods, too.

The next section continued "Major Periods of Armenian History."
- Independent Kingdom of Bagradoonis: 9th–11th centuries
- Cilician Armenia: 11th–14th centuries
- Seljuk and Persian Rule: 15th century
- Ottoman Turkish Rule: 16th–20th centuries
- Republic of Armenia: 1918–1920
- Soviet Armenia: 1921–1991
- Republic of Armenia: September 1991–present

Here, again, I walked very briefly through the various time periods.

The fourth slide was titled, "The Armenian Empire of Dikran the Great in 70 B.C.," which showed how vast an area original Armenia occupied.

The fifth part was titled, "Armenia, First Christian Nation in the World—301 A.D." Here, too, I explained how adoption of this came to be.

The next section was called, "Cathedral of Etchmiadzin in Armenia," and had a picture of the Cathedral. The church was built by King Drtad III and St. Gregory the Illuminator in 314 A.D. There is a Khatchkar (stone cross) on the side. Again, I very succinctly explained the significance of this church.

Slide 7 showed my visit to Etchmiadzin in April of 1986 and meeting Vasken I, Catholicos of all the Armenians. Slide 8 had the "Armenian Alphabet" invented by Mesrob Mashdots, 404–406 A.D. I read this aloud so they could hear the different sounds, unlike any other language. The next slide was "The Armenian Prayer."

Slide 10 was "Battle of Vartanantz, 451 A.D.," with a picture of Vartan Mamigonian. Here, I explained about his faith and how he fought the Persians. Sad to say, he gave his life during that battle.

The next slide contained "The First Genocide of 20th Century—The Armenian Genocide" by the Turkish Ottoman Empire 1915–1923. Here, I had Ambassador Morgenthau's picture, because he had witnessed the atrocities of the Turks, and informed our government during the time of his tenure, 1913–1916.

Number 12 was my visit to Ainjar, Lebanon, where I saw the "18 black boxes" of our heroes' ashes and bones at the St. Paul Armenian Apostolic Church, who had given their lives fighting on Musa Dagh (Mt. Moses) in Turkey during the Genocide in 1915. I had the picture of all 18 boxes, and I was sadly gazing at them. And, on the other side of the slide, I had the picture of *40 Days of Musa Dagh* book by Franz Werfel.

I moved on to "Virginia's Trip to Musa Dagh, 1991." I explained that I wanted to go back and search the land where I was born, and to see the monument built on Musa Dagh for the 18 heroes. I talked about this grueling trip of one whole day to get on top of that famous shrine. Sorry to say, it was no longer there; it had been destroyed by the Turks.

Number 14 showed independent Armenia today, with a map and, at the time, President Robert Kocharian, our second one since our independence.

The last frame showed my credits, that I was a member of the NJ Governor's Ethnic Advisory Council Member, president of Union County College Alumni Association, and member of the Board of Governors, and Foundation Trustee of the College.

This media presentation's technical work was prepared by the able hands of Amarjit Kaur of the UCC's Technical Department of the Media Center. She was a very able person to put all this together for me in a lucid way and it was visible throughout the auditorium.

Next, a film was shown called, "Everyone's Not Here," a very moving story of three genocide survivors who told their stories of being spared from the Armenian Genocide, except all three of them lost family members. It was not an easy story to tell their grandchildren here in the U.S.

Shushi dancers enter the auditorium.

After the film, I introduced the artistic dance leader and choreographer, Mrs. Seta Kantardjjan with the Shushi Dance Ensemble of the Armenian Diocese of NYC. She thanked me to have given them this opportunity to perform their beloved traditional dances for us. The first number of the

59

dance was called "Black Dark Clouds" symbolizing the Armenian struggle and genocide. The dancers were dressed in black, and each carried a bouquet of white roses, plus a lit flashlight and marched into the auditorium down the center aisle, while Miss Talia Jebejian, one of the dancers, eloquently recited very softly, the meaning of our plight with verses taken from our Armenian poets to somber Armenian music playing in the background. As the dancers arrived at the stage, they very gracefully placed their bouquets at the apron of the stage and raised their arms to the heavens—at which point Miss Jebejian's recitation and the music stopped. The audience could not contain themselves; they stood up and applauded enthusiastically. This was only the beginning, more colorful costume dances followed. The audience was on 'cloud nine' in sheer admiration.

Shushi dancers on stage.

After the last dance number, the "Armenian Flag Dance," the audience stood up again and applauded a long time. Soon after, I came to the microphone, and called the director of Shushi Dance Ensemble to the stage, presenting her with a bouquet of flowers and thanking her for the excellent job she had done with the dancers. At that point, she called all the different dance presenters to come on stage, and the applause continued.

I announced that refreshments would be served at the Faculty Dining Room. Everyone gleefully joined us there for a beautiful reception of Armenian pastries: *paklava* and *choreg* were abundant to the visitors' delight. All these pastries were donated by Anahid Krichian's delicatessen in Paterson.

Everyone left the college quite pleased, at about 10:00 p.m. I had this great feeling of satisfaction that there were lessons learned this evening, and talents enjoyed by all. And this was what it felt like to be proud of your heritage. I certainly was.

Dancers on stage taking a bow.

Having thanked Anahid with a letter of mine, I also visited her store a week later with a bouquet of fresh flowers for her kindness.

To this day, in 2011, my alumni friends and others still talk about the evening of that rich cultural program on February 27, 2001. The newspapers headlined it as "February 27 Was a Glorious Evening for All Armenians to Stand Proud," and "Armenian Program a Hit", and many more accolades were given.

On Wednesday, February 28, at 3:30 p.m. and 7:30 p.m. in the Roy Smith Theater, the George Street Playhouse presented performances of the socio-drama, *And Then They Came for Me*. This powerful play was about two surviving friends of Anne Frank.

On Thursday, March 1, at 7:30 p.m. at the Roy Smith Theater, we had panelists representing different ethnic groups who have had experience with atrocities and different forms of discrimination. The panel consisted of Dr. Qaaim Saalik, a specialist in African culture and history, Rutgers University; Rev. In Cheoh, of the Korean Calvary Presbyterian Church in Livingston; Chief Roy Crazy Horse, of the Powhatan Renape Indian Nation of Mahwah (a friend of mine from the New Jersey Ethnic Advisory Council); and Eric Freedman, president of Ahavas Shalom, the last synagogue in Newark.

Thus, the week's celebrations ended with high spirits, and kudos to all the participants who worked so hard to make these programs possible. Special events such as these are priceless. To cultivate human dignity in all nations is a necessity. To educate the general public is highly essential against all tides of resistance that try to thwart that possibility. We must all be dedicated to teach our youth and educate the general public that they, too, will walk in integrity in honor of all who have suffered unjustly. Then, only then, we all will have the everlasting, cherished dreams we all long for: peace and harmony.

PART TWO:

A Brief History of Armenia

5

The Land, the People, and the Culture

The Land

Urartu was one of the large kingdoms of the Ancient East, around 1288–1286 B.C. It was a feudal kingdom located near Lake Van, and on its shore stood the capital city of Van, the first capital of Armenia. Eleven more capitals followed: 2) Armavir; 3) Yervantashad; 4) Ardashad; 5) Dickranagerd; 6) Vagharshabad: 7) Tvin; 8) Pakaran; 9) Shiragavan; 10) Gars; 11) Ani; and 12) Yerevan.

The present day capital of Armenia is Yerevan, which is also ancient, but today it has many modern edifices—such as the government buildings, the Opera House, new hotels, libraries, the American University of Armenia and many others. Yerevan was built at the foot of Mount Ararat. It is as old as Babylon and Nineveh of the Bible, and older than Rome by thirty years. Yerevan was founded by Urartian King Argishti I in 782 B.C. Much of Armenia's industry is concentrated in Yerevan. Also, the city is a famous tourist attraction, drawing people from all over the world, due to its unique ancient history and amazing old churches with their characteristic domes, still standing of thousand years.

The Urartu Kingdom arose with the slow fading of the Nayiri Kingdom, which preceded it. David Marshall Lang, the famous author and professor of Caucasian Studies at the University of London, has written many books, but he has had a keen interest in Armenian history for over a quarter of a century. He has done intricate historical research on Armenia, culminating in his book, *Armenia: The Cradle of Civilization*. The book is written with such expertise and detail; it is a fountain of knowledge on Armenian history. I will share some of it here with you.

Armenians call themselves *Hi*, and their country Hiasdan after Haig. Haig was a legendary archer, and grandson of Japhet, who was son of Noah (Genesis 10:11) whose ark came to rest on Mount Ararat (Masis) at the end of the flood (Genesis 8:41). It was Haig, according to Movses Khorenatzi (a 15th century Armenian historian who traces Armenian origins as far back as Noah, and even Adam), who led his people from the tyranny of Pel in the plain of Shinar (Mesopotamia) to the cold mountains of Armenia. Khorenatzi has said the traditional site of the Garden of Eden was in Armenia. For many years, scholars were generally of the opinion that Khorenatzi, in an effort to preserve all he could, may have included in his history many legends which have little or nothing to do with historical reality. However, recent years' archeological discoveries on the plains of Mount Ararat have, perhaps, enhanced his credibility.

Last year, the oldest leather shoe was discovered in an Armenian cave of 5,500 years old. This year, 2011, a prehistoric winery was discovered in an Armenian cave in Vayots Dzor province, which is considered to be 6,100 years old. These news items were given in major newspapers, on CBS radio, and in the newsletter of Armenian Eastern Diocese.

Writer Arnold J. Toynbee says, "The Armenians are perhaps the oldest established of the civilized races in Western Asia." This British historian had done much research regarding the Armenians. Also, N. Mikhailov, a Russian scholar, calls Armenia, "The oldest state to have existed on the territory of all of Russia and one of the most ancient in the world." Historic Armenia was located between the Black, Caspian, and Mediterranean seas, and has been the homeland of a nation over 3,000 years.

The present Armenia, after numerous map changes, now is located in Western Asia. It is slightly larger than the state of Maryland, occupying only an area of 11,500 square miles, 225 miles at its longest part and 150 miles in width. With an annual number of sunshine hours in Ararat Valley of 2,700, Armenia is termed the land of sunshine. It is almost 70 percent mountainous, 13 percent forest, and only 17 percent rich, arable land. Among the rivers and lakes is the beautiful Sevan Lake, one of the highest lakes in the world and famous for its "prince of fishes," the golden trout. In 1986 I had the pleasure to dine near Sevan Lake, on that very tasty trout cooked with Armenian fine cuisine.

Turkey borders Armenia to the west, Azerbaijan to the east, Georgia to the north, and Iran to the south.

Mount Ararat, having been in its past history a major Armenian landmark, is now in modern Turkey. However, it is quite visible from Yerevan from any angle. When I visited Armenia in 1986, I stood on our hotel balcony and gazed at it, repeating Armenian poetry about it that I had learned in school in Ainjar. It was a bittersweet feeling that Mt. Ararat no longer belongs to Armenia. Its snow-clad summit rises majestically to over 17,000 feet (5,000 meters).

In February 1988, a peaceful democratic movement for the reunification with Armenia began in Nagorno-Karabagh. The regional assembly of the Nagorno-Karabagh Autonomous Region adopted a resolution seeking a transfer of Karabagh from Azerbaijan to Armenia, as a realization of the right of self-determination. Nagorno-Karabagh had always been inhabited by 85–90 percent Armenians. Historians tell us that Stalin's machinations separated that part from Armenia for political reasons when Armenia became part of the USSR.

Map of Armenia today.

The Azeris did not like that idea—to have Karabagh united with Armenia. Therefore, the Azeris responded by Armenian massacres in the Azeri cities of Sumgait, Kirovabad, and Baku, turning the peaceful movement to a violent conflict and committing acts of military aggression against the Armenian population of Karabagh. However, with much work and fighting, the newly proclaimed Republic of Nagorno-Karabagh defeated the Azeri forces. To keep the peace, the Armistice of Karabagh took place in 1994, but Armenians are always vigilant lest any new problems arise on the horizon regarding this issue of uniting Nagorno-Karabagh to Armenia.

Today, there are eleven marzes (provinces) of Armenia, which contain a total of 900 villages.

There are eleven *marzes*, provinces or regions, of Armenia. The chief executive of the eleven marzes is a *marzbed* (marz governor), who is appointed by the government of Armenia. In Yerevan, the chief executive is the mayor, appointed by the president. The eleven marzes, or provinces, are Aragasotn, Ararat, Armavir, Gegharkunik (including Lake Sevan), Kotayk, Lori, Shirak, Syunik, Tavush, Vayots Dzor and Yerevan.

The People

After seventy years as a Soviet Republic, Armenia became independent on September 21, 1991. Also, it joined the UN on March 2, 1992. On January 25, 2001, Armenia also became a member of the Council of Europe.

Armenia's flag, the Tricolor (red, blue, and orange), flies alongside the official flags of the world of the UN, where it evokes pride and regenerates faith rooted in past Armenian generations. It symbolizes the inalienable right to a free, independent, and united Armenia. Armenia's first elected president was Dr. Levon Der Bedrossian, a descendant of Musa Dagh. The second president was Robert Kocharian, and the current president is Serge Sarkissian.

When President Der Bedrossian visited America, I was very elated and attended the public rally held for him at the Marriott Marquis Hotel in New York City on September 25, 1994. He was a dynamic speaker. He did not paint a rosy picture that everything was great now, but that there was much work to be done on everyone's part. Armenia had suffered with its 1988 earthquake, which was devastating, about 100,000 people were reported as having lost their lives, thousands were injured, and many orphans were left behind. The United States was one of the countries that helped in supporting the orphans, and brought groups of children to the U.S. for certain medical operations and needs. Many Armenian doctors and nurses from America volunteered their services after the earthquake. They went to Armenia and stayed for a month or two. Also, pharmaceutical companies donated antibiotics and other medicines for the Armenians in this emergency. I know for a fact that Schering-Plough Corp. donated a large amount of medicines at this time. My husband was employed at Schering then.

Armenians are resilient and very hard-working people. This was a natural catastrophe that they were going through. No matter where they are or in whatever situation, they never lose faith in God. No matter how tough things get in their homeland or any other country, they make their mark prominently.

Let's not forget our five dynasties and twenty-six great kings, one of whom was Dikran the Great, 95–56 B.C. who expanded the Armenian territory. Armenia reached the zenith of its power and glory under his rule. He built a new Hellenistic capital of Dickranagerd. During his reign, the people in Armenia wore elegant clothing and they were prosperous. However, his reign was short-lived.

Armenians are one of the most literate peoples in the world, with a 99.4 percent literacy rate (2001 census). Their main objectives in life are their faith, family, heritage, and education. There are new modern schools in Armenia; for example, there are German and French high schools, and the American University of Armenia, in addition to private church schools.

People still do farming, but not as much as before. Armenian people produce the best cognac and brandy, also computer software. There are mineral spas for health and pleasure. Yes, they even have skiing in the northern part of Armenia. The Opera House in Yerevan always has a full audience. I was interested to notice that the opera is made possible for everyone's pleasure. People come home from their daily chores and jobs at the end of the day, get cleaned up, put on their best attire, and then head to the opera. The price of attending the opera was much more reasonable than the prices here in U.S. Armenians love music and the arts, and they attend the opera in droves. That was something very interesting and worth seeing.

Another good thing for the Armenians is that now Americans and Europeans are investing in Armenia, and tourism is increasing. My dear Jewish friend Gilberta Fass visits Armenia at least twice a year. To this writing, she has been in Yerevan at least twenty-five times. She and her family plan their vacation each year to spend it in Armenia. She loves the Armenian people and she is also learning the Armenian language in New York City. She even has taken on the responsibility to have godchildren in Armenia.

Armenians are accomplished artisans of producing the superior rugs. Also, they are creators of exquisite jewelry. Diamond merchants bring their goods for fine workmanship to Armenia. When I visited there, I was surprised to see items made out of ordinary things that people will throw away here in this country: the seeds of fruits, instead of being discarded, are collected, shellacked, and made into photo frames and jewelry. They utilize anything and everything to make it purchasable. They are innovative and patient, a happy people even though they have gone through so many struggles. God has shed his grace on them. They are not rich, but what they have, they enjoy thoroughly.

In 1986, when we were in Armenia, my husband's cousins invited us to their home. They had emigrated in 1946. They were so overjoyed, and prepared a king's feast for us several nights. They would put all they had on the table to make us happy. The atmosphere was joyful. They played musical instruments for us, and the children, dressed in their best clothing, recited Armenian poetry for us. The dinner lasted with all this entertainment and merriment until 2:00 a.m. When I think of them, my heart rejoices as to how much they enjoyed life with so little. That is a God-given grace we should all practice.

The Culture

The 4th and 5th centuries were the Golden Age in Armenian cultural and political life. Kings and dynasties governed ancient Armenia. Dikran the Great was one of Armenia's greatest kings, whose reign ended only with the coming of the Romans. For two centuries, Armenia became an ally of Rome and a fortress against Persia.

Armenians contributed tremendously to the culture and economic life of Byzantium, with some of the greatest Byzantine emperors and commanders of the army being of Armenian descent. As traders, Armenians were among the first to enter China with King Hetum of Armenia visiting the Great Khan in 1255. Armenian traders established colonies in Kabul, Afghanistan; Calcutta, India; Singapore; and Malaysia in the 16th century. They also established trading centers in Rome, Venice, Paris and Amsterdam. In fact, Patrick the Armenian, first brought coffee to Paris, and opened the first café.

The Armenian Kingdom of Cilicia was the last one for the Armenians. This Christian state, surrounded by Muslim states hostile to its existence, had a stormy history of about 300 years, giving valuable support to the crusaders all along, and trading with the great commercial cities of Italy. Also known as "Little Armenia" or "Kingdom of Lesser Armenia," it was a bastion of Christendom in the East. This region was north and west of the Gulf of Alexandretta of the Mediterranean Sea. Today, that area is southern Turkey. So, as the Crusader states disintegrated in the 12th and 13th centuries, this kingdom was left without any regional allies. Continued attacks by the Memluks of Egypt took place in the 14th century, and the Armenians fought with great courage. The Memluks never stopped their heavy bombardment. At the same time, the imams destroyed the fortresses chanting "Allah Akbar," urging their troops to destroy the enemies of Mohammed. The Cilician kingdom finally fell in 1375, and King Leo V was the last king of all the Armenians.

However, during this kingdom, important links with Europe, mainly France, brought important new influences on Armenian culture. The Cilician nobility eagerly adopted many aspects of western European life, including chivalry, fashions in clothing, and the use of French Christian names. Also, European tradition was adopted in the knighting of Armenian nobles. Jousts and tournaments became popular in Cilician Armenia. In addition, two letters were added to the Armenian alphabet, and new Latin-based words incorporated into the Armenian language. Most importantly, during the 13th to 15th centuries, Armenian illuminated manuscripts were created. Nikoghos, the finest 17th century illuminator of the Cilician school, used elegant Cilician figure types in new arrangements. This particular artist was identified in some thirty-four manuscripts dating from 1640–1690. He profusely decorated the Gospels of 1656, and has over 200 illuminations. The production of manuscripts was a very complicated, labor-intensive and expensive matter. However, it was accomplished through skilled craftsmen.

71

Armenian manuscripts were usually copied, illuminated, and bound in monasteries by monks or priests who handed down their knowledge from master to student, from one generation to another.

Khatchkar (cross-bearing stone) was a Calvary cross placed on manuscripts. But the real monuments with stone crosses were carved almost everywhere. It is believed that in Armenia there are at least 5,000 stone crosses. When I visited Armenia in 1986, I saw these crosses everywhere on church walls, cemeteries and artifacts. They are carved stones, and we were told that no *katchkar* is like another; they are unique. I have a replica of a stone cross plus copies of illuminated manuscripts. The copies are on good paper, but the originals were done on parchment or animal skins with certain prepared mineral pigments for enduring brilliance of their illuminations. Then, they would be bound. Armenian bookbinding was quite distinguishable in their characteristic wooden covers with decorated leather.

Exhibitions of these unique manuscripts can be found in major libraries in the U.S., when exploring the art and culture of medieval Armenia. The exhibition's focus is the Gospel books, for over 1,000 years the most important visual expression of Armenian civilization. Throughout Armenia's turbulent history of invasions and deportations, which has scattered Armenians from their homeland, these illuminated manuscripts have played a key role in preserving cultural continuity by transmitting religious doctrines. In addition, they depict all the historical records with brilliant pictures.

However, sad to say, after 14th–20th centuries, Armenians had fallen under the tyranny of Turkish rule. Then came the genocide, and after that a brief independence (1918–1920). The Armenians succumbed to Soviet rule from 1921–1991. Armenians were industrious people. Even though they were a Soviet republic, they produced more in creative ways in business and the economy than any of the other fourteen soviet republics. In 1986, when I visited Armenia, it was still a Soviet republic, yet St. Etchmiadzin was packed with worshippers. That was a very interesting and pleasant sight to see.

In the olden days, Armenia had its troubadours, traveling minstrels of the 18th century who wrote the songs of love in the Armenian, Georgian, and Azerbaijani languages. One of my favorites is Sayat-Nova (1712–1795) or "King of Songs" in Persian. He essentially was a humane poet, and his works were first published in 1852 in a volume called "Daftar" (folio). He has won international fame and admiration. He was considered as the "prince" of all the troubadours. Also, some poetically minded clergy's compositins in imitation of the troubadours were quite popular, too. During the 5th–14th centuries when the Armenians had terrible struggles for their very existence, they never dropped out from the scientific and literary movements. In the monasteries, freedom of the mind still found expression. Armenians looked up to their writers as champions of their national independence. Armenian literature was always abundant, but persecutions made the works of the past all the more highly treasured.

Having had numerous difficulties at the time, Armenians were stressed trying to keep up with the general advancement of thought of the civilized world. This progress in various centers was quite different. St. Etchmiadzin, Constantinople, Moscow, Tiflis, St. Lazarus in Venice, and the Armenian Monastery in Vienna were for many years in the forefront of the movement. Venice for a long time was the leading center. In the city of Doges, the Makhitarists found not only freedom to express their thoughts in writing, but also discovered the resources of the Western world for men of science and letters. So, for these reasons, St. Lazarus during the 18th century and the first half of the 19th was considered the intellectual center of the Armenian people. The teaching of St. Lazarus included the study of the best ancient and modern authors, whom the Mekhitarists specialized in translating. Most of the Mekhitarists became eminent in the literary world and achieved positions of distinction in Armenia's national life. Mekhitar was the founder of St. Lazarus.

After Stalin's death in 1953, the new Communist regime in Moscow brought in a new era of cultural and scientific achievements with the hope for a better life. Thus, soon after, Armenia became one of the most industrialized republics of Soviet Union. In cultural and scientific accomplishments, Armenia surpassed most of the countries in the Communist world. Literature, ballet, opera, and art were all in "full gear." The poetry of Yeghisheh Charents and other writers' works banned during the fierce rule of 1930s were reinstated. The Soviets built hydroelectric, thermal and nuclear power stations in Armenia. The country became an important producer of power transmitters, electric motors, machine tools, computers, instruments, leather goods, carpets, textiles, high quality wine and cognac, food, and fruit preserves.

Many new schools, colleges, theaters, museums and libraries were opened, and philharmonic societies were established. Armenia made great strides in the fields of science, astrophysics, stellar astronomy, chemistry of silicates, and polymers, with scientists, such as Victor Ambartzumian of world renown. Thus, the Armenian Academy of Sciences made Yerevan one of the most leading centers of scientific research in the Soviet Union. Also, Aram Khatchadurian received international accolades for his musical talents. Stalin and Beria were gone, and the Armenians began to produce and excel in everything they were doing, especially considering they had endured the harsh regime of the 1930s.

However, there was something missing in the Armenians' life. Even though Krushchev presented himself as a good ruler with new policies, the Soviet society was still a closed society, and Communist rigidity continued. The Armenians were still prevented from observing their national holidays, and signs of religious matters were halted. These oppressive acts did not sit right with the Armenians at all. Even though Armenians were in a Communist country, without any choice and had done their best to survive, they still would not succumb to that oppression. They loved their freedom and liberty. So, in 1965, over a million Armenians went on strike and marched in the streets of Yerevan in defiance of Soviet orders not to mark the 50th anniversary of the Armenian Genocide. In the history of Soviet Union, this mass demonstration of nationalism was unheard of. The Kremlin could do nothing, and the demonstration went on as planned. Not long after this demonstration, the Armenians were allowed to build a monument in the memory of their martyrs, called Tsitsernagapert (Castle of Swallows), in commemoration of the 1915 Armenian Genocide near Yerevan. My husband and I visited Tsitsernagapert on top of a hill on April 24, 1986. That is an unforgettable memory in my mind. After the buses let us out at the bottom of the hill, we had to walk uphill to the area where the eternal flame burns. We laid down our flowers and gave special prayers. It was such a sight to see all the people winding up in a long trail. I was looking after a sweet old Armenian lady from the USA who took this trip with us. She stopped several times out of breath, until she got to the top. People thought she was my mother, because I was caring so dearly for her. But she made it to the top.

I met this sweet lady, Mrs. Armenouhi Melikian, in Nevada in 1997 at an Armenian gathering. It was sad to see her almost blind, but when she heard my name, she called out, "Is that my Virginia Apelian?" It brought tears to my eyes as I went and hugged her—she would not let me go for a while from her warm hug. Her son Gregory and his wife were there, too. They were so happy finally to meet me. They said that she continually talked about me because of so many incidents in which I was nearby to help her. I am so glad that I did get to know her, and thanked God for the opportunity to see her again.

Also, it was during this period in 1965 that the Armenians demanded that Karabagh to come back to them. That section with 85–90 percent Armenian inhabitants was given to the Azeris. Later on, after Armenia became an independent republic, separate from the USSR, they got Nagorno-Karabach back, also called Artsagh, after fighting for it. In 1994 the Armistice was attained and fighting ceased.

Armenian music is one element of the Armenian culture that has been transmitted from one generation to the next, continuously for thousands of years. Early on, we had the troubadours, but later, many talented musicians surfaced in Armenia, such as Aram Khathadurian, whose work is well-known all over the world. The famous Charles Aznavour, the Frank Sinatra of France, is an international talent. And let's not forget Komitas Vartabed (clergy), and many more in the Diaspora. World famous composer Alan Hovhannes is another gifted musician, born in Massachusetts of an Armenian father and a Scottish mother.

Pertinent to Armenian culture, I'd like to mention some other personalities with outstanding scholarly backgrounds.

Dr. Vartan Gregorian. I have met this erudite gentleman twice—both times I was impressed greatly. The first time was at the requiem of our dear Catholicos Karekin I at the St. Vartan Cathedral in NYC.

Dr. Gregorian and the author.

The second time, I was at Rutgers University at a Mason Welch Gross Lecture, at which he spoke enthusiastically about education and its sources of strengths. At present, Dr. Gregorian is president of the Carnegie Corporation of NY, the grant-making, institution founded by Andrew Carnegie in 1911. Prior to assuming this role in 1997, he was the president of Brown University (1980–1997). Also, he was the president of the New York Public Library (1981–1989). Dr. Gregorian was born in Tabriz, Iran of Armenian parents. He received primary education in Iran and secondary education in Lebanon. He received his Ph.D. from Stanford University in 1964, in humanities and history. Dr. Gregorian is a fellow of the American Academy of Arts and Sciences and of the American Philosophical Society. He has received numerous academic and civic honors, including the Ellis Island Medal of Honor and the American Academy of the Institute of Arts and Letters Gold Medal for Service to the Arts.

William Saroyan. A Californian, born of Armenian parents, Saroyan's father was a minister. Saroyan was a novelist and playwright, winning a Pulitzer Prize and the New York Drama Critics' Circle Award. He passed away in May 1981.

George Mardigian. Another Californian, Mardigan was owner of the famous Omar Khayam restaurant in San Francisco. My husband and I dined in his restaurant years ago with his fine cuisine.

Edward Mardigian. Was an engineer in Michigan, working for both Ford and Chrysler before starting a tool and die company, Oakman Engineering, which later became Mardigian Corp. He was a large philanthropist to U. of Mich., Beaumont Hosp. and the Armenian community. He was a great American citizen and a happy Armenian with his rich heritage.

George Deukmejian. He was a California State Senator, Attorney General and, in 1983–1991, Governor.

Kirk Kerkorian. CEO of Tracinda Corp, Kerkorian splits his time between Beverly Hills and Las Vegas. He is credited with development of "megaresorts" in Las Vegas. He is a self-made business magnate who has become a multi-billionaire.

Vosdanig Adoian (Arshile Gorky). A painter, he took as his professional name that of the renowned Russian writer Maxim Gorky. His works have been shown in numerous museums in the U.S. and overseas. Arshile Gorky was born in Armenia in 1905, and passed away in 1948. He came to this country during WWI when he was 16. He went to schools here in USA, and developed a very unique abstract art style. He was a highly depressed person, remembering all the atrocities of the Armenian Genocide. Also, he was saddened that his mother had died of starvation in Russia after the genocide. He was very talented, but showed his sadness through his paintings. After a series of calamities, including accidental burning of his later works in 1946, he could not bear the burden of it all and committed suicide.

Other known Armenians in the USA are—

Peter Paul Halijian of Connecticut invented the Mounds candy bar. With other Armenian investors, Peter Paul Candy Co. was formed in 1919. In 1946, Almond Joy was added.

Dr. Varaztad Kazanjian who began as a dentist, pioneered techniques of plastic surgery during WWI, and finally became the first professor of plastic surgery at Harvard Medical School in 1941.

The four *Hovnanian brothers* of New Jersey have built thousands of homes in U.S., and one of the brothers built homes and a light emission manufacturing center in Armenia.

Ara Parseghian, the legendary Notre Dame Football coach of 1964–74. During eleven years at Notre Dame, his teams won 94 games and finished among the top ten college teams.

Michael Kermoyan, Broadway musical star; *Lucine Amara (Armaganian)* and *Lili Chookasian* were great opera singers with the Metropolitan Opera, NYC.

Adrienne Barbeau, actress

Eric Bogosian, performance artist and playwright

Arlene Francis (Kazanjian), actress

Mike Connors (Krekor Ohanian), actor, film and TV (*Mannix* show).

Rouben Mamoulian, a director of films, who also staged *Oklahoma*. He was instrumental in launching the careers of Rita Hayworth, Claude Rains, and William Holden. He started his American directing career on Broadway in 1929 with the play, *Porgy,* and later in 1935 to stage the original musical production of *Porgy and Bess.*

Dr. Raymond Damadian of New York invented the magnetic resonance (MR) scanning machine, which led to MRIs.

Dr. Hampar Kelikian, physician, was known as the healer of shattered bodies. He was instrumental in helping Senator Robert Dole when Dole returned from WWII with severe injuries that had left his right arm useless and about to be amputated. Dr. Kelikian had invented a medical technique that saved Senator Dole's shattered shoulder and gave him some ability to his arm.

Andre Agassi, tennis star

Armen Keteyian, reporter

Roger Tatarian, vice president of United Press International

Mark Geragos, defense attorney in California.

Rose and Sarkis Colombosian, founders of Colombo Yogurt.

Alex Manoogian, businessman and a great philanthropist. He arrived in Ellis Island at 19 and settled in Bridgeport, Connecticut. He became the inventor of one-prong faucet under the Delta label, and the sale of this faucet became very popular. He was a life member of Armenian General Benevolent Union (AGBU). He contributed generously to the church, charitable and educational institutions.

Michel Legrand. French-Armenian composer and musical performer in philharmonic orchestras. He has done film scores and acclaimed albums. I used to listen to his albums a great deal. As jazz pianist and conductor, he has won Grammies and two Academy Awards.

Garry Kasparov, World Chess Champion. He was born in Baku, Azerbaijan to a Jewish father, and an Armenian mother (Kasparian). In 1985, Kasparov became the youngest chess champion in history at the age of 22. He changed his name from "Weinstein" to the Russian version of his mother's name, "Kasparov." His father died when he was only seven years old.

Nune (Yesayan) was named Armenia's Top Female Singer during this past decade. I have seen this young lady numerous times on the Armenia channel here in this country. Her voice is very melodious and she is quite dramatic. She is a great performer.

Also, let us not forget our U.S. Armenian astronaut, Dr. James Philip Bagian. He was born in Philadelphia, on February 22, 1952. He graduated from Central High School in Philadelphia in 1969. He received a B.S. degree in mechanical engineering from Drexel University in 1977 and an M.D. from Thomas Jefferson Univ., where he was a member of Alpha Omega Alpha. While a USAF colonel, Bagian became a NASA astronaut in July 1980. He has been in space twice: once on March 13, 1989, aboard the Orbiter *Discovery*, and the second time on June 14, 1991, aboard *Columbia*. He left NASA in 1995 and currently is director, VA National Center for Patient Safety and is trustee at Detroit Science Center.

At this point, I want to end my listing of famous Armenians here and abroad who have added to our culture. Nevertheless, there are many more that I will leave to your own discretion and knowledge to pursue.

Armenian culture has been blessed with numerous talents, and the Armenian heritage is rich with its culture of language, church and traditional customs of cooking, marriage ceremonies, and unique Biblical manuscripts. American society's reception of Armenians is friendly. Armenians have experienced little prejudice in the United States. They are a tiny minority, barely noticed by most Americans, because Armenian newcomers are mostly multilingual. Armenian culture obviously encourages education of girls since so many women have training and work experience. Armenians were dubbed "The Anglo-Saxons of the Middle East" by British writers in the 1800s, because they had the reputation of being industrious, God-fearing, creative, family-oriented, business people and, especially, they leaned towards conservatism and smooth adaptation of society.

Armenians quickly adapt to their society, learning the language, attending school, and adjusting to economic and political life. However, they are highly resistant to assimilation, maintaining their own schools, churches, language, and networks. Armenians are proud to be Americans, yet with a nostalgic pride in their heritage.

And, finally, anthropologist Margaret Mead suggested that over the centuries, Diaspora Armenians (like Jews) have developed a tight-knit family structure to serve as a bulwark against extinction and assimilation There is merit to this sentiment for some Armenians; America's culture has evolved for less than four centuries, whereas the Armenian culture is already 2,500 years into its evolution.

On the lighter side, Armenians have many proverbs that they repeat to teach a lesson. The Holy Bible is the source of many Armenian adages. Here are some:

- You cannot draw a straight line with a crooked ruler.
- A lie has short legs.
- A cut of the sword will heal, but not a cut of the tongue.
- Lock your door well; don't make a thief of your neighbor.
- He who steals a needle, will steal a camel.
- The fish begins to smell from its head.
- Do not burn the house to catch a mouse.
- A narrow mind has a broad tongue.
- A wine shop is not founded on one grape.
- A person cannot clap with one hand.
- The serpent changes its shirt, but not its nature.
- Fear the person who does not fear God.
- Gold will shine even in mud.

In each of these proverbs, there is a great lesson. Hopefully, we revere the Ten Commandments, and some of these also will come in handy to teach a lesson. All of us need to observe our actions daily, lest we fall in a trap of delusion or falsification.

It is important to know where we have come from and where we are heading. To know who we are and what we individually can contribute to society is important. This is not only granted to one nation, but also to all who see the grandeur work of God and want to be a part of it. We all have the right to participate by God's grace and loving care.

Religion and Language

Religion

As a nation, Armenia was the first government in the world to accept Christianity, in 301 A.D. This occurred during King Dertad III's reign, 238–314 A.D. In keeping their beloved faith, it is not by accident that the Armenian nation has survived the overwhelming odds of so many centuries. Our ancestors were strong morally, intellectually, and spiritually. Here lies the foundation of the vitality of Armenians. In peacetime, they are industrious and productive. In war, on the battlefield, they are valiant fighters to their last breath. They have immigrated to other lands because of persecutions and deportations. Wherever they have landed, they have embraced careers and professions to make a happy and stable life.

Who brought Christianity to Armenia? Often people ask me that when I give lectures about our history. Almost 2,000 years ago, Apostles Thaddeus and Bartholomew preached the Gospel in Armenia from 60–40 A.D., forty years after our Lord's ascension. Armenian people embraced Christ's love through the personal ministry of His apostles. At that time, faithful believers in Christ gathered secretly, since others and the king were still pagans. At the end of third century, St. Gregory was preaching already about Christianity in 285 A.D. However, since King Dertad III was still a pagan, he threw St. Gregory in Khor Virab (deep pit), a dungeon, for thirteen years. Later, at Khor Virab a monastery was built. St. Gregory was fed through a hole in the dungeon throughout those years, by Christian women in disguise. When I visited Armenia, I went to Khor Virab. It is a historical place, and it has become a tourist attraction and a shrine. I went halfway to the narrow stairway to see where the pit was, but could not finish it because it was too narrow and dangerous. People from all over the world come to see where St. Gregory was imprisoned.

With Mt. Ararat in the background, Khor Virab monastery was built near the dungeon by the same name.

After King Dertad III became a Christian, he released St. Gregory from the dungeon and officially Christianized his Armenian Kingdom. Sourp Krekor Lousavoritch (St. Gregory the Illuminator) through his imprisonment and suffering finally brought Christianity to the Armenian nation in 301 A.D. St. Gregory the Illuminator is considered Armenia's saint because he brought Christianity to Armenia through his undying faith, and the suffering he went through. For this reason, sometimes people call the original church "Lousavorchagan" (Illuminated). When one talks about the Mother Church of Armenia, which is the Armenian Apostolic Church, it may also be called the Lousavorchagan Church. St. Gregory the Illuminator had traveled from Caesarea, where he was baptized and ordained in Ani, Armenia's ancient capital. Because he was so dedicated and firm in his faith, he became the First Catholicos for all Armenians (302–325). Right away, in 302 A.D, the first Christian cathedral in the world was built in Armenia, called St. Etchmiadzin.

The *New York Times* on May 29, 2001, headlined an article written by Michael Wines that caught my eye: "From a Dungeon, a Birth of National Christianity." I was so elated that this story would live on forevermore. In brief summary, the article stated that Khor Virab is indeed a very important

Christian shrine for all people to see how Christianity began in an ancient land. Also, he noted that during Soviet rule, the Armenian churches were repressed and the worshippers were always monitored closely by KGB. It is so sad to learn that the church headquarters was converted to military offices, and some of the church relics were awarded as gifts to Communist bureaucrats. Armenia once had thousands of churches; only sixteen were functioning at the time. However, Soviet Prime Minister Mikhail Gorbachev eased the restrictions on religion in the mid-1980s. Thank goodness for that; that is why we saw the churches full in 1986 when my husband and I visited Armenia with a group of Armenians from the New York area, under the leadership of Archbishop Mesrob Ashjian of the Armenian Prelacy of NYC.

A hundred years later in 405 A.D., Armenia got its own alphabet, which I will talk about more in detail later. This was a great asset, to have the Bible translated into their language. It made Christianity more understandable to the people, who could read all about our Lord, Jesus Christ in their own tongue.

King Dertad III's conversion to Christianity came 10 years before the Roman Empire granted Christianity, and 36 years later, Constantine was baptized. So, after the fall of the Armenian Kingdom in 428 A.D., most of Armenia was incorporated within the Sassanid Persian Empire (present-day Iran). During this Marzbanic period, the Persians launched a series of persecutions against the Christian Armenians. Especially, King Yazdegert II (438-457) wanted to pressure the Armenians to accept Zoroastrianism, which included the worship of supreme god Ahura Mazda, sometimes called Mazdaism.

That was not good news for the Armenians. They did not want the pagan religion that worshipped the sun and fire. Now this was to be the real test of the Armenians' religion. After only 150 years of Christianity, would they take the big risk and face the Persian Empire's might to oppose them? So, King Yazdegert was determined to get the Armenians converted. He sent an edict in 449 A.D. asking Armenian nobles to his court to give up their erroneous decision of remaining Christian.

Soon after the nobles returned to their country, they had a general assembly in Ardashat to answer the edict. Gatoghigos Hovsep (Catholicos Joseph) presided over the meeting. It was attended by 17 bishops, 18 major noblemen, and prominent priests whose courageous spokesman was Ghevont Yeretz (Leon priest). The Council's reply was respectful, but firm; they rejected Yazdegert's edict and presented the following manifesto to the Persian king:

"Neither angels, nor man, neither fire nor sword can make us renounce our Christian faith. All our earthly possessions are in your hands; our bodies are before you, dispose of them as you will. If you let us live in our faith, we will on earth choose no other lord in your place, but to heaven choose not other God in place of Jesus. Because for us there is no other God than Him. But should you require anything beyond the great sacrifice our bodies are in your hands, do with them as you please. Generations ago our forefathers surrendered their goods, their possessions, and their bodies for the sake of the Christian faith. We are no better than our fathers. We are prepared to die for the love of Christ. But if we die as mortals Jesus may accept us as immortals."

On May 26, 451, Kachn Vartan (brave Vartan) Mamigonian was the general. On this day of preparation for the upcoming attack, Kachn Vartan, who from childhood on was well-versed in the Holy Bible, read aloud the heroic deeds of the Jewish Maccabees, who successfully fought against the Seleucid (Syria) tyrant in defense of their faith. So, Vartan Mamigonian, as the commander-in-chief of the Armenian forces, crossed the Arax River and placed the Armenian army of 66,000 at the Armenian frontier, with cavalry and infantry, thousands of civilian volunteers, and clergy. The army was prepared with professionalism into squadrons and companies of able archers. They were skilled troops with such dedication to uphold their faith. They had courage and profound respect for ancestral customs and the principles of liberty.

On June 2, 451, the Battle of Avarayr began. Vartan divided the army into four legionary formations to make sure each one had a crucial and important task to perform as follows: 1) The right side with Commander Prince Khoren; 2) The center with Commander N. Ardzruni; 3) Vartan took the left wing himself; 4) The reserve division with Commander Hamazasp, Vartan's brother.

The foot soldiers were armed with bows and arrows, spears and swords; the heavy cavalry was armor clad. There were civilian volunteers, people from all walks of life, who were armed with clubs, slings and pitchforks. Ghevont Yeretz, the good priest, who had galvanized the priests to join the army, offered prayers and made the invocation before the battle started: "May God have mercy upon us," he chanted, "and may He not deliver our Church into the hands of the heathen."

Now, let's see what the Persians had. On the other side of the river, there were 300,000 Persian soldiers, one of which was an Armenian traitor, Vassak Suni, who had helped the Persians burn some churches and put some clergy in jail. He was hoping that the Persian Empire would give him an important position to rule the Armenians. He did not succeed with his conniving ways, and finally he was put in jail at the end. Because the battle took place in an open field near the village of Avarayr, it is often called the Battle of Avarayr.

Vartan Mamigonian & Ghevont Yeretz
Before The Holy Battle of Avarayr

(451 A. D.)

St. Vartan Mamigonian
and St. Ghevont Yeretz
Defenders of Our Faith

Vartan Mamigonian. (Courtesy of M.E.B. Enterprises of Watertown, Mass.)

In addition to the enormous army, the Persians had 10,000 horsemen and a herd of trained elephants, each carrying an iron tower with a bowman guiding the animal. The battle was fierce; imagine 66,000 against the mighty power of 300,000. It was not even a fair match, but Vartan's soldiers fought valiantly, and there were dead bodies all over the field. The Armenian troops could do little but adjust their positions as the Persians fiercely kept fighting and continued their attacks. There was immeasurable confusion on both sides because there were so many bodies piled up on the field. Some soldiers retreated to the mountains. Seeing the confusion of the Persians, Vartan rallied his reserves and led a counterattack. Soon Vartan and his warriors were surrounded by the Persian vanguard and went down fighting.

The fighting ceased at dark. The beloved Armenian General Vartan was now a martyr with his commanders and soldiers having given their lives, all 1,036 of them, on this historic day, in their courageous and faithful battle to keep their Christian faith. There was much damage done to the Persian army, too; 3,544 Persians had fallen dead.

"I have fought a good fight, I have finished my course, I have kept the faith." (2 Timothy 4:7)

Yes, indeed, Vartan Mamigonian had fought the Persians; even though he died on the battlefield on that first day, the spirit and faith of the Armenians still live on. St. Vartanantz is a sacred holiday for all the Armenians since that battle was the sealing of our Christian faith for so long, being the first Christian nation in the world.

In Armenian church history, there have been two women declared as saints. St. Santoukht, daughter of King Sanadrug, was supposed to be the first Armenian martyr in Armenian church history. The other was St. Shoushanig, the daughter of Kachn Vartan. She died in prison for her faith. There was a third virtuous woman whose name was Sahaganoush. She was the daughter of Catholicos Sahag, the mother of Vartan Mamigonian.

St. Vartanantz is commemorated each year in February in all of the Armenian churches in Armenia and the Diaspora. This is the glue that has kept Armenia's faith so strong through so many centuries, that it cannot get weakened or unglued. The question may be asked, "Who, then, won this battle?" Well, it did not end that day in 451, but continued with Persian pursuit to still convert the Armenians to Zoroastrianism. For thirty-three more years, the battle continued on and off, with Vahan Mamigonian leading the armies. Vahan was a nephew of Vartan.

Finally, the Persians gave up in 484. They could not win this war to make Armenia abdicate their religion. So a peace treaty was made between Armenia and Persia: the Treaty of Nevarsag in 484. The Armenians destroyed all the pagan altars in their provinces and were free to build more churches and worship as they pleased. Yes, it took thirty-three years in addition to the Battle of Avarayr. The model of Christianity had shown its durability in a great, exemplary way.

Armenian illuminated manuscripts play an important role in Armenian history and religion. The Gospel Book is its most significant cultural artifact, both its history and the strength of the native traditions. Armenian worship designates a major role to the Gospels of Matthew, Mark, Luke, and John. During the liturgy of the Mass, priests or deacons elevate the book, carry it in procession around the altar, and read passages at burials, engagements, baptisms, and read it at visits to the sick as blessings, in homes, and at graves. The earliest Armenian illuminations date from about 7th century. These devotions were in writing and picture form.

At the present, there are three distinct denominations in Armenian Christianity. They are as follows:
- Armenian Apostolic Church
- Armenian Catholic Church
- Armenian Protestant Evangelical Church

They include eight independent organizations which are the following:
- Armenian Catholicate of All Armenians in Etchmiadzin
- Armenian Catholicate of Jerusalem
- The Armenian Catholicate of the Great House of Cilicia
- Armenian Patriarchate of Constantinople
- Armenian Catholic Church
- Mekhitarist Orders of Venice and Vienna
- Armenian Evangelical Church
- Armenian Evangelical Brotherhood

The majority of the Armenians belong to the Armenian Apostolic Church, which is the Mother Church. Then, there are the Catholics of the Pope followers and the Mekhitarist Catholics. The Armenian Protestants is the group that became established after American and European missionaries had gone to Turkey in the 19th century trying to convert the Turks. Although that did not happen, some of the Apostolic members liked the educational and church polity introduced through the missionaries. They built their Evangelical Churches, both in Armenia and the Diaspora.

In the Armenian Protestant Church there are not many denominations as there are in the USA, such as the Lutherans, Methodists, Baptists, Presbyterians, Congregationalists, etc. However, here I would like to state that the church that I grew up in and went to get my primary education in Ainjar, Lebanon, was the Armenian Evangelical Church and the polity was the same as the Presbyterian Church (USA). My mother was of the Armenian Apostolic Church, and my father was an elder in the Armenian

87

Protestant Evangelical Church. My mom enjoyed the Evangelical Church sermons and the simplicity of the church order, but during Christmas and Easter, she enjoyed going to the Apostolic Church to hear the Gregorian chants and the ceremonial mass with colorful silk gowns and jeweled crown, and the smell of incense. I went with her sometimes and I enjoyed the *sharagans* (the chants). *"Der Voghormia, Der Voghormia"* ("Lord, have mercy," repeated) in beautiful melodious chants. The priests in the apostolic churches always had very strong and beautiful voices. The Armenian Apostolic Church is the original Mother Church of Armenia.

The spiritual head of the Armenian Church resides in Etchmiadzin in Armenia. At this time, the Catholicos of all Armenians is Karekin II. He is number 132. Our First Catholicos was the founder of our Christianity, St. Gregory the Illuminator.

At this point, I would like to speak of Catholicos Karekin I. First of all, I knew him better than any other Catholicos that I had met or heard of. To be exact, I only have met two Catholicoi: Catholicos Vazken I (1955–1994) in 1986 in Etchmiadizin and Catholicos Karekin I (1995–1999). The latter's untimely death on June 29 was mourned by all Armenians in Armenia and the Diaspora.

His Holiness Karekin I was born in Kessab, Syria on August 27, 1932. He was baptized Nishan Sarkissian. In Kessab when he was growing up, a Musa Daghtsi priest was the priest. His name was Rev. Father Movses Shrikian. When Rev. Shrikian saw the ability and dedication young Nishan demonstrated, Rev. Shrikian became his mentor telling Nishan that he should go to Antilias and study there. Taking Rev. Shrikian's advice, Nishan Sarkissian attended the Seminary of the Armenian Catholicate of Cilicia located in Antelias, Beirut, Lebanon. Thus, during his priestly ordination in 1952, he was renamed "Karekin" in memory of the late Catholicos Karekin Hovsepian. He continued his studies at Oxford University and, later on, he became an outstanding aide to Catholicos Khoren I of Cilicia. In that capacity, he served as an observer to the Second Vatican Council (1963–1965). He served in Iran and America, then, he was elected Catholicos of Cilicia on May 22, 1977. During his tenure there for eighteen years, his Holiness served as one of the three presidents of the Middle East Council of Churches. His numerous writings in English, French, and, of course, Armenian were collected in several volumes.

On June 3, 1983, my husband Henry and I were invited to a special reception at the Lebanese Embassy in New York City by the Consul General of Lebanon. This was in honor of Karekin II, Great House of Cilicia. Only about 50 couples and some other guests were invited from all over U.S,, and Canada. This was a very interesting and glorious fanfare for the honor of

Catholicos Karekin II. As always, he spoke very graciously and enthusiastically, thanking everyone and appreciating the Lebanese Embassy's great honor bestowed upon him. The guests had a marvelous time. I also had a wonderful chat with the Consul General, Miss Samira Hanna-el Daher and thanked her personally for the invitation and the honor they presented for our Catholicos of the Great House of Cilicia that is at Antelias, Lebanon. She graciously accepted my expressions.

In 1973, his Holiness was elected to be the Prelate of the Armenian Prelacy in New York City, and on April 26, 1973, he was ordained Archbishop. With this title, he served four years in U.S. and Canada.

His Holiness Karekin II, Catholicos of the Great House of Cilicia, and the author.

The Lebanese Consul General, Hanna-el Daher received a Lebanese flag made of fresh carnations from His Holiness Karekin Catholicos of the Great House of Cilicia.

On August 4, 1995, the National Ecclesiastical Assembly chose Catholicos Karekin as the new Supreme Patriarch and Catholicos of All Armenians. This was right after His Holiness Vazken I died after a 39-year reign as the pontiff of the Armenian Church. Karekin I became the most traveled Armenian Church Pontiff in the Armenian Church History. In 1996, he had pontifical visits in the Armenian Diaspora to meet with his flocks, their heads of state, and ecclesiastical hierarchs. He met Pope John Paul II; Russian Orthodox Patriarch Aleksy II; and the Archbishop of Canterbury, George Carey. His inspirational visits to America in January 1996 and May 1998 attracted hundreds of thousands of Armenians in over a dozen major cities. Of all the dynamic speakers I have heard, no one comes close to His Holiness Karekin I. When my husband and I went to see him in NYC on one of his visits, he had the audience spellbound. Not only that, he was a great unifier. He also wanted to cater to the youth to guide and encourage them in their endeavors with Christian ideology. Too bad his life was a bit too short, but his memory and good deeds will always be alive in people's minds and hearts.

Henry Apelian, the author and His Eminence Archbishop Khajag Barsamian, Primate of the St. Vartan Cathedral of NYC.

At the requiem on June 9, 2002, with Hasmig and
Vahakn Hovnanian, Henry Apelian and the author.

We don't often think how very fortunate we all are in USA to have the freedom of speech and freedom of worship. We can belong to any church or choose any religion that we want. There are no persecutions connected to it. We may have neighbors of all different religions, and we still get along and respect them. That was not so in 451 A.D. with the Armenians. Let us not take any of our freedoms for granted.

Language

Language is one of the most important factors of life. If you don't have it, you cannot communicate any knowledge you want to pass on to people, generation to generation, and progress stops. The Armenian language belongs to the Indo-European family of languages.

With the support of Catholicos Sahag and King of Eastern Armenia, Vramshapuh, Mesrob Mashdotz started on an important mission to invent an alphabet for his people. Mesrob had begun teaching the Christian faith in the mountainous areas of Armenia where he found pockets of people still continuing to worship the pagan gods. He was upset, and wanted to deliver

91

his sermons in the Armenian language so that they could read the Gospels in their own tongue. Mesrob, being a polyglot, spoke Greek, Syriac, and Persian languages. He served as a royal secretary to the king, but later he entered into the service of the church. He was a respected intellectual who wanted to pursue a career devoting his life to the teachings of Jesus Christ.

Mesrob started an intense search around all cultural centers of Asia Minor and the Near East to develop some type of letters that would be obvious with the phonetic sounds of the Armenian language. King Vramshapuh had heard that there was a certain bishop, Daniel, the Syrian who had devised characters for the Armenian language. Mesrob immediately sent for those characters to study them with his pupils, and soon he discovered that they were unsuitable for the phonetic system of the Armenian language. Mesrob thought that Daniel's system was based on Syriac, which was written from right to left, and it basically had the same twenty-two characters as Hebrew. The Syriac alphabet failed to supply a complete system for writing vowels. Mesrob searched for an alphabet that contained at least thirty-six characters suitable for Armenian language sounds.

Therefore, Mesrob and his group of disciples started working tirelessly to devise a fresh system for Armenian. They retained a number of Greek letters and changed others to fit better Armenian patterns they identified. Also, they decided to write the characters from left to right, as in Greek. Mesrob retained the order of the Greek alphabet, while adding a number of new, non-existent signs, which had to have the sounds which occur in Armenian and Georgian, but not present in Greek. The work finally was completed in Samosata, probably between 404-406 A.D. with the thirty-six characters or letters. Later on, two more letters were added to make a total of thirty-eight characters during the Cilician Kingdom, which was the last kingdom of Armenia.

Soon after, Mesrob and his pupils devised an alphabet for the Germans and for the Albanians of the Caucasus. The Armenian and Georgian alphabets have continued in use with the original sets of characters up to the present day. However, today they are written in modern, cursive script. This is an amazing task that was completed by this great erudite man who passed away of old age in the year 440 A.D. He is buried in the crypt of the church in Oshagan, near Etchmiadzin.

The Armenian classical language as written down by St. Mesrob and his group of disciples is known as *Krapar* (written or book language). From the 15th century on, poets and other writers began to use the popular spoken idiom of the people called *Ashkharapar* and to write it down. During the 19th century, two main literary languages were spoken—Eastern and Western Armenian. The Eastern Armenian is based on the Ararat region: Russia and Iran. The Western Armenian is based on the idiom of the Armenians in the Diaspora. I speak the Western Armenian, but one can understand the Eastern Armenian, too, even though its pronunciation may be slightly different and the conjugation terms may vary.

The Armenian alphabet.

St. Mesrob's style was followed by a brilliant school of disciples who created a new Christian literature, covering main fields of knowledge, including theology, philosophy, history, geography, and astronomy. These classical writers of the 5th century are known as the "interpreters" or the "translators," because they brought knowledge to the people. During the 5th and the following centuries, Armenian literature was greatly enriched by many translations from Greek and other languages. Many classics of ancient philosophy were also translated, even though they had pagan content. It is

93

interesting that the originals have perished, and the Armenian translations are the only ones that survived. However, great attention was paid depicting the Bible and early Church Fathers into Armenian. It is important to note that education in medieval Armenia was not confined to theology only, but also progressed in studies of history, and mathematics. Also, science and especially medicine were very well-developed.

Further revival of culture and learning began during the 18th century under the sponsorship of the Armenian Catholic order of the Mekhitarists. The founder of this order was Abbot Mekhitar of Sepastia. He was born in 1676 and entered the priesthood at an early age, soon coming under the influence of the Roman Catholic Church. Even though he won fame as a preacher in Istanbul, he was suspect in the eyes of the authorities of the Armenian National Church. He resolved the issue by setting up a new Armenian Brotherhood, directly subject to Rome. They settled at San Lazzaro in the bay in Italy. Mekhitar and his disciples had the task of being intermediaries between Armenia and advanced countries of the West. Soon, they set up their own printing press and built a great library filled with many treasures of Armenian calligraphy and learning. In the 19th century, Lord Byron visited San Lazzaro to learn Armenian, and it has been told that the stone table in the monastery garden is still there where he used to sit and study.

After Mekhitar's death in 1749, dissension occurred among the Venice Fathers. Some of them seceded and formed a separate monastery in Trieste in 1773. However, during the invasion of Italy by Napoleon, the Armenian Fathers were driven from Trieste and settled in Vienna. They were accommodated by the Austrian government. My husband and I visited this monastery in the city center in Vienna in 1988. The late Archbishop Mesrob Habozian was a distinguished expert on ancient Armenian coins and a promoter of Armenian studies all around the world. After his death, even up to the present, writers are very much indebted to him.

The Armenian Church was blest with another outstanding personality—Bishop, later Catholicos, Khrimian Hairig (Little Father). He was born in Van in 1820. He began his career as a teacher and became the Bishop of Van. He established a printing press in Van and in 1856, he started publishing patriotic journals. He also founded several schools. In 1869, Khrimian Hairig was elected Patriarch of Constantinople. Soon after, the Turkish government made him resign and in 1889, this eloquent preacher was exiled in Jerusalem. Three years later, he was elected as Catholicos in Etchmiadzin. He died in 1907, and is dearly revered to the present day by all Armenians as an outstanding architect and patriot of the Armenian spiritual life.

In Constantinople, there were numerous Armenian intellectuals. Two of which were Daniel Varujan and Siamanto. Their lives were cut short during 1915 by the Young Turks. Daniel Varujan studied in Belgium at the University of Ghent, where there is a monument erected in his honor for this talented poet killed at the age of 31. Among his patriotic poems was "The Heart of a Nation." He devoted his time and talent to the continuous struggle of the Armenian people. Siamanto was the pen-name of Atom Yariarian, whose poems were sad. In "Agony and Torch of Hope," he dealt with the Adana Massacre of 1909, during which thousands and thousands of Armenians were killed by the Turks. He also wrote in celebration of the heroic struggle and actions of Armenian fighters of General Antranig and others. Another poet, Avedik Issahagian (1875–1957), was born in Leninagan, studied in Germany, and lived for many years in France. He came back to te Soviet Union in 1938 and was awarded the Order of Lenin in 1945. He was a very close friend of Komitas, another talented personality.

There are many learning centers in Yerevan, such as the Armenian Academy of Sciences, established in 1943. It is the leading center of scientific research and has about thirty subsidiary institutes. The Institute of Physics in Yerevan has a unique electronic accelerator, with which Armenian physicists have earned many achievements to their credit. The Armenian scientists were scholars and mathematicians, and they had made their mark in the Soviet Republic of Armenia.

The Armenian written alphabet looks very unique, unlike any other nation's alphabet. It is attractive, and when written in its cursive form, has a loopy, artful form. When pronounced, the letters come out with sweet sounds of clarity of the desired pronunciation. To learn Armenian is quite easy; the sounds of the letters never change or vary, as they do in English. Once one adapts to the soft and hard sounds of the letters, it is very easy to comprehend the reading and the meaning of the words. The Armenian language does not combine letters to make a certain sound or diphthong. We, not only have a letter for each sound, but a softer one and a harder one in each case. Thus, words with the soft and hard sounds will have different meanings. For example, for the "czar" of Russia, we would use soft "z" for that word; a hard "z" would be used for the word "tree" as in *tzar* in Armenian. There are more differentiations to separate words with different meanings It has been said often that the American anthropologist Margaret Mead even has suggested making Armenian an international language because of its easy and distinct rules.

Armenian is flourishing in the educational arena. The American University of Armenia (AUA) has graduate programs now in business and law among other curriculums. This institution owes its establishment to the combined efforts of the Government of Armenia, the Armenian General Benevolent Union (AGBU), and the Boalt Hall School of Law at the University of California, Berkeley. Many of the country's most successful young entrepreneurs are graduates of this institution. Also, the English language studies are expanding through the extension programs and the library is forming a new focal point to that end which is succeeding. In Armenia, 96–97 percent of the people speak Armenian, and of those about 76 percent also speak Russian as a result of the Soviet language policy. The adult literacy rate in Armenia is 99 percent. Most adults in Yerevan can communicate in Russian, while English is becoming quite popular now.

As I mentioned before, the Armenian alphabet does not combine letters to make a certain sound. For example, to make "sh" sound in the word "she" in English takes two letters. In Armenian, there is a letter for that sound called "*sha*." Another example is "ch" sound in the English word "chat"; Armenian has the letter "cha," and other sound letters. Once the ears are able to differentiate the sounds, soft or hard, it is easy to use the correct letter to form the word. And to some people's surprise, many Armenian words are the same root as in the English language. Here are a few examples:

English	*Armenian*
foot	vodk
mother	mair
daughter	douster
son	san
ass	esh

And English "tion" endings of a word become "tioun" in Armenian as in "organization" changing to "gasmagerbutioun."

The invention of the alphabet was a most remarkable act from the point of Christian history. It was a salutation toward an ancient civilization and independence, especially when the Bible was translated in 434 A.D. According to a European scholar who thought that the Armenian Bible was the "Queen of all translations." Thus, the Armenian Bible became with its translation and the illuminated manuscripts the link between religion and human consciousness.

Our Christian religion was firmly enhanced by having our alphabet being invented. As was noted, there were still some mountainous folk who were remaining pagans, because they did not have their own language. After St. Mesrob and his devoted students worked tirelessly to get the Armenian alphabet of thirty-six letters, things changed dramatically. Those two are linked together in the Armenian psyche in such a way that Bible reading had become a pleasure to understand the Gospels and their meaning. Also, having a sound religious foundation to sustain itself, the language component was most essential to complement both aspects, religion and language, which facilitated the survival of Armenian Christianity these many years.

PART THREE:

My Parents' Youth

Mom and Dad

How I wish I had some photos of my parents when they were growing up. However, in those days of the early 20th century, there were no professional photographers in their villages. One had to go to Antioch, Alexandrette, or Aleppo to get some photographs taken. Those cities were miles and miles away, about 4-5 hours' ride.

My parents were engaged in 1911, when my dad was 21 and my mom was 16. They were engaged for 10 years before they were married, because of major circumstances. In those days, people remained engaged longer than they do today. As long as they were spoken for, the commitment was sealed. It seems very strange in today's world to make arranged marriages or be engaged for a long time. There are some countries that still have arranged marriages today, but not in Western countries.

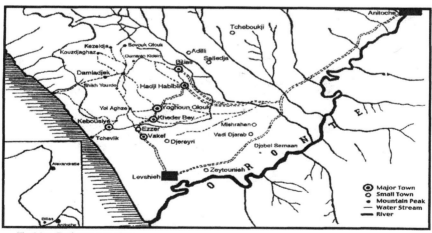

The Musa Dagh region in 1915.

Map of Musa Dagh villages. (Courtesy of Musa Ler Assoc. of Calif.)

When I was 11 years old, I had the following conversation with my mother.

"How did you meet dad?"

"Huh?" She laughed gently, and continued. "Everyone knew everyone else in the village of Yoghoun-Olouk, or any other village."

"Had you ever talked with him?" I urged her to tell me.

"Of course not," she asserted to me.

"Then…how…how did you know that he was the one to marry?"

"Oh, I knew…he was the one. He was the handsomest guy, and all the young girls longed for having their hands asked for."

"What? Hands asked for?"

"Yes, when a young man wanted to be engaged to a young lady, there would be some old wise people visit the house of the young lady, and ask for her hands to be engaged."

"That is so weird, mom."

"Yes, maybe so, but that's the way it was. As a matter of fact, we have had three parties who have come and asked for your hands to be engaged."

"What!" I exclaimed. "Who were they?"

"Oh, that is not important, because your dad and I laughed it off, and said '*no!*'"

"I am glad you said '*no.*'"

"Of course, your dad and I have had a good life, but we would never subject our children to impose such rules in the old-fashioned way."

"OK, let's go back to the reasons you wanted to get engaged to dad, besides he was very handsome. I know that."

"Oh, yes, that alone is not enough. Your dad was a very caring son and helped his parents with their properties, which they had a lot, like orange orchards, olive orchards, etc. Also, he was from a very good family and attended church with his parents every Sunday, and was active in the church. You know all these things become very obvious to everyone in a small community. As they say, he was a 'good catch.'"

"Ha, ha, that's funny, mom."

"But I want you to know that our engagement was not an arranged one."

"That's good, I feel better now."

"Let me tell you, *janiges* (my sweetie) that many others had asked my hands, and I vehemently had said, '*No*' to all of the others. Thank God, my parents did not force me. I would never, never have married anyone that I did not want to marry."

"Good, I am glad," then I gave her a big lingering hug approving her actions.

Then, she told me of her engagement ceremony. Both the village minister and the priest came to bless this future union. Both the boy's relatives and the girl's relatives usually gather, and wedding rings are exchanged. The gold wedding rings are placed on each right hand and later, during the wedding, they are transferred to the left hand, close to the heart. The girl's family makes many traditional Armenian pastries, such as *paklava*, *choreg*, olive oil layered donuts, milk and sugar donuts, and surrounds all of these with Jordan almonds. They are placed in a *debough* (a deep basket handmade with wheat straws). The goodies are placed very carefully, and distributed to close friends and neighbors in celebration of the engagement. Mom said all this was done in a week's time before the engagement ceremony.

The *paklava* (the Greeks call it *baklava*) is made in a tray and baked, layer upon layer of fine dough filled with walnuts, homemade syrup, and a touch of cinnamon; and cut in diamond-shaped pieces. It is great to the taste buds. *Paklava* was done on an open fire. The rest of the pastries were baked in the *"toneer,"* which was a brick construction, ground up, for the items to be placed on heated bricks until baked. Their other breads were prepared that way, too, in the toneer.

Toneer (outdoor oven) in Ainjar, built the same way as in Musa Dagh. Author took this photo when she visited Ainjar in 1996.

Then a question remained in my head to know why there were two clergies blessing the engagement ceremony.

"Why were there a priest and a minister officiating at the engagement ceremony?"

"Because your dad and I did not go to the same church." Mom continued, "I was 'Loosavorchagan' [Armenian Apostolic Church, the Mother Church] and your father was and is Protestant."

"Did that make any difference to you?"

"*Anshoushd, che, che.*" (Of course not, no.) She said, "We both believed in the same God, Jesus Christ and the Holy Spirit."

"Oh, I see. Is that why we are Protestant, and belong to the Armenian Evangelical Church?" Hesitating a bit, then I continued, "Did dad make you belong to this church?"

"*Che, che.*" (No, no.)"

"Then, how come you changed?"

"Well, until I was married, I still attended the Loosavorchagan Church. After we got married, in America, I enjoyed the Protestant church services very much."

"You mean you did not enjoy the Loosavorchagan Church mass?"

"*Che, che*, I love the 'Badarak' [the liturgy of Mass] and all the chants, but some of the sermons were in 'Krapar' [written old Armenian] and I did not understand it."

"Oh, I see. Now tell me about what happened after the engagement?"

"Well, all girls that get engaged, they start making their dowry."

"What's that?"

"You start making things like curtains, tablecloths, embroidered and lacy pillowcases, handmade hankies for women and men to give as *ojid* [gifts] from the bride."

"Oh, my, my—that is a lot of work, and where do you keep everything?"

"It is a lot of fun to be creative and make beautiful items. I had made numerous beautiful things. Oh, you keep them all in a 'hope chest.'"

"That's so nice. What else? What else?"

"Do you want to know everything this afternoon?" she asked. "Let me tell you something very important then I have to start supper."

"OK, mom, I am listening."

"You see these earrings I am wearing?"

"Yes, mother, you always wear those earrings, I meant to ask you about them."

"Well, they are pure gold and your father picked them out and gave them to me at our engagement celebration as a gift."

My mom's earrings.

"Oh, mom, Dad gave you those—they are so beautiful."

"Yes, that's not all. Your grandma Rose and grandpa Matthew gave me a long golden necklace with many gold coins."

"Real gold?"

"*Anshoushd.*" (Of course.)

My grandma Rose Matosian. She was 100 years old in this picture.

105

I never knew Grandma Rose Matosian. She died before I was born. I am sorry to say that I do not have a picture of my paternal grandfather and my maternal grandparents.

"I also got a long necklace made with gold coins, as a gift from your dad's parents."

"Did you ever wear it?"

"*Che*, it was too fancy and shiny and eye-catching. That is only for prosperity."

"Oh, that's sweet."

Now at that point, I learned a great deal about the customs of yesteryear. That was very interesting to me.

After 1911, the years went by quite quickly; mom was building her 'hope chest' and happy as a lark, as they say. My father was helping his dad with the essentials of keeping up with their orchards. My grandpa Matos (Matthew), I understand was the pillar of his church in Yoghoun-Olouk. My father was a big helping hand to him, and to the young people. "Your dad loved hunting, as a sport," mom told me. He would bring a string of birds that he shot and mom would barbecue them. They would have a special gathering at mom's house to enjoy the delicacies. My five uncles were loving and caring people who got along with my father very well. My dad's sister Florence was married to a young entrepreneur, Dikran Kuyumdjian. After they got married, they went to USA.

All my uncles had biblical names. Bedros (Peter), the oldest, was very well-respected. I never knew him; he had passed away before I was born. The next in line was Kapriel (Gabriel). I knew him well; he lived in Ainjar for a long time. He was the kindest and most fun uncle I ever had.

My other three uncles: Setrak, Missak and Hapet Atamian (Shadrack, Meshach and Abednego of Daniel 3:13-14).

My eldest uncle, Peter Atamian,   *My uncle, Kapriel Atamian.*
a cheteh, *one of the most*
trained soldiers on Musa Dagh.

World War I had begun in August 1914. There was much turmoil and uneasiness in the world. The Young Turks took advantage of the situation, to get rid of the Armenians in Ottoman Turkey. Turkey had begun recruiting young Armenian men from the age of 20–40. Initially, these men had high ranking positions, but all that changed very quickly. The young Armenian recruits were being used for hard labor, as carriers of ammunition and as road builders. The Turks only used their services until they were too sick or weak to continue—then they were either hung or shot.

This horrendous news was dripping in little by little in the Musa Dagh villages. It was very scary. Especially, when Rev. Dikran Antreassian returned from Zeitoun where he was the pastor of a Protestant church. He was able to leave Zeitoun, to save his family with the help of American missionaries. But he saw firsthand what was happening to the Armenians. Zeitoun was the first town to be deported when the Armenian Genocide started. Rev. Antreassian was a young man of 27 and he warned the people in Yoghoun-Olouk and the other villages of terrible things to become reality very soon, even for Musa Dagh folks. Hearing all this was bad news, but it was the truth. My grandparents, having only one son, could not bear the thought of losing him. So, Grandma and Grandpa Matosian took some of their savings and prepared to send their son, my father, to America to save his life. My aunt Florence, who was there already, would be a great help. Therefore, early in 1915, my father had set sail for America. He became established in Philadelphia.

However, my mother was extremely sad. My mom told me that when my father came to bid her "Goodbye," by tradition, all her family members were present: her parents and brothers. My mom's older sister Iskuhi was married already to the Yoghoun-Olouk chief priest's son, Bedros Der Kaloustian. My mom and dad said goodbye. Mom gave my dad six silk handkerchiefs that she had made with his initials. Mom said dad was very moved and thanked her saying, "I will always cherish these and soon I will send for you to come to America." After he left, mom went to her room and sobbed. She said she was happy that he would be safe, but only God knew when she would see him again. Soon after, her brother Missak wanted to leave for America also. He did not want to be in Turkey and fight or be slaughtered by the Turks. Soon, he left for America, too. As a matter of fact, Uncle Missak and my dad lived in an apartment as single guys in Philadelphia for a while.

Uncle Hapet was mom's youngest brother. He did not worry too much. My uncles Bedros and Setrak were ready to fight the Turks. They were very brave and fearless. Uncle Kapriel had severe asthma and could not be a fighter, but he helped in other ways. I did not know my uncles, other than Hapet and Kapriel.

I did not know my mom's younger sister since she had died at a young age. Iskuhi, my mom's older sister, lived in Ainjar, and we visited often. Later on, she came to America to visit my mom and us, and visited her adult grand-children in California, Mrs. Houry Dorian, and Jirayr Der Kaloustian.

Bad news was arriving on a daily basis in Yoghoun-Olouk of the Turks deporting Armenians from all over Turkey. Finally, the Musa Dagh people got their decree to leave their long-lived homes for deportation. The sad day arrived in the summer of 1915.

My parents' past is very important to me. We all can learn from our past, and better appreciate the things that come in the future. A few years ago, I was watching my Armenian TV station direct from Armenia when the following phrases came on the screen:

"Jantsek Anstyale" (Recognize the Past)
"Vayeletsek Nergan" (Enjoy the Present)
"Abrink Abakan" (Let's Live for the Future)

What beautiful thoughts these are. Let us live them honorably.

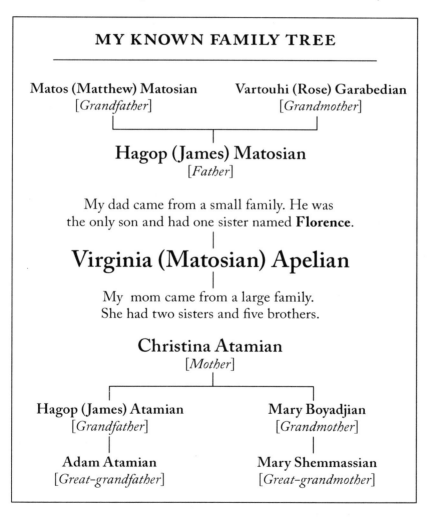

MY KNOWN FAMILY TREE

Matos (Matthew) Matosian
[Grandfather]

Vartouhi (Rose) Garabedian
[Grandmother]

Hagop (James) Matosian
[Father]

My dad came from a small family. He was
the only son and had one sister named **Florence.**

Virginia (Matosian) Apelian

My mom came from a large family.
She had two sisters and five brothers.

Christina Atamian
[Mother]

Hagop (James) Atamian
[Grandfather]

Mary Boyadjian
[Grandmother]

Adam Atamian
[Great-grandfather]

Mary Shemmassian
[Great-grandmother]

The author's family tree.

Musa Dagh Battle

"But they that wait upon the Lord shall renew their strength;
they shall mount up with wings as eagles;
they shall run, and not be weary;
and they shall walk, and not faint."

(Isaiah 40:31)

This is the story of a most historic battle of resistance by a small group of people who revolted against an established empire, the Ottoman Turkish Empire. Franz Werfel, the Austrian-Jewish novelist, depicted these people's plight in *The Forty Days of Musa Dagh*. He was visiting Damascus, Syria in the late 1920s, when he noticed maimed Armenian orphans working in factories. He wanted to know the story behind those sad faces. When he learned about the Musa Dagh people—how they fought on that mountain so valiantly against the Turkish Ottoman Empire—he was inspired by these folks' bravery. Thus, he wrote his famous classic in 1934.

MGM Hollywood was going to make a great movie about this book, before machinations by the Turkish government began to exert pressure through their lobbyists, and their government, to not allow this movie to become a reality. It was a long battle. Our State Department succumbed to the Turkish pressures and the movie was not allowed to be made by MGM. Much later on, John Kurkjian, a small business owner, made the movie after all, but not with the same enormity that Hollywood would have done it. Nevertheless, we were all happy and so was Mr. Kurkjian, who had always wanted to tell the story. It is my opinion that no matter how hard the Turkish government has tried, and are still trying to hide their guilt, it will never work in the long run. Recently, it is obvious that some very well-known Turkish writers and journalists are coming forth to admit that in 1915 there was the Armenian Genocide by the Ottoman Empire. All outward physical proofs and sealed documentations are obvious that it took place. Also, thus far, it is not well-taken with many people that the U.S. government has had to bend their human rights policies to appease the Turks.

My mother was a young lady on Musa Dagh during the battle and witnessed the hardships they all went through. That was astonishing and heartbreaking. They took livestock with them. Also, they carried their loads of needed items: clothing, mattresses, food items, wheat, flour, and many other utensils to set the bare-ground kitchens. Their bedrooms were near the rocks to be their pillows. Let alone, wild animals, and snakes crawling about their young in the late hours of darkness. No one could have any kerosene lamps or fires at night, or they would be noticed by the enemy. We are talking about people who had lovely, comfortable homes for many years in their villages. They had not done anything wrong. Why, oh why, was this happening. However, having the dilemma at hand, this was the only solution for them.

With all the hardships, they never lost faith. They had worship services and mass every Saturday and Sunday throughout their stay on the mountain. My uncle Setrak Atamian carried his grandma all the way to the top of Musa Dagh, because she was very frail and weak; she couldn't possibly climb those winding roads to their destination. My two grandfathers were great helpers, too, in more than one way. My maternal grandfather Hagop Atamian was on the Executive Council. His sons, my two uncles Setrak and Bedros, were dedicated fighters. Bedros Atamian was one of the thirty-three *chetehs* (guerrillas).

They were very well-trained, fearless men and the best sharpshooters. All the women, young and old, kept it all together with their housekeeping chores, cooking, sewing, washing, and getting the water, etc.

The story begins with the seven villages of Musa Dagh: Yoghoun-Olouk, Vakef, Khederbeg, Bitias, Hadji-Habli, Kebusye, and Izzir (very small, two-part village). Some people refer to only six Musa Dagh villages, because of the very small size of Izzir.

These villages' total population was about 6,000 people. The name Musa Dagh is Turkish for "Mt. Moses." The Armenian word for mountain is *"ler,"* so sometimes we call it "Mousa Ler." However, it has been said that there is another meaning. *Musa* may be from a Greek root word meaning "meditation, poetic inspiration" so some people call Musa Dagh (Mount of Inspiration). Since the battle was fought there, that seems to me a better explanation.

However, with all that has been said, today, the Turks call it *Saman Dagh* (Straw Mountain). Sad to say, that is not the only name the Turks have changed to erase any record or memory of the Armenians. They have changed all Armenian names and architectural work done by Armenians or any related monuments or churches having to do with Armenian history. They have tried very hard and continue to distort history. They are ashamed of their brutal past, but all the worldwide archival records will not allow that destruction to be continued forever.

So, the Turkish decree had been received by the leaders of Musa Dagh in Yoghoun-Olouk on July 13, and to all the other village leaders, that they should evacuate by July 21. It was a cunning decree, issued with many false premises to deceive the Musa Dagh people into being deported from their homes. Immediately, the leaders had many important meetings one after another to discuss this very serious matter. A special meeting with all seven village leaders present, except the leader for Kebusye, took place on July 14. They did not want to attend. Rev. Dikran Antreassian, a young 27-year-old minister was elected chairman of the Central Administrative Council. He would oversee the general activities of their agenda. Twenty-year-old Movses Der Kaloustian, an intelligent and dedicated son of the Chief Priest, Apraham Der Kaloustian, was chosen commander of the military front. All of these mentioned leaders were from the village of Yoghoun-Olouk.

The decision was made to ascend Musa Dagh for defending themselves. The climb began on Thursday, July 15. More than 4,000 in number were on top of the mountain by the end of July 15, 1915. Some of the Bitias, Hadji-Habli and Kebusye folks followed the Turkish decree and were deported to the Syrian desert of Der Zor.

By Sunday, July 18, the Central Administrative Council was firmly set and prepared for defense.

L–R: Leaders of Yoghoun-Olouk on Musa Dagh: Rev. Father Apraham Der Kaloustian, Movses Der Kaloustian, and Rev. Dikran Antreassian.

The young Protestant minister, Rev. Antreassian had just returned from Zeitun, where he had a church. Zeitun was the first Armenian town that had the decree to be deported. Rev. Antreassian was able to leave and head to Musa Dagh, the village of Yoghoun-Olouk, with the help of American

113

missionaries. If the American missionaries did not intervene with the Turkish government at the time, Rev. Antreassian and his family would have perished with the Zeitun population. However, that was meant to be—that he would return to his hometown and be one of the leaders to lead the Musa Dagh people in their fight for freedom. At follow-up meetings, the leaders of each village fervently discussed all possibilities in order to make a sound decision regarding this decree of deportation. Everyone present agreed not to subject their people, young and old to starvation and slaughter, and not have their women be raped and tortured by this barbaric people. The decision was made that they would go on top of Musa Dagh and fight. With God's help, they would go forward without any hesitation, except those few families in Kebusye, Hadji-Habli and Bitias who wanted to follow the decree and were deported. The following reasoning was discussed and decided upon by the leaders at this emergency meeting.

- That Musa Dagh was a special site for self-defense. They all knew every corner of this mountain.
- Because Turkey had joined the Central Powers during WWI, there were always many allied ships cruising near the Musa Dagh coast. So it was a great possibility of those allies helping them.
- Nevertheless, if either of these two points did not happen, it would be better to die with honor than be subjected to being slaughtered one by one, or buried alive in some ditch.

The meeting closed a bit in a somber note, because there was much work to be done and planned carefully. They were determined in their decision, and prayed for God's mercy and guidance.

In summary, the Ottoman Empire decree stated the following:

- Within seven days, everyone should arrange personal affairs to be ready for transportation.
- The gendarmes will provide help and safety along the way to the destination.
- For poor people, the government will provide food and transportation.
- Whatever you leave behind will be sold and the money will be sent to the rightful owner.
- All deportees will be settled at their destinations and be protected.
- All personal belongings you leave behind will be listed in books for the record.
- You should trust the government and cooperate in every way. It will be simply moving from one place to another.

114

- And if these orders are not followed, those shall be arrested and punished.

Signed by the Mayor of Antioch, "Magroof"

What a cunning and deceitful document this was! Where were they taking these people—and why? There was no doubt in Musa Dagh leaders' minds; they knew one thing for sure that they had to get ready in one week to climb that mountain with all the necessary things they had. It was very sad that some people were fooled by the rhetoric of the Turks' decree and stayed behind, like Kebusye and part of Bitias and Hadji-Habli. They were deported on Sunday, August 15. They foolishly thought, they would be spared, but that, obviously, was not to happen.

On Sunday, July 25, the eighth day after the delivery of the decree, the first of the Turkish attacks begun. This was not a major attack, because they did not know which roads or areas to attack. They were not as familiar as our soldiers with all the areas and the strategic points of Musa Dagh.

Soon, very carefully, the first self-defense groups were organized by our leaders and put in place. Plans were also drawn and there were four different camps arranged, about one mile apart from each other. Most of the people planned to stay in Damlajik which was the largest safe area to hold the people.

On August 7, the first major confrontation began. Several hundred Turkish soldiers were on their way. They had about six of their men killed, and the Musa Dagh people had no one killed on their side The Musa Dagh soldiers were told, "Aim exactly, then shoot, we cannot waste any bullets." So to aim precisely was very important so that they did not run out of bullets and ammunition, since their supply was a lot lower than that of the Turks.

Again, on August 10 at sunrise, the Turkish soldiers appeared from a different direction. This time they came with ten times more force, about 2,000 soldiers. Musa Dagh people had border guards who evaluated the situation beforehand. However, in the middle of the day, it started raining very hard. The Musa Dagh soldiers were drenched completely, but there was more trouble for them—about 75 percent of their firearms were not usable. The enemy's rifles were more modern, and they had more of them. Also, the Turks had two cannons. This made a horrific scare with the camp people when the cannons roared with a big bang. Soon after, one of the Musa Dagh sharpshooters eliminated the gunner and his three replacements, one after another. This quick thinking and ably aimed bullets paid off. The cannons stopped. Not only were the camp people terrified with all the fighting going on, but also the heavy rain had damaged their beds and their makeshift sheet tents, little shacks and all were under water from the fierce rainfall. Many of their food supplies were ruined also.

Dear reader, put yourself in that scene. How does one cope with all that—not knowing what the next hour or day will bring? The fear of it all gives me the chills when I think about my mom telling me her experiences. But then, going through these types of situations, makes one endure it all, and it builds character. I truly believe this. The next day, mom continued telling me that it was the nicest day on Musa Dagh. The sun shone brightly and everyone dried out their items, and even some people were whistling and singing. That's the spirit that the Lord plants in people's minds and hearts, "Praise be to His Name."

There were men called "The Workers Brigade," who were either a little old or did not have guns. They did other important tasks: clearing some brush from the camps' areas for better visibility of the enemies, digging trenches, and making ramparts. Also, they would add big trunks of wood and branches on main passageways to make the enemy's advance much more difficult. In addition, there were "telephone boys" 10-12 years old who transferred information, delivering news of enemy attacks from the trenches to the center. However, the main information was heard by the camp people by the "*moonedig ganchoghs*" (the town criers). Arakel Gobeshian was chosen for this job because he had a distinct, loud voice. He would warn the people of special dangers, traveling from one camp to the other with his warnings. Musa Dagh encompassed about 80 square miles. This was a large area to defend.

On August 19–20, again there was heavy fighting against the Turkish army. The casualties were three wounded and two men killed on the Musa Dagh side. It was estimated that the Turks lost about a hundred soldiers in those two days. Mom told me that from one day to another, they never knew what would happen next. The women went to get their water supplies from the springs, quite a distance from the camps, and the jugs were very heavy to carry. The trip to and from the springs was dangerous. If they met Turkish soldiers, they were instructed to do the following, mom said sadly, tears in her eyes:

"If we were confronted by the Turkish fighters, and had no way to get away—we were told to run to the nearest cliff and throw ourselves down."

"Oh, mom, how awful!" I started crying.

"*Me lar, siroones.*" (Don't cry, my pretty one) "I am here, aren't I?"

"I know, I know, thank God, but it must have been very hard to think you'd do that maybe."

"Yes, it was, and I often thought of your father, will I ever see him again?" she choked a bit saying that.

"Oh, mom, I love you so much, and I am glad you did not have to jump off a cliff and that you married dad, after all." I smiled and gave mom a lingering hug.

To have heard all of this made me appreciate mom more for her enduring strength.

By the way, after the fighting on those two days, August 19–20, the Turkish army retreated. However, no way were the Musa Dagh people "out of the woods" yet (interesting phrase to use here); their food supply was diminishing rapidly.

The conditions of sanitation were not good. People who became sick did not have medical attention or any medication, so a number of people were lost. The women started laboriously crushing wheat with rocks to make flour for bread and *pelav* (a wheat side dish). Things were getting very difficult. However, they did have meat, which is protein and that sustained them pretty well. Each day, the butchers would slaughter a couple of bulls for food for everyone.

The following days, the enemy fought continuously, with 3,000 regular forces, and a large crowd consisting of about 4,000 people covered the Musa Dagh fighters with continuous bullets shouting: "Allah Akbar" and praying. And their cannons repeatedly bombarded each rock and tree where smoke coming from trenches revealed where the Musa Dagh fighters were. However, by nightfall, few of the enemy had succeeded in getting to the Musa Dagh fighters' fields.

At this point, with complete assurance, our fighters answered "Allah Akbar" with our national songs ringing in the air. Soon after, bullets rang out again from the enemy, onto our armory and surrounding, petrifying the people, who ran scared into the forest. Several of our *chetehs* (guerrillas) were able to control the situation and sent the enemy into a retreat. This reversal calmed our anxious people. Our soldiers were able to capture two Armenian traitors from the Kebusye village who had guided the enemy to the camps. Then, these traitors were executed for their disloyal act upon their own people.

Two of Musa Dagh soldiers that died during this attack were killed by friendly fire. In a mountainous situation, this sad event was understandable. Hagop Havatian was wounded badly and died later. Movses Hanessian and Tovmas Kalmeshian were wounded, but survived.

117

Sad to say, there was no medical doctor or a pharmacist to help the wounded. The makeshift doctors were Hovhannes Koboorian and Levon Kazanjian, who were not familiar with the medical field.

As the enemy moved closer and closer, things became very bad. Some people were becoming too distraught and other people started acting in weird ways. For example, a man nicknamed "Sekhtor," who did not want his wife to be taken by the Turks, came after her with a big hand knife to kill her. But he missed, and she ran out of their hut screaming. A woman was crying out saying,

"I will never surrender to the enemy. First, I will throw my four-year-old child down a cliff, and then I will jump myself."

Rev. Antreassian tells of this horrendous happening. The little girl cried, saying, "Mama, please don't throw me down, I will carry a bundle." Sometimes the human mind can take just so much. When losing all hope, strange manifestations come forth. My dear reader, how would you have handled all this?

During most critical moments, despair had dominated all the sensibilities of various groups pushing them into extreme, sudden action without knowing exactly what each one was doing. They started firing on the enemy as if this was their last moment of life. This attack lasted one hour, around dusk. Amazingly, the enemy forces did not know what hit them. In confusion, they scattered hopelessly and helplessly into the darkness. The next day, our happy fighters searched the battlefield and discovered many of the enemy dead, a mule, and food items, like bread, cheese, medicine and many other items which came in handy. Our fighters apprehended booty of seven rifles and about 3,000 bullets. During this day's casualties, the Armenians totaled three dead and four wounded. According the information our fighters received, about 1,020 of the enemy had been killed and 190 wounded. It became obvious that the Turkish government found our fighters to be quite different than they expected.

The enemy had attacked the Musa Dagh people about five times with complete confidence that they would destroy our people, but at each battle attack, they retreated with very large losses. The enemy thought for sure our people would either surrender or die of starvation. Thank God, neither happened. However, there came a point when the executive body decided that the food items would have to be rationed. They gathered all the foodstuffs and placed them in one depot. They did not have a salt shortage, because they could boil seawater by the seashore.

However, there were other disturbances. When the people became desperate and hopeless, and now starvation was in the picture, they started complaining to the leaders. All had different ideas about what they should do now. In desperation, the morale was very low at this point.

One major task remained. Rev. Antreassian wanted to make a sign that would be visible from the mountain to the passing ships. A widow, reluctantly, lent her large white sheet for that purpose. Added to it was a little boy's red apron that was given to him by his Catholic Fathers as a gift, taken away from him to use as a red cross. Rev. Antreassian's sister cut a cross from the red apron and sewed it on the sheet. And on another sheet, they wrote: "CHRISTIANS IN NEED – HELP!" This was written in pencil first and then young ladies embroidered it with red thread. The two sheets were connected and sent down by the shore area with guards. They had to make sure that they were not noticed by the enemy, but as soon as they saw a ship passing, they would wave it back and forth to be noticed. Also, Rev. Antreassian had written a long petition in English, describing who they were and that the Turkish government wanted to destroy them just as the Turks were killing many other Armenian towns' people. He addressed this petition to English, French, Italian, Russian and American admirals, captains and nations—to whomever this petition reached.

"We appeal to the name of God and human brotherhood; we appeal to the name of Christ and Christianity." The petition continued stating that they were people from Yoghoun-Olouk and six other villages, totaling about 6,000 people. This figure lacks a census count, but we have a total number of 4,200 on the field of Damlajik. "We are certain that you are aware of the Turks' policy to exterminate the Armenians in the Ottoman Empire. Now the massacres have spread their horrors. . . . please save us. If that is not possible, provide us weapons so we can defend ourselves the rest of the time." The appeal was strong and asked the world to save their lives, and honor before it is too late. This was the summary of what Rev. Antreassian had written in August 1915.

This appeal was put in a tin can and sealed and was left with the guards at the shore of the Mediterranean Sea. When they saw a ship, they would swim and bring the can tied to their back to the ship. One of the guards would do that, whoever's turn it was at the time. In their desperation, two carpenters even built a boat to send people at sea, perhaps to Cypress or other cities to seek some help. The boat was built, but only one person volunteered to take the trip. There was the need of another person, but no one wanted to do it.

Then another disappointment set in when a ship appeared at the shore toward evening. Soon the ship disappeared into the fog. Again despair set in. The people waved banners, burned piles of wood and cried out loud to no avail. The leadership sent swimmers with appeals in a can attached to their backs to Eskenderoun. Before they received a reply from the swimmers, liturgy took place on Sunday September 5, a beautiful sunny day. The singing of *"Der Voghormia, Der Voghormia"* ("Lord have mercy, Lord have mercy") filled the air. People sang sadly with tears in their eyes, as if death was near.

Suddenly, the air was filled with a loud rumbling of shouts, which turned to joyous outbursts. This was about noon. The shouts filled the air, "The ship is here! The ship is here!" The ship had docked at the shore. What a miracle, finally, everyone was shouting in joy and raising their arms toward heaven, thanking God. What a precious moment that was! The ship crew had seen the Musa Dagh banners from a distance. The vessel soon arrived, in an hour, to see what this was all about. Our scouts delivered the petition, plus Katcher Deumanian boarded the French battleship *Le Guichen* and spoke to the authorities in the ship. Katcher was fluent in French, explaining the whole situation they had been in since July. Soon Bedros Demlakian arrived and boarded the ship also. He, too, spoke fluent French, and informed the Captain that the Turks had occupied one of Musa Dagh villages, Kebusye, and the church now had become an ammunition depot. Thus, in a few hours, *Le Guichen* bombarded the village Kebusye, hitting the church with all the ammunition, which exploded. The Turks ran in all directions, confused as to what had happened. After the bombardment, *Le Guichen* returned and sent boats to the shore. Immediately, bullets poured on the boats. Those bullets came from a wooded area, from the Turkish forces from Chanaklek, who had arrived at the Musa Dagh campsite. Again, there was much confusion with the Turkish forces. While the fighting was still continuing on the mountain, the Executive Body proceeded with their invitation to see Vice Admiral Dartige du Fournet. He was on the cruiser *Jeanne d'Arc*, and he was specifically coming for a meeting with the Executive Council to check the area. He shook each leader's hand and said encouraging words to them and left.

As a last resort, the Turkish government again tried to lie, saying that our people would be saved if they surrendered to them. Of course, our leaders knew better than that; the Turks could not be trusted, yet they wanted a reply. But before our people even replied, the Turks resumed their battle until evening. Soon, our fighters showered them with bullets. At this battle, two of our fighters did especially well: Mardiros Jansijian and Mardiros Habeshian who killed a few of the enemy at one time without changing from their post. Our soldiers had fought so valiantly that they received a letter congratulating them. Their work was excellent, but on September 10, about 9:00 p.m., two of the French battleships, *Le Guichen* and *Le De*

Seks, began bombarding the Turkish armory of Suedia and other points, and Kebusye. Soon, all this area had become a pile of ashes. The French government did not supply the Musa Dagh people with ammunition, but they came to our people's rescue

Thus, two days later, on Sunday, September 12, all the Musa Dagh people were being boarded on the French ships to freedom. The French ships that transported the Armenians from this terrible siege were the *Guichen,* the *De Seks,* the *Destre,* the *Amiral Shame,* and the *Foder.* The *Foder* transferred its people to the British carrier, the *Raifin* and then the *Foder* left.

Le Guichen, *a French battleship, saving the Musa Dagh people to freedom on Sept. 12, 1915.* (Courtesy of the Musa Ler Association of Los Angeles)

Could anyone imagine the joy and the feeling of being free and alive with hope? All the soldiers gazed for a long time at the mountain. How they fought with faith and, at times with fear, not knowing how it would

121

all end. All the people gazed longingly and wistfully. They had to leave their comfortable homes, orchards, and some family members because they did not make it. But, thanks be to God, now they were on a journey to a freedom that will, hopefully, last forever.

The chivalrous French help will never be forgotten in Armenian hearts, and Admiral Dartige du Fournet's name will forever be remembered in all Armenian circles. All the people on the ships were given clean clothes and good food, and they showered for the first time in almost two months. They felt alive again, after fifty-eight days of terrible ordeals. Thanks to our Almighty God. They reached Port Said, Egypt, on September 15, 1915.

Zeitoun, Sasssoun, Malatia, Marash, and Van were other Armenian towns whose people fought back as had the Musa Dagh people, but they did not succeed. Those innocent people were tortured and killed.

Musa Dagh lost eighteen valiant and dedicated fighters; the memory of them will never fade from our Armenian history. Every year in the second week of September, caldrons of *herisah* are cooked all night, a special Musa Dagh dish with shelled wheat and lamb. This dish is served to everyone who comes for the commemoration. This event is also commemorated in Armenia, in the town called Moussa Ler (Mt. Moses, *Movses* in Armenian) each year. Here, too, numerous caldrons are prepared with *herisah* and served to all.

All Musa Dagh people honor and revere these 18 heroes for giving their lives for the freedom of their people. Here are the names of our heroes:

Names	*Age*
1. Hagop Karageozian	27
2. Hovhannes Lourchian	24
3. Krikor Nkrourian	40
4. Baghdasar Mardigian	29
5. Hovhannes Kojanian	41
6. Boghos Andekian	21
7. Bedros Penenian	60
8. Jabra Kheoian	28
9. Krikor Kebourian	61
10. Sarkis Shannakian	27
11. Apraham Seklemian	17
12. Bedros Havatian	33
13. Samuel Boyadjian	41
14. Samuel Markarian	24
15. Hapet Vanaian	26
16. Hagop Havatian	30

17. Hampartsoum Khoshian   41
18. Misak Bayramian   21

The 18 Memoriam boxes of our heroes who gave their lives for the freedom of our people.

In 1996, I visited Ainjar, and paid special tribute to these eighteen heroes by visiting the memorial boxes of their ashes and bones, which are placed in St. Paul Armenian Apostolic Church of Ainjar.

Those honorable men will never be forgotten; they gave their lives for freedom, for others to have life. Just as in the Battle of Avarayr of 451, even though good people were lost in that battle to keep our Christian faith, including our commander, brave Vartan, they won the war. It took thirty-three more years, nevertheless, it was worth it and that is why our faith stayed so strong. Here, too, the Musa Dagh battle was fought with faith; they carried all these harsh days with extreme hardship and fear. Even though things became desperate at the end of days on the mountain, Almighty God sent help, and they were on their way to FREEDOM. And by the grace of God, these folks were made even stronger in their faith and were given stronger character.

"The Lord shall preserve thy going out and thy coming in from this time forth, and even for evermore." (Psalms 121:8)

If you believe in the Lord, miracles will happen. People will not perish if they have the vision of the strength of the Lord.

"Where there is no vision, the people perish." (Proverbs 29:18a)

Certainly the Musa Dagh people were shown that vision by Almighty God who came to their rescue. You may call it Providence, Faith, or a Miracle, and with all its combination, it is the Power of Almighty God.

"He shall cover these with his feathers, and under his wings shall thou trust his truth shall be thy shield and buckler.

"Thou shall not be afraid for the terror by night nor for the arrow that flieth by day." (Psalms 91:4-5)

Port Said, Egypt
and Return to Musa Dagh

ow the Musa Dagh people were in safe hands, in French ships and one British one. People took a long sigh to release their anxieties. The carefree children were running on the decks as if nothing had happened. They were happy, because they had good food to eat and pastries and candy were offered to them by the French sailors. The parents were happy to see their children's faces with big smiles. But many people did not know where they were headed, and they did not care to know immediately, as long as they were not under fire of the Turks' bullets and cannons bursting and petrifying them. Anywhere to head to was a safer place. At this point, that is all they needed.

Soon, they found out that it would be a nice place near the Suez Canal. At first, some people thought that they were heading to Cyprus, but that was not true. The French ships had started embarking these tired and physically weak people on September 12, and they all arrived at the East Bank of the Suez Canal, close to Port Said, Egypt on September 15.

Le Guichen *bringing the refugees to Port Said.*

Arrival of Musa Dagh refugees to Port Said.

Musa Dagh refugees' first Mass.

Oh, what sweet freedom, even though covered with dusty sand. The French sailors worked tirelessly and gently with all the people to get them out of the ships with their belongings. Some elderly had become seasick, because of the tremendous speed of the ships. After all, it was wartime, and they were cautious about German submarines. The captains were in a hurry to get these poor exhausted people to their safe destination. And they did.

All the tents were ready in a very organized manner. Each village's people were assigned their own section, just as they had been on Musa Dagh. It was an enormous responsibility on the part of the organizers and the volunteers to settle these folks in an orderly manner. There were Red Cross groups from Cairo, France and England to help everyone. This is important to mention: all the food, three times a day for everyone, was provided by the British. The Armenian General Benevolent Union (AGBU) was a major helping hand also in many ways. They had contributed much to make these folks stay safe, healthy, and happy. They provided Sisvan School for the youngsters up to 16 years old, which became a very popular place for the young people.

The main camp was called Lazaret. Besides the tent arrangements, there were some brick buildings to be used as a hospital, and another building to be utilized as the quarters for the administrators. Teachers from Cairo had special tents.

Each quarter of the camp had separate showers, sheds and lavatories for men and women. Also, there was a British military group at the campsite. They kept watch so that no camper would wander out of the camp, and no strange outside folks could get in. The whole Camp Lazaret was governed by a British General Douglas Haig.

A big tent was set for 12-15 men to police the camp and keep order, just in case there was a need.

School children and their masters.

At the Sisvan School, they were learning Armenian, French, English, ancient history, geography, mathematics, economics, music, etc. Mr. Karakashian was the first principal, and a very able and experienced educator. He had an immense task to classify and designate each group. He had 2,000 students to deal with. Boys and girls had separate classes. Several of the teachers were from Musa Dagh, but the rest of the teachers were from the outside. They were all dedicated educators. Also, a large shed was built for the elderly so that they can go there and socialize. As the years went by, people were reasonably happy, but they still longed for the original homes that they had left behind. However, at Camp Lazaret, they continued their church mass on a regular basis.

Mr. Reynolds, an Englishman, was a very patient and experienced man with children's sports. He formed the Boy Scout groups and trained leaders.

127

The Scout marches and ceremonies were watched by the population with admiration. Also, football and soccer teams were formed to keep the boys happy and out of mischief. Reynolds also started a swim team with the boys. All these interesting sports were a novelty for them and they enjoyed them tremendously.

Women waiting to bathe.

The laundromats and lavatories.

On November 11, 1918, WWI was over. This brought joy to the people; now they could go to their own homes in Musa Dagh. They would not have to water the sand down every so often so that it would not blow on their faces. They were thankful for what they had received in Camp Lazaret, but the thought of returning home was very exciting.

Well, that time had arrived. From the beginning to the middle of the month of November 1919, Camp Lazaret nearly became empty. The Armenians had remained at Camp Lazaret for four years. That was certainly long enough for them. Now, Sisvan School was closed and the tents were gone. They were ready to leave; with faith, there is always hope—hope for living and being happy again.

"This is when I really thought I was being born anew," my mother said, when she was telling me about Port Said. This is when her hopes and dreams would be a reality; she would join my father soon.

The authorities had arranged for ships to take them to Alexandretta, and from there people decided to go to different areas. Some left for Beirut and others to other areas, but most of them headed to Musa Dagh via Antioch. From there with bumpy horse cart rides, they reached their destination. They had to stop quite a few times for feeding and watering the horses. Those animals, too, needed care to transport people through to their destinations. Each family went to their previous villages, except those who were "deported" by the Turks were not there any longer. However, as expected, the rest of the people did not find their homes intact. They found pieces of furniture missing, doors unhinged, and many other losses. But they were happy to be back; they could now start anew fixing and refurbishing their properties. They all started fixing and cleaning their properties with great zest. After all, they were very happy to be back.

"I was not sure if this whole thing was a dream, or a nightmare that I had just awakened from," mom said to me later as she was telling me her story again. All her dowry and her hope chest had disappeared. She had to start over. Very soon, my mom received encouraging letters from my dad telling her that he was working on her papers to bring her to America. Mom was overjoyed with that news, and began impatiently waiting for that special day.

This whole period, from July 1915 to November, 1919, seemed like a thousand years at times to these brave people, but now they were back. They had kept the zest to carry on with their plans to rebuild with hope and dignity. The fierce experiences of the battle on Musa Dagh and the refugee camp in Port Said—both of these experiences—humbled and strengthened them, young and old alike. What an enduring and precious lesson of life.

10

My Parents' Marriage

B arely two years had passed, before my dad sent a special delivery letter to my mom that everything was set. This exciting news came in the beginning of 1921. My dad had prepared the necessary papers for mom to join him in America. That was simply music to my mom's ears. She couldn't contain herself; she ran to my grandparents' house to tell them the good news. Both Grandpa Matos and Grandma Rose were delighted. They all hugged and happy tears fell down their three faces. My mom was prepared; she had some hankies with her that she had embroidered—she gave them to my grandparents. They laughed saying, "Oh, you came prepared!" Mom said she laughed shyly, saying nothing.

Soon, family and relatives gathered at the Atamian household, each bringing a present to my mom as a wedding gift. Also, my mom invited her close friends over for a farewell party. Those 10–12 young ladies serenaded her all night with special national songs, which are always sung at weddings. They giggled and cried, mom said, but it was a very happy part of her life. After all, she had stayed true and faithful to my dad for ten years. The day had finally arrived. She had to go to Aleppo to get her passport picture taken, plus other signatures from the local government, prior to her departure via France. She was twenty-five years old. Her birthday had just passed on May 12. This was one of her happiest birthdays, and more happiness was on its way.

She took the ship from Beirut, and it stopped at Cherbourg, France. After a few days, she was on another ship, the *Orbita*, bound for to New York City. She sailed first class and arrived in New York City on June 24, 1921. This ship was built by Harlan and Wolff Limited, Belfast, Ireland. Mom was delayed at Ellis Island for a few days until all the examinations were completed. About two percent of the people were sent back to their original countries, because of disease. Ellis Island was open to immigrants from 1892–1954. Thank goodness for that immigration center; it helped my mother join my father.

Of course, my dad was in New York City a couple of days earlier to greet my mom. My father had such great anticipation that he welcomed her with a big bouquet of roses. Then, they went straight to the justice of the peace

131

in Manhattan and got married on June 26, 1921. Mom told me they went to a nice hotel to rest and to get reacquainted. It was a very happy night and neither got any sleep.

Dear reader, I will leave the rest to your imagination. They stayed in New York for a brief honeymoon. They went to a photo studio and had an official wedding photo taken, and then they prepared to leave for Philadelphia. Mom had an enlarged photo of that wedding picture. Since they traveled so much, it was folded. I received the photo in that state many years later before her death. At that point, it was damaged, but I kept it and it is still very dear to me.

Dad gave mom a wedding gift: a beautiful Oscar de la Renta ivory silk scarf with light pink roses embroidered on it. Mom cherished that scarf throughout her life. She gave it to me during the last years when she lived with me. I took care of her after my dad's death. That scarf is priceless to me; I use it on very special occasions.

When they arrived in Philadelphia after their honeymoon, everyone was delighted to see them. Especially, mom was happy to see her brother Missak, who now was also married to Zabelle, a pretty young local Armenian. They often visited each other and lived close by.

The first year, mom became pregnant. They were so excited, they planned to call the baby "Movses," if it was a boy, since mom had been on Musa Dagh, and "Musa" was *Movses* in Armenian. Nearly on their first anniversary, the baby was born and it was a boy. Sad to say, he was a breech baby and did not make it. Both mom and dad were very sad. They both loved children. So, two years later in May 1924, they had a beautiful, healthy girl. She was named after the two grandmothers: Rose and Mary, so they called her "Rosemary."

In 1926, mom and dad were blessed with another healthy baby girl. She was named Alice. Rosemary had pretty dark brown eyes and dark hair like my dad; Alice was fair with hazel eyes like mom. Mom said Alice was very adorable, too.

Mom and dad were very happy that they had started their beautiful family. Dad established a very good business in Philadelphia, having purchased the large store of dry cleaning firm with many workers. He was also very creative in being able to mix dyes to get certain desired coloring for people's coats and jackets. Business was growing. He had originally started working there as one of the employees, when he first arrived in America, and now he was the owner of this business. Mom had the best of clothing and household goods that were not attainable by others as yet. They had the first upright phonograph, on which neighbors used to come and listen to their favorite records. Life was good, and they were thankful for all of God's blessings.

Mom, Dad and their first two children:
Rosemary in dad's lap and Alice with mom.

PART FOUR:

Return to Musa Dagh

11

Bad News about
Grandpa Matos

In 1928, dad got news from Turkey that his father's health was failing rapidly. The whole family prepared to go to Musa Dagh together, since my mom wanted to visit her family, too. Just a month before their departure, mom gave birth to another baby girl, whom they named Dawn. At this time, a family of five was on their way to a long journey to see their grandparents, and dad wanted to be near his father at this crucial time. Dad knew that his mother would need help very urgently.

When they arrived there safely, thank goodness, Grandpa Matos was still alive, but very weak. He was elated to see his son and the whole family. He was such a genuine Christian that he raised his hands and thanked God for this opportunity to see his son and family. Shortly, after a few days, he went to his heavenly rest. Dad was thankful that he had been able to get there on time so that his father had seen and enjoyed our family. Now, dad had his hands full with the funeral and putting things in order for his mother.

Soon after that, another tragedy occurred: Dawn developed pneumonia. Before they could bring her to a doctor, she, too, died. There were no doctors in the villages. They had to get her to Antioch or Aleppo, which would have taken hours reach. This was a very sad time for mom. Both mom and dad handled it very well, mom told me. They wanted to stay on another year to make sure Grandma Rose was well-settled in her situation before they returned tor America. At this point, Rosemary, now about five years old, complained about the stones in the street when she walked. They did not have paved roads. Also, she did not understand people; she said they talked funny. Mom said, she often cried and said, "I want to go back to Philadelphia." However, they could not leave yet, because my father had to make sure that the orchards were taken care of. He had to find people to be in charge when he left.

During this year of 1928, there was a modern fountain built in Yoghoun-Olouk for the villagers to obtain their supply of cool spring water.

The Yoghoun-Olouk new fountain built in 1928.

Mom had another baby in the spring of 1929. This time the baby was a boy; they named him Movses. In Musa Dagh, many people named their sons Musa, or *Movses*, Armenian for Moses, especially after the famous battle of Musa Dagh.

Having put everything in order, my father was happy that his mom felt assured that everything would be fine. Also, dad and mom were sad by having lost Dawn early in 1928, but now God had given them a son, a year later. They were very thankful for that. To make Grandma Rose happy, little Movses was baptized in the Yoghoun-Olouk Protestant Church before they journeyed back to the USA in the fall.

Life is beautiful, but it certainly has its ups and downs and sad incidents. If we count all the positive and good things we all have, that is a much bigger number than our disappointments. The positives always outnumber the negatives we experience. My parents lost a baby, and the Lord gave them a new child to love.

12

Back to the USA

It was time to get back to America, but things did not look good in the USA at that time. The Great Depression was on its way. Thank goodness dad had his business, but that, too, would suffer. When dad talked about the Depression, he had hope that it would not stay that way forever. Interestingly, dad told me that his dyeing of coats and jackets was now even more in demand, because people were not buying new coats but refurbishing their old ones. Dad and mom managed well. They both knew how to economize and dad's business was still operable. My siblings were growing very nicely. Mom was very handy; she could make them beautiful clothes. Here is a photo taken in 1931, where you can see how she had dressed my sisters and brother by the innovative clothing she made.

My two sisters, Rosemary and Alice, and little Moses, taken in 1931.

Dad had a very nice disposition and a good heart. He would make possible jobs for his close friends at his business so they could buy some food for their families. Things were getting a little better gradually. However, it was a slow process and many people suffered greatly because of lack of money and jobs. Grandma Rose was getting older, and now she was 95 years old. She was quite healthy except her eyes were getting very weak. Dad received a special letter regarding this matter, and he wanted to go back and see his mom again.

After all, he was the only son. He felt the obligation and love to see his mom at that old age. My parents both thought that it would be a good opportunity for their children to learn Armenian with their cousins and bond with family members. Now that they were getting a little older, they could appreciate visiting more. In addition, it would be a great adventure for them!

13

Returning to Musa Dagh

I get tired of telling the story as to how many times my parents went back and forth across the ocean to visit their loved ones in Turkey. But no amount of money or time can equal the love of family. That was very exemplary on both of my parents' parts. In 1934, they were back in Yoghoun-Olouk, in the beloved village where both of my parents were born.

My father became very active again in his church and so did mom. Mom had enjoyed her Protestant church sermons in Philadelphia, and was very willing to go to church with my dad and siblings as a family. My sisters and brother went to school in Yoghoun-Olouk that was a church-sponsored school. My brother was very young; he was only in *Gogon* class (Kindergarten).

My sisters were very bright at learning the Armenian language. Actually, in two years, my older sister Rosemary was reading college-level Armenian books, dad had told me. Alice was catching up to her, too. Because of the situation in America with the Great Depression, my parents, especially my dad, did not want to rush back to the USA. Instead, he built a beautiful villa in Yoghoun-Olouk, near that newly built public fountain. And he asked one of his good friends to keep and operate his dry cleaning firm in Philadelphia.

My father soon attained the nickname of *Hairenagits* (compatriot). He greeted everyone he met with a smile with that word saying, "*Parev*, ("Hello") *Hairenagits*." That stayed with him until the very last time when we came to the USA in 1950. Dad was quite generous, too. He contributed money for the eighteen fallen heroes' monument on Musa Dagh, which was built in 1935 in their honor. He often talked about it to me in Ainjar, and I wanted to go and see it some day to pay my own respects to those brave men.

Dad had already constructed a villa for his family about 200 feet away from the new fountain of Yoghoun-Olouk. I was told by dad that our beautiful house had a Spanish tile roof and balconies all around. Not only that, but also American-style toilets, which became a special show place. When word got around, people wanted to see the toilets in our home. Mom told me that it was very annoying after awhile when people would stop to see the toilets. They were a novelty for the village people.

Dad had many workers to harvest the oranges and olives. He sold the produce and managed the whole thing quite profitably. Life was good and everyone seemed to be doing well. The girls went to summer school at the Protestant church and they had a very nice young teacher by the name of Hovhannes Hajian. He taught them music and crafts, and some Bible study. This was in 1936 and 1937. In California in 1994—fifty-seven years later—I interviewed this gentleman about the Musa Dagh battle. Life is quite interesting and intertwined with amazing circumstances. Life is so beautiful with all its ups and downs, if only we can stop and savor every bit of it, and learn from it.

The villages were prospering and people were happy again and building and renovating their homes. Life was good.

But soon, in 1939, newspapers were covering the invasion of Poland by Hitler. At this time, tragedy hit the Matosian family again. My sister Alice, who was born in 1926, died of an ear infection at the age of 13. Also, my grandmother Rose passed away at the age of 100. Now, I was a toddler, and then mom had another girl, which they named after the first Alice. They had named me Virginia, an American name, translated to Verjine in Armenian. Since mom and dad were American citizens, all of the last children that mom had after were automatically American citizens.

Tragedy and death steered life's journey in some troubled waters. Grandma Rose was nearly blind at age 100. Mom and dad took good care of her until the end. At this point, my parents had four children, Rosemary, Movses, Virginia, and baby Alice. My parents still thanked God for all they had. All in all, mom bore seven children. Christina, my mom, was a strong person in character and integrity. I think she and dad were a perfect match. She was the outspoken one, and dad very reserved, but when he spoke, everyone listened.

The following years were quite historical, too, for the Musa Dagh people. But again, everything was in God's hands. WWII was in its early stages, and the world was experiencing uncertainty as to what was yet to happen.

PART FIVE:

Refugees Again

14

Bassit, Syria to Ainjar, Lebanon

So WWII winds were blowing in the air, and the world political situation was not stable. At this time in 1939, about 30,000 Armenians were to be evacuated from Sanjak which covered the following areas— Alexandretta, Antioch and Musa Dagh. Some people call this a deportation, but I will call it a political evacuation, because this was different in essence than the 1915 deportations. In 1915, the aim of the Young Turks' plan was to exterminate all the Armenians in the Ottoman Empire. This 1939 evacuation was a sheer political move by France and Turkey. After WWI had ended, the Musa Dagh area was taken from Turkey and it had become a part of Syria. Both Syria and Lebanon were ruled as a French mandate, just as Palestine was a British mandate. Thus, an agreement was made between Turkey and France to give Musa Dagh to Turkey. Then France made an offer to the Musa Dagh people that whoever did not want to stay in Turkey under Turkish rule could move and settle in Ainjar, Lebanon.

Some of the other folks from Antioch and Alexandretta chose to go to Syria or other parts of Lebanon. And still others emigrated to Europe or the Americas.

Only the Musa Dagh people, about 6,000 of them, were to settle in Ainjar, Lebanon. They were to be given homes and property in Ainjar. Ainjar is located in Bekaa Valley in Lebanon. They would go and establish themselves there. After leaving their homes in Turkey with whatever belongings they could carry with them, the people from Musa Dagh were stationed at Bassit, Syria for a brief period of forty days until preparations were finalized in Ainjar. Bassit was a wooded area near the sea. Even though the stay was not long in Bassit, it was a devastating experience. In those forty days, these poor people suffered unbearable conditions: sickness and flooding made their huts fall apart. Mom told me this sad story. They had terrible winds and no sanitary conditions. She thought she was going to lose her children, especially my baby sister and me, in this chaotic situation.

My sister Rosemary wanted to go back to America. She cried a lot about these terrible conditions we were all in. Mom was a bit annoyed with dad at that point, saying, "Why aren't we heading to America, for heavens sake?" She added, "We are American citizens." Even though, my brother, my baby sister and I were born in Yoghoun-Olouk, Turkey, we automatically were born American citizens, because of our parents' citizenship. However, dad had this strong feeling to be with his people now, whatever their fate would bring them. Thank God, they did not lose any of their children in Bassit, but many other children died. And thank God, also, that I have no memory of it at all. I was just a little over a year old.

After much agony and suffering, they were told they were leaving for Ainjar. Dad wanted our family to go to Beirut first and rent an apartment with some other Musa Dagh folk who were able to pay, before we would be transferred to Ainjar.

The majority of the people were brought to Ainjar. It was very dusty and hot. There were no houses yet, but tents were ready to be divided with among the villagers as they were in the Musa Dagh villages' plan. The properties were divided with Khederbeg and Vakef villages being on top at the right side, near the mountains. Hadji-Habli was below them. The top left side was the Kebusye and the center part was Yoghoun-Olouk. Below Yoghoun-Olouk was Bitias. My father had examined the situation well, and decided to stay a little longer in Beirut, until things were settled.

Another family was sharing the apartment complex with our family, Mardiros Habeshian and his family. Their eldest son Hrant was seventeen years old and was wooing my sister Rosemary continuously. The family came and asked for her hand in marriage. Having gone through so many fierce situations, my parents reluctantly agreed, but first they wanted to ask my sister's consent. My sister finally said "Yes" and so it was decided to have this union take place. My mother had second thoughts and did not want my sister to be married at 15, so young. She changed her mind, saying that "our daughter is too young" and that there was plenty of time later to make such a serious decision.

My father went to check the Ainjar situation again and when he returned, he told mom the conditions were deplorable in Ainjar. People were under tents. There were no sanitary conditions and practically no privacy. The mosquitoes were rampant and sure enough malaria was taking many people's lives. Thinking over my sister's wedding plan, mom finally agreed that the wedding could take place, in view of the trouble ahead in Ainjar.

The Ainjar tents for Musa Dagh people.

Rosemary and Hrant Habeshian were married in 1939, and the large Habeshian family moved to Latakia, Syria. This was a very affluent family and they did not want to be subjected to any of those agonizing conditions in Ainjar. My parents felt good, thinking that Rosemary was willing to marry Hrant, and that she would not go to Ainjar and suffer badly. In the back of mom's mind she was never 100 percent sure if they should have allowed it to happen. First of all, Rosemary was very young and a cultured young lady and she would be far away from them all. However, it seemed the better decision. So, after a simple ceremony by the local priest, my sister was wed and they moved to Latakia, Syria. Later on, mom told me numerous times that this decision was not a wise one. Our family learned later on that my sister was not happy and she died young.

Then my father took another trip to Ainjar to assess the situation. He had more money than the villagers, so he went to the bank in Beirut and cashed some of his American stocks. Then, he went to Ainjar as the houses were being built and added some more conveniences to our house. For instance, he had some workers add an extra room to the side of the house for a kitchen. On the back, he built a shed for some animals and chickens. Because mom liked gardening, he had an upper level wall built for a spacious garden area. Below it was a narrow strip for more flowers to be planted later on and a nice stone porch with a pathway to the bathroom. Next to the upper-level garden, he had another area picked out for fruit trees. He had this knowledge of

147

orchards when he was in Turkey. The property was fenced for safety and privacy. Everyone was going to get one large room, with a front door and a large window. Also, about twelve feet away, a separate bathroom was situated. Each family received that one square room to function as the bedroom, kitchen and everything else one would need in a household. There was no luxury here, just the bare essentials for survival.

In Ainjar, all the houses looked, and were, exactly the same, like square boxes with flat roofs.

Every family had the same size lot, and other properties were distributed to each family for their future living and income. That was all good and fine, but things initially were very rough and in a rudimentary state. While all this was happening and the buildings were being completed, dad had rented a house in Zahleh, another town facing the Bekaa Valley, across from Ainjar, about ten miles away. This was a much closer location from which to keep an eye on things. Also, this was an established town below Mt. Sannine that had cleaner conditions. Dad made sure that mom would not go through more hardships after having enjoyed a luxurious life in America, and having gone through the Musa Dagh Battle experience. Ainjar had great possibilities of fertile fields with water nearby, and a location at the slope of mountains facing the wide Bekaa Valley. These were good thoughts to have, because at this immediate time, those possibilities seemed far away. People were dying every day from malaria and the elderly, from heat exhaustion. The folks' morale was quite shaken.

As years went by, conditions improved; people started farming, buying cattle, and making a living. Still, there was much work to be done health-wise and organizing in other ways. For example, schools needed to be established.

However, our people had survived centuries by having faith in God, so they built churches, three of them. The St. Paul Armenian Apostolic Church was built at the very top of Ainjar, at the slope of the mountains above Khederbeg and Vakef. The main road entering Ainjar led to the top of the mountainside where St. Paul Church was erected. The St. Joseph Catholic Church was built on the right-hand side of Ainjar near Hadji-Habli. The Armenian Evangelical Protestant Church was in the center area near Yoghoun-Olouk village, below Kebusye and above Bitias. Even though there still was much work to be done, people were thankful that they would not be under Turkish rule and persecutions. And that alone for many was a freedom that they had longed for for many years ago.

Let me explain where this new place, Ainjar, was. The Arabs and some other folks write the name as Anjar, but initially it was called Ainjar, which means "flowing spring" in Arabic. Many people still use the spelling "Ainjar," as I do. When the Musa Dagh people arrived there in 1939, it was a wide area called Bekaa Valley of Lebanon. Little did we know what this town was built on. When I visited Ainjar in 1996, there were newly found ruins established right at the foot of Ainjar. A pamphlet written in French was given to us, which explained the whole discovery as we entered the gates of the Umayyad Ruins. I read and understood most of it, but I wanted to be extra sure to have an expert translate it for me. When I came back home to the USA, I asked my former French professor, Roger A. Poirier of Union College, to translate the brochure for me. He graciously did so.

I had learned so much since I left Ainjar as a preteen. However, we all knew from the beginning when we lived there that there was something unique and strange around Ainjar. The soil near the mountainside and the fields was a reddish color. The surrounding area with thick walls had ashy gray soil. This was very close to our town, and we called this area "The Soor." I remember later on, when the father of one of my friends was digging near the Soor, he found some human bones and a skull. This was all an enigma to us then. No one knew the historic value of our newfound town.

Ainjar was a city built in the 7th century, sixty kilometers from Beirut and near the highways of Damascus. There is a large flowing spring, which is one of the sources of the Litani River. This city was built in 650 A.D. by the first Umayyad Caliph. It had four main gates, one on each side: east, west, north and south. The city was surrounded by two-meter thick walls, reinforced by thirty-eight semicircular towers. It had two main streets: one running north to south, and the other, east to west. In the middle of each main street was a large storm drain in the shape of a tunnel, 9.0 meters wide and 1.40 meters deep. The two main streets intersected in the middle of the city, where four columns stood, joined at the top by arches. There were more than 600 stores in the city, which told of its history as an important commercial center. However, most of the southeast section in the city was an empty space, probably an area where the animals of the caravans, such as the camels, horses, mules, and donkeys, were parked during their journey.

The author at the Umayyad Ruins in Ainjar, 1996.

The author sitting on the left historical rock at the ruins.

The palace of the city (City Hall) was situated in the southeast section. The mosque of the city was situated north of the palace. And the *mihrab* (the altar) was built in the middle of the south wall, facing Mecca, the holy Moslem city. In the middle of the courtyard, water was transported in brick pipes from the great spring of Litani River. There was a smaller palace, known as the Harem. This palace was decorated more elaborately with heads and bodies of naked women, which indicated this palace was reserved for women. In the northeast section of the city near the north gate, the Roman baths were located. All of the construction and plans are similar to Byzantine architecture.

Finally, this city was destroyed in 744 A.D. by Merwan II, the last of the Umayyad caliphs and was never rebuilt. Archeological digs began in 1953, assisted by U.S. President Truman's Point Four program and supervised by the Department of Antiquities of the Lebanese government.

A very interesting fact remains about Ainjar: this purely Armenian town is the only representative of the period of the Umayyads, the beginning of Islam. All the described areas at this place were completely guarded, surrounded by thick walls. Today, Ainjar has become one of the historical attractions for many foreign tourists and the local Lebanese population.

151

15

My Early Childhood

L iving in Zahleh was not bad. Dad traveled a great deal back and forth to Ainjar to make our housing situation more bearable for mom and all of us. At the same time, mom made new friends in Zahleh, and we often visited them and vice versa. Mom always told me cheerfully that when we would visit those friends, I always wanted to pick flowers—and bring some to mom and to the guests.

Here author is about 2, holding some posies.

Dad finally thought it safe to move his family to Ainjar in the fall of 1940. He had a gardener plant poplar trees along the side of the house, towards the pathway to the bathroom, plus rosebushes in front of the house, and couple of fruit trees on the upper level of the garden. Dad told me later on, when I was older, that he wanted to make Ainjar a very pleasant place for mom to live, because she had gone through so much. That was very thoughtful of him.

I have very faint memories of our first year in Ainjar. I remember one thing clearly: there was so much snow during the winter that we could not even open our door. We cuddled up to get warm. Dad would prepare a mangal (a charcoal burner), first outdoors until the charcoal was burning and turning red, so all the carbon monoxide would be out completely. Then dad would bring the mangal inside. Mom would put a table over the mangal and cover it with a blanket. We would sit around it with our bodies covered with the blanket. This would create heat for us to be warm during the winter. There was no central heating, electricity, or running water in any of the houses. We would sleep with long

153

flannel pajamas and long-sleeve sweaters under a couple of thick blankets at night. Our large room was partitioned with a curtain for mom and dad's bed; our beds were on the other side of the room, side by side. By the way, our neighbors and many of our relatives did not have beds, but slept on mattresses on the floor. These conditions may sound strange to the reader, but that is the way it was—the life of refugees.

These were hard times. Mom would prepare the kerosene lamps to produce light at night for doing some reading or having special family time by reading the Bible or singing hymns. As a routine, we had our Bible-study time, with dad teaching us Bible verses and Bible stories, and mom leading us in our singing. I remember once dad's friend from church stopped by, and he was so happy when he came in. My dad asked him what made him so happy. He smiled and said,

"You know, hearing you all singing hymns so enthusiastically like that made my heart rejoice, and I could hear you all the way down the hill."

"You should join us sometime," dad replied.

By the time I was four, and my little sister was starting to talk, dad had taught us Psalm 23. One day, my little sister Alice and I were sitting by our doorstep and had the Bible open to the marking for Psalm 23. We were repeating the psalm as a neighbor was passing. He stopped short and asked our father if we were really reading the Bible at this young age. My dad smiled and said, "No, they know it by heart."

"Oh," said the neighbor, "I thought they were geniuses, reading at such an early age."

"Yes, they are, because they're learning the Bible," said my father, smiling.

Every day we recited Psalm 23: "*Dere eem Hovives eh, Yes pani ma garo-dutiun bede chounenam....*" (The Lord is my shepherd, I shall not want.)

The roads were not paved, either, so it was hard to play outdoors during the summer with all the stones, dust and the thistles growing everywhere. Dad found someone to prepare a cement play area for us behind the house. It was quite a large area, because we could draw with chalk on it and play hopscotch. There were a couple of benches made for sitting and resting. After school, my friends would come over almost every day to play with me in my backyard. Mom would have healthy snacks for us, such as dates, figs, sunflower seeds, and walnuts.

Across from our backyard was the Yoghoun-Olouk fountain, with its four sides with four separate faucets. The fountain was high, about ten feet tall from the ground, but the faucets were low at reachable height. Women would come with their jugs and tins to fill with spring water for cooking, washing, and bathing. The other villages had their own fountains. Sometimes, the lines of women fetching their water would be so long, about fifty feet. While waiting on line, the ladies would catch up with the social events of the village: who had a newborn and who got engaged, etc. I noticed during my 1996 visit to Ainjar that those fountains are still there, but no longer in use. (Of course, the water is shut off.) The villagers now had running water in their homes.

The fountain from which the villagers got water. This photo was taken of the author in front of it in 1996.

By 1942, the three schools from the churches were quite well-organized. Our church minister was Rev. Aram Hadidian and he had tallied a good group of teachers, both from Musa Dagh people and from Beirut, Lebanon. He was a very good shepherd of the Armenian Evangelical Church. He visited his flock regularly to tend their needs, in addition to giving Sunday sermons and running Sunday school classes. He was not of Musa Dagh extraction, but had been with our people from the beginning of our strife. He was also given property: a house and a large garden near the main road to the springs that produced our water supply. I could see his house from our house. There was an open field leading down to the main road. Rev. Hadidian had the best rose garden you ever saw, surrounded by fir trees. He had a gardener who took care of it on a daily basis during the summer.

He did not live there with his family. His family lived in Zahleh, which was a better established town with red-roofed houses set among the eastern foothills of Mount Sannine. Zahleh enjoys a prime location in Bekaa Valley. Snow-covered mountains tower above it in winter, and in summer, its high elevation keeps the air light and dry.

Our church, the Armenian Evangelical Protestant Church.

When I was in grade school in Ainjar, the school took us on outings on Mt. Sannine. I have climbed it with joy, gathering wild violets with such fragrance, and bountiful cyclamen flowers of pink and crimson. Little wild oregano plants grew abundantly on Mt. Sannine foothills, which were useful herbs. After we settled in Ainjar, my parents took us to Zahleh for shopping and to its beautiful public parks. We would sit under fragrant-flower trellises of peacock jasmine and other varieties of flowers and enjoy a nice lunch and watch people scurry around.

Thus, in 1942, all three denominations were established. The Armenian Evangelical Protestant Church had about 250 enrolled students. The main photo was taken by our church at the end of August.

The first picture of the Armenian Evangelical Church of Ainjar. Mom had kept this special photo. I am supposed to be the sixth child sitting, front row, on the right.

Rev. Aram Hadidian and most of the teachers are sitting in the center of the second row. To the left of the photo is Barkev Philian and on the right-hand side is Papken Zanoian, both of Musa Dagh. Some of the other teachers sitting with Rev. Hadidian were from Beirut.

I was put in Kindergarten at four years old. In 1943, I was in grade one. I loved school. Learning became a hobby of mine. My brother Movses, now called Mike, did not like school at all. He finished 6th grade, and then stopped. However, he was very creative with his hands. He once took a piece of tin and made a beautiful bus for my dolls. He chiseled out the windows, put plastic for glass parts, made wooden tires, and painted the bus pink. I was thrilled. All my friends came to see my dolls' bus. Too bad I don't have a picture of it. He also loved American Western movies. Since there was no movie house in Ainjar, he would rent a bike and go to Zahleh to see those movies. Not only did he go there for movies, but also he used the bike to pick up medicines for family and relatives from Zahleh's pharmacies. The distance from Ainjar to Zahleh was a good ten miles.

The next year, 1944, I was put in third grade; I had skipped second grade. Even though I had skipped second grade, I did pretty well with God's help.

157

That year, I was awarded the most prestigious gift of all, a wooden egg made in Jerusalem with wood from the Garden of Gethsemane. I still have this special gift, kept it all these years. I used it in mending socks. This gift was for having the highest grades of all classes from grade 1-6. I was very happy, but most of the knowledge I learned from my father. He would tell me not only the Bible stories and help me with my homework, but also teach me world knowledge and geography. He encouraged me in drawing and painting. He was very experienced in creating color shades by mixing colors as he had done in America at his workplace. I enjoyed all of this knowledge.

Mom was also talented; she made us all beautiful clothes. She taught me how to crochet and sew at a very young age. She was an expert knitter and, in addition, she made beautiful embroidery pieces. At an early age, I learned how to cross-stitch and made beautiful things. I often watched her, and soon I was making creations for my dolls. She was very proud that I would concentrate and be able to do that at a young age.

"Some day, you can make all the nice things you want for yourself," she would tell me lovingly.

"Can I use the sewing machine, mommy?"

"*Che che dagavin toon shad bzdig es*," (No, not yet, you are still very little.) she added gently, and continued saying, "Your legs cannot touch the pedal yet, *bedk e sbases*" (you need to wait).

I could not wait to get my own Singer machine. Mom had two of them from America, and told me that she would give me the older model. I was simply elated. But, I guess I had to wait for a while until I grew some more and would be able to reach the foot pedal in order to operate it.

My parents decided to grant my brother's wish to go to America. Mom had a first cousin who was married to Mihran Atamian, a distant cousin of mom's family. He had agreed to have my brother stay with them for a while. My brother came to the USA in 1945, and stayed with our relatives in Paterson, N.J. Mom and dad were also planning some day to return to the USA, but they did not know yet exactly when that would be. My brother found a job designing and printing fabrics in a factory. He was creative and loved his job. Mom and dad were happy for him.

Now I was in fourth grade, and had a very nice and pretty teacher, Mary Sherbetjian from Bitias. I was merely seven. All of my classmates were older than me, because their parents would keep them to work with them at the farm for a year or two and then send them to school for a year or so. The other students' ages ranged from 13-20 years old in this grade four. I am very thankful that my parents valued education and we did not have to waste any years. My dad took outside jobs to afford the schooling for me and my sister. That is because we did not have free public education. We had to pay from kindergarten to the higher grades. That is why other people could not send their children to school every year so readily.

Virginia is standing on the church stairs on the left by the teacher. (4th Grade)

Then Armenians started migrating to Soviet Armenia in 1946. I was very saddened by this happening. Two of my best friends' families had signed up to leave for good. I loved my two very best friends: Lucine and Iskuhi. Lucine was from Bitias, and Iskuhi was from Kebusye. I cried and cried and asked dad to go and register. He said we could not go for two major reasons. First, my brother now was in the USA, and second, when dad was younger he belonged to the Tashnag party youth group. The Soviets did not want any of the Tashnags to go, because the Tashnag philosophy was quite contrary to the Soviet regime. Needless to say, we could not go. I had other friends, too, but those two were at our house every day and we would play hopscotch and other games until dark in our backyard.

In 1946, I was in fifth grade. Missing my two best friends, I concentrated and was getting real good in the recitation period, which we had every Friday, open to all classes. I was eight years old, and I loved singing and dramatics, too. At one of the pageants, I played the part of a little boy, since no little boy was chosen to play the part. I had my hair cut short for the part. Especially when I wore a beret, no one could tell there was a little girl under those boyish clothes. I played the part of this little boy who was physically abused by a drunken father. When he seemingly beat me up, I had to shed real tears and sob. I got accolades for the part I played.

From then on, I played different roles at pageants, including the part of Mary, the mother of Jesus. I made other friends during 1946 and I played a great deal with my cousins who lived on the same block. They all went to another school, the one run by Apostolic Church.

In 1947, conditions changed quite drastically. First of all, there was some kind of vaccine being given to all of the children in the six villages. My sister, my cousins and I all took this unknown vaccine, which I think to this date, no one knows what it was for, but it was quite fatal. Because we were still called refugees, we were being tested with this vaccine. In Lebanon, there was no official authority that could determine to whom and when this vaccine should be administered. Not like here in the U.S. where there are Boards of Health, Health Departments and the FDA to check everything beforehand, to determine and supervise such actions.

Second, Rev. Aram Hadidian announced that he had received a call to Beruit to be the pastor of the Eshrefieh Evangelical Protestant Church. He no longer was going to be our pastor; we would have visiting ministers to preach every Sunday. However, there was some good news on the horizon: a missionary was going to be with the Ainjar people, a person who was also a nurse. She would help our church and the group of villages. Before Rev. Hadidian left for good, many of the children who were vaccinated with this unknown vaccine became violently ill. I was one of them. I was only nine years old, and reacted to this vaccine very badly. Thank God, my sister was not affected or my cousins, but many other children were. Many children died in less than a week after the vaccination. When I became very sick, my mother told me later, I was not able to move or open my eyes, just lie in bed. Mom told me how she wished that my dad was there in this horrific period. She told me later that she could not bear the thought of losing another child. Rev. Hadidian came after hearing about me to say a prayer over me, and then he had to leave and visit other children who were very sick also.

My father was gone for a job out of town, and he would be gone two to three weeks at a time to translate for workers who were building barracks for the British soldiers in neighboring towns. WWII had ended in 1945, but there were many remnants of unrest between the Arabs and the Jews. And in those days, the French and the British were in competition to gain Syria as perhaps a colony. There were a lot of plane fights over the Syrian and Lebanese borders in conjunction with their disputes. These plane maneuvers were also taking place over Ainjar many times. My father had a ditch prepared by some construction workers for us to hide in. We were to pull the top cover over it, which was a large green sheet of tin. If necessary, we would jump in and hide there until the plane fights were over. As a matter of fact, one of my friends from school, in the village of Bitias got one eye blinded. She was cooking outside on an open fire, helping her mother, when a bullet dropped in the fire near where she was standing. The bullet bounced back and pierced her right eye. That was so sad. She was such a pretty girl; her name was Asdghig (little star).

There was a definite effort on Britain's part to expel France from Syria. As usual, Lebanon was always in the middle, innocently, paying the bigger brunt of damages, especially during the Arab-Jewish conflict. My dad was gone, earning a living. Since he was fluent in English and Arabic, he was guiding construction workers properly. Of course, my dad did not know of me being very ill, dying. There were no telephones to inform him of this dire situation.

Mom told me that she stayed by my bedside all night and prayed. She cried and sang soft hymns to make me comfortable and encouraged me to come to life. She said that I had become limp and motionless; she did not see any signs of me breathing.

"Please Lord, make her come back to me," she prayed, and she repeated this over and over all night.

All I remember was I took the vaccine and came home; the rest is all blank. During the time that mom was describing, the time I was not responding, I later on told her there was this pleasant light, and I was blown

161

into a whirlwind that pulled me up and up, so high in this lighted area. But soon, I was falling down, and pulled up again, and down again. When finally she told me that, I squeezed her hand and a cold sweat came over me. Mom said she was so happy to see my eyes open. She hugged me and cried out:

"Thank you, Lord, Thank you. You did not take her now."

I remember vividly the way I was being pulled up through this tunnel of light, and then let go. It felt like my body was not with me, but just my feeling of going up by a force that I could not control. I guess one can call this a near-death experience. Mom said she immediately changed my clothing, which was completely soaked. Whatever that was, I thank the Lord now to be able to write about it. I think after that my mother's faith was strengthened even more. Praise be to His Holy name.

The time arrived when Rev. Hadidian had to leave his flock in Ainjar. We were saddened about that, but something good came out of it. He had asked a missionary to come and look at Ainjar to see if she would like to work there with his people. Well, that missionary was from the Hilfsbund Mission of Germany. This Mission was founded by Rev. Erst Loman in 1896. It was a Christian organization, which produced missionaries to send into countries where Armenian refugees were deported to through the atrocities of the Ottoman Empire. Rev. Loman had gathered funds from German Evangelical churches and some of the Swiss Evangelicals to create a strong Christian mission of men and women to send to countries where Armenian refugees were scattered. But above all, the mission had sent missionaries during the actual happenings of the massacres to witness the brutal acts of the Turks and bring out into the open all the stories. Such was the love of Christ at the core of their dedicated work for the Armenians, this Christian nation that was being brutalized.

Sister Hedwig Aenishanslin

After my parents, whom I adored, loved and respected, Sister Hedwig came next. I admired her so much. First of all, she had the love and the dedication to not only help us, the Ainjar people in great need, but also to assist the neighboring Muslim villages. She was always ready to help anyone. She was a trained nurse, a Christian teacher, and a motivator. I understood that when Rev. Hadidian first brought her to Ainjar, she did not like the place. Ainjar did not have the facilities for the things that she wanted to do. But after much thought and sacrifice, she was willing to plunge in and serve the Ainjar people.

She was born in Switzerland and was schooled there to be a nurse and midwife. In Germany, she went to Bible school to prepare for being a missionary. She came to Ainjar in 1947, when she was forty-seven years old and immediately delved into the church matters. She held Bible study for the young people and weekly evening services for everybody. She would prepare the study schedule, as I recall studying the Book of Acts, in detail. As I would listen intently to every word she uttered, I would write them down in a notebook. One day, she asked to see my notes, since everybody did not take notes. She was so impressed that from that day on, she borrowed my notes to make her spelling corrections and to observe the way I had organized and prepared my notes. She praised me often for being a good listener. From then on, she would borrow my notebook, and give it back to me before the next lesson.

However, I can tell you of two incidents when she scolded me very intensely, which I have never forgotten, but I learned a good lesson each time.

The first time, I had injured my finger and I was rushed to her clinic, which was also her house—the house originally belonged to Rev. Hadidian. I went down to have her clean my wound and bandage it for me. I knocked on the door, but there was no answer. I was determined to get my wound taken care of so I stood there by her gate and waited. I waited and waited, and, finally, I saw from a distance that she was walking towards her house. She had a package in each hand, and you could see that she looked tired As she came near me, she did not even ask why I was waiting for her, but instead she raised her voice and said,

"Why did you not come and try to help me with my packages?"

I did not know what to say. If I had said, "I was waiting for you to fix my injured finger," that would sound very selfish and dumb, so I said nothing.

"You ought to always look and see if people need help," she continued.

"Uh, huh," I said quietly.

"What is it that I can help you with?" she now said softly.

By that time, I was so embarrassed that I did not want to tell her.

"C'mon, why were you here waiting for me?" she repeated.

I was at a loss for words, but just extended my finger to show her the cut that was wrapped with a blood-stained cloth. She signaled me to follow her. She put her two packages down, turned her key in and opened the door. She asked me to go in, and immediately took care of the cut on my finger gently. As she finished, she put her hand over my head gently, and said the following.

"I hope this will be a lesson to you."

"Yes, definitely, and thank you." I left very humbled that I should always remember the lesson to help people. In my mind, I was trying to justify that

I had an injured finger and could not have done what she asked for. Then I thought I really could have assisted her with my other hand. But I did not want to go there, because that would have been a lame excuse. From that day on, I was always alert to look for situations in which I could help someone. I never forgot that incident. It was a good lesson.

The second time, I was scolded not for ignoring someone who needed help, but for something else. Here is the story. We were celebrating Harvest Time in October, and we had to go door to door asking people for some of their well-earned crops to bring to church. After a ceremonial service, we took the goods to the poor people in the villages. There were large burlap bags of grain and legumes—wheat, barley, lentil, corn—and vegetables, such as, tomatoes, peppers, and pumpkins. After the service, we all had to help making different stacks of portions to bring to the poor. I was working very diligently to get the items put in order. When the wheat portion was being divided, some fell on the floor. Sister Hedwig asked me to gather it and put it in the portion to be given out. The church altar floor was clean, so I enthusiastically, gathered the spilled wheat grains and placed them in the portion to be given out.

Then I cheerfully swept the floor clean. She must have been watching me through all this. She came and tapped me on my shoulder saying,

"Do not throw that in the garbage."

I looked at her in surprise as to what she was talking about.

"You see those two grains of wheat, you should not throw them out in the garbage!" And she meant what she said.

I still did not understand how she could make such a fuss when there were bags and bags of wheat around.

"You see," she said, "the ocean is so big, but it consists of many little drops, and they are all important to be there to complete the ocean." And she looked at me, and then looked straight at those tiny kernels of grain and left me.

I had a hunch that she was still watching me, so I bent down, picked up those two kernels of wheat, and put them in the big bag. Then I swept the other refuse into the garbage bin. Immediately, she came and commended me for doing a great job. I was right; she was watching to see what I would be doing. Yes, definitely, I learned a big lesson that time, too. She was very sweet and giving, but also quite a disciplinarian. I admired her for that.

To this date, 2011, my husband always kids me, saying that I am a little squirrel who keeps everything. That is true; if I can make something out of anything, I keep it. For example, I kept toilet paper rolls for a long time, and I knew that I would have some use for them someday. I did. I taught Sunday school for forty-two years, and those items that I saved, always were utilized wisely. One primary class I had made Jesus' twelve disciples. I used those rolls. In the hollow part, I showed the children to make the head with paper tissue. Then we drew the face, glued some yarn on top, and put on a piece of cloth and tied it. We put a straight stick across the neck and tied it and put a cloth as a robe over the arms. Finally, we placed a belt made out of yarn in the middle of the robe, and *voila!*—we had made a disciple of Jesus.

The children had so much fun doing this, and, of course, we needed to have the Jesus figure. This time, I brought a hand towel roll, which made a bigger figure, and we dressed Jesus with a white robe. This whole project had made a big display which adorned the Sunday school hallway for a long time. When I look at the pictures I took of the display, it brings back beautiful memories of the children.

Jesus and His Disciples display that we made in Sunday school.

Even when I am sewing, I never throw away pieces of materials. I use them later as appliqués on tablecloths that I make or on clothing to decorate them. I have done this with curtains, too. And there are many other projects that can use leftover items not thrown away. This I call creativity and economizing.

I graduated from sixth grade, which at the time was the end of grade school classes. Then, in 1948 I attended seventh grade, equivalent to the first year of high school. At this point, I was ten years old. Sister Hedwig gave me many responsibilities; for example, I was to make the Symbol of Jesus Christ in Greek on a maroon velvet runner for the pulpit, the two Greek letters were the chi and rho. She wore this symbol on her clothes as a silver pin at the center of her collar. She always wore her long white nurse's gown with shoulder straps and a dark blouse under it. In the middle of her white collar was the pin described previously. I gladly embroidered the chi and rho in orange-gold thread on that velvet runner.

To my surprise, when my husband and I visited Ainjar in 1996, I saw the velvet runner that I had made on the sanctuary pulpit. It brought back tender memories for me. Too bad, Sister Hedwig had already gone to her heavenly rest in 1983 in Germany where she was transferred to a home for retired missionaries.

She had bestowed upon me other responsibilities, which I gladly performed. She gathered young girls on a weekly basis to help them learn embroidery so that they could earn supplementary wages for their families. The items were sent to Switzerland as a business. She had me supervise small groups and check their work. Doing that at that early age gave me great confidence to administer and be in charge of responsibility. I would give her a report with all the data. In 1949, another missionary arrived in Ainjar. Her name was Marie Rock. She, too, was a very dedicated nurse and a Biblical teacher. At the time, I did not work very closely with her, because she specialized in taking care of pregnant women. She was the midwife for delivering healthy babies throughout the six villages. If there were any complications, she would refer them to a nearby hospital in another town. She was three years older than Sister Hedwig and was a very sweet and kind person. I had not noticed that disciplinary trait in her.

Sister Hedwig (left) and Sister Marie (right).

Also, during 1949, I was very active in the Christian Endeavor (CE) group of our church youth. This was the young group of Christians who did many important chores for the church and the community. We had Bible studies and took trips to special events and special church functions. Also, there were socials and picnics when we all contributed our talents by making desserts and other tasty items. We had two Saturdays in a year to clean the church thoroughly from top to bottom.

A special location was Eshtora, not too far from Ainjar. It was an advanced town where there were good hotels and banks to do business, especially for travelers. Eshtora had many beautiful picnic areas we visited often. It is located between Ainjar and Zahleh at the Bekaa Valley.

I had a leadership role in the CE group, and many times, I conducted worship service for the group. In addition to all this, I was paid a special stipend for helping the teachers at the Armenian Evangelical Protestant School. I used to help the students with their vocabulary, giving definitions to the words, so that they knew how to use them in a sentence. One student from each class would write down all the vocabulary words they did not know and bring me their notebooks. At night, I would put all the meanings on them and bring them back the next day. After they received them, they were expected to learn all the words. They would be quizzed on the words at the end of the week. Also, I prepared projects for the kindergarten classes, and made samples and how-to instructions for the children. I sang in the choir and presented programs at the church on special occasions.

I enjoyed all these activities and expressed to my parents that I wanted to be a missionary. I liked working with people and helping them in any way. When I expressed this idea to Sister Hedwig, she was so happy to hear that. She even suggested that I get my higher education in Germany or Switzerland on a scholarship, and that I would not pay anything. I was so excited, but I wanted to discuss it with my parents. They did not agree with the idea of me going to a foreign land all by myself to become a missionary. I could not understand it. They emphasized that it is not a woman's job to go far away, and that I could be just as helpful and useful where I was. I can see that even though they were education-minded, they were not sufficiently liberated from their own upbringing to send their daughter to a foreign country to work. I did not want to continue arguing the issue; however, they suggested that I could go to the city high school in Beirut to continue my education for pursuing a profession. This was also a suggestion given to them by Rev. Hadidian, who had told my parents that I was like a "shiny nail to be utilized, but not left alone to get rusted."

At this point, I told them that I would like to go into the ministry. Both of my parents said, "That is for men. Do you see any women ministers coming and preaching at our church?" I went back and forth with this argument that it is not right for only men to be ministers. They were not moved. I told my parents they were living in the past, and it was sad for me to see that. That was the first time that I had answered them back, but it was the truth.

We did not argue about it any longer, but I got registered in city high school in Beirut, and I was ready to leave for my studies in September 1950. Now, I was twelve, but quite mature for my age. Rev. Hadidian still kept in touch and encouraged me to enter the Beirut high school. I was excited about it. I figured, after I finish high school, then I can still go to college and seminary. Then I would be an adult, and I could make my own decisions. That thought left me satisfied.

That summer there was so much turmoil in the neighboring towns—both in Syria and Lebanon—that several governmental leaders were assassinated, some government buildings were burned, and traveling became scary. I noticed lately my parents were getting in many long discussions concerning the politics of the Middle East and its volatility. Soon after that, my dad took a trip to Beirut, to sort out things. He had gone to the American Embassy for some matters. When he came back, he and mom declared that we were going to America in this year. I was surprised, but happy, too, since I would see my brother. I had heard so much about the good old USA; I was ready to see it, even though I was a bit disappointed since I had to cancel going to high school in Beirut. So, that plan fell apart. After all that, I really believed and thought, "Let it be God's will, whatever is ahead of me, and of us all."

My father took me aside, and talked to me very seriously and lovingly. He said that I was very intelligent and that I would do well no matter what school I would attend. He continued saying that

"You and your sister will not have any future in this country. The government is so unstable, and one does not know from one day to the other what will happen. Lord willing, we will go to America and stay there this time. I know that you will like it there, and you will have many opportunities to do the things that you like to do." I listened intently and hoped for the best. I trusted my parents.

For the last time, we went to the *agge* (water springs) of Ainjar, the second week of September, to celebrate in honor of our eighteen heroes who gave their lives fighting the Turks on Musa Dagh. There were caldrons and caldrons of *herisah* (a special Armenian dish prepared with wheat and lamb) served all night long to whoever comes to the commemoration of this event. Special mass takes place, and then people celebrate their freedom from the pangs of Turkish rule with temboug and zurna (drum and fife) being played, and people dancing in round-group form holding hands.

168

The pulsating rhythm fills the air and everyone has a great time. We attended with our relatives for the last time before we prepared to leave for the USA. Some people were very happy for us, calling us lucky to have been American citizens all this time, and that we were able to have this opportunity. Others were very sad that we no longer would be there. Sister Hedwig had big plans for me, so she was very unhappy about the whole thing.

I had such wonderful memories of my childhood, but as we grow older, nothing stays the same. I think dad and mom made a wise decision to get out of the Middle East when they did, because things got a lot worse after we had left. The Syrian soldiers had set their headquarters and secret service headquarters in Ainjar and those soldiers were doing lots of damage to my people. Also, the Syrian government was meddling in the Lebanese government. Furthermore, beautiful Lebanon, which was considered the Switzerland of the Middle East, was nearly wrecked between the Jewish and Arab conflict. No one was completely safe. Many of the Beirut modern buildings were destroyed during this time. When we visited the Middle East in 1991 and 1996, the Lebanese government was trying to fix the demolished roads and the buildings. No question, it did look like a war zone.

Those dedicated missionary sisters gave twenty-five of their precious years to my people in Ainjar. They both retired in 1972. Sister Hedwig and Sister Mary were very much loved by most, including the Muslim inhabitants of neighboring towns, such as Mejdel and others. Initially, from the other denominations of Ainjar, some people resented those missionaries thinking that they were taking over, but soon they discovered that they were angels sent from God to help them all. Other missionary sisters joined them later, which I have only read about, two sisters, both named Hanna. They not only attended the sick and the poor, helping them all, but started a secondary school with housing and major curriculums for the students who came from far and near places, even Kuwait. Those sweet sisters even had prayer meetings with the Muslim students and they got their education in a loving Christian atmosphere.

What more can one ask than to be blessed so abundantly? All praise be to Almighty God. I will cherish these nine years of my life in Ainjar with super memories, when my formative years were being established with such a nice Christian surrounding. I praise and thank my Lord for everything, and especially saving my life, so that my parents did not suffer having to lose another child.

PART SIX:

My Early Life in the USA

16

Culture Shock

In getting ready for the move to the United States, my parents gave most of our belongings to friends and relatives. The only thing that was sold at a high price was our upright phonograph. When we played records, all the village children would come and sit under our house window, row by row to listen to the music. We had English and Armenian records, and played them often. They, having listened to them many times, would join the chorus and sing along with the record. It was quite an enjoyable scene and kind of funny, too, as if we had our own chorus. The reason I am explaining this is because many of the people who wanted to have this piece of furniture, started the bidding on it. So, this was one item that we gladly made some spare spending money. Finally, the bidding was getting out of hand, until my father put an end to it, saying "The next call is the last one." And that is how it ended. This was a novel piece of furniture that no one else had. Of course, all the records that we had went with it.

Soon, a few days later, all the neighbors and relatives gathered at our house and outside to bid us "Good-bye" the day that we were leaving. Sister Hedwig was there, too. She kept caressing my hair and told my mom to please take good care of me. She gave me a hug and said good-bye to my parents and left. As the car that took us to Beirut started to move, I looked at everyone longingly and started to cry. I was happy that we were going to America, which I had dreamt about since I was a little girl. On the other hand, I thought: *Would I ever see these friends again?* That thought saddened me. We just took bare essentials with us—a change of clothing and some souvenirs people brought us. The night before, my CE youth group had given a warm and cordial party for me, which was so lovely, and sad in a way. They presented me with a silver CE pin, which I was very thankful for. I would cherish all those memories the rest of my life.

We got to Beirut and stayed overnight at my mom's aunt's house. The next day we boarded the ship, Greek liner, *Nea Hellas*.

The Greek liner, Nea Hellas, *that brought the author to America.*

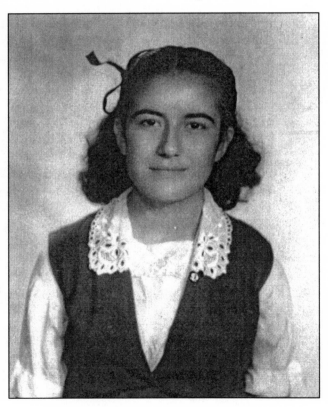

This is a photo of when she came to America.

This is how the author's mom and dad looked when arriving to the USA.

The ship was huge. It was interesting to walk on the deck and enjoy the ocean air. It seemed like a long trip, because there was not much to do, but it was a novel experience. I can see my parents' expressions of relief to be free of the Middle East, where the governments were always either at war or not stable. When I grew up in Ainjar, my teachers knew that I was an American citizen, so they used to call me "*Pokrig Amergouhi*" (little American female). So, I was thinking, finally, I will be that little American female.

Our cousins, my brother and my mom's first cousin were all waiting for us at the New York port. I had never seen so many neon lights. And the streets were crowded with cars and people. We were to be the guests of the Atamian family, where my brother had originally come to live. Friends and relatives from Philadelphia came over the next few days and greeted us lovingly. They invited us to stay with them after we spent Thanksgiving with Evelyn Atamian's family. After that, former Musa Dagh compatriots came to see us almost every night and day. It was a big reunion for my parents.

After all the greetings and visitations, we had to look for a place to rent so we could start our new life in America. Initially, my father had a lucrative business in Philadelphia, but my parents now wanted to stay in Paterson, since there were many Musa Dagh folks there, also my mom's first cousin. So, it was settled that we will be living in Paterson, New Jersey.

Mom and dad found a nice house to rent on the second floor, 9 Timothy Street, right across from School No. 9. We all thought that it was heaven-sent to have the school so close to our new residence, which would make things easier. We had to start from scratch with furniture and all. Before we moved in, my parents purchased three bedroom sets, a kitchen set, and two couches. Immediately, they both looked for jobs, so that they could pay for their new furniture and pay the rent. Thank God, they both got jobs right away. For the time being, mom's job was part-time where my aunt used to work. It was a baby blanket factory in Paterson. Mom was to knot the loose fringes on the tiny blankets. My dad got a job at the Bright Star Industries in Clifton. They used to make flashlights. He was the new elevator operator. It was not a difficult job, but he had to walk to work and back. It was a three-mile walk. He did not mind. He used to get up early and start walking. Mom took the bus on Main Street and went to work, at first, three days a week, Monday through Wednesday. Much later on, she was full-time. She was a good worker and was producing twice as much as the other workers.

At that point, my brother joined the Army; this was during the Korean War.

Author's brother Movses (Mike) in the U.S. Army.

My sister and I were enrolled at School No. 9 in December 1950. Because of our language barrier, they placed us in second grade. That made me so sad. Here I was with seven-year-old children who were just learning the times tables and simple work that seemed so elementary to me. I felt bad and I felt like screaming. But I knew that I must learn the English language well so I could express myself. One great thing was that I had a very nice teacher, Miss Wilson, a young black woman. I had never seen a black person before. I knew black people existed, because I had learned in Sunday school that God loves everybody, whether they are black, white, yellow, or red. So, I was never exposed to being prejudiced against anyone.

Miss Wilson was my first teacher in a new land and I looked forward to learning. Not only was she nice, but also she was very neat and fashionable. As a young girl, I really liked that. Also, she was extremely patient with me and my sister to explain things to us slowly.

One day she asked the class to make a picture and she would hang all of them around the walls. But the picture had to be about Christmas, something about the Christmas spirit, she said. I understood that much, because those were words my father had taught me. I started drawing. As I was still drawing and coloring, Miss Wilson walked by the students to see the work being created by each one. She came to me and stopped; she called me, "Virginia, the little artist." I looked up and she was smiling, then she said,

"Would you make pictures like that on all of the windows of our classroom, facing the street?"

"Windows?" I replied, inquisitively, because I had never painted on glass before.

"Yes, paint on the windows." She pointed at them.

"Paint, what paint?"

"Don't worry, I have the paints and brushes, wait..." she headed to the closet in the back of the room, and pointed at me to go there. I got up, and she pointed at the paints and the brushes that I could use to paint designs on the windows that I had drawn on paper.

This was exciting to me, but I did not know how it would turn out on the glass. I started making Christmas trees with pretty ornaments on them. Then at the next window, I made baby Jesus in the manger. The next window, I made some shepherds and a few lambs. I continued with other pictures of angels, and made notes on one window, and put the title of the Christmas song that I knew in English, "Silent Night, Holy Night" and made branches around it and a big red bow. I finished all this in couple of days.

Miss Wilson called the other teachers and showed all the decorated windows to them. They, too, wanted me to do their windows that were facing the Timothy Street side. Miss Wilson was on "cloud nine," she was so happy and she continuously praised me. I felt good that I had done something that made everybody happy. So, I was labeled as the "Little Artist" around the other classes, too. This was, indeed, a very joyous time of the year. It made me think, however, about what my friends in Ainjar were doing at this time. Probably, they were getting ready for the Christmas pageant, which I had always had a part in and had sung in the choir. And they would be going around caroling, which I enjoyed very much. All these flashbacks were coming to me, and I missed it all.

One day, after Christmas, I went to Miss Wilson and told her the following with my broken English,

"Miss Wilson, you are very nice, and I like you, but I think this class is easy for my education." I was hoping that she would understand what I was trying to tell her—that I needed to go to a higher grade. My goodness, she did understand, and she put her arms around me and said,

"I will see what I can do about it. But I am going to miss you," she said, smiling.

"Thank you, thank you," I said gently. I left that thought alone for a bit, while the students were still being tested on the times tables, etc. My sister Alice did not mind staying in the class. That was fine with my parents, but they knew that I was not happy.

After the Christmas vacation, in January of 1951, I was told that I would be in Miss Connolly's fifth grade class, which made me feel better. These students were ten years old, not too bad. I figured I needed to deal with it even though I still thought I did not belong there. My major problem was communicating and having a good command of the English language. I figured out that I would do all the homework that Miss Connolly assigned me, which was better than being in second grade.

I began learning American history. This was a fascinating subject for me, learning about the presidents of the USA, and the different states, and the capitals of each state. I was feeling better now that I was learning something more than I knew. Also, Miss Connolly was quite persistent to teach us good penmanship. Through her teaching process, I developed a very legible and good writing habit. She was an older person than Miss Wilson, but she, too, was very sweet and kind. I liked her very much. I learned quite a bit in this class, yet still in my mind, I did not want to go to the sixth grade next.

I made a plan for myself. My brother had bought a brand new dictionary for me and my sister. It was the *New American College Dictionary*. This dictionary became my second Bible. Let me explain: I would get the newspapers and start reading. Any words that I did not understand, I would put in a special notebook. Then I would look them up, find the meanings, and jot them down. At times, I did not even understand the given meanings; I had to look up the meaning, too. Now, here was my system. I made myself learn at least ten words a day. Then I wrote sentences to learn to use the new words. When my father came home from work, after helping my mom with the supper, I would ask dad to quiz me on the vocabulary words. This was almost every night. My dad was very patient and proud of what I was doing. My mom thought I was pushing myself too much, but I explained to her that I really wanted to do it. My report card showed the proof of this hard work; I got straight A's from Miss Connolly.

But there were times, especially when school recessed for the summer, when I saw my age group of young people gathered around and having fun. I felt left out. Now, at thirteen years old, I was thinking about my friends in Ainjar and all the activities and fun I was missing. First of all, being in fifth grade with ten-year-olds was not my "cup a tea"; I could not make close friends with them. They were all nice to me, but I was lonesome for friends my age. Many a night after studying very hard, I would go to bed, close my bedroom door, and cry myself to sleep. I went to church with my family, then Sunday school at an American church near our house. Those people were very nice and I felt better being in Sunday school class with students my own age. My parents went to the Armenian Presbyterian church which was held at an American Presbyterian church in the afternoon. Rev. Makhitar came to give the sermon for the Armenian congregation, since we did not have our own church building. Here, too, there were no young people. It was a small congregation for all the emigrated people, mostly from overseas. There were many Sundays that I sang solos in Armenian, hymns that I knew by ear. They enjoyed that coming from a young person in fluent Armenian. It made me happy to see them happy.

On the weekends, mom and dad took us up to Garret Mountain, which was very nice. We all walked there, sometimes with our relatives, and had picnics. We always visited Lambert Castle, too. This castle was built in the late 19th century by a local silk tycoon. Its location is in Passaic County, New Jersey. One can view the scenery from up there clearly for many of the towns of Passaic and Bergen counties.

As the summer was progressing, I was still learning all those words that I had assigned to myself from the dictionary. It felt good that I was preparing for the next session of school. I really wanted to go to high school in September, but my cousins, and even my parents, said I would not be able to go to high school, because I had not graduated from grammar school yet. I knew that, but I was learning more and more every day. I had to think of something.

During the summer, I usually sat by my bedroom window and watched the street for different summer activities. The entrance of School No. 9 faced my room. I remember clearly, because I recorded all this in my journal. On Thursday, August 30, 1951, there was much activity going on. Secretaries were going in, and then I noticed that Dr. Alfred Knopf went in. He was the school principal. That being a Thursday, mom was home because at this time she was working part-time. I went over and asked her the following:

"Mom, I want to go to the school, and ask Dr. Knopf if he would allow me to go to high school in the fall."

"*Inch, gadag geness?*" (What, are you kidding?)

"No, mom, I am serious," I said emphatically.

"*Shad love, kna,*" (Very well, go) she relented, and continued, "Why aren't you doing some puzzles like your sister is?"

"Oh, mom, please. I already have done that," I responded.

"*Payts dun yegour should.*" (But come home right away.)

"*Oor bede yertam? Hos paregam choonim.*" (Where am I going to go? I have no friends here.)

"*Kna, kna.*" (Go, go.)

I ran out of the door and down a flight of stairs. My heart was beating fast, because I was excited, but I did not know how to approach Dr. Knopf. I thought it was definitely worth a try.

I looked both ways, then I ran across the street, up some stairs, and there I was at the front door of the school. I hesitated for a second or two, opened the big door, and headed to the office on the first floor. I knocked on the door.

Dr. Knopf noticed me and came to the door. The secretaries were busy typing.

"I want to ask you something, please."

"Sure, little artist, what can I do for you?"

"I want to go to high school." I thought I would come right to the point and ask what I wanted before I made a mistake."

"Huh? You really want to go to high school?"

"Yes, yes."

"Let me see now, take a seat."

He continued talking with me. I became so happy. He knew that I had a very good report card from Miss Connolly, and now he wanted more assurance from me about this high school issue. He wanted to know if I was serious about wanting to go and if I would do well.

I shook my head and said, "Yes, yes, I will try very hard."

He looked at me with a smile on his face and headed to the phone. He was on the phone at least five minutes. Then he came to me and said the following:

"Take this address," it was an address on Broadway in Paterson, "and go to Dr. Louis J. Schmerber's office. He is the Superintendent of Schools in Paterson."

"When?" I said, anxiously.

"Now. He will be waiting for you."

"Thank you, thank you." I shook his hand and ran out quickly.

I ran home, up the stairs in one breath, and knocked on the door, excitedly,

"Mom, mom," I shouted. "Do you know that Dr. Knopf said I can go and see Dr. Schmerber?"

"Who is this Mr. She-m-m-burg?" mom mumbled.

"It is Dr. Schmerber, the Superintendent of the Schools. You know what that means? Mom, please give me a dime for my bus fare; I have to leave right now."

"Have lunch first."

"No, I am too excited, I'll have lunch after."

Mom gave me a dime for 5 cents each way. I said thank you, gave her a kiss and ran out to catch the bus from Main Street, a block from our house.

I took the bus and got off on Broadway. I had to walk at least four long blocks before I reached the address and went up to the second floor. Dr. Schmerber's name was on the door. I knocked gently. After I waited a few seconds, Dr. Schmerber opened the door with a wide smile,

"Come in, young lady."

He had such a kind face. I knew I could talk with him without any fear. But I thought, *what is he going to ask me, I wonder?* I said to myself, *Patience, patience.* He was not a very big man, but walked confidently and had a nice head of gray hair. He looked very distinguished.

"Sit at this desk, young lady, and I want to talk with you." He pulled up his chair and sat next to me.

"Fine," I said, softly, and sat down.

He asked me why I wanted to go to high school. I explained to him that I already had a year of high school overseas, and that I was working very hard now to read, speak and write English, but that I still had a lot to learn. I continued, saying that I know I would do fine in high school, and I don't want to waste any more time in grade school.

He looked at me with a caring look, and said, "Let's see what you can do."

He already had some papers ready to start testing me. He first gave me a map of the world with no country names, and he pointed at certain locations to see if I knew where they were, what country. I named every country accurately, with an accent, of course. Then he asked me some general questions. I answered them with my broken English. He nodded, occasionally correcting my diction. Then, he said, he would say words, and that I should write them down. I did not do so well. I spelled them phonetically, but most of the words were spelled wrong. The math test was last, which was my favorite subject. I knew I would do well. There were several long divisions, multiplications, and fractional problems. I did them quite speedily, and they were all correct.

He took a little while, checking everything and turned around and said, "Young lady, as a whole, you did marvelously. Also, I admire your desire to learn and work hard. After you leave, I am going to make a call to Dr. Knopf. You go and see him when you leave my office." And he said nothing more.

I was so excited. I wanted to go straight to Dr. Knopf's office before I went home so I could see what this is all about.

"Thank you," I said cheerfully. I shook his hand and left. I walked those long blocks quickly and hopped on the bus to Main Street, paying my nickel fare to head home. Soon I got off, and went straight to School No. 9. Dr. Knopf was waiting for me.

I knocked on the door and he let me in:

"Congratulations, young lady, here is your diploma. You are awarded this diploma after having passed the required examination, and you are recommended for graduation."

He smiled and gave me my diploma, saying "After Labor Day, soon, go to Central High School and register. Take this diploma with you, and if they have any questions, they can call either me or Dr. Schmerber."

"Thank you, very much," I replied as I took the diploma from him, and shook his hand. With happy tears in my eyes, I left.

I ran across the street, up those stairs quickly, and banged on the door rapidly, calling "Mom, mom."

"*Inch yeghav?* (What happened?) You kept me on pins and needles. Tell me the whole thing."

I did, and she was delighted to hear it all. She said, "*Park Asdutso, ekhset ounetsar.*" (Praise God, you got your wish.) She hugged me and kissed me.

I was so excited. She continued saying that I should eat something now. She said my sister Alice and she had already eaten. I told her that I wanted to put my pretty pink organdy dress on and go downtown again to get a graduation photo with my diploma.

She said, "Do you have to do that today?"

I said, "Yes, mom—today is a very special day for me and I am going to remember this day the rest of my life." I then added, "Lord willing, I will make you and dad proud."

I just grabbed an apple, ate it with some peanut butter, and drank some milk. Then I went to my room, searched for a red ribbon to tie my diploma with a bow. I changed my clothes. Mom gave me a dollar for the photos

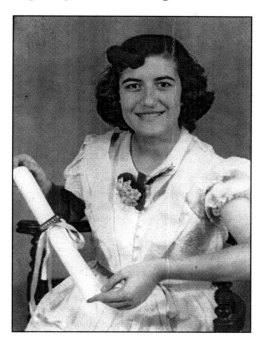

Author with School No. 9 diploma, taken on August 30, 1951.

and an extra dime for my fare again. I was ready to hop on the bus again, this time with no surprised anticipation. Now, I had my diploma! It was all rolled up in a bag. I was going to go to Central High School in the fall. I felt really good. I got my photos at a quick photo place for 10 cents a piece, ten of them. Some to send to my friends overseas, and some to mom and dad, and I kept a few.

Now the day was complete for me. I could not wait until dad got home. As a matter of fact, I asked my mom if I could start walking to meet dad on the way home. Mom said "yes." I still had my pink organdy dress on, and cheerfully I went to Getty Avenue, where dad's route was. He was surprised to see me all dressed up, but looked happy. I gave him the good news, he put his arms around me and we walked all the way home like that. He said that he was very proud of me, and he knew how much I loved school and learning. He also added that things will change now. He said

Author's diploma.

I would make new friends that are at my age level. He knew I was still homesick, missing my dear friends overseas. Dad was a very wise man. He continued, saying that as time passes, I will have so many opportunities that I will love this country.

"I still do," he said, "even though I had to be with my people for a while. I don't feel that I abandoned them, but I had to think about my children's future. It was not going to be good overseas. I really don't think it would have worked."

"God willing, we will make the best that we can now," I said softly. He looked at me and nodded in agreement.

"I am very proud of you, what you did today. That took lots of guts to go and see the principal and ask him to allow you to go to high school next semester. I know how hard you are studying to improve your language and vocabulary; that is very good."

I truly believe that with God's help, we all can do anything we set our minds to, whatever our hearts' desire doing for ourselves and for others. This will make a better life and, of course, a better world for all.

17

Central High School

I was so excited. I did not know what to take with me the first day, other than my diploma, a couple of notebooks, pencils and pens. The place was buzzing with students scurrying around. I finally found the office and the registrar asked me who I was. I showed her my diploma. She had to place me in a curriculum, which I did not have. I did not know what she was talking about when she asked me:

"Do you want to take the Academic, Commercial, or Home Economics courses?"

These choices were not explained to me beforehand. I had no idea what she meant, but my reply was,

"I like mathematics, and languages...." I hesitated not knowing what else I needed to add to my statement.

"What language would you like?"

"French and..." She interrupted me, saying you can only take one language.

"That's fine, French."

"I will put you in the Commercial curriculum," she said, and continued, "that has mathematics, and you can also take French and other subjects."

I waited while she prepared a schedule for me so that I knew where I would go for my homeroom and other classes. I took the schedule, but I felt like a little lost sheep. I checked some of the room numbers; they were not even close to what I had in my hand. Finally, I stopped and asked some people where Room 86 was. They told me that it was not in that building, but at the Annex. Oh, my! What a beginning this was. This first day was simply overwhelming. I got to that building, which was across from the main high school building. I found the room, and most of the students were already there. I presented my schedule. The teacher made a note of it, added my name to the list, and showed me my seat. The confusion went on all day. It was a hard day for me, not knowing anyone yet. I did not know where the rooms were and I did not know what the teachers were going to be like. We received our books in each class, and were assigned lockers so that we did not have to carry our books around all day. I knew that once I learned the system, I would be fine. I told myself to be patient and everything will fall in place.

That first year of high school was not easy at all. I wanted to make friends, but first I had to have my routine under control. Only then, would I be able to concentrate, make friends, and meet my classmates. Soon, I would know the teachers a little better.

While in my first year of high school, my mom made a very good Christian friend. Her name was Mrs. Katabian. She visited us often. One day she asked my mother if I could write her letters for her correspondence with her many close friends and relatives overseas. They could only understand Armenian. I said that I could help her with writing her letters, since I am fluent in Armenian. She was so happy. In an hour one day, I wrote about ten letters for her. She was pleased, and relieved that she had answered these letters finally. After I finished, she offered me money. I said, "No, I want to help you whenever you need me. It made me happy to do so." She insisted, but I still did not take any money.

The next day she visited us, she brought me a gift: a desktop radio with a clock. I accepted it graciously and I was delighted with it. Number one, we did not have a radio or a TV or even a telephone yet. I figured if I listen to the news every day, I would learn the English language easier, learning and listening to the way that the words were being pronounced. Now I had three valuable things that I cherished: the Bible, which I read every day (in Armenian); my dictionary, where I learned all the new words; and now a radio, which was also teaching me the spoken language in its correct pronunciation.

I enjoyed the music stations a great deal. Before bedtime, I would listen to classical music, and during the day, I loved listening to popular music with all the new records. I used to sing along with the songs, and that gave me confidence in pronouncing the words correctly and gave me the knowledge of which songs were popular and number one. The radio became a good tool for me to have conversations with my friends in school. You see one must find some common ground to utilize in making a connection to pursue friendships, to have something in common.

Also, there was another way that I gained friends—by being nice and patient with them and helping them with their math problems. They were thankful and I was happy; we became good friends. Sometimes, when I did not understand something well with the English language, they did not make fun of me, which was so dear to me.

What I am about to tell you is very comical. One of my newfound friends in high school asked me if I would go on a blind date with her and her boyfriend. I immediately said "No." She said, fine, I thought we could have fun to do something together. When I went home that day, I was thinking, *"Why, oh why does she want me to go out with a blind person, and think that I would have fun? Is she crazy or something?*" Later on, I learned that "blind date" is an expression in English that means a "surprise date"; however, this phrase cannot be translated in Armenian other than what I thought. You see, the English language has its ups and downs, in having to translate it to one's own language, the meaning changes completely. I laughed at myself, having thought what I thought. Even though I knew the real meaning of a "blind date" later on, the prospect did not appeal to me. I had to know the person and to have things in common before I would go out with them. That's what I thought anyway. Maybe you, the reader, have a different opinion about the issue; that is fine with me. I think it is a matter of choice.

Speaking of having to learn English, in some ways it is an easy language, because its alphabet is the same as the French alphabet characters. However, in English, I learned that there were exceptions to the exceptions to the rules. In the Armenian language, we do not have that problem. The rules and the sounds stay the same almost always. I was trying so hard to be proficient in English, when I learned that there were more changes that I was not aware of. For example, for "book," the plural becomes "books," just add an "s." "Foot" does not become "foots," but instead it is changed to "feet." Also, for "box," the plural becomes "boxes," but for "ox" the plural becomes "oxen," then "mouse" becomes "mice" in the plural. Another example: listen to the pronunciation of "bough" then that for the word "rough". The pronunciation of sound for each is not even a close match. And listen to this: What is the difference between the meaning of a "wise man" and a "wise guy"? Well, there is a difference. If a new learner does not know the difference, she or he could use the wrong choice in attempting to pick the right one. I could go on and on, mentioning the differences that I have noticed, but I think you get what I am talking about. For a foreigner to learn correct English is not an easy task. How could a "slim chance" and "fat chance" mean the same thing? One can get lost in the idiomatic process of the English language. You simply have to memorize and be aware of the context and the format. Linguistics can be quite a challenging science.

My first year's English teacher was not a cordial person. He was tough and he called me in one day after class, and was scolding me for having used the wrong tense in the sentences. I very quietly told him that I was trying very hard, and that this was a new language for me. He felt bad, tried not to criticize me so bluntly, and became a little more tolerant in correcting my mistakes.

My second year of high school seemed and felt better than the first year. My language annunciation was improving greatly, and I had some very good teachers during my second year. I had Miss Saal for English—she was great. She was the adviser for the Literary Debating Society (LDS) club.

She asked me to join this club. I was a little hesitant, but was honored that she thought I would be worthy of handling this.

"I know you can do it, Virginia," she told me cheerfully.

"You think so, Miss Saal? After all, I have to think what words I have to use so carefully, and I would have to debate challenging, good speakers."

"Yes, I know you can. The way you do your homework, listen so intently in class, and express yourself so thoughtfully—you will be fine."

"Thank you for your trust in me, Miss Saal. Yes, I will try it."

She was glad that I would try. That coming Friday, I was in a debate. She was so impressed, she told me later, "You will be president of this club very soon."

I did not believe her at first, but I did become president of the debating club by the end of the school year. Through the encouragement of Miss Saal, I gained so much confidence. However, if I had refused to take that leap, confidence would not have revealed itself to me. Confidence is not something you buy or a quality given to you as a gift. By challenging yourself with a task and succeeding in doing it, that is how confidence is attained.

I had some other wonderful teachers whom I admired dearly. One was Mr. Walters, a tall, handsome gentleman, one of my English teachers. He would never embarrass me by calling on me unless I had my hand up. And when I answered correctly, he would always commend me. Another fine gentleman was my homeroom teacher, Rev. William Turnbull. He was the kindest of all the teachers. One day, he was talking with me, and he noticed that I was wearing my CE (Christian Endeavor) pin. He did not want to assume, so he asked me what the "CE" stood for. I said "Christian Endeavor." He said, "I thought so." I told him that I belonged to CE in Lebanon, and that I was a very active member of it. I said they gave me this pin as a going away souvenir. After that, he would have very nice conversations with me before homeroom time. I really trusted him.

One day, Rev. Turnbull came over and told me that he was glad students were looking up to me, because I was helping them with their homework and had a very kind attitude towards everyone. He said that quality of leadership was a special gift. He told me that Student Government Association (SGA) elections would be held soon and that I should run for office. I was very surprised. But he continued to encourage me; he believed I would be a good representative for the students.

I thought about it for a while, and I said, "Why not? I have nothing to lose and everything to gain by experience. I will learn new things. It would be good experience and I would enjoy helping the school any way I can."

So, I submitted my name to the SGA adviser, who at the time was Mr. Walters. Then, all the names were distributed to the homerooms prior to election. My friends, whom I often helped with math, became my advocates and the word got around. They assisted me in making posters and hung them all around different areas: hallways, the cafeteria, and in classrooms. The first time I ran for SGA office was for the position of Secretary. This would be a truly big challenge for me, because I would have to take the minutes of the meetings, and to read them back at each meeting. I thought even if I did not win, it was a great experience in learning the process and meeting many students. We also had to be introduced and make a brief speech at an Assembly, so that the students knew the candidates. There was a very nice young lady named Louise Shultz, who was a senior and well-spoken. I was running against her. I wanted to do a good job, but I really thought she was going to win. Nevertheless, I continued campaigning with goodwill and hard work.

The election took place and to my surprise, the results were a landslide for little old me. Rev. Turnbull took me aside and showed me that each homeroom had about 23-25 students, and in each of them, 20-21 votes were cast for me. I could not believe it. From that incident, I was humbled to be serving the students.

There were trips to take to Eastside High School for different programs, and meetings with their SGA students, interacting with them and giving reports. The next year, I was elected again, this time as Commissioner of Elections to oversee the election process. When newly elected, I did not imagine the amount of work behind the process.

Each of these experiences improved my knowledge and confidence, love of friends, and provided great opportunities regarding this new role that I was getting acquainted with. Now, I was beginning to see what my dad had been telling me all along, about loving this country with all its abundant opportunities. The opportunities are open to anyone willing to take the leap to savor them. My father was a smart man to instill those seeds of faith in me.

Two of my best friends were Veronica Oleshko, a quiet but a very nice and intelligent young lady, originally from Poland, and Martha Moore, a cheerful and happy Irish redhead. Martha's parents invited me to their Ocean Grove house at the Jersey Shore many times. My third friend was Helen Piccolo. We had many things in common and always hung around. I also corresponded with my dear friends in Lebanon, but that initial sadness of mine had disappeared already. Now I was enjoying my new friends very much.

I have to mention another great teacher I had. She was my math teacher in my third year, Miss Mary Alward. We became such good friends that she took me to the United Nations. That was an intriguing trip for me.

She took me all around the UN, and we attended the General Assembly. Not only that, but we observed the Security Council. It fascinated me as to how one could switch from one language to another on the earphones and listen to what was going on. To top it off, she introduced me to the Lebanese delegate, Miss Laure Shabet, a fine, educated woman who had such a sweet face. Miss Alward was telling her about my schoolwork, and the ambassador said she was very proud that I was doing so well. This was really a very scintillating day for me. The Central High School reporter had a special story on it with Miss Shabet and me and describing how one of their high school students attended the UN Security Council. If I perfected my English, I thought perhaps I could become a linguist and become a translator in UN. I thought UN translator might be a good and interesting job. Miss Alward was a committee member of an American organization at the UN. I cannot recall what it exactly was, but that is why she had access to the many areas at the UN.

By the way, Miss Alward and I remained friends even after my graduation. She was invited to my parents' house on Christmas a couple of times after my graduation from high school. Also, she came to my first child's christening in Mt. Vernon, N.Y. in 1960. She was a very sweet and friendly lady.

However, I had a science teacher at this time that was a scatterbrain. I won't give his name, even though it is crystal clear in my mind, lest a grandchild of his read this book. I do not want to dishonor him. What he did was so unfair. I had studied very hard for a test. I had all the questions answered correctly, and the test was done neatly with diagrams. He brought the test papers back in a few days and distributed all of them to my classmates, except mine. He said he misplaced it, and could not find it. He added, "I will give you a 'C.'"

I did not like that statement at all. I asked him to give me the same test or another one if he wanted to, because I knew that I had all the answers right. He refused. I was very upset, because he would have left me out of my honor roll status. If I was willing to take the same test or another one of his choosing, why was he refusing those ideas? I really wanted to take the test. He insisted: "No, you can't take it again."

That did not sit right with me, and left me with no other choice but see Mr. Matteson, the principal of Central High. I went to Mr. Matteson's office after my classes, but he was not there. Mr. Foley, the vice principal was there. I told him the whole story. He shook his head in amazement, and said "I will take care of it, young lady."

"Thank you very much, Mr. Foley," I said, and shook his hand and left.

The next day, my science teacher said nothing to me. I realized that Mr. Foley had not talked to him yet. As usual, no matter what kind of day it was, he would always greet the class saying, "It's a nice day if it don't [sic] rain." Always, he said that in the beginning of the class. I often wondered where he learned his English, and I did not think that he should be a teacher. But, of course, that was not my job, and I tried to live my life the way I saw fit. I wanted justice, and I had to do something about it. That was my right. I did not want to bother my parents about it, because they had their hands full trying to make a living.

I took my normal seat the next day. Mr. _____ came and told me discreetly to see him after class. So, I did.

"I don't want to give you another test. I know you are an excellent student, so you will not get a 'C' but an 'A,'" he said in a low voice.

I said "Thank you" and was about to leave.

He said, "I'm sorry to have lost your paper, to have caused you frustration."

"Don't let it happen again, Mr. _____." I had the courage to tell him that.

"It won't," he laughed, mildly.

"Thanks," then I left quickly, because I did not want to be late for my next class.

I did not hold a grudge against him, but I knew that he had a different personality than the other teachers that I loved dearly.

My third year of high school continued to be very interesting and successful. By this time, I had many friends, and I found the English language quite challenging and in a way intriguing. I started comparing idiomatic differences, which were fascinating to me by translating them from English to Armenian, and vice versa. For example, in English we say we have "no room"; in Armenian you say we have "no place." If one translates literally, the "room" is a place like a bedroom, living room, etc. That translation in Armenian would sound silly, because in the Armenian translation, the emphasis is on "space," which I think makes more sense.

However, in Armenian, there are some ridiculous idioms, too. For example, in colloquial Armenian, if a person loves someone very dearly, they would say to that person "love your liver." This, translated to English, is absolutely crazy. How could one love someone so much that the liver comes to mind? It is ludicrous. But again, it is an accepted expression of endearment for the person receiving that compliment.

Also, in English, the two letter word "up" has many connotations according to the different ways it is used. For example, you "look up" a number, you "look up to" someone, or "building up" a list, or "shut up", or "open up" a store, or we can "warm up", the congressman is "up" for election or people "stir up" trouble, "warm up" in doing a chore, or "work up" an appetite, and its meanings go on and on. If English learners do not know all these usages, they can get really "fouled up."

Also, during the end of my third year of high school in 1954, I was chosen as a delegate to the Jersey Girls State to be held at Rutgers University, New Brunswick, N.J. This was sponsored by the American Legion Auxiliary of New Jersey. The Director of Girls State was Mrs. Elizabeth Sharpley. The Vesper Service was the opening session on June 27, 1954. This service took place at the Voorhees Chapel at the New Jersey College for Women, what is called today Douglass Residential College of Rutgers University.

The service started with the hymn, "Faith of Our Fathers," then the invocation, and another hymn followed: "Softly Now the Light of Day." After that, the Scripture reading took place which was found in the Gospel of Matthew 20:20-28. A prayer followed and after that we sang another hymn "The Lord Is My Shepherd." After this hymn, I sang a solo, called "The Love of God." The Vesper message was given by Rev. William Turnbull (my high school teacher), the Pastor of the First Christian Church of Paterson, N.J. He spoke about service, which he presented very eloquently as service to God and service to humanity. That message became embedded in my psyche. After Rev. Turnbull, another hymn was sung by all, "Now the Day Is Over," and the Benediction ended the Vespers. Now, our initial program was over, and we were assigned to our cottages for the week's duration.

We had assistant directors giving a hand to Mrs. Sharpley during the week. They were as follows: Mrs. R. Graham Huntington, Mrs. Harry Kellerman, and Mrs. Charles Phillips, who was also the department president, and of course, Mrs. Samuel J. Sharpley was the Director of the Jersey Girls State. All of the students picked for this assemblage had to be scholastically bright students and on the honor roll in their given high schools. As a matter of fact, Central High School of Paterson was well-represented by other students, such as Doris Roffino, Janice Broglio and Barbara Jahreis.

The week turned out to be very busy, but very well-organized with all the sessions. We were obliged to study all phases of United States government. I learned about the process of elections and the different offices in each level of government: local, county, and state. Based on our U.S. government, we had two political parties called Federal and National. Then, all the girls were divided in different fictional counties, such as Nimitz, Eisenhower,

The initial Vesper Service at Voorhees Chapel. Far right: Mrs. Sharpley, onstage; middle, Rev. Turnbull; and the author, facing the audience, singing "The Love of God."

and MacArthur. I was assigned to Eisenhower County. There were primary and general elections, with members running for different offices. Offices would be filled by girls who were running for certain positions in city, county or state government. All officers needed to be registered and processed properly for each given office. I was elected as the City Clerk of Washington. All the other offices were modeled precisely on our local, county and state governmental offices. At the finale, we elected a governor, Lee Hillenbach on July 1 at 11:30 a.m. This whole process taught me so much about government—how each office is necessary and how each department functions. After the governor's election, there was the Governor's Ball, and we all were dressed in formal gowns in celebration of the occasion. July 2, 1954, was our last day. At 12:00 noon was the final assembly for retreat. We had the Farewell Luncheon at 12:30 p.m. and at 1:15 p.m. every citizen checked out with her cottage counselor.

Cottage "N"—L–R: The author as City Clerk of Washington and Gail as the Sheriff of Eisenhower County.

This was such an educational and scintillating week that left a big impression on me and guided my future years as an adult public servant.

As we grow older, each phase has its ups and downs and each phase takes us to a different plateau in life. The secret is to allow ourselves to enjoy each and every phase. With God's help, and our determination, we can all attain whatever we are working toward. Sometimes, our goal is attained easier and sometimes not; however, the journey we take is a learning process. If we are willing to take the chance, and utilize the opportunities presented to us, with God's help, the possibilities of having to reach one's goals are limitless. And that kind of determination and perseverance takes us to higher levels of learning. For me, learning was never a chore, but satisfying a thirst for knowledge. Even to this date, I try to learn something new all the time. I do not think that anyone knows everything, but we must always strive to learn more, no matter what our individual pursuits are. Truly, if continuous learning is done lovingly and sincerely, the quest is a great gift, a way to enjoy life fully. That has been my philosophy, thus far, it has worked for me.

18

High School Graduation and Meeting My Husband

At this point of my life, I am absolutely thrilled to be a senior at Central High School, Paterson, N.J. My parents are doing well with their jobs and now they are contemplating buying a house. The year is 1955. Just four years ago we had landed in the United States. I think if people have faith, determination and work hard, they can do just about anything.

Our new house was purchased with hope, love, and hard work. It was a bungalow house at the corner of Knickerbocker and Getty avenues. To top it off, a nice church, the Lakeview Presbyterian Church stood right across from our new house. We became members of this church. I sang in the choir and taught Sunday school classes. My sister joined the youth activities. Now, truly, I had found the niche I was hoping and searching for. I became a youth counselor at the Presbyterian Camp at Island Heights, N.J. I enjoyed all these activities immensely. Everything at the church gave me so much pleasure. I enjoyed helping out in whatever way I could to make a difference.

I thought one more year of high school, and then I will go to college. This year was another challenge for me to do well in order to be accepted by a good college. I wanted to serve people in some facet. That was my main desire. I was asked to run for SGA office again, and I did and won. This role became second nature to me and I worked for the students diligently in any way I could. Also, I became president of the Bible Club, while remaining president of the Literary Debating Society. This last year, my English teacher was Miss O'Neil, a very petite woman who was a very astute and sweet person. She encouraged me in writing my term paper, or my senior thesis, hoping that I would be the valedictorian. She knew of my experience as an articulate debater.

But that did not happen, because I had chosen a religious topic, and she was cautious to use that. My topic was "Children of God." It was sprinkled with many Biblical verses and issues. She told me that she loved it and it was written well, and I got an "A" for it. It really did not matter to me if I was not picked to deliver the paper as a valedictory address. I had the satisfaction and the love of having written what I wanted to express about my faith.

I did very well in all of my subjects and was preparing to apply for colleges when my dad became ill. At that point, I wanted to take a break and get a job to help the family first. My mom and dad had sacrificed so much for us. The least I could do was help them now.

I made my availability known to the business department of the high school where seniors were informed of job possibilities. Mrs. Elliott was in charge; she called to say there would be two bank officers from their personnel department to interview seniors for jobs. I wanted to be interviewed, because I wanted a steady job. A bank seemed like a nice place to work. From 150 students, they chose two students to be employed with the County Bank and Trust Company in downtown Paterson.

But before graduation, I had a part-time job at a diaper factory not too far from my house. I walked there, about six long blocks each way, to save bus fare. I did this during the summer vacations when I was not doing youth counseling at the Island Heights Camp. My job at the diaper factory was that when the sterilized hot Birdseye diapers came out of the machines, I had to quickly count and package them in a brown paper cover and label them as to how many diapers were in each packet. I had a chart to follow. They were packaged in groups of one dozen, two dozen or three dozen diapers. When I got home, I would have to soak my fingers in cool water, because they would be tingling and burning with pain after constantly touching those extremely hot diapers. It was hard, but I survived it.

I was very happy, however, to be one of the two students who got the bank jobs. I was thrilled about that.

Aside from wearing a cap and gown for graduation, the girls had to have a pretty dress to wear at "Class Day" marching down the aisle for the student assembly. Mom was working very hard, and did not have time to make me a dress. I did not have the money to buy an expensive dress, so I decided I would design and make my own dress. I did. It was a soft white silk material with silver leaf designs on it. I made it dressy enough to have a red, soft crepe shoulder sash and a tiny red satin waistband with silver sequins sewn on it. I did this all by myself on mom's sewing machine. Then I bought a pair of silver shoes with five-inch heels, and a silver evening bag. As a matter of fact, it was in this dress that I met my husband after graduation at a dinner dance in September of 1955.

The author's Class Day dress. This is how her husband Henry saw her for the first time.

Graduation was in June 1955, right around the corner. It was an exciting day for me dressed in a white gown and a white cap.

The author's high school graduation.

During graduation I received the highest service point award, having attained by any student thus far for curricular activities in school besides my actual class work. I also received a gold medallion for being in the National Honor Society. My parents and I were very happy for all these honors.

Two weeks after graduation, I started working at the County Bank and Trust Co. in Paterson. Prior to starting to work, we moved to 504 Getty Avenue, our new home. I would walk up Knickerbocker Avenue to get to Main Street and catch the bus each day to go to work.

My father was such a terrific dresser. He always looked great. Unless he

Mom and dad sitting in the kitchen of our new home.

was working in the yard, or at bedtime, he wore a suit, white shirt and a tie. He always looked like an executive. I loved him for many reasons, but that was an additional thing that I really enjoyed seeing. Even when he went to work, he dressed like that and many times he would also wear a fedora on his head. Then he would change at work into his work uniform, and change back when he came home. To church, he always dressed immaculately and mom did, too. But mom did not fuss as much as did dad.

*A 1956 portrait of Matosian family: mom, dad,
Mike, Alice and the author at the left.*

I worked on the fifth floor of the bank in the Loan and Rebate
Department as a file clerk. I immediately got used to it, and filing became
a very easy task for me. I knew from the beginning that I would not stay
there just filing. However, that initial job acquainted me with the loan
process, reading ledgers, and knowing which accounts were faulty by not
having paid their loans on time. Soon, there was a paper circulating from
the main office that the American Institute of Banking (AIB) was offering
courses at Central High School in the evenings. The courses were to improve
our status and knowledge of banking in many ways. I was really interested
and I was told that if we got a grade of 90 or over in any of the courses, the
bank would pay for the class.

I thought, "*Oh, my Lord, what more could one ask for?*" I immediately
decided to sign up for courses. There were varied courses: Fundamentals of
Banking, Customer Interaction, Public Speaking, Commercial Law, etc. All
of these appealed to me. However, I could not sign up for more than one at
a time, because they were taught at the same time in different classrooms
by different professors. I decided to take Fundamentals of Banking first. I
asked some of my new friends in the department if they wanted to take
some courses, too, but they did not want to.

When I was given the schedule, I had no idea who would be in my class,
but I did not mind or care. That was fine with me, even though I did not

have any friends there. When I walked into the first class at 7:30 p.m., I was very surprised to see that there were no young people my age there at all. They mostly were department heads and some older men and women from different departments. Again, I thought I could learn from them all, of course. They had a lot more experience than I had. The classes went very well; they were from 7:30 to 9:00 p.m. each night for a semester. I received a grade of 95; therefore, I did not have to pay one penny for the course. I learned quite a bit, and I met many department heads, which was very interesting.

Before the fall started, my supervisor promoted me to be in charge of the Rebate Department. In this department, we had certain officers who were in charge of giving loans out for cars and boats. My task was to keep abreast of all the loans being paid on time each month; those in arrears would pay a penalty, a late charge. Also, there were those who paid in advance before their term was up, several months in advance. Then I would calculate how much rebate they would receive, send them a check, and close the account. Having learned all this gave me such confidence. In addition, I was able to help my family with bills, including paying the mortgage.

There were many Musa Dagh people in Paterson—that was one of the reasons why my parents settled there. Some were cousins of my parents and others good friends. During the summer, a committee was formed to commemorate the 40th anniversary of the Battle of Musa Dagh when my people fought the Turks on Mt. Moses. This commemoration always takes place the second weekend of September, because that is when in 1915 my people were saved by a French battleship, *Le Guichen*. We were also going to honor the memory of the eighteen heroes who died to save their people from the Turks who were going to massacre the Armenians. Thank God that did not happen.

At this commemoration, there were two bands to entertain the guests: one was an American band, and the other was an Armenian band. The Armenian music was mostly for the older people and the American band played for mostly the young people. It was a very jovial evening, and many guests showed up from the tri-state areas and even further: New Jersey, of course; New York; Pennsylvania; Connecticut; and Massachusetts. I was an usherette standing by the door passing out programs, after the folks' names were checked and the table assignments were given.

The evening progressed very nicely. The tables were getting occupied quickly. There were some late arrivals having come from a distance. The music filled the large auditorium with melodious Armenian music, and the sound of people talking filled the place with white noise. Soon, the host of the evening came out, asking everyone to rise and sing the "Lord's Prayer" in Armenian. After that, dinner was served. My name was on the program, because I was going to sing a solo in Armenian. I noticed that a table in the center back row was signaling me to go there. I complied, and I was asked for more forks; they said they were short. Being an usherette and a good sport, I went to the kitchen and I got some forks. They thanked me, but as I was leaving, they called me back saying—

"Miss Matosian, we don't have knives either."

"I am surprised that you are the only table that is missing some utensils," I said inquisitively. As I looked at them, they were smiling.

"Is there something funny? Was this a joke?" I asked.

"No, no, not a joke. Thank you."

I walked away and went to my table where my parents were. After dinner, the program started. We had a couple of speakers commemorating this special Musa Dagh celebration of Fortieth Anniversary. Then my name was announced to go up on the stage and sing. I did, and they wanted more. I sang another song, and then went back to my seat. The applause was very enthusiastic because the people there wanted to hear Armenian songs by a young person. Afterwards, many people came and congratulated me, including a young blond man with blue eyes who did not even look Armenian. I thanked them all and did not remember who they were. As the band started playing Armenian dance music, I wanted to join the "pinky dance," in which everyone holds the pinky finger of the person next to them. It is a quite enthusiastic circular dance. As I was enjoying this *shourchbar* (circular dance), the blond young man came in and cut through the line and held my pinky and started dancing next to me. He began talking with me, telling me how much he enjoyed my singing. I did not pay too much attention. I thought he liked dancing, and he was being kind to chat.

After the dance was over, I went back to my table. A little later, he came by and wanted to chat some more with me. He told me that he was studying at Columbia University, and that his name was Henry Apelian. He was here in the USA to pursue a medical degree, but there were no openings in the medical schools, so he was studying pharmaceuticals at Columbia. He said his brother Robert insisted that he take a break from his studies to come to this affair. I said, "How nice. Everyone needs a break sometimes." Our chat continued for a while, I thought he was a very nice young man, but after that I never thought of the incident anymore.

Two weeks later, he called to ask me for a date. I was curious as to how he got my number since he did not ask me that night.

"Who gave you my number?" I wanted to know.

"Oh, I have ways—my aunt gave it to me. She belongs to the Armenian Relief Society [ARS, equivalent to Armenian Red Cross] that you belong to, and you are the secretary," he said very surely.

"That's right, I belong to the ARS, and I must add, I am the youngest member there. Who is your aunt, there are many women there."

"Her name is Manoushag (Violet)," he replied, briskly.

"Oh, she is very friendly. I know her."

So the conversation continued, and I said that he should come and meet my parents personally since my parents are very traditional in their ways. He agreed, and a beautiful friendship began that continued on a higher level in the future. He was very polite and a real gentleman. My parents liked him right away, unlike other young men who wanted to date me. They always got the third-degree interrogation. Dating Henry was very nice, but I wanted to take my time slowly since I was just out of high school. After the first date, he visited me every weekend, and was very romantic with his gifts and flowers always.

It is very interesting how life has its twists and turns, and somehow all things fall in their proper places. I had my strength first from Almighty God, and then I had my parents, Sister Hedwig, and many great teachers to get encouragement from to continue my young life with hope and determination. This type of healthy concept about life in general, can sustain anyone through any situation until they are the victor. I thank my Lord and Savior for all His blessings thus far, and I am looking forward to a more abundant life hereafter.

PART SEVEN:

Marriage and Family

19

My Wedding and Move
to Mt. Vernon, N.Y.

I continued working in the bank and I loved it. It was a large bank and there were many possibilities to advance. Not only were work obligations in the picture, but also the bank had many other activities that one could join and enjoy. Some of them were singing in their choir, square dancing, picnics, drama presentations, and ballroom dancing. Of course, all of these were possible after work hours. I took advantage of many of these activities and they were much fun. I also made new friends from different departments. In 1956, I bought my own car, a 1953 Dodge, black top and cream colors.

Author sitting on her car.

In 1958, I was promoted twice and, at this point, I was moved to the sixth floor to assist one of the vice presidents, Mr. Miller. This position had given me a wide range of that department's activities, which were being in charge of the insurance part of the department, dealing face to face with customers and handling telephone disputes. Under Mr. Miller's jurisdiction was the responsibility of the money safe on the sixth floor. I was put in charge to open and close the safe for transactions.

Soon after, our bank merged with New Jersey Bank and Trust Co. whose main office was in Clifton. Many changes occurred and some people were let go. I did not lose my job; instead, they made me Branch Manager in one of their walk-in offices. I enjoyed that, too, and the travel was about the same distance for me, since our house was on the border of Paterson and Clifton. The only difference was that I

Author was now engaged in 1958.

had to take the bus to go east instead of west to Main St., which became Main Avenue in Clifton.

By this time, Henry and I were dating steadily, and we soon got engaged. We were very happy for our future plans. Now that my father was feeling better, I wanted still to pursue my education by going to college, other than just the AIB courses. I made my wishes clear to Henry that I had taken a break to help out the family, but I still wanted to go to college.

He was not against the idea, but suggested that even if we got married, I could still pursue my wishes. That made me feel better, and thus, we set a date for getting married on April 4, 1959. I wanted to give myself ample time to make my own wedding gown.

Henry graduated from the Pharmacy College of Columbia University in the summer of 1958 and found a job with Vick Chemical Co. in Bloomfield, N.J. It seemed our plan would work perfectly: he had a job and I could continue my education. Vick Chemical Co. gave a special luncheon in our honor, a day before our wedding on April 3, 1959.

In honor of author's wedding, April 3, 1959, Vick Chemical Company held a special luncheon with Henry's coworkers.

Things were progressing well at the bank, and Henry had begun his work at Vick. I was busy looking for special materials and lace for my wedding gown. I found the very best French satin and lace and beads that I would hand sew on the bodice of the gown. The next step was to create the design and get started. Between work and my activities in church—singing in the choir and teaching Sunday school—sewing the gown became a tedious job. But it was an exciting one that I enjoyed doing.

While still dating, Henry and I went to his relatives' house in Jackson Heights, N.Y. and other family functions. We had planned a big wedding, because the Apelian family was quite a large one. Most of the wedding guests were Apelians; the rest were friends and my family. Since my father was the only son, we did not have any relatives from my dad's side. My mother's side of family members was mostly overseas, except for one cousin and her family. We had two bands, an American one and an Armenian one.

We got married at the Lakeview Presbyterian Church where I taught Sunday school and sang in the choir. The wedding ceremony was conducted by two ministers: one, the Pastor of this church, Rev. Robert Sackmann, and the other, an uncle of Henry's, Rev. Bedros Apelian, who had his church in Fairlawn, N.J.

Rev. Robert Sackmann and Rev. Bedros Apelian marrying the author and Henry Apelian at the Lakeview Presbyterian Church.

Henry Apelian and Virginia Matosian getting married.

We went to Florida on our honeymoon for a week, and then went to Atlantic City for a week, where there was a pharmaceutical convention that Henry attended while the wives were being entertained by day trips and shows. In the evening, we had private times and dinners with friends of the Vick Chemical Company.

Soon we were back to our jobs. Then word got out that Vick was going to move to Mt. Vernon, N.Y. Since that was the situation, we lived at our parents' house for three months before the move. My parents had three bedrooms and there was ample room and a big yard. We did not have any furniture since we did not know where we would be living in Mt. Vernon or how big an apartment we would have. However, we started looking almost every weekend.

Henry and author cooking shish-kebob in her parents' backyard in July of 1959.

We found a very nice house where the owners lived on the first floor. We rented the second floor on Summit Street in a very nice neighborhood. It was close to the parks, and Henry's new work place at the Walker Labs building. I began to look for colleges so that I could start immediately. It was most probable that I would travel to New York City by train. Soon, to our surprise, we discovered that I was about three-months pregnant. This was about the end of October 1959. Both Henry and I wanted to have a family; however, this situation was going to delay my plans for going to college. I simply accepted it, "Let it be God's will." We often talked about having a nice sized family, so this was going to be the beginning of a nice journey to parenthood.

Life is so interesting and full of surprises at times. As long as the surprises are something of a happy nature one can deal with, with God's help and grace, anything can be worked out. Now I was going to cross another bridge in life, which was part of my dreams some day. We bought new furniture and settled in our first apartment. I sewed the curtains and couch covers, and made some embroidered pillowcases for the throw pillows of the couch. To many folks' surprise, I still use and cherish those pillowcases that have such fond memories. Life is beautiful, and if we learn to enjoy every phase of it without any complaints, we can establish that heavenly rapport with our Maker.

20

Four Blessed Miracles

Since I knew that very soon I was going to be a parent, I inquired through the Mt. Vernon Hospital if there were any classes held for prospective parents. Yes, indeed, there were. I enrolled Henry and me for ten evening sessions. Neither one of us was familiar with taking care of an infant, so it was important for us, especially me, to know everything about a baby's needs and care. We began the course with many other couples. This was a nice relationship with young couples to compare notes and ideas.

However, during this time, I did not want to stay idle at home during my pregnancy, so Henry mentioned at work that I would be willing to work at the office for that time being. The Vick Co. people had no openings, but recommended to the Walker Labs personnel that I had an extensive office experience and that I needed a job. Mr. Quinn, the personnel director of Walker Labs contacted me to arrange an interview. After the interview, he offered me a job to help in the personnel office. He also said they would need a switchboard operator soon since the person there was going to have a major operation. She was going to be out nearly six months. That sounded fine and plausible with me and I accepted the job.

After a few weeks of work in the personnel office, Margy started training me on the switchboard. At first I sat next to her and watched her closely. Oh, my, I was mesmerized to see so many wires and holes on the switchboard; it looked so confusing to me. That was the switchboard for both companies' personnel, Vick and Walker Labs. One could easily be intimidated just looking at this complex board of wires crossed over each other, and to know the names of all of the two companies' officers and workers. I thought: *Oh, my goodness, this is going to be much more difficult than I imagined—having to deal with over 100 switchboard holes to connect the right calls and remembering if there were callers on 'hold,' waiting to be connected to the right person.* You had to go on and off telling the person holding that the line was still busy. Although I had succeeded in doing many challenging jobs, this one as switchboard operator seemed almost impossible.

But then I said to myself, *if Margy can do it, I certainly can do it, too.* She was actually older than I and I looked much healthier. With that attitude,

I concentrated very hard, and thank God, having a good memory helped a great deal. Margy sat aside me, put the headphone on me, and said,

"You are in charge now; answer the next call."

"I am?" I said timidly.

"Yes, my dear, you are, and just remember I am here next to you. Believe me, the sky will not fall down on you." She chuckled.

"OK, here we go." I put the main switch in the flashing light hole, and gave my salutation, "Good morning, Walker Laboratories, how may I help you?"

"That sounded great," Margy whispered.

I continued to place the call on the proper switch connection while I checked Margy's expression to see some approval. She nodded her head meaning it was fine. I continued with the other calls. I was a bit hassled at the end of the hour, but no major mistakes had occurred. I was happy for that, and I wanted to go back in the afternoon for a longer period to get the knack of it. That was arranged and in one week, I was conducting myself quite well. But I still did not have Margy's speed. I knew that would come by doing it over and over.

In the beginning, I shuddered when Mr. Quinn was to get a call; I did not want to mess up. By the time Margy left, I was pretty confident. I was also gaining weight now, and I thought this was the perfect job for the time being.

Soon, I started getting compliments from Mr. Quinn and even Dr. Walker, who was the CEO of the company. As a matter of fact, he came down to praise me for the good job I was doing. That really made my day. He even gave me a raise.

I look back and compare that system with how easy things are presently when calling a big company with their electronic, automated switchboards. This may sound a little funny, but I prefer the old-fashioned way, because you talked to a real person, and there was that personal connection and interaction. Whereas, now, even though it is faster, you could be talking to a machine, and be transferred numerous times before you can speak to a human being, and maybe not ever reach a person. Sometimes the automated system is quite frustrating.

I was gaining a little more weight now, but not that much. I had a very strict doctor. Dr. Baker instructed me to gain no more than two pounds a month, or a limit of only twenty pounds total. And that was an order! He believed by not gaining too much weight, I would have an easier delivery when the time came. I was very good at listening to his advice and had a special skimpy diet that he suggested. I could not have any white bread, but had dark whole wheat bread, only one piece at each meal. For breakfast, I could have a soft-boiled egg with no salt added. I could drink all the fresh juices I wanted, but absolutely no sodas. For lunch, I could have two pieces of cheese, one piece of bread, a glass of skim milk, and a piece of fresh fruit. At dinner, I could have a broiled hamburger with a baked potato, no butter or sour cream added, with a leafy vegetable and again a glass of skim milk. There were to be absolutely no desserts of any kind, but I could have a fresh fruit.

These were the orders, and our parenthood classes emphasized that. Before Christmas, Henry and I graduated from that class, and we were given a diploma for having completed the "Parenthood Class." This was a new start for us for being new parents. It was an exciting time, and we were preparing the baby's room with a nice crib and whatever goes with it. In those days, we were not able to take a sonogram to find out the baby's sex or any other type of picture-taking of the fetus. We had picked names for a girl and a boy to be sure we were ready with a name. For a girl, the name was "Arminee" and for a boy, we would choose either Krekor (Gregory) or Raffi, all Armenian names.

I felt very healthy and energetic even though I was carrying a child. I used to dress nicely for work, even wore heels—they did not bother me. Some people, including my mom, said I should wear flats. I knew that I would be wearing flats when I took care of my baby very soon.

Having customary pink or blue colors for babies, I purchased and made things in neutral colors, such as pale yellow or green. I had made a very adorable sweater set, hat and booties all in white. I knitted them during the evenings when I was watching television.

The days were passing very quickly, and I was enjoying my new job, even though I knew it was temporary until Margy returned. Margy had her operation and she was doing well, but needed rest. Occasionally, she would call me on the switchboard and compliment me saying that others tried to learn the operation of the switchboard, but did not last. They all quit. That was interesting to hear. She and I became good friends, and would tell each other things, which friends would trust in each other.

April 1960 soon arrived. I had gained nineteen pounds and felt a bit uncomfortable, especially when I slept. I thought: *Well, soon, I will have a bouncing baby in my arms so I had better rest as much as I can.* Dr. Baker had predicted that the baby would be born April 10–15. Thus, I stopped working after the first week of April. That was close, but it worked out fine. If anything happened during the day, my husband was on hand on the second floor of Vick Chemical Company's section, and there were doctors around his workplace. So, I did not worry.

The day arrived that contractions were coming more so, and, thank goodness, it happened after dinner on April 11th. Doctor Baker was informed and he said that I should get to the hospital right away. That was at 8:00 p.m. I took my valise with my packed items and headed to the Mt. Vernon Hospital. My husband seemed a bit nervous, I even asked him not to be. He replied that he was not nervous, but soon he passed the hospital.

"Honey, where are you taking me?" I said nervously.

"To the hospital, of course," he said quickly.

"Oh, my goodness, you just passed the hospital."

"OK, OK, don't worry, I will turn back."

"Uh-h," I sighed.

Soon we were at the hospital and went straight to the Labor Room. The doctor was there already. To make a short story of the long labor, I was in pain for thirteen and half hours. Dr. Baker said that was a common length for a first child. While I was agonizing with my pain, the woman across the hall, who was also in labor, was no help at all, because she kept screaming all along, saying "Oh, Mario, Mario, never again." Even though I was in agony with my pain, to hear that was comical and made me laugh for a second or two.

Eventually, my first blessed miracle arrived, a little baby girl of 8 lbs. and 9 oz. She was now in my arms. This little bundle of joy was going to be called "Arminee." She was healthy and I had her by natural childbirth. That is what Dr. Baker was talking about when he had said the delivery would be smooth if I did not gain too much weight. He was right. My newborn was so beautiful. I guess every mother thinks so. Truly, she looked so healthy and had dark hair and seemed to have blue eyes. I figured she had my dark hair and dad's blue eyes, and that would be such a nice combination.

Soon enough I learned from the pediatrician, Dr. Aronson, that the eye color might not stay the same. She told me that it usually becomes obvious after six months. I was kind of disappointed to learn that, but as long as she was a healthy baby, I did not mind. I stayed in the hospital about five days, and Henry came with a big pink bunny for our adorable little girl who was born on April 12, 1960. It was Easter, and she was our Easter Bunny. Actually, she was also our first anniversary gift from God.

I wanted to nurse her, and every time the nurse brought her through the hallway to me, I knew when she was coming. When she was hungry, the whole floor heard her crying. I immediately would sit up and get ready to be at her command. Once her tummy was full, she would purr like a little kitty. So sweet and content, it was such a pleasant sight to watch her.

Before my release, Henry brought my mom over to our house to help me for a week or so. She was delighted to see Arminee. This was mom's seventh grandchild. She had made a beautiful blanket for her. Mom was very handy and creative.

I was enjoying motherhood so much, and started a normal routine. I ordered a diaper service for her. Soon mom had to go back to dad and back to her chores. A very good pediatrician, Dr. Aronson, was recommended to me. She taught me a great deal, because I knew very little about taking care of an infant. She was always ready to answer my questions and teach me in a very patient way the proper way to do things.

One night, Arminee cried incessantly and I became alarmed. First, I took her temperature, but she had no fever. I changed her diaper; she was fine. I also burped her, thinking that she might have some gas; that did not help. I offered to nurse her, and she did not want that either. Of course, I could not reach the doctor at 3:00 a.m., so I sat on my bed and cried, saying, "What is wrong with my baby?"

Henry assured me that there was nothing major that should concern us, but the poor guy could not sleep either. He was exhausted for the next day's work. Welcome to parenthood! I knew there would be moments like this. I prayed to God: *please Lord, let there be nothing wrong with my baby*. The next day, I called the doctor as soon as I could and left a message with the answering service that it was urgent. She called me back within a half hour. She asked me all the things I had already checked. Everything was done, except one last question she asked me:

"What did you have for dinner last night?"

"What did I have for dinner?" I asked with puzzlement.

"Yes, describe everything that you ate."

"I had steak, baked potato, and a green salad."

"What was in the salad, what vegetables?"

"Oh, I had lettuce, cucumbers, tomatoes, scallions, and I had a jalapeño on the side."

"Oh, my goodness, your little one had cramps all night from what you ate. You see whatever you eat goes in your system, so after you nursed her in the evening, she started having cramps."

"Oh, my Lord, so I caused all that."

"Yes, I am so sorry, but you did. Now, let me tell you what not to eat while you'll be nursing. Make a list of the following: cucumbers, peppers, onions or scallions, cabbage, and, especially, no jalapeños, definitely."

"Of course, of course, Dr. Aronson, then my baby is fine. There is nothing wrong with her."

"Yes, indeed, I had just seen her last week."

"Thank you, so much, I'm learning."

"Fine." She said "good bye" and hung up.

What a relief! In our family, only my father and I liked spicy hot food. My mother would not touch the stuff, and yet I learned to eat spicy hot food from my grandmother Mary, my mom's mother. When I was little in Ainjar, every time my grandma had her meals, she would say to me, "Honey, go pick some jalapeños for me from the garden." I would do it, and one time I asked her if I could taste a jalapeño. She allowed me, and then she would share some of her lunch with me, and share her hot peppers, too. After that, I developed a great taste for hot peppers. Food tasted so much better with spice. But at this juncture of my life, I promised myself not to eat spicy food until I stopped nursing. And for my child's sake, that was not such a big sacrifice. I could do without those items that the doctor mentioned to me.

Arminee was growing beautifully, and she started speaking when a year old. She was a happy child, and loved dancing to the music that I would play for her.

Henry and I wanted three children, so we tried again and had a son this time. We named him Gregory after Saint Gregory the Illuminator, a very prominent clergy in the Armenian Church and the First Catholicos of all the Armenians.

I was due to have this second child in the beginning of June 1962. On June 4, 1962, after dinner, I received a call that some of Henry's relatives were on their way to visit us. I was happy, set up a table of goodies with coffee, and sat and waited on the living room couch. Now we had moved from Summit Avenue to 7 Bradford Rd., near Walker Labs. There was a big public park and swimming pool close to our house. This was a duplex house that we rented from Walker Labs. Anyway, as Henry walked into the living room, I was holding my midriff because I had a few painful episodes. He got concerned and said,

"Are you OK?"

"Yes, I am fine, really." Soon after I said that, I felt another twinge of pain. He looked at me.

"I'm calling Dr. Baker."

"No, no, the company will be here soon. This may be false alarm; the pain is not steady."

"No, I am not waiting, I will call the doctor and we will leave right away." He meant it.

We told the next-door neighbor, Mrs. Cowan, that we were heading to the hospital, and leaving our door open. We said soon our guests would be arriving, and to please let them in. She got so excited, and said, she would let them in, and "good luck."

Henry rushed me out so quickly that I did not even take my valise with me. It was ready in the bedroom, but I did not think I was going to have my baby that night, since I did not have regular contractions. Anyway, we left. I walked briskly with my husband through the hospital door. I had barely reached the entrance desk when my water broke. Oh, my goodness, I did not have that experience before. Hot water was gushing down my legs—I was embarrassed, but it all goes with motherhood. They immediately rushed me to the delivery room.

With no big effort, a son of ours was born in two hours. It was amazing. Again, I had only gained only 19 lbs. He was a beautiful baby, too, 8 lbs. and 2 oz., again dark hair and dark eyes. Now we had our Gregory. I was doing great.

Again, Henry brought my mom from Paterson to help us after Greg was born. He stopped at the house first to give the good news to our guests, and stayed with them briefly. They left, but my husband asked Mrs. Cowan to watch our daughter Arminee until he and my mom returned. He dropped my valise at the hospital and went to get my mom.

The next day, I was released and went home. This time it was so easy, I could not get over it. Now we had our second miracle, thank the Lord. Gregory was also a happy child and he was always singing with a melodious sound. I knew he would be very musical some day.

Here I have Arminee, 2, and Greg, almost one year old, at the frozen lake for a stroll.

Our Bradford Rd. house had many attractions both in the summertime and winter. During the summer, I used to take Arminee who was two, and Greg who was only one, to the public pool. During the winter, we would go to the frozen lake where children used to skate. This was right next to our rented house.

I am reading bedtime stories for my Arminee and Gregory.

A year later, visiting grandma and grandpa in Paterson during Christmas 1964. Virginia was pregnant again.

During the next and last pregnancy, I felt very tight and full. Dr. Baker still insisted on my strict diet, since I had done well with the first two babies. However, at my 7th month when I saw the doctor, I had jumped the poundage to seven pounds. He was very annoyed and asked me if I was eating extra things. I said definitely not. He then examined me more thoroughly. He said that he felt two heads, but heard only one heartbeat.

I was so upset that night, because his statement made me worry. In the beginning of the pregnancy, I had lost weight because I had morning sickness and with the other two pregnancies, I did not. As I mentioned before, in the 1960s, there were no sonograms to tell you more information. The last few months, I had too much activity. I could not sleep comfortably, because it seemed like I had two boxers in my tummy.

So much activity was going on that this time the doctor told me that he thought I was having twins. I was excited, but his first statement was still bothering me. Nevertheless, Henry and I went to buy another crib. We had chosen one girl's name and one boy's name: Christopher and Christine. Also, we had two girls' names: Christine and Lucine.

Anyway, I felt quite energetic during the day, until I went to bed. I did not know which way to place my body, it was so uncomfortable. Easter Sunday April 18, 1965, I had invited my parents and sister and family over for Easter dinner. But first, we all went to church at the First Presbyterian Church of Mt. Vernon. From our duplex, we needed to go down twelve steps. I was the first one to go down, and had my little ones' hands as we went to the car.

"I don't think you are having those twins quite yet," my mom said, assuredly.

"No? The doctor said it will happen soon, maybe this week or next week."

"*Che, che*, (no, no) look at you, how quickly and easily you went down those stairs. No way will you have the twins in two weeks."

"OK, mom, if you say so," I laughed.

We had a fantastic time at church, stayed for the social hour, and then came home to enjoy a pleasant family gathering. The night before, I had worked hard to make *dolma* and other Armenian delicacies for my guests. Everyone went home happy. Toward the end of the day, I was a little tired, but that was expected.

Monday morning, April 19, there was more activity in my womb, and then I started staining slightly. When my husband called the doctor, he was told that Dr. Baker was away and that the head of the gynecology department would handle the deliveries. We were told to get to the hospital immediately.

This time, we did not go to the Mt. Vernon Hospital, but to the newly built Yonkers Hospital. So, the twins were born, two adorable sons. However, we did not have two boys' names. Also, there was a problem this time during the delivery. This other doctor was a bit older than Dr. Baker. He had his hands full in delivering two babies at once. In the rush, he had scratched me; that made me bleed heavily. Therefore, two pints of blood had to be given to me. For several days, I felt weak, but bounced back to my normal self. The hospital was so gorgeous, like a resort hotel. I wanted to stay there awhile.

When the twins were being delivered, Henry waited awhile. When it was not happening yet, Henry left again to get my mom, and arranged for Mrs. Cowan to watch the other little ones. My mom was shocked that I had them the day after Easter. There they were Easter bunnies too. We were so delighted. Here we had our two sons, but only one boy's name. We thought and thought and came to the conclusion that one of the babies seemed taller and had dark hair. We would call him Christopher. The other one was chubbier and had more fair skin and hair, so we would call him David, as a Biblical name, also Sassountsi Tavit (David of Sassoun) was an Armenian legendary hero.

Here, Virginia is feeding the twins. David is in her arm and Christopher is waiting patiently.

Here are Virginia's four "blessed miracles" and she thanks the Lord for them.

All our four beautiful miracles were born in Westchester County. I nursed all four of them as long as I could: our daughter for six and a half months and our first son four and a half months. I could not go any longer, because both of them had two teeth each, and it was unbearable to deal with it. The twins also were nursed by me for one and a half months. This was a shocking surprise to my pediatrician, since she had never seen twins being nursed before. I wanted to do it, because I did not want to deprive them of that privilege just because they were twins.

The reason nursing lasted only one and a half months was not because the twins had teeth, but because it was an exorbitant task on my part. After a few weeks, I did not even sleep, because they would wake up at the same time day and night and need to be fed. This was nearly comical to a degree that I did not even know what day it was. To keep my sanity and health, I said, "Fine, I will stop." Then, when both of them awakened, I would take one, and my husband would take one—feeding them at the same time with bottles. What a relief that was. Nursed babies hardly get sick; none of my little ones ever became ill when I nursed them. Their immune system is protected by the mother's milk. Of course, I had to watch my diet very carefully and eat healthy foods. That was no problem. It was an important benefit that I enjoyed providing.

It was not easy while they were growing up, because I had no steady help near me. Our daughter was four years old, our first son was two, and I had two babies in my arms. Being a very organized person, I would feed the two oldest first, then give them projects to color, or I let Greg ride the white horse he loved. If I put on their favorite music, they were happy.

At this point, I would change and feed the little ones, David first, because he screamed more and was always hungrier. And then I would feed Christopher, who was more patient. This method worked beautifully. After breakfast, I would take them for a stroll in the park, the twins in a twin carriage, Arminee and Greg picking leaves and flowers on the way. This was our routine, and we all got our fresh air daily. Arminee danced all day to music, so I enrolled her in ballet and tap dance school. She loved it.

At this time, my husband was going to Columbia two evenings a week towards his Masters degree. Those two nights were very difficult for me to get them all bathed and fed and put to bed without any assistance. Somehow, when you are young, healthy, and willing and enjoy life, those little hindrances do not matter. Truly, I enjoyed my motherhood, and savored every moment of it.

At the same time, when my husband was home in the evenings and weekends, I wanted to do something creative that I would enjoy. When in high school, I had won art contests and had won trophies for my original paintings. Even in School No. 9, I was known as the little artist. Now having four children, I enrolled at the Famous Artists School in Westport, Connecticut with a correspondence program. I had always loved art, drawing,

Arminee in her ballet costume.

and designing clothes. I thought it would be a very nice thing for me to pursue other than just changing diapers and dealing with formulas. I wanted some time for myself to enjoy doing something I truly liked: creating.

So, my books and instructions were sent to me, and I began my course enthusiastically. I had marvelous famous artists as critics such as Jon Whitcomb, Al Dornan, Al Parker, Peter Helck, Austin Briggs, and, of course the famous Norman Rockwell. I just loved this happy interlude in my life. I would finish the required assignment and send it to the school. I would receive comments back, good or bad. Remember, these were professional artists, and they knew what they were talking about. I took their criticism and praise with a serious frame of mind and completed my work, and received my diploma from them. I extended the course for over a few years according to my own agenda and time. Once I had paid my tuition, there was no strict rule to finish my assignments at a confined date. I liked that. It did not pressure me.

After I finished that curriculum, I then enrolled at the Famous Writers School of Westport, Connecticut. I also loved writing. I had written articles in the newsletters when I worked in the bank. Also, I wrote in church periodicals, and later on, I also wrote in *Hi Sird* (Armenian Heart), an Armenian Relief Society (ARS) magazine. So, these were things I enjoyed and cultivated.

There are many things in life that we can enjoy doing to have a fruitful and happy life. Many of these things were instilled in me by my dear parents, and I had the discipline to pursue matters with love and determination to get results. My zeal in helping others was taught to me by Sister Hedwig, who, next to my parents, I respected dearly. She was a perfect model to live by the rule of God. She had also sacrificed as much as my parents had in their life journey to get where they were. Things were not always easy and comfortable, but the end result of surviving it all, was strength and happiness. I truly mean this. When I help someone without expecting something in return, the action is very fulfilling for me and makes me happy. In summary, no matter how hard some days were with my four children with no additional help, I still praised God for His abundant love and endurance to have gifted me those four beautiful miracles.

21

Musa Dagh Educational Association of America (MEAA)

The year was 1965. Ten years before, I had met my husband at the Musa Dagh heroes' commemoration when I was just out of high school. I never imagined then that in ten years I would be a mother of four and establish an organization all by myself to further educational arenas for the Musa Dagh children in Ainjar.

When I approached Musa Dagh people in New Jersey, New York, Massachusetts, Pennsylvania and Connecticut, many people were excited and loved the idea. However, some told me, "Why bother with it? It is too much work." I went with my gut feeling that we should keep the memory going, and make our young generation aware of this historical event. Most importantly, we would be able to help Ainjar church schools of all three denominations: The Armenian Apostolic School, The Armenian Protestant Evangelical School, and the Catholic Church School. When I say church school, I do not mean only Sunday school, but daily regular school as well.

Since most Musa Dagh people lived in Paterson, N.J. at the time, I had my initial meeting at the Armenian Club hall on Main St. where ARS and other groups, such as the Tashnags (ARF), used to meet. After the 40th anniversary in 1955, the Musa Dagh folks had not commemorated that Musa Dagh resistance. It bothered me that no one took the responsibility to do something. Now that I had my four children and our family was complete, I made every effort to call many people from those other states to form this organization, the Musa Dagh Educational Association of America (MEAA). At this time, I was still living in Mt. Vernon, New York.

The initial flyer prepared by me had a drawn picture of the Musa Dagh memorial monument on it, with an open book with the eighteen names of the heroes of this battle. The chosen dates of commemoration were Sept. 25-26, 1965, the 50th anniversary of this heroic battle. I took on the task to make reservations at the Van Hotel, 6th Avenue, near the Boardwalk in Asbury Park, N.J.

The volunteer committee members were as follows:

- Mrs. Hermine Techoian of Worcester, Mass. (Father Movses Shrikian's daughter). We were neighbors in Ainjar when we were growing up. Sad to say, when I had not heard from her for a while and wanted to reach her this past year, her brother, Priest Gorun, told me Hermine had passed away with cancer.
- Armen Hanissian, Clifton, N.J. He too has passed away now.
- Stephen Panossian, Upper Darby, Penn.
- Andrew Hanesian, Newington, Conn., and
- Me, Mrs. Virginia Apelian, Mt. Vernon, N.Y.

Flyers were sent to all known Musa Dagh people, and committee members tallied the reservations for the occasion. It was a great success. We had several speakers: Dr. Vazken Der Kaloustian and Arthur Giragosian. Also, we had a young Musa Dagh singer, Kevork Boursalian.

On Saturday evening, September 25th, we had the famous Musa Dagh *herisee* that everyone was looking forward to tasting. Also, much fun was ahead with an Armenian band that played numerous Armenian favorites, encouraging people to dance all night through.

MEAA on Sept. 26, 1965. 1st row of adults: Movses Matosian, left; Stepan Panossian, far right. 3rd row: author's dad, left, with a fedora, and mom, four from right, beaming, near center; back row, right of tallest man, Dr. Vazken Der Kaloustian. (Author took photo)

*Sept. 26, 1965 at dinner. L–R: Arthur Giragosian,
Stepan Panossian, and the author.*

*At dinner time, L–R: Dr. Vazken Der Kaloustian,
Mrs. Boursalian, Mr. and Mrs. Techoian, and
Kevork Boursalian.*

The MEAA continued successfully year after year, even after I moved with my family to Clark, N.J. in 1966. Thereafter, the meetings took place at my house at 85 Rutgers Rd. in Clark. The group grew for a while, but gradually the survivors of the genocide were leaving for their heavenly rest. Many had moved to warmer climates (including my parents who died in the mid-1970s) such as Florida or to assisted living. Few survivors remained.

After 1975, it was very difficult to continue the MEAA. All the gathered monies were sent directly to the three schools of Ainjar. I received appreciation letters from all three of the school principals with photos of their schools and students. We were very happy to be able to help with moral and monetary support. However, after 1975, we could not continue any longer, since most of our members were deceased. Life goes on, but their memory stays fresh in our hearts and minds.

Later, in 1994, Nazaret Emlikian had a few Armenian gatherings, calling them "Hye Time" (Armenian Time), in Atlantic City where other groups of Armenians and some Musa Dagh Armenians, too, attended.

In 1994, at Atlantic City "Hye Time": Virginia Apelian and Mr. and Mrs. Nazaret Emlikian.

Many immigrants of Musa Dagh extraction have settled in California, mostly from Lebanon and Armenia. An active group there was formed by Dr. Vahram Shemmassian. This group is called Mousa Ler Association of California. ("Mousa" is spelled as in French, and "Ler" means mountain in Armenian.) I often correspond with some of their members. I am glad that there is an organization that keeps the memory of the Musa Dagh heroic battle living on. They also have cultural programs and news from Lebanon regarding Musa Dagh people that live there, especially those in Ainjar.

For ten years, I was able to lead the MEAA group. I was happy to be able to do it, and made many friends near and far because of it. Life goes on, and the memories we make because of these special events tell a story of our past and enrich the present, passing on our heritage to our children and the next generation. Thanks be to God for His enormous love for all those beloved people who survived it all.

PART EIGHT:

Back to New Jersey

22

A Near-Death Experience

Near the end of 1965, my husband Henry got a better paying job in his field at Merck and Co. in Rahway, N.J. He began his job there after the twins were six months old. In December, we took all our children to Gimbels to get a photo with Santa.

The four Apelian children with Santa, December 1965.

However, harsh winter weather made travel to New Jersey on a daily basis difficult. Travel from Mt. Vernon, N.Y. to Rahway daily was becoming quite a hassle for Henry. Thus, we started looking for a house in New Jersey to move to as soon as we could. We looked and looked, but could not find one that we liked for our growing family. My mother loved our children and she was so kind to watch them all as Henry and I traveled to numerous towns to see what we could find. We discovered that one of the towns connected to Rahway was Clark, which had a very good school system. That appealed to us. By investigating further, we found there was a nice section of Clark, a new development being constructed with four to five different model homes. We wanted to take a look, and we were so pleased with the area.

We liked the split-level model immediately, so we made a down payment and picked our lot. We were very satisfied with our decision.

The builder promised us that our house would be ready in March 1966. Thus, we made plans to put our furniture in storage in February. We came to our parents' house that month to wait until the final papers were signed for the new house, at which time, of course, we would move into our new home.

After we all came to Paterson to stay only for a month with mom and dad, things changed drastically. There were delays in receiving building materials; they were not going to complete our dream house on time. That was a big disappointment to us. However, mom and dad did not mind; they were happy that this would give them a great chance to bond with the children.

They had three bedrooms, so it worked out fine. I helped with the cooking and mom helped by babysitting; it was a good tradeoff. Of course, not knowing how long we would be there, Henry and I decided to help mom and dad with the mortgage and the food. That worked out fine too. But we needed to know when the house was going to be completed. Henry and I took weekend trips to see the progress being made. We finally learned that by the end of May, our home would be finished. It was good news that our waiting period would not continue much longer.

Since we were going to stay there four months, I decided I would teach Sunday school again at the church where we were married and where I taught before. As I mentioned, the church was across from my parents' house. I also registered our daughter in kindergarten at School No. 9, where I had originally attended when I arrived in America. This plan was going to work out fine. I enrolled our two older children, Arminee and Gregory, in Sunday school, mom watched the twins, and I taught Sunday school.

In April 1966, there was a terrible epidemic of measles. I called our family doctor, Dr. Dibsie, to ask if he could give us all the measles vaccine. He said he would not even give it to his own children, because he thought the vaccine was not perfected yet. I thought, *Well, if he will not give it to his own children, we should not take a chance on it.* As I continued teaching, several of my students were out with the measles. The bad news went around that grown-ups were getting it, too, and that many had died from it. I hoped we would not get the measles.

However, little Martina came to my class one Sunday having had it already. You could see the scabs on her face. She came and sat right next to me and she seemed fine. Next week after that, I became very ill with the measles. Not only I, but all my four children, came down with it. I guess the time for passing measles to another person was *not* over yet for little third grade Martina when she came back to Sunday school.

Even though I was not up to it, I cared for my little ones. Christopher, one of the twins, was covered with red spots from head to toe. The second worst case was our daughter Arminee, crying, "Mommy, mommy, I can't see." I had to put dark blankets over the window curtains to keep out the light. The next bad case was our eldest son, Greg, who was only three and half years old. The lightest one was David, the other twin who had about six red spots on his tummy, and that was all.

My parents' house was like a mini hospital. My husband took off from work a couple of days to give my mom some assistance. I was not doing well at all. I had measles spots all over me and a burning sensation everywhere, especially internally, which was hard to describe. I could imagine how badly the children, and especially the babies, were feeling, without being able to describe the horrific internal pain. This went on for several days quite intensely.

One night, as the children were getting a little better, I was out of it completely while I slept. My mom told me she kept watch over me, while Henry was tending the children, and that I was almost gone. She first thought I was asleep, but with no movement, nothing was apparent. She said she went to her room and cried, "Oh, dear Lord, please don't take my Verjine (Virginia) away. The children really need her." She said, she went on her knees and prayed desperately.

Soon, she and my husband heard me screaming that I heard a big bang; my pillow was covered with blood. I heard a big pounding-with-pressure sound, which had caused the rupture of the measles bump in my ear. My husband called the doctor. He said, "Please bring her to the hospital immediately." My husband carried me to the car, while mom and dad cared for the children.

As we arrived at the emergency room of St. Joseph's Hospital on Main Street, our doctor met us. Immediately, I was thoroughly examined and given antibiotics. He cleansed my ear of all the blood still oozing out. He applied compresses with medication and instructed my husband to use the antibiotic drops. What had happened was this: because of my high fever, the measles in my ear had busted and started bleeding. The doctor said he was happy my husband brought me to the emergency room so quickly; otherwise, it might have been too late.

Thank God, this was the second time that my life was spared. This near-death experience, if it had resulted in my passing, would have been devastating to my husband, our children and my parents.

Life is a journey, on which we all are travelers. It is by the Grace of God that we are able to go through turbulences and make it to the end. In my opinion, no one should take anything for granted, but rather enjoy every moment of each day, because it is a gift from God. What treasures we may have in this world are useless unless we have good health and enjoy life by thanking our Maker. I have learned to appreciate life more after these near-death experiences, since I realized how, in a fleeting moment, I could lose all.

23

The Move to Clark, N.J. and Raising a Family

We were all recuperating from our horrendous measles episode except Henry. He must have had the measles when he was little. Thank God, he was fine.

With our last walk to check our new house in Clark at 85 Rutgers Rd., everything seemed to be fine. We finalized our deed and other documents, signing everything at the end of May. We made arrangements to have our furniture delivered on June 6, and we moved on that day with the family. The house was new and beautiful, but the outside was dusty and barren with no vegetation yet. In a situation like this, one must be patient for everything to fall into its proper place.

We spent a little time getting acquainted with our new town—where the needed services existed. For that reason, I had bought about three dozen Birdseye cloth diapers for my twins, since they were only a year old. I was running short of diapers for them. Until I found a diaper service, I washed the soiled diapers. I hung them on a stick-in-the-ground laundry line. It was a beautiful June day, the sun was shining brightly, and I thought for sure, the diapers would be dry shortly.

However, it became very windy in the afternoon. I fed the children their lunch, and the older two were watching a children's show on TV. I put the twins down for their afternoon nap. Then I thought I would go out, fetch the diapers and I would be set until I ordered a new diaper service that day or the next. I went out to the backyard—*surprise!*—no diapers or clothesline in sight. I searched and searched all around the house, but there was nothing.

I came in to check on the twins; they were still asleep in their cribs. I took our daughter and son with me to go around one more time searching for the diapers. They noticed something sticking out by Oakridge Rd., which was the back street running parallel to ours. We ran towards it. Sure enough, there was our stick-in-the-ground laundry line with all the diapers down on the ground and dirty. Wow! We all helped dragging the line with all the diapers attached to our backyard. I let the children in, and checked the twins again. They were still asleep, thank God.

I hurried downstairs, went out, collected the diapers, and put them back in the washing machine. What a day! I called the nearest pharmacy to see if they could deliver four dozen disposable diapers. They could, thank goodness, but, oh, those diapers were not what they have on the market today. They were so flimsy the twins went through them quickly; they were used by morning. Thank God, I was able to get a diaper service started the next day. What an interesting day that was, but I was glad it was over.

In a few months, the roads were paved; no more dust floating around. Also, the township tree department started planting trees by the curbs.

Soon I had to register our daughter in school. She would start first grade in September. Since she was three years old, she had played school with me at home. She knew the Pledge of Allegiance by heart and nursery songs. Using picture cards, she knew the whole alphabet and an item to recognize each letter. She loved music and had a special time that she danced and sang. I had her enrolled in the local dance studio, to take ballet and tap dancing. She loved it and did very well.

Other new home buyers moved into the neighborhood with many children. This was heaven-sent, because they all needed new friends to go to school with and play. At first, I drove our daughter Arminee to school. After she made friends and was familiar with neighborhood, they all walked home from school. The Frank K. Hehnly Elementary School was only two blocks away from Rutgers Rd.

Gregory was only four years old. There were no preschool classes at the time. I had coached him, too. He knew the alphabet and had knowledge about other things. He was very inquisitive and always asked, "Why?" Of course, I answered him in a way a four-year-old could understand. He was very bright, too, and eager to learn in a fun way.

The twins were still very little, but both of them started walking when they were a year old. So, I had my hands full running after them all the time. However, we had a nice routine every day. After their sister would go to school after breakfast, I would take the boys on a nice walk every morning. I had the twins in their double carriage and Greg would follow us on his tricycle.

Refreshed from our morning walk, we would come home and play in the backyard with swings and the sliding board. While I watched them, I would do some gardening or reading. And in the evening, when Henry came home from work, he would play with them, especially Greg with baseball, and the little ones would be running around. At dinner time, we all sat together, and had pleasant conversations, and played games. After all that, my husband would give me a hand with the dishes, and then I would take our daughter to her ballet lessons early evening.

At bedtime, there was a special curfew hour to be in bed by 8 p.m., and the older ones no later than 9:00 p.m. They all would say their prayers, and off to sleep. The twins would kneel by their cribs and pray before bedtime.

Here, the twins are praying before bedtime. As the photo flash went on, Chris noticed it, but David is still praying. These were such precious moments.

Time was passing by, and the children were making many friends in the neighborhood. I met many of the young mothers. We would all have birthday parties for our children and invite the neighborhood friends over. Now my twins were two, and at this age, I dressed them the same without any complaint. But as they grew older, they had their individuality and did not want the same thing. That was understandable.

Mom is reading a bedtime story to the twins in their room.

I painted murals on the walls of the children's rooms of the three bears, the Flintstones, and other happy scenes. When they would wake up in the morning, I would hear them talking to their imaginary friends on the wall. It was so adorable to hear that. They would entertain themselves for a while. Then after breakfast, after Arminee would go to school, we would all go out and take a walk and play.

On the porch of our Clark house, getting ready for a walk with the three boys.

They were growing up so quickly. We all would go to Sunday school, then come home and spend time with the family and visit my parents in Paterson.

Going to Sunday school. L–R: Arminee, mom, Greg, and the twins, Chris and David.

My husband and I planted foundation bushes and trees around our property, which was a good size at 100 x 150 ft. Soon things were growing beautifully. Also, our children were growing and showing many talents as they all entered school. Arminee won art contests and trophies for her ballet excellence. Gregory and the boys joined the church young people's Cherub Choir. Greg won writing contests and received U.S. bonds as prizes.

The twins were chosen to appear on television by Dr Robert W. Scott, a well-known Presbyterian minister, for three Sundays. This program was sponsored by the N.J. Council of Churches and the Protestant Council of the City of New York. The show aired on WNBC on April 13, 20, and 27, with the first date exactly on their tenth birthdays.

We were members of the Osceola Presbyterian Church of Clark, N.J. Greg belonged to the Boy Scouts of America; the twins belonged to Cub Scout Pack No. 245. All the boys were very athletic and belonged to the Clark Minor League. Greg and David also played football in high school, and Chris was an avid golfer. Arminee was getting many accolades in school in drama and ballet.

The twins won *Woman's Day* magazine's 1972 Children's Poster Contest for painting original posters on the ecology theme, "How to Save the World for Me." This contest was open nationally to all youngsters in the USA. Christopher chose the theme of "Fresh Air" and used magic markers and crayons for his poster. David wanted to concentrate on the theme of "Clean Water" and used watercolors for his poster. The twins were thrilled when they each received high-power binoculars as an award.

The children were growing beautifully, both physically, and spiritually. It was my pleasure to run four different directions on a daily basis to encourage their talents and aspirations.

Christopher and David won Woman's Day *magazine's contest* (Courtesy of *Suburban News.*)

At times, it was not easy, since I had to time myself in quite an organized way to be at five different places in one day. I say five, because when they were all in school full time, I enrolled at Union College in Cranford as a full-time student myself. Now my long-yearned wish was going to be fulfilled. I knew what I was getting into: every moment of my time would be extremely valuable.

As time went by, I established a good routine, and everything fell in its own place. I even taught Sunday school, and was an elder at Osceola Presbyterian Church of Clark. I was very active in the Parent-Teacher Organization (PTO) and was the chair of the Legislative Committee. I truly believe that if one has good health, determination and faith in God and one's self, everything is possible.

In several years, our Clark house looked very well-landscaped, too, and we had a happy living at 85 Rutgers Rd., thanks be to God, where all our children grew up.

Our house in Clark where all our children grew up.

Community Involvement
and College

I had given myself a real big task now. As my children were all in school full time, I registered at Union College in Cranford as a full-time student. When my husband came home, I told him that he was looking at a full-fledged college student.

"Great!" he said. He was happy for me, except he thought it was a very heavy load upon me with all that I was doing.

"I will be fine, Lord willing," I assured him.

"If it's fine with you, that's it. Good luck" and he gave me a gentle kiss.

I would drive all of our children to school at 7:45 a.m.: the boys to Hehnly Elementary School on Raritan Rd, and my daughter to Kumpf Middle School. Then I would rush to Cranford, N.J. to Union College for my first class, which started at 8:30 a.m. I had arranged with my guidance counselor to be out by 2:30 p.m. to pick up my little flock from their schools at 3:00-3:15 p.m. Thank God, it worked fine. I had Wednesdays off, and that was heaven-sent to do all the laundry, the food shopping, and miscellaneous things.

Now, another situation was created. In a way it was great, and in another, things became more hectic. My husband was promoted at his job at Schering-Plough Pharmaceuticals to be the new Director of International Laboratories. I was happy that he had advanced and they respected his work. On the other hand, he would be traveling overseas and to South America to check on their other labs.

I ran after school to bring the children to their extracurricular activities, such as our daughter to ballet lessons and the boys to piano lessons with a nice German lady in the neighborhood. Also, there were the Cub Scout meetings and birthday parties they attended. I would prepare dinner and feed them. Sometimes, I would attend school activities they were in, like plays and the chorus. There was not a dull moment at the Apelian household. After their daily routine was done, I would make sure their school work was completed. Next, they took showers and went to bed by 9:00 p.m. Around 9:30 p.m., I would sit down to do my homework until 1-2:00 a.m.

When morning came, the whole routine started again: getting ready, having breakfast, fixing their lunches, and out in the car. During this time, I was also active in the community and organizations that were dear to me. I belonged to the Paterson Chapter of the Armenian Relief Society (ARS). This is equivalent to the American Red Cross, which helps other countries in their time of need. ARS helped with the Plate of Food program and other ways of assisting people in need. We mostly helped people in the Middle East. I was the youngest member and their president. All of the *shercha-peragans* (monthly bulletins) would come from the Boston headquarters. They had to be read, explained and digested with the whole membership for evaluation—to see what our status was for helping whatever way we could. I was the only one that could fluently read and write both Armenian and English for them. I had to make sure that everything was done properly and the headquarters in Boston received everything on time. Thank goodness, these monthly meetings took place in Paterson on Saturdays. I would take all the children with me, and they visited grandma and grandpa. Grandma would cater to them with their favorite dishes, and grandpa would take them for ice cream afterwards. This was a big treat for them and for my parents.

The other officers and I consulted often to have a fundraiser to make some money for the charitable work that we were working on. We decided

Apelian family portrait in 1972.

252

to have a dinner dance at the Champagne Towers in Lodi. We had a very successful fundraiser and we made a good sum of money for the orphans and the poor of Lebanon and Syria. The headquarters received our donations with great appreciation.

Meanwhile, Henry was traveling quite regularly to Paris, France, and Lucerne, Switzerland. Sometimes, he traveled to Japan and to South America. Each trip would last about eight days. When he came home, the children would make confetti and throw it all over him when he entered the door. They knew when he would arrive, thus, they would sit behind the living room balcony railing and yell "Welcome home, daddy" and sprinkle confetti all over him. Also, they made large signs inside the house saying, "We missed you, daddy," and "Welcome Home." Henry always enjoyed seeing how the children reacted when he came home. Those are such sweet memories. At this point, we had our family portrait taken by Lorstan Studio in Union, N.J.

When I graduated from UC, I was very happy and so were my family members. I was on the Dean's List and the President's List. There were very few married adults attending full time at the colleges in those days. The local newspapers did special articles about me, a mother of four children, graduating with honors, The *Daily Journal* put the headline this way: "Mother Completing College Exacts Time's Full Worth." The *Rahway-News Record* and *Clark Patriot* had the same headline: "Mother of Four Finds Time to Gain Degree and Be Involved in Causes." Both papers were published in June 1973. Both articles began as follows: "Most husbands may wonder what their wives do all day, but for Henry Apelian of 85 Rutgers Road, Clark, it's the opposite. It's a wonder how his wife, Virginia, does what she does all day."

Virginia's graduation photo from Union College, June 9, 1973.

253

The family proudly attended the Union College graduation of their mom.

After graduation, we, as a family, took a nice vacation to Disney World, in Florida. We all had a marvelous time. Everyone was rejuvenated when we got back, and began getting ready for school. I was ready to start my fall session at Rutgers University, Douglass College. I followed a psychology curriculum, heavy on political science courses. Also, I took Constitutional Law which I enjoyed tremendously. As I was preparing my term schedule, I lacked two credits, so for the first semester I took International Folk Dancing. This was such a happy and relaxing course to learn all the folk dances of different countries. I was asked by the teacher to teach them an Armenian folk dance. I brought a cassette tape, and taught them the "*debke,*" a certain Armenian line dance. I taught them the repetitious steps, and they caught on very quickly.

On nicer days, the teacher would put the music on real loud and open the gymnasium doors, allowing us to go outdoors from the gym and do the dances under the trees at the beautiful Douglass Campus. There were times when the ongoing cars from George St. would slow down to get a little glimpse of an original folk dance, such as the Greek serpentine dance. The folk dancing broke the monotony of serious classes that were more cerebral.

However, when my daily classes ended, I did not linger around as my classmates did. I had to hurry home to get my children out of school, and yonder to all their activities. This trip home was much longer than the Cranford route from Clark. To get to New Brunswick, not only was a longer trip, but also there was major truck traffic daily. Initially, the truck traffic bothered me on Route 1 and 9, but soon I got used to it, and zoomed right through the traffic without thinking about it. My courses were very tense at Douglass. I would need to read several books for one report, and I studied very hard. Douglass was a very demanding college. One had to be better than the professor in order to get an "A". My second semester was very busy.

Aside from my scholastic obligations, I was asked to present a program for Mother's Day. It was called "A Tribute to Our Moms" on Sunday, April 28, 1974, at the Douglass Commuter Lounge, College Center.

*Arminee and mom are ready to go to Douglass
for the Mother's Day program.*

Models picked for Mother's Day program and Virginia.

This was a special program for the commuter students. Mrs. Dorothy Cole was the adviser of the Mom's Day event. Activities began at 10:00 a.m. with registration, a tour of the Douglass Campus, and a service at Voorhees Chapel, followed by coffee hour. A turkey luncheon was served at noon in the Commuter Lounge. Following the luncheon, Adele Young, a celebrated opera star, and Pat Collins, star of her own television show, were the speakers. Then original creations by Virginia Apelian were highlighted, with my fourteen-year-old daughter Arminee, as one of several models. All the creations were designed and made by me, even the attire my daughter and I were wearing. The models were handpicked by me to fit my size on each of the student models. This was a very creative and entertaining day as the Douglass Woodwind Quartet played on. Throughout the day, there was an art exhibit provided by Mark Howard of the Douglass Art Department to be enjoyed by all.

One more year of a full schedule was awaiting me before I could graduate from Douglass. I sometimes would enjoy eating lunch at the cafeteria with friends. During other lunch hours, I would grab my home-prepared lunch and go find a cubicle in the library and study. The cubicles were very quiet and private; I could study there without any distractions from nearby wanderers or whisperers. One day, I was studying in one of the cubicles and after reading a while, my eyes were really tired. I stopped reading and noticed different messages carved on the study desk. Some of the messages were quite obvious: gals leaving their phone numbers and hints for replies. I became curious, so I found an empty spot and wrote my own message. I wrote, "Jesus Saves," hoping maybe to see some sort of reply to it someday. A few days later, I happened to get the same cubicle again to do some studying, when I noticed right under my two-word inscription there was the following: "but Moses invests." I had a nice chuckle and continued studying.

For the last year, I needed two more credits again to complete my studies at Douglass. This time I took up fencing—yes, fencing, I thought this should be lots of fun and challenging. In the class was a very tall, young woman who seemed to be the champion fencer. She was so cocky that she intimidated even the best of the students. I want to add that the girls chosen for Douglass were of the highest caliber and intellect. This college was known for its scholastic acumen. I did not like seeing this arrogant young woman, time after time petrifying the other students. The other students were fearful to do a match with her, even though everyone was in that class to learn fencing. Thus, it was in my nature to do something about a situation like that. I don't know if it was the "mother" in me or the "fair teacher." I wanted to put my inability at fencing on the line, and give a good lesson to those who were afraid of this so-called "fencing queen"—that they should try harder to compete with her. I also think the gym teacher did not handle matters correctly.

So, I watched this fencing star's technique very carefully. I liked challenging myself. I told my gym teacher that I would like a bout with her, "What can I lose?" I thought. It would be quite an experience. Besides, even if I lost, they can just say I was not as agile as a twenty-year-old woman anymore, so be it. That would not bother me at all. The rules were again explained to me. I definitely thought the teacher was sort of implying that I would be clobbered. However, I was ready to try this challenge.

As I had watched this young woman closely, I had some hints as to how I could make her lose points. She always fenced offensively. As she would lunge at me, within the realm of my space, I took one little step aside and occasionally tilted my head slightly. Thus, she would miss her target, which was me, although I was protected by my vest and helmet. I could see how annoyed she was as that happened time after time.

Well, she lost that day. I was utterly shocked, and I am sorry that her pride was hurt badly. She did not take it too kindly. But I had followed the rules and did not feel sorry that she lost. The match was just to prove the point for the other girls that if you want to pursue something, study it and put your all in it. That is how one succeeds in doing—taking some risks and forgetting your pride. I strongly felt that this taught the other students that they should try to do their best and not be intimidated by anything or anybody.

Believe me, besides me, there were others after I won my match who tried and won. I felt this was a good lesson learned—mission accomplished. I never wanted to fence with this young woman again. Here I was a mother of four, in her thirties, fencing a young woman in her prime twenties. This was not only a lesson at the gym class, but also a lesson of life for later on in the workplace.

I even have fun today, teaching my little granddaughters how to fence with a long cardboard tube. We have fun doing it, and it brings back fond memories for me.

The year came to an end, June 1975, when I graduated with a B.A. degree in Psychology. I wanted to continue getting my Ph.D. right away, but my eyes needed a rest. The psychology curriculum is abundant of reading many books. My husband said, "Why don't you take a little break first, and see what you want to do next."

"Fine, I think that's a good idea." I said.

The preparations for graduation were made outdoors, but there was the threat of rain, so the dark clouds made the decision for us to have the graduation at the Voorhees Chapel. My immediate family was again present and they were very happy for me. Also, my parents came to the house for a special celebration. My father said to me that he was really very proud of me and that he always knew that I would climb the ladder of opportunities in this great land of ours and succeed. He was very patriotic and an exemplary Christian. My mom did not think that it was necessary for me to go to college after I had children.

"You are beautiful, and have a wonderful husband, gorgeous children, and a fantastic home and life, why bother with a college education at this stage of your life?"

"Oh, mom, that is so old-fashioned," I responded, lovingly. I gave her a hug and a soft, tender kiss. I loved her, but she came from such a different perspective and generation. However, on graduation day, she was really happy for me.

Virginia's Douglass College graduation photo.

The author's graduation dinner in 1975. This was the last picture of her mom and dad together.

All during this time and thereafter, from 1975 on to many years beyond, I was involved with many volunteer activities, which gave me so much knowledge for serving the public effectively. Here are some of the involvements that I had:

- Chair for the Heart Fund Drive in Clark in 1977.
- Chair of the Cancer Fund Drive in Clark, 1978. This task took much time to coordinate with volunteer teams, both adults and high

school students to complete the work to hand over all the donations to the Cancer Society.

- First woman president of the Clark Republican Club.

I increased the Republican Club membership by having wide involvement of the community served. I established essay contests to encourage the youth of the township to be involved in writing about patriotic themes, and rewarded each of them with a U.S. Savings Bond. Also, when I was elected, we had little money in our treasury. That was fixed also by having fun events where everybody joined and the public was invited. For example, we netted quite a bit of money for the club by holding Fruit Festivals during the summer. We had designated weekends, and the crew purchased fresh fruit from the farms, then prepared it with ice cream and whipped cream. *Voilà*, that presented an outing for all members of a family to enjoy.

Then during February, we would have Valentine's Day Dance, where many people attended to dance the night through with reasonable prices and great music and snacks. In December, I would organize a White Elephant sale, which was a complete profit-making event, since all the items were donated by the people and some businesses. Our treasury was filled with a substantial sum of money to help us do more for the community and to donate moneys to eligible candidates who were running for office.

- I was a member of the Clark Historical Society, and later became its president in 1993-1994.

This Society was formed in 1970 and it did marvels with a historical house located at 593 Madison Hill Rd., Clark, as a local museum. The house was built circa 1690 by Dr. William Robinson, the area's first physician. He had emigrated from Scotland. His original tool chest is still intact, and visitors marvel of their use in those times, unlike the medical implements doctors use now. Costumed guides, as docents, give tours of the museum the first Saturday of each month. I have served as docent many times. We had many tours for schoolchildren to tell them about their town and Dr. Robinson.

Dr. Thomas Brown, president of the Union County College, a historian himself, installed me as their president in 1993. During my tenure as president, the membership doubled.

Through the assistance of the Clark Historical Society's membership and other interested parties, we saved the Oak Ridge Golf Course house, known as Homestead Farm at Oak Ridge, which is on another landscape of historical value. William Fidurski and I worked diligently through the efforts of State of N.J. Historical Society. When I was the president of the Clark Historical Society, we went to Trenton to a special hearing regarding this matter to keep this building as a historical sight. We also submitted documentation to the Federal Government to prevent the destruction of this building that the Union County freeholders had decided to demolish. At that point, I was very much disappointed with the Union County Board of Freeholders. The members were mostly Republicans, sad to say. They did not listen to the public's wishes. There was too much politicking going on and I did not like it one bit. For a major issue of this sort, I put aside my party affiliation, and did not vote for them, and the feeling was mutual with other people, too. All of them who opposed saving the property lost in the upcoming election—all of them were Republican.

The only two freeholders that helped us were, Linda Lee Kelly, a Republican, and Linda Stender, a Democrat. They did not lose the election. I must also mention a good friend of mine, N.J. Assemblyman Alan M. Augustine, who helped us keep the Oak Ridge House. He was also a member of the Board of Governors of Union County College with me. I asked him if he would urge the Freeholder Board not to raze the Oak Ridge House. He wrote them a nice letter, but the freeholders did not pay any heed to their Republican assemblyman. Alan was a very thoughtful gentleman, and it was great working with him on the UCC Board. I am sorry to say that he is no longer with us. He passed away a few years ago. That was a big loss for our community.

The Homestead Farm of Oak Ridge was founded in the early 1700s by descendants of John Smith of Massachusetts, one of the original founders of Woodbridge Township. The more than 200 acres this site comprised had served as home for six generations of prestigious Quaker families. This Quaker lineage included the Smith, Hartshorne, Bowne, and Robinson families. These owners of the Homestead Farm at Oak Ridge were related to four Colonial governors, which included Thomas Hinckley of Plymouth Colony, and three Winthrops, who served as governors of either Massachusetts Bay Colony or Connecticut Colony. The families descended of John Bowne of Flushing, New York, a Quaker who was imprisoned and exiled for his faith by the governor of New York, Peter Stuyvesant. Bowne's persecution is considered a motivating factor for passage of the Bill of Rights of the United States Constitution.

In the 19th century, Homestead Farm at Oak Ridge served as the lifelong home of Judge Hugh Hartshorne Bowne, abolitionist and prominent New Jersey statesman, who served as justice of the peace, Judge of Common Pleas, Clark Township mayor, member of the N.J. Assembly and delegate to the Southern Reconstruction Convention at Philadelphia in 1866. Judge Bowne was the founder of the Republican Party in Essex and Union counties, also a delegate to the First Republican Party National Convention of 1856. At the second Republican National Convention in 1860, Judge Bowne participated in the nomination of his cousin, Abraham Lincoln, to the Presidency of the United States. Thomas Edison was friendly with the Bowne and Robinson families. He often visited Homestead Farm at Oak Ridge by horse and buggy when he was at his Menlo Park Laboratory. All this history was attained by the hard work and research of William Fidurski.

Homestead Farm at Oak Ridge,
William Fidurski and author, 1995.

I love history. We can see its importance from generation to generation in knowing about the places we live in. Through research, we knew who occupied this magnificent, unusual Victorian farm. First of all, the location of the Homestead Farm of Oak Ridge was not even a block away from our Clark house. It was called the Oak Ridge Golf Course. My son Greg often golfed there, and I worked in that mansion as the director of the Union County Senior Citizens. This was such a historical, monumental edifice that we could not understand the reasoning of the freeholders' decision to demolish it.

The late Professor Richard Cohen, William Fidurski and I went to Trenton to another hearing about saving it and were able to list it on the National Register of Historic Places. At the present time, it is considered a park, and many concerts and other entertainments are offered there for everyone to enjoy the premises, and it is not a golf course anymore.

My precious parents' deaths

Between January 12, 1976 and September 13, 1977, I lost my dear parents. My dad went to his heavenly rest first. He died in his sleep with congestive heart failure, did not suffer at all. It was a great loss for us all, and especially for my mom. They were married for a beautiful 55 years. Even though they had gone through much grief having lost four children, they found peace in God's mercy for all that they had. They had good times, happy times, and sad times with deportations and being refugees in a strange land. But nothing dampened their enthusiasm for life. They were my true models showing me the determination in life that one could not buy with any amount of money.

After dad died, I saw that mom was too lonesome, thus, I wanted to take care of her. She moved to be with me and my family in Clark, N.J., where she was very happy. She would sit under our apple tree, which my father had planted, have a bowl of fresh fruit on her lap, eating it and enjoying the birds and the flowers in the yard. It was such a great feeling to see her so content. Other times, I would catch her with her hymnbook singing hymns as in the past she did often with my dad. She would pray that when her time was up, "Dear Lord, take me as my dear Hagop (James) in my sleep." I hate to say this, but that is exactly how she died. She passed away peacefully in her sleep of congestive heart failure at the Rahway Hospital. I took her there, because she had fainted the day before.

Even though I miss them terribly, their presence is with me in many instances. It was my sincere act of deep love that I took care of my mom during her last eighteen months. My husband Henry was with me all along on this issue. Mom enjoyed being with my children, and was with our family at all times vacationing and being part of our everyday life. I am sorry to say that my sister and my brother, even though they had fewer children than I, did not take care of mom in any way; they were not there for her. They were even in closer proximity to her when our father died. That is all I have to say about this issue.

After my parents passed away, I became more involved in church activities. It gave me a special peacefulness. I did not want to simply tell my Sunday school class a story from the Bible, but I wanted to show them by Jesus' example, the way my parents' examples of life were revealed to me.

To show humility and being humble was my task as a Sunday school teacher. As is well-known, it is not so much what one says, but what one

Washing the feet of my Sunday school class.

does as a good example. Even as a parent, you can model a good example to get your children's moral compass started and set, rather than preaching to them all day long.

I led Presbyterian Women's retreat at the Poconos, as a Fanwood Presbyterian Church member and an Elder. When we moved to Manchester, N.J. after our children graduated from college and married, we first belonged to the Lakehurst Presbyterian Church. It was a medium-size church with 300 members, but their activities as a church was dormant. I asked the minister, Rev. Dr. David Emery if it would be fine if I would increase the enrollment of the Sunday school from 3 pupils to 20 or more the first year. I put out articles in the newspapers, inviting the neighborhood children to join. During the summer, I started a Vacation Bible School (VBS). Being the director, I had to choose the curriculum and select teachers—those who were willing but needed direction—and train them. Also, I made large color posters and we put them up by the church to invite the community children. This was a big task again, but I wanted to do it.

I made an appeal to the congregation about the children's snacks for the VBS. It did not cost the church anything, and the children had all the juice and cookies they needed. The congregation members were happy to do it and got involved.

Also, I wanted to know if this congregation had special dinners for special occasions. I was told, "Yes, 20-30 years ago, but not anymore." That bothered me. Here there were some young families and more of the elderly, but a church should not stop functioning. So, I took the church directory, and started calling people to volunteer in making a certain dish. I formed a few committees, and we were all set. I asked Rev. Emery to pick a date or two for a big congregational dinner. My wish was granted.

My committee worked with me to get the menu list prepared. That was needed so that we knew who was preparing meat dishes, salads and desserts. The church had a closet full of paper dishes and cups that had not been used for years. Now they would be. I also picked a crew of six women to clean the kitchen, the stove, and the refrigerators for safekeeping of our foods. We made everything sparkle. We opened closets where things were stuck in there for 20 years, and no one knew where these things were. We unlocked them, and threw away much of their contents, but saved a few items that still could be used.

I wanted to have people make reservations so we would know how many people we would be serving. The food was being donated, and there was no charge to come. I asked the choir to have a medley of songs to entertain us. Rev. Dr. Emery was very happy about this, and appointed me as the superintendent of the Sunday school.

Needless to say, we had a most successful congregational dinner. The people's smiles and interactions made it obvious that they were having a great time. What more can anyone ask; the joy of friendship in church which spills out to the neighborhood, too. Now, more families were joining us.

However, I noticed a certain small element of a very few people who wanted to make things difficult for Rev. Emery. They were talked to, but to no avail. They had their unreasonable reasons, and this discontented feeling had been there for a long time, for years. Instead of resolving their issues, they just opposed any suggestion that had come from Rev. Emery. This attitude by some continued, and it was not healthy. I had private talks with Rev. Emery when he was thinking of leaving his pastorate from this church. I, of course, kept this confidential until he had another position, then he revealed it himself.

That day arrived, when he announced that he would be leaving and that he had found another church. Most people were sad, and some who did not like him were very happy. But now we had no pastor to preach every Sunday and our budget was not so great to have an interim minister or a pulpit supply minister each Sunday.

Rev. Emery had written a letter to the Session that he was sorry, but that he needed to move on. He also suggested that "Virginia Apelian, having had past experience at the Osceola Presbyterian Church in Clark as lay person preacher, would be available for the church's needs." Also, there was another gentleman, "Chuck Bodo, who could alternate Sundays with Virginia to help out with the sermons, until the church found a new minister." He said that he felt good about this suggestion because he trusted both of us.

So, now, there was this very special need to be taken care of, to fill the pulpit every Sunday. Chuck and I conferred with each other and decided we would take turns delivering the sermons every other Sunday. That would give us time for the preparation, among other things that I was involved with at the church and outside the church.

A medley of Virginia's church sermon photos.

This went on almost two years, until they hired a new minister. At that point, nothing seemed the same anymore. First of all, she and her husband had a house already. Our manse was vacant.

Hurricane Katrina was the reason I left Lakehurst Presbyterian Church. Let me explain. I was on the Session, and I knew how devastating Hurricane Katrina was in New Orleans in August 2005. I suggested to the Session that since we had an empty manse with two floors with bedrooms and all the necessary rooms, and all were furnished, to utilize the space for a family destitute from the Hurricane.

All the session members looked at each other and said, "We don't think that the Lakehurst government would allow it."

I told them that I would take care of that. I went to the Lakehurst Borough and spoke to their business administrator and the town building inspector. They both agreed. As a matter of fact, the inspector came with me to see the manse, examined it thoroughly, and found it to be in good condition, except a railing for the basement stairs had to be fixed and one of the windows needed adjusting. All that needed about a half-hour's work.

I thought this was fantastic news; we could help a family at least six months to a year with donations from nearby businesses and other fund-raising. I even took that responsibility to do so. Furthermore, I was ready to approach some of my attorney friends to draw the papers for the terms involved. The church would only allow the manse to be used for a certain period. We set a special meeting the first week of September 2005 to do a Christian deed for a desperate family—at least, I thought so.

The meeting was a shocker. Here are some of the comments: "It is a nice idea you have, Virginia, but it is too risky." Here is another dumb comment, "We don't want to open a can of worms." And on and on it went with lame excuses. And the new minister (I won't mention her name) was as inept and spineless. She said absolutely nothing. I thought: *Oh, my Lord, to be a Christian by name only is a horrible and pathetic thing.*

They were all afraid to take that step to do this good deed. The meeting ended without voting on this issue, even though I had the inspector's report in hand, and he did not even charge us a fee, which usually he would have. The Lakehurst Borough would allow us to do this good deed. I left the meeting very disappointed. The next day, the minister called me and said that she agreed with my recommendation, but. . . .

I said, "How come you gave no encouragement to the Session in doing so?"

"My hands were tied," she said.

"How so?" I asked firmly.

She said nothing after that. I courteously said "Good-bye" and hung up on her. Then I thought: *If she will be their leader, their shepherd, this was a very poor way of handling it.*

After that, I thought about all this over and over, and it just did not sit right with me. If I wrote a letter of resignation from the Session, all my other activities there would cease also. I really hated to do it, but I had to. I could not work with people who did not practice the word of God. Of course, no one is perfect, but to me this was a major principle of Christian ethics.

I delivered the letter of my resignation to the secretary personally so that it wouldn't take long in the mailing process, and I wanted to thank the secretary who had worked with me amicably in the past. Then, the next day, calls were pouring in to have me go back. The new minister, said, "What will we do with all the things that you do here? Who will take the role of doing all of them?"

"I am sorry, I don't see the Christian spirit, either in you or the governing body of the Session. That is all I have to say," I ended my last call to them. But, I was still praying that they would change their minds and have the empathy to utilize that empty building to do some good.

After a while of not hearing from them, my husband and I joined the Toms River Presbyterian Church, and loved the Christian spirit cultivated there. It was a much bigger church, but so well-organized; everyone was important in that church, young and old. I soon was elected president of the Fellowship Club, which met once a month with special programs with outside guest speakers on pertinent topics. We would bring our lunch, and socialize each month, with the Hospitality Committee taking care of coffee and cake. I believe a church should be a place of nurturing love and compassion to help those in need. There was a new building constructed on this church's property for all kinds of mission work for the needy. We had church volunteers manning it daily.

I also belonged to the Manchester Friends of the Library. Through the Library volunteering, I learned there was an Armenian-American Club in Ocean County that had meetings every month on social issues and fun things. At this stage in 2003, since my husband and I were retired now from our daily jobs, we inquired about the Club and joined it. The meetings were held in the Toms River Municipal Building. In 2003, 2004, and 2006, in September, I was asked to be the Keynote Speaker of the day for raising the Armenian Tricolor Flag at our Independence Day from the USSR. That event had taken place in September of 1991, when Armenia became an independent country, free from the USSR's subjugation and oppression lasting 70 years. I also was elected president of this club from 2005-2007.

The Ocean County Freeholders had the most efficient and interesting county government I have ever witnessed. They are so wary of their ethnic citizenry that they honored all nationalities' independence. The programs were very well-advertised and administered from the Freeholders' and the Sheriff's offices. It was a joy to see the enthusiasm of the people involved.

We went afterwards to the club area, and had a reception for all the guests who attended the flag raising ceremony and the program at the Municipal Building. People socialized and enjoyed Armenian pastries, such as *paklava*, *choreg*, and other goodies, coffee and tea.

I had a wonderful group of people to work with. The American-born members asked me if I would take some time each month during the meetings and teach them conversational Armenian. I was delighted to do that. They would come to the meeting with pads and pens and write what they learned. It was beautiful to see their desire for learning.

Father Mamigor always said the Armenian Lord's Prayer to start the meeting. Pictured are the author and her Jewish Armenian friend, Gilberta Fass.

The Tricolor Armenian Flag is being raised at the Toms River Municipal Building, to fly for three days in honor of Armenia, with Father Mamigon, Elberon Armenian Apostolic Church, the Ocean County Freeholders, Sheriff, and the author, 2005.

The author giving the keynote speech, October 2, 2006 (delayed due to September flooding).

Kudos goes to the Ocean County Board of Freeholders for doing this very important deed for their constituency, in honoring them. The Greeks, the Ukrainians, Asian Indians and many other nationalities all had their day.

Ocean County Freeholder Director Joseph Vicari is presenting a proclamation in honor of Armenia's 15th anniversary of independence to the author. On the left is Sheriff Polhamus and on the far right, Freeholder Jerry Little.

I had other community involvements. I was appointed to the Union County Environmental Health Board from 1983-1984, and served as its Research Chairperson. From 1980-1984, I served on the Consumer Affairs Board. From 1980-2001, I served on the Juvenile Advisory Board of the Family Division of the Elizabeth Superior Court, and was Chair of the Clark Juvenile Advisory Council. All these were on volunteer basis.

First term, Virginia Apelian, President of UCC Alumni Association.

I served as the editor of *The Presbyterian* of the Elizabeth Presbytery from 1989-1991, working closely with the Executive Presbyter Rev. Richard Giffen.

My volunteer work for Union County College (UCC) was as follows: I served as president of the Alumni Association for two, three-year terms: July 1, 1993 to June 30, 1995, and July 1, 1998 to June 30, 2001. The UCC Alumni Association is a private non-profit organization with the purpose "to assist in advancing the mission of UCC by maintaining a continuing relationship between alumni and the College and by strengthening the relationship between the College and the community."

In 2001 during my second term of presidency, before my husband and I moved to Manchester, N.J., I installed the new officers of the Alumni Association.

L–R: 1st Vice President Gail Ann Denman; 2nd Vice President Bonnie Bendlin; Treasurer Suzanne Covine; outgoing President Virginia Apelian handing the gavel to the new President Naomi Mirlocca; Corresponding Secretary Maureen Invacare; Recording Secretary Linda Kurdilla; and Board of Directors member Cathy Meyers. (Absent: Brian Reilly, member of the Board of Directors.)

Then I served as the Alumni Representative to the Union County College's Board of Governors from July 1, 1992 to June 30, 2001. We met monthly, and many times had to meet more often on emergency basis. The two boards, Board of Governors and Board of Trustees, had major roles in making very important decisions pertinent to the College. I also served on the Personnel Committees of the boards.

I served on the Union County College Foundation Board as a trustee from July 1, 1999 to June 30, 2001. This role had specific duties pertaining to Foundation matters, the budget and fundraising issues.

At the third major UCC Gala in 1995, I was honored as the UCC Alumni Association president and for my dedicated service to the College. As usual, at this third Gala, we raised major amount of scholarships for the needy and bright students.

My family had donated a plaque for "The Tree of Education," which you can see behind us on the wall in the photo. It was inscribed "In Honor of Virginia Apelian, by her husband Henry, and the children, Arminee, Gregory, Christopher and David."

Effective July 1, 1990, the Union County College Board of Trustees and Board of Governors announced the appointment of Dr. Thomas H. Brown as the new president. The April 26, 1991 Inaugural Ceremony took place on the outside of the campus to accommodate more attendees. All of the teaching staff, plus the Boards, were officially in procession to the stage area where the ceremony was to take place. The procession was lined up alphabetically, and we were dressed in our specific college regalia.

Dr. Brown's Inaugural Procession. The author is front row, right.

Author's husband Henry and she at the 1995 UCC Gala.

Sitting and listening to the ceremony. The author is in second row from back, fifth person from left.

Dr. Brown is a historian, and he has taught U.S., Civil War, Latin American, and Immigration history courses and State and Local Government classes. He was the chairman of the Cumberland County Cultural and Heritage Commission and wrote for the Department of Education's Ethnic Oral History Program, which prepared 2,600 oral history tapes on immigration to the United States. His twenty-year tenure as President of Union County College 1990-2010 expanded UCC enormously, to four campuses. The main campus is in Cranford with satellite campuses in Plainfield, Elizabeth, and Scotch Plains. During his tenure, UCC's enrollment increased from 22,836 to 33,226 students. In addition to full-time and part-time students, there are also students enrolled in continuing education courses. The College has gained recognition for its scholastic standards for its students and for its students being accepted to any major college. In Dr. Brown's 2010 graduation address, he emphasized the enormous strides made at the College: any graduate from UCC may take advantage of one of 86 articulation/transfer agreements with four-year colleges to move on and continue their education. This guarantees the UCC graduate to junior status and has been an enormous advantage for those wanting to continue their education.

With Dr. Brown's persistent dedication as president, UCC is one of the very best of county colleges in N.J. It is the only N.J. county college with four full campuses. When I attended this College, it was called Union College, and in 1982 it merged with Union County Technical Institute, located in Scotch Plains, N.J., to become a county entity.

Working closely with Dr. Brown, I found he was very gregarious and complimentary with the people who are dedicated to the College agenda. When I was the Alumni President, he never refused to be a part of our special functions of the Alumni Association, no matter how busy he was. Union County College stands proud for being "A Leader Among Its Peers" thanks to Dr. Brown and many other dedicated Board members and staff, and faculty, also. All this is a reflection of the leadership and dedication of the people involved.

L–R, The author has finished Alumni Holiday Party decorations with the enthusiastic support of VP Gina Cavaino and Suzanne Covine, a most efficient treasurer.

When I was president of the Alumni in 1993, we had a marvelous Holiday Party for all alumni. First, I would make sure that we would have the Alumni room decorated in cheerful Holiday décor. We would have catered food by our College kitchen, and many members would bring all kinds of cookies. One of our members, Marion Menzer, would even make homemade ice cream to our delight. We had donated door prizes so that everyone would leave with something nice. We had games for fun and enjoyment while holiday music played in the background.

There were numerous other meetings for me to attend. Sometimes, I brought my seven-month-old grandson with me, because I had the obligation to watch him while my daughter was tied up with her other two children. Little T.J. Curran was a real trooper who would not make any noise or fuss while we discussed plans of fund-raising and other topics.

277

UCC Foundation committee at work with a 7-month-old future student. Executive Development Director Nadine Brechner was delighted to have little T.J. (November 1995)

At the beginning of 1997, I was selected to be on The Committee to Reinvest in New Jersey Community Colleges. At the time, there were twenty-nine members on this committee from all over New Jersey, in addition to the co-chairmen, Raymond Bateman and William T. Hiering, both former N.J. State Senators. The members of this committee were chosen from different fields, such as banks, corporations, county executives, hospital administrators, and from the N.J. State Chamber of Commerce. I was the only representative from a community college board. Launching of this "Reinvest" campaign took place on December 4, at Middlesex County College in Edison. The major component of this campaign was the establishment of the "Blue Ribbon Committee" comprised of business, government and education leaders from around the state.

The participation and the leadership of members of this committee helped create higher education opportunities for New Jersey folks and was a great benefit to the business community and the skilled workforce.

The Alumni Association of Union County College sponsored "Back-to-College Day II" "Pride in Our Past and Faith in Our Future, 1933-1993." On this spring day of 1993, the program was as follows:

- *Pledge to Flag*
- *Welcoming Words* – Virginia Apelian, President of Union County College Alumni Association

278

- *Remarks* – Dr. Thomas Brown, President, Union County College
- *Presentations of Awards* – Virginia Apelian and Dr. Thomas Brown

The Alumni Association of Union County College recognized 119 members of the UCC community following the Back-to-College Day program on March 6, 1993, at the Cranford campus. Honorees were 25 presidents of the Alumni Association, 19 had served on the College's governing boards and 65 alumni who were members of the faculty and staff.

Nine prominent UCC alumni who had achieved success in their respective careers presented seminars on selected topics related to their fields on this special day, prior to the awards presentations. Yours truly, as Alumni Association president and member of the Board of Governors, presented a seminar on "Stress Management," plus presided as mistress of ceremonies at the awards presentations. When I received the Alumni Association Service Award, I was being recognized for my multifaceted duties and honored as the current president of the Alumni Association.

Virginia receiving the Alumni Association Service Award from Dr. Thomas Brown. (Courtesy of Bogard Studio, Elizabeth, N.J.)

279

In 1990, $2 million was distributed to UCC students as scholarships through different donors. In 2010, that whole picture changed immensely to a figure of $40 million dollars. This is an extraordinary success. All this happened during Dr. Brown's tenure.

In 1997, my husband Henry and I started a scholarship called the "Virginia and Henry Apelian Scholarship" with two scholarships awarded annually according to the following rules:

One scholarship recipient must be of Armenian descent, with a priority given to financial need for their academic work. This recipient must have a minimum cumulative GPA of 2.8 and must have completed at least fifteen credits.

The second scholarship will be awarded based upon academic achievement and financial need. This recipient must have a minimum GPA of 3.0 and must have at least fifteen credits.

A modification was made in 2010 that if no Armenian-descent student is eligible for the first scholarship, a student from any former USSR republic will be eligible. This was decided by us, knowing that all these former USSR republics had been under aggressive rule, and now their children should get a break.

At the Donor Reception in 1997. L–R: Dr. Thomas Brown, Virginia and Henry Apelian, and Victor Richel, chair of Trustee Board.

At the 1998 Alumni picnic at Nomehegan Park, Cranford, across from the College. L–R: Treasurer Sue Covine; President Virginia Apelian; and Exec. Director of Development Nadine Brechner.

Graduations at Union County College were always very ceremonial and important for the Alumni Association, since I had to present a special scholarship to a graduating student with the highest GPA in the whole graduating class. Each year, as the Alumni president, I was given the opportunity in my six-year tenure to present such an award with a talk given to the graduating students, too, to make them aware of joining our Alumni Association. Also, I wished all of them a successful continuation of their studies in four-year universities or on their job hunt.

Graduation 2000: Dr. Brown and the author are getting ready to join on the Procession line.

UCC Graduation 2000. L–R: The author presenting the Alumni scholarship. Professor Regina Simoneit announced names of the graduates as they received their diplomas.

In May, 2001, the author delivers a special talk to the graduates before giving the Student Award. At this time, she was still teaching at Union County College.

I would like to mention here the favorite teachers I had at Union County College. They have left a good impression on me both scholarly and in friendly ways. They are Dr. Bernard Solon who was my biology professor, a very kind and knowledgeable person. Psychology teachers stand out: Professor Regina Simoneit, who was a very direct and fun person, and Dr. Barbara Engler, who was very thorough and kind. English Professor Margaret Gill was a very sweet person. Professor William Dunscombe, another biology teacher, was very outgoing and had a good sense of humor. Professor Roger Poirier, my French teacher, was very nice and patient. I cannot forget Professor Oscar Fishtein, who was the Head of the English Department, and a very knowledgeable human

My last Holiday Party of Alumni in 2001, with Dr. Brown, Pres. and the officers and members.

283

being. Some of these nice teachers have become very good friends of mine. Professor Frishtein stands out, because while some of my other professors knew nothing about Armenian history, he was familiar with our past. He and I worked closely on the first program "Overcoming Hatred, Creating Community" at UCC on February 26–March 1, 2001.

Professor Oscar Fishtein and the author.

Professor Fishtein was born in London in 1906. He had written a book called *I Will Sell You a Million Jews*, which was a novel inspired by history. Professor Fishtein is no longer with us; he passed away on July 30, 2004, but left a great legacy.

In 2001, when I moved from Clark to Manchester, N.J., I was honored by the Board of Governors, Board of Trustees and the President of Union County College on September 25. I humbly received a gold sealed and framed resolution emphasizing many contributions to the College and the community as well as activities motivated for love of my Armenian heritage. It was mentioned in this "Resolution" that "Mrs. Apelian was the first person ever to have introduced an Armenian program at Union County College, with detailed information of the 'Armenian Case' and its history, enhanced by PowerPoints, pictures, film and a cultural program. All this was presented to a large audience on February 27, 2001." The auditorium was full to its capacity.

The Resolution also declared that Virginia Apelian be a permanent member of the UCC community. I received other gifts that day, a UCC cap and shirt, which I cherish with all their great memories.

During this day, I was asked to speak. The summary of my speech was as follows. I thanked them all sincerely for this honor and good wishes, and that UCC will always be a part of me no matter where I go. But I did not want to forget to say a few important words about this great country of ours, which at this time was in mourning. No one will forget the 9/11 destructive act upon our country by the terrorists. I felt then, and I still do feel, the great loss that this country suffered on that horrific day. Even though this was a special meeting to honor me, I wanted everyone to rise and have a few moments of silence in the honor and memory of those precious people who lost their lives at the Twin Towers, the Pentagon, and in the fallen plane in Pennsylvania. I wanted to recognize all the agencies and folks who tried to help the people from that carnage, many of whom also lost their lives—*honor to them all*. After I finished, with tears in my eyes, I just sat down quietly.

In our American history, that day will go down with such individual accounts that no one will be able to eradicate it from their psyche. My husband and I later on in 2003 went especially to the area and visited the sight of banners, flowers, and photos of loved ones displayed in honor to those who lost their lives. It was very sad, but to see so many people there paying their respect was a special sign of compassion and patriotism.

When we were settled in our Manchester home, my husband and I hosted a Hawaiian luau for our UCC Alumni friends in 2003. Here is a scene of that luau.

L–R: standing, the author's husband and Judge Covine; sitting, Karen, Mary Lou, Gina, and the author.

Presedential sextet at UCC Alumni Assoc. Holiday Party, 2002. L–R: Former Pres. Linda Kurdilla; current (and former) Pres. Naomi Mirlocca; UCC Pres. Dr. Thomas Brown; Immediate Past Pres. Virginia Apelian; and former presidents Suzanne Covine and Anthony Paglia.

Throughout 2009, there were many celebrations at UCC for its 75th Anniversary. The College had grown and advanced tremendously by the efforts of the many dedicated people who worked for it. Dr. Thomas Brown contributed immensely to this College's growth. Having worked closely with Dr. Brown and the Boards, I was part of this worthwhile cause for furthering education and building a great community.

I also have been active with Douglass Alumnae Association of Rutgers, having been to many receptions to further Rutgers' goals for fund-raising and speaking to legislators about not cutting funds for Rutgers. When Dr. Richard L. McCormick returned to Rutgers as

The author and husband at the 2006 UCC Gala.

its nineteenth president, there was a special banquet held in his honor to introduce him to local, active Rutgers Alumni members. Since my graduation from Douglass, I had been an active member of "The Pride in Rutgers Network" and I was often invited with my husband to the special receptions. Also, we were invited to this special gala on February 20, 2003, at Chateau Grand in Ocean County, to have the new Rutgers President introduced to the community. I had a special time to discuss with him matters of Rutgers endeavors. He is a very cordial person.

Dr. Richard L. McCormick, Pres. of Rutgers University and Virginia Apelian on February 20, 2003 at Chateau Grand in Ocean County.

I have been to several Douglass reunions, and have helped mentor students to enter their needed fields, by phone and in person. I have attended several of the Founders Day parades to the Voorhees Chapel after having private breakfast at the Dean's residence with all other Douglass Society members.

My collegiate life has been very fruitful, and enjoyable. Whatever I got involved in was not because I had to, but because I wanted to. When one sacrifices time willingly and lovingly, it becomes a pleasure, a pleasure of doing it and helping others. All these experiences generated love of people in me, and I see that involvement in my community to help any way I could makes a difference. That difference makes each situation a little better than it was before.

Jobs and Politics

Even though I was attending college, I was quite visible in the community with many volunteer works and church involvement. I was offered a job immediately after college graduation by Assemblyman William Maguire, for the 22nd District of the New Jersey Legislature. I wanted to be sure that I would work only until 3:00 p.m. every day so that I could cater to my children's needs for school and otherwise. That was no problem; I was told and that I could start as soon as the children were back in school, which was the fall of 1975. I wanted to try this for a while, and then decide what to do about continuing my education for my doctorate degree later. I took some graduate courses here and there, but wanted to do a full-time job with the Assembly office first. As I remembered from when I was at Jersey Girls State in 1954, in the third year of high school, now was my chance to see government work and to be a part of it. I was very interested and willing to do this job for the benefit of the community, and all the knowledge that I would receive.

So, I became the Office Manager and Administrative Assistant for this District 22 Legislative Office. Not only would I manage the numerous issues handled by this office, but also I would attend all the sessions of the General Assembly in Trenton with Mr. Maguire. Plus, he was on several important committees to oversee state matters, one of which was the Appropriations Committee. This was one of the most important committees. It determined the budgets of the State for distribution to each municipality of New Jersey, which is comprised of 566 municipalities. There are, of course, three levels of government oversight: the local government, which is the Council-Mayor format or a revision of sort; the county government, the freeholders; and the state government, assembly persons and senators, per district.

It is fascinating to learn how a bill becomes law. During each session of the legislature, 7,000-8,000 bills are filed to both state bodies. However, few of them make it all the way into law.

First of all, there has to be a sponsor or sponsors. Then the bill goes to the Secretary or the Speaker of the Assembly, and the bill is assigned a number. It is examined for corrections. The General Assembly Clerk does the first reading. It is referred to committee. After that, public hearings are conducted, with possible amendments added. When the committee approves of the bill, it receives a second reading on the floor for amendments. Finally, after the third reading, the floor debate and vote takes place. If passed, an Assembly bill is sent to the Senate. The same committee procedure is followed in the Senate as the Assembly, until after both bodies approve, the bill is sent to the Governor. The governor may sign, veto, or apply a conditional veto until certain changes are made. However, if the Governor signs it, the bill becomes law. If the Governor vetoes the bill, then the Houses may override the veto by two-thirds vote, which would be 27 votes in the Senate, and 54 in the Assembly, and then it becomes law. Bills returning to the Houses with conditional vetoes can also become law by being modified. All this is an interesting and time-consuming process, but in the end, it is hoped the resulting law is the right decision to make for the benefit of the people.

Some people do not know, as I discovered while working in this legislative office, that any citizen has the right to call the Office of the Legislative Services and receive copies of bills and other information. This information is available to all, but many people do not utilize it and stay in the dark. I always got so many calls as to what bill was passed or what were the contents of each, and by whom. All that information is available to everyone just for the asking.

Sitting in those legislative sessions, one sees how much work is done or not done. There is also a waste of time and repetition of ideas if the sponsors of the bill have not done their homework to begin with. Also, on major issues, at the legislative office where I worked, I would be the determining person as to who may come and see the legislator in our district. And there were times I had to determine the dire issue at hand to pursue further. Then I would make arrangements for the public meeting to occur with news media invited so that the information was made available to the general public.

For example, I noticed in one of the newspapers that the Arthur Brisbane Child Treatment Center, Farmingdale, N.J., was suffering from insufficient funds and lack of proper departmental faculty. I thought this would be a very special place to visit to find out the core problems. I discussed it with Assemblyman Maguire and made it clear to him that it would be a very good idea to see what was happening there. He agreed, and then I made all the arrangements for us to visit this institution. It was an eye-opener to find out that they had a crowded situation, first of all, with only one faculty member who was qualified to be in charge, whereas two people should have been with each group because of the nature of problems that had occurred in the past, and may again arise should only one person be present with the special groups. There were many other issues to be corrected. The Assemblyman and I spent the whole day there as I made notes about important issues that were to be corrected. Soon many major papers covered the visit—that in 30 years no governmental agency had ever visited there, and now this certain Assemblyman had. Of course, the story did not end there. Mr. Maguire brought this to the attention of N.J. Assembly and the Appropriations Committee, and soon help was given to Brisbane. By then, Assemblyman Maguire was getting very well-known for his good deed for the institution. I felt good that we had assisted helpless young people. There were many other types of issues where this office would intervene for productive results for the constituents.

I remained in this job from 1975 to 1978. It was a tremendous job and I gained knowledge about the procedural steps to follow to achieve results. However, the State did not allow a big stipend for the legislative staff and, at this point, there were many expenses for our children's needs as they were growing up. There were other opportunities for me to pursue.

I found a job as manager of the Electronic Corporation of America working with six engineers. I had the responsibility of the whole office's transactions and the personnel. Red Wagner was my supervisor. He had offered me the job at the interview and said that I could start the next day. I would not do that until I gave at least a two-week notice to the Assemblyman. Mr. Maguire was sorry to see me leave, but he understood I had four children and they had many needs. He said personally, "I could not match the salary that you will be getting now, fourfold."

"I really liked working here, and your office was so close to my house. I truly appreciate your understanding." I shook his hand and thanked him for having given me this opportunity to work for him.

We kept in touch, and he encouraged me to run for public office. At the time, there were other candidates from the Republican Party who wanted the Clark Council seat. I won the primary, having the backing by Mr. Maguire. I worked very hard to beat the incumbent Democratic candidate. I had a strategy unlike the others, which depended too much on written rhetoric in newspapers only. In addition to my newspaper statements, I went house to house on foot to meet the constituents face to face. Most of them were happy that I took the time to meet them personally, especially when they had questions pertaining to legislation and protocol about certain issues. I had the answers for them, and they were impressed. Also, there were those who were typical male chauvinists, saying to me, "Why would a nice young lady want to run for office; that is a man's job."

When I first ran for public office. (Courtesy of
photographer Roy Graves)

"Thank you for your time, sir." I would say very calmly and move on.

Here I would like to mention something that someone had told me, "If
a woman wants to run for office, better develop thick skin." I did not like
that expression. First of all, idiomatically, it did not translate well with me
in Armenian. Second, I wanted to run for office in a respectable way as a
knowledgeable person no matter what gender I was. When you train yourself
to not heed comments such as that, you don't get aggravated, but pursue
your wishes. And that is what I did.

BEST WISHES
TO ALL THE PEOPLE
OF CLARK

BERNARD G. YARUSAVAGE, Mayor

CLARK MUNICIPAL COUNCIL

JOSEPH B. POZNIAK
Council President

BERNARD R. HAYDEN   DON LABELLA

JOSEPH FARRELL   MANUEL S. DIOS

JOHN BODNAR, JR.   VIRGINIA APELIAN

Clark Township Council, 1980.

In 1980, I was newly elected to the Clark Township Council, plus I was working full-time for Electronic Corporation of America (ECA).

293

Our son Gregory, a senior at Arthur L. Johnson High School, won the essay contest sponsored by the Union County Bar Association, Union County. The topic was "What Does the Law Mean to Me?" This competition was open to all Union County high school students. Greg was honored at a special ceremony and presented a $100 U.S. Savings Bond by Superior Court Judge V. William Di Buono at the Union County Court House in Elizabeth, N.J. All the N.J. Superior Court judges were present at this special presentation. Greg graduated from A.L.J. High School with high honors. He was also named a National Merit Scholar. The next fall, he attended University of Delaware to pursue a pre-law curriculum in their Honors Program. Both my husband and I took off from work to be at our son's side. Our minister from Osceola Presbyterian Church also attended. We were all very happy for Greg.

Greg, Rev. Kopp and the author at the Court House in Elizabeth. Author's husband Henry took the photo.

My job at ECA was great. This was a different type of work as compared to legislative duties, but had many personal interactions on the telephone with other company heads. My boss, Mr. Wagner, would give me the hardest of the disputes to settle on the phone with the other companies' personnel. And later he would come and congratulate me saying, "I don't know what you said to them, but they are now happy and satisfied." That made me happy. It was in my nature to listen to people completely and attentively. I would make notes as I spoke with them about their troubles and issues. Then, I would ask them to kindly now to listen to me. And ninety-nine percent of the time, they were willing to listen and comply with my suggestions and explanations. That was a method I had used while I worked in the banks in my early years.

Just installed as Clark Township Council President; Virginia confers with the Mayor (middle) and the City Clerk.

While still working for ECA, Virginia was elected as the first woman Council President of Clark Township. Here, the Mayor and well-wishers are celebrating with her, January 1, 1982.

295

I was in the main office of ECA where Mr. Wagner would be most of the time, but the six engineers came and went on daily basis to different companies, selling and demonstrating our gadgets and products. I kept all their records and files, and answered their correspondence. In the other end of our building was the shipping department, which I had no connection with, except when their shipments were delayed, I had to find out why. They better have had a good reason; if not, it would go to Mr. Wagner. I was in charge of the big safe of all the moneys, and needed purchases for the office supplies. Most of the time, I would be in the office all by myself. This office was located in Springfield, N.J. off Route 22, which was a very hard road to drive on, with narrow lanes and much traffic. I worked for ECA for three years until they moved their offices to Boston. Of course, my roots were in New Jersey, so I started looking for another job.

CHANGING OF THE GUARD - At the Township Council meeting of Jan. 18 the newly-elected officers of the Clark Volunteer Fire Dept. were sworn in by Mayor Bernard G. Yarusavage, left, for a two-year term of office. The officers and their families attending the meeting with the mayor, left to right, are: The director of public safety, Robert Taylor; the Council president; Mrs. Virginia Apelian; a deputy chief, Robert Volpe; the chief, Vincent Pereira; the assistant chief, Howard Payne; a deputy chief, Arthur Slinger, and a deputy chief, Frank Brattole, Sr.

Mayor and Clark Council President Virginia Apelian with the newly elected Clark Volunteer Fire Dept.

My next job was with the U.S. Defense Department, Quality Assurance Offices located in Springfield, N.J. at 240 Route 22. This was interesting work, but I thought too much waste in paperwork took place. When I suggested that out of a six-step project, four steps could be eliminated easily, and the same result accomplished with two steps, no one wanted to hear of it. Now I understood why the government could spend all these extra dollars creating more paperwork while hiring more people to do it. At that point, I saw how a corporation works to save money by deleting unnecessary steps in getting their work done. What a difference! When I worked at ECA, Mr. Wagner was delighted when I made changes to save time and money.

While at the Defense Department job, my Party wanted me to run for office again. Although I declared to run, yet because of the Hatch Act of 1939, I could not run for public office and still work for the Federal Government. So, I left that Defense position after a year. I served as the Council President of Clark Township, the *first woman* ever to be elected to that office.

While in office, I did a number of other jobs in the community to keep close to my family's needs. I was a consultant for Total Quality Education (TQE). I had weekly seminars with various corporations' personnel, lecturing on one's full potential, how to control stress, and ways of economizing time. My approach has always been "individual centered," with each course being both self-help and an enjoyable experience for the participants. Role-playing was a major part of my style of teaching. By being able to rehearse for that which has been difficult in the past, a person can attain the result one wants. My courses, as a psychologist and educator, have always stressed the human condition, user-friendly method. This unique method has been very productive in helping many people: corporate employees; students of all professional backgrounds at Union County College; or members of different organizations in private sessions.

Because my courses gained such popularity, I was asked by Union County College to teach classes for young adults, ages 12–17 and younger children, ages 7-11. The essence of these Saturday young people classes, "College for Kids," was to energize students within their own talents to full potential with assertiveness.

Assertiveness is the opposite of aggressiveness. Lord willing, after I am done with this book, I will write one on all of my experiences teaching and developing my own programs on "positive self-image." If all of us are given the chance and the opportunity to be the best that we can be, and we believe it—it will happen. God has created us all in His image; we are all very special, no matter where we come from or what color of skin we each have. None of that matters. If you know your worth, others will recognize it too.

I had many other workshops on a freelance basis. The good thing about this type of work was that I made my own hours. Not only was I getting paid for it nicely, but also it was very fulfilling for me to see the joy in people after having attained their desire of self-assuredness.

I have worn many other hats, so to speak. (By the way, I really love hats. I guess you can tell by now viewing my photos.) I have done other jobs and have been paid for them quite well. For example, I was Youth Director at the Central Presbyterian Church, Summit, N.J. Also, I have taught nursery school at Temple Emanu-El in Westfield, N.J. This was the first time I had served in a Jewish temple. It was very interesting for me as each Friday we would prepare for the Shabbat. We would light the candle, present the challah, and then repeat the kiddush prayers:

> *"Baruch ata adonai elohanu melech ha olam,*
> *Hamotzi lechem min haartz."*

I have learned to love challah. Since then, I always buy it at Shop-Rite when I do my food shopping.

Also, I was the nursery school director of the Scotch Plains Baptist Church in 1983. I took this position for a year, to organize the parents' group and the agenda for immunization records, which I found in poorly recorded condition, in terms of filing with the State. Also, I tested the children's ability for learning to see if areas of special attention needed by certain children were taken care of.

In 1984, I was offered the directorship for the Coordinator of the Senior Citizens Center of Union County, at Oak Ridge Golf Course, which provided for all kinds of programs for the needs of seniors in twenty-one municipalities. I called large, local companies, such as Merck and Co. and Schering-Plough Pharmaceuticals, and asked them to donate furniture, a ping-pong table, clocks, television set and other miscellaneous items for the Center, without a penny's cost to the County. Many other private firms and individuals donated in addition to the Clark Library providing books. Special services and programs were donated by the police department, doctors, school choruses, and private dance schools. We had a fantastic curriculum. The Parks and Recreation Department of Union County was exhilarated with all these special events at the Oak Ridge Golf Course Center.

I served as Vacation Bible School Director at United Presbyterian Church of Plainfield. This was a very large group of children, and it was a pleasure and a delight to work with such a large group with many different ethnic backgrounds.

On a volunteer basis, I have helped the Mayor's Committee on Drug Abuse. I went to different schools and various classes to talk on the negative aspects of drugs. I have also lectured to church groups and school PTAs, presenting a "Parenting Skills Forum." Aside from teaching Sunday school classes, from K-adults for forty-two years and seeing the need of a group for seniors.

I established a group called "The Owls" at the Osceola Presbyterian Church in Clark. Rev. Robert Kopp was the minister at the time; he was thrilled with the idea. The seniors elected their officers, and felt very important by having a special place in church. I arranged very good monthly programs for them, such as doctors giving them good advice on diet and medical care issues. We had fun trips and socials.

When I belonged to Clark Alliance Against Drugs, we had many open forums for parents and young people. I coordinated a special joint program with the Clark Board of Education and the Garwood Alliance at The Westwood in Garwood. Some committee members participating were Principal David Carl of Arthur L. Johnson High School and Assistant Superintendent Susan Miksza, of Clark; and Dr. Maryann Moy, guidance counselor of Kumpf Middle School. Dr. Moy and I worked very closely with the students. She was a wonderful person to work with, as I also did substitute teaching at the Kumpf Middle School then during the day, as a certified teacher. I assisted Dr. Moy with her problematic students who needed help.

Being in politics was an eye-opener. The people that I knew in social situations, so friendly and nice, were not so as you worked with them. Let me explain, although I will give no names. It is not my intent to embarrass anyone, but I learned that some elected officials do not have the knowledge or the desire to help the people who elected them. So, I came to the conclusion that there are four types of people who run for elected office. That goes for any level of government. The first type wants the status symbol of the position, nothing else. The second group of people who desire to be elected would sell their soul to profit by negotiating a gift of jobs in exchange for bribes. A third type of office seeker aims for a certain agenda. They push their own person to be elected, to get their way. The last type is the most important one: that person wants to be a "A Genuine Public Servant" and to help people as best as she/he can. They have ethics and a moral compass to follow. Those are the types of people—men and women—we should seek to elect, for they will help people, but not their egos.

When I became council president with my own merits, I literally can say I got my Ph.D. in politics. The things that I witnessed and dealt with were incredible. I will give you a few examples to show you what I mean. First of all, I learned that you never call a politician colleague and tell them something of importance on the telephone; especially, if they are inept or have a different agenda to pursue. They will come up and deny your call completely. At first, that was so frustrating to me, and I thought: *Where is everyone's integrity?* Soon, I developed my style of delivering a message or an action to be pursued by interoffice memos only. I would explain my request or order, and send copies to all department heads involved. Oh, my goodness! Things would work out like magic. Everyone knew what I was talking about, and no denials were possible, whereas before they so quickly forgot what I had said to them on the telephone.

Another incident, I was the chair of the Rent-Control Committee. We met on a certain date and the agenda was obvious, and there were major statements made at the meeting pertinent to the renters of apartments. During these meetings, the newspaper reporters would often attend to give the summary of the meeting the next day to the public. This particular time, a certain councilman, quoted as saying something leading at this meeting, was not there. That immediately caught my eye, and I took the news clipping with me to the Executive Board Public Meeting the next evening. After finishing our usual set agenda, I usually asked if any of the council members had any comments or statements other than what was in our main agenda. Each one gave his comments, and now it was my turn. The reporter who wrote the article about our committee meeting was sitting right on the first row of the meeting hall, practically right across from me.

"There was an erroneous reporting on *The Journal's* part yesterday about our meeting content." I looked straight at the reporter, and turned around and looked at the councilman who had not been there the day before. I continued saying,

"Councilman _____, do you know anything about this?"

"No, I don't," he replied.

"Well, have you read the article by Mr. _____, and did you not notice anything unusual?"

"No, I did not notice anything unusual."

"Oh, let me read it to you all," and I took the clipping and read the part about this particular councilman was there, and that he said such and such. I continued saying that this said councilman "was *not* there!" I could hear the people in the audience whispering.

The council member said nothing after my comment. And I said nothing additional—the message had gotten through, and it was recorded in the records for good. The reporter, at that point, walked out of the meeting and we never saw him again.

In politics, if one is not prepared to face the music, she/he should not run for office. However, integrity and honesty must be established right from the beginning. If I had called this councilman the night before and asked him about it, he would have denied it and that would be all. But to save it and bring it up at the public meeting is a different story. At such a meeting everything is recorded for a permanent record and the public witnesses it, too. I want to emphasize that this type of occurrence never happened again.

Here is another incident. A harsh winter storm had come about, and we had about twenty inches of snow. People shoveled themselves out of their driveways to get to work. At the end of our Rutgers Road was a cul-de-sac at the Roberts Rd. entrance. The Gelorminis had cleared their driveway, and Frank Gelormini was supposed to go to work. When he came in to have breakfast, the town's people came and put all of the street's snow in front of his driveway, over a twenty-foot mound. He was very upset, and called the mayor. The mayor did not respond well, saying,

"Well, there is a lot of snow to plow, and the guys are on the opposite side of town now, maybe later."

That had made Frank Gelormini furious, and so he called me explaining the whole situation and that he had to get to work. He reported that the mayor had said, "The crew cannot come now, maybe later."

I said, "I will see what I can do for you." I called the captain of the snow removal team. I told him without any delay, you'd better get your crew and come and take that mound of snow from off the front of the Gelormini's driveway.

"No questions asked, do it now," I said firmly. I thanked him and hung up the phone.

The crew was there in fifteen minutes and cleared the whole view of the driveway. By the way, the Gelorminis were Democrats, but they were endorsing me to run for mayor, the next time around. They never forgot that good deed for them. Recently, at a gathering, they saw me and told the whole story to the other people, as if it had happened just yesterday. You see, when you respect the people you represent, it leaves a mark of trust and caring for them. We happened to move from Clark soon after that, sorry to say that I could not grant the Gelorminis' wish for me to run for mayor of Clark.

There are many incidents that I can talk about, but just one more will give you a clear picture as to what an elected person should do for the people who elected him or her. On Raritan Rd., near Hehnly School where all of our children attended, and I was on the PTA, and the Legislative Committee Chair. There was a little boy caught in a large cement easement pipe outside the field of the school, and adjacent to the Lewis' property. The parents of the little boy were suing Mr. and Mrs. Lewis for negligence, because this large pipe had been exposed when the child got stuck in it. This gentleman,

Mr. Lewis, had written to the Clark Township mayors and council members for nine and half years.

When I got elected, he wanted to write to me to fix this long-awaited problem he was still facing. He told me that his wife said to him, "Don't bother wasting your time, she will be just like the others."

But he said, "I wanted to try to write to you, too."

When I got the letter, I brought it to the executive meeting where we usually set the agenda for the main public meeting. As each one of us brought issues to put on the agenda for the public meeting, I said I had received this very urgent letter from Mr. Lewis, regarding his receding property next to the Township easement of this large cement pipe being exposed near his property. Right after, I brought this out, they all said,

"Yeh, we know about Mr. Lewis, what's next?"

I became absolutely furious, and said, "What have you done about it?" as loudly as I could. All of a sudden, they stopped talking, and they were stunned to hear my interrogative question asked so strongly. I don't know what they thought, but truly, I did not care about their evasiveness.

"What have you done about it?" I repeated.

"Well, that has been a chronic complaint."

"A complaint for nine and half years and you never looked into the matter?" I looked at everyone very sternly. I added, "That is just so incredible to me, I just can't believe it."

They, in turn, mumbled that I could take it over and see what I can do with it if I wanted.

"I am very disappointed what I hear about this," I told them.

Democrat and Republican alike, these were guys who had been elected time after time. It seemed to me that it was a nice niche to come each month and do nothing, but meet like a club for them, to exchange niceties. This position was just a status symbol, for them to be at certain store openings, at ribbon cuttings, and at sport games where their names were announced over the microphone system. How very sad, I thought, to be so artificial.

To continue this saga, I met with our Clark Township engineer, a very nice, conscientious young man who wanted to work with me wholeheartedly. We both went and got the County engineer, and found the deed of this house, and met Mr. Lewis. We compared the house deed to the one on file; everything was in good order. After the engineers measured and figured the cost of fixing this problem, filling with dirt the receded area, which was quite a bit, at least eight feet of property from Mr. Lewis' yard. In addition, the large cement pipe had to be covered with dirt, and the opening part that would release floodwaters out downhill, but the opening would have a strong mesh cover to prevent any creatures or little boys getting stuck in the pipe. This project took me three months, back and forth with the engineers and the pricing. The final estimate was to fix it all for $17,000. I was glad to inform the Lewises and he was very appreciative.

"Do you think the rest of the Council would go along with it?" he said, doubtfully.

"They better," I said firmly.

I could not wait until our next executive meeting. I had all the engineers' reports, the deed and the pricing: $17,000. As I mentioned the cost, they all raised their eyebrows, "What, $17,000 it will cost us?"

"Yes, only $17,000. Would you like to be sued for $100,000 or $200,000 if a child is hurt or, God forbid, dies in that pipe?"

Silence prevailed.

Then, I continued, saying, "Let's vote on it and put it on the agenda right now."

We placed it on the agenda that very evening.

"Thank you, gentlemen, for your cooperation," I said graciously.

The Clark Council and the author.

I had to inform Mr. Lewis that soon work was going to be started to fill his yard with dirt, and restore his property to its original state of about ten years ago.

"You are a miracle worker, Mrs. Apelian," he said joyfully.

"No, I am not a miracle worker, I just did my job."

"Thank you, thank you so much for everything you did."

"You are welcome," I said, and added, "Please call again if you have any other requests where I can be of any help."

When I was running for office again, he stopped by my house to ask what he could do for my campaign. He took a big bundle of car bumper stickers to distribute. I did not ask him to do that for me, but he wanted to do it. A friend of mine in Rahway remarked to me that there were *so many* of my stickers on cars visible when she traveled to and from jobs around our town and in the next town. I knew it must have been Mr. Lewis' work.

Well, there are many more stories to tell, but I think you have a good sample of matters I had to go through. One more thing, when I was in elected office, I hardly had a warm meal. I was always interrupted, even at late hours until midnight. To be a public servant is to be dedicated in helping people. There is much sacrifice of time and energy, but in the long run, the service is worth it, because you are making a difference. As you know, in this country, we have two major political parties, Republican and Democratic, and many other smaller parties. However, people sometimes forget what each party stands for. That is a major issue in choosing the party one supports, but there is another major issue: to choose people to run who are of high caliber, with honesty and sincerity to help their constituents. Even when I was the president of Clark Republican Club, and later in Manchester, N.J., when I was elected as the Republican Club president, I always strived to do something a lot more than to be a partisan person.

In Clark, I used to encourage young high school students to write essays about patriotic issues, such topics as "What Democracy Means to Me," or "What Ways Can I Honor My Country?" or "This Land Is My Land." All the high school students were able to participate. I wanted the students to submit their essays, by merely attaching a number on it, but no name, so it would be a fair judging. Only the teacher would know what number corresponded to what name and essay. I always chose educators of high caliber to be the judges, such as the Superintendent of the Schools, a minister, and me.

The student submitting the winning essay would receive a $50 U.S. Savings Bond and have a special meeting for her/him with all their friends and family to join us as they would read their essay. This way, they would feel the honor and the opportunity to savor their hard work. Also, I would arrange a visit to the N.J. Assembly to get a resolution in honor of the student's winning the essay contest. She or he would read the essay to the Assembly session and get a big ovation. Who could forget such an experience at their young age?

I was also a member of the steering committee of the New Jersey Association for Elected Women Officials. This was an organization that encouraged capable women to run for public office. I made many friends there, both Republican and Democrat. These were very able women who had many good things in their communities, and were always alert to the government's role, whether they were in local, county or state government. Each of these roles was very important. When Assemblywoman Leanna Brown was elected the president, I was elected as First Vice President. Prior to that, I was the Treasurer. Assemblywoman Brown was a very hard-working and astute person. Later on, she ran for a N.J. Senate seat and won. She is retired now, but we still correspond and talk on occasion about important issues. We usually met at Eagleton Institute at Rutgers University, at the Douglass Campus. We have had Governor Kean of N.J. as one of our speakers, who was always a great advocate for Women's causes.

Also, I coordinated and chaired a Celebrity Auction by inviting both Republican and Democratic elected officials to donate some things of value to be auctioned off at a big gala. This affair was sponsored by the Republican Women of Union County. Here again, because this was an all-out effort to have fun and raise funds, the donations were used for the Battered Women of Union County. Some zealous Democratic personnel were trying to make trouble saying that we created a big fund-raiser to aid the Republican candidates. This was not true of course. A popular Democratic State Senator called me saying that he just wanted to be sure where the money went. He told me that because he had contributed towards this function, he was being criticized. I assured him that he can check with the Battered Women of Union County to verify the truth. He thanked me, and that notion of a falsehood was put to an end.

No matter how hard one tries to benefit the community with a nice gesture such as this, some people would always like to make trouble. This is one of the reasons why some people would say, "Politics is dirty," but it does not have to be. There are good politicians, who are great public servants. We had two great ones in Union County: Congressman Matthew Rinaldo, who was a long-term legislator who did numerous good deeds for the people, and another, freshman Congressman Bob Franks was an honest public servant who always returned the people's calls and letters in a timely manner. They were both people-oriented men, who always treated their constituents with respect. When you respect people, they in turn will respect you.

Congressman Bob Franks congratulating author on election as Clark Township Council President. On the left is Freeholder Miller at our home celebration (1982).

Congressman Matthew Rinaldo and the author at one of his rallies. (Courtesy of Roy Graves, photographer)

They both have been to my house on different occasions, such as, congratulating me when I became the first woman Council President of Clark Township. My husband and I were always invited to their inaugural parties in Washington, D.C. When people say all politicians are crooks, it is not so. Kudos to those two; they will be sorely missed. They both passed away recently: Rinaldo, at about age 77, in 2008, and Franks in 2010 at a young age of 58, with an unusual cancer.

There are times when it is fun to help colleagues in their endeavors in politics: such as when Union County Freeholder Edward J. Slomkowski invited me as the Clark Council representative to be his aide and march in the Pulaski Day Parade in New York City. Freeholder Slomkowski was the Grand Marshal. He invited all the guests to dinner at the Polish Center in Elizabeth after the parade that evening. There was much merriment and happy people around.

Grand Marshal Ed Slomkowski and Virginia Apelian as aide at the Pulaski Day Parade, November 1981.

CIA Job Offer in 1985

I received a job offer from Central Intelligence Agency (CIA) with an official letter, and an application for my submission to the Office of the Personnel. It was interesting that the letter was not dated, but the postmark on the letter was February of 1985. I

307

received the letter in the beginning of March of 1985. I won't reveal the name of the Personnel Officer, but I was asked to a personal interview, also. The letter gave all the information of unique rewards and educational opportunities that the nation will appreciate. They had enclosed a self-

Congressman Rinaldo and Virginia and Henry Apelian.

addressed, stamped envelope for me to use when returning the application. First of all, I had not applied for this job, and the only way they could have had my information was from the *Who's Who* that I am listed in. Second of all, I was a mother of four children at the time. Although our daughter Arminee was married in 1982, our three sons were still in college. I was honored that I was thought about, but I did not reply. I kept the letter, the application, and the return envelope just in case some day I need to show it to my grandchildren for proof. Anyway, I thought this was very interesting. If I had been single, I might have considered it, maybe. The letter came from Washington, D.C., but I was to be meeting them in their New York City office. To this day, this has been an enigma to me.

In October 1982, when I was still president of Clark Council, I met with my friend, Assemblywoman Leanna Brown; the Vice President's wife, Mrs. Barbara Bush, a very gracious lady; and elegant Congresswoman Millicent Fenwick, for a Republican Women's Task Force celebration at the Parsippany Hilton.

L–R: Standing Virginia Apelian and Leanna Brown; sitting, Mrs. Barbara Bush and Congresswoman Millicent M. Fenwick.

Congresswoman Fenwick was called the "conscience of Congress." Congresswoman Fenwick passed away at 82 in 1992. She was a champion of human rights.

Armenian Assembly of America 2002 Advocacy Conference

My husband Henry and I were invited to be delegates to the 2002 Armenian Assembly of America (AAA) Advocacy Conference, April 19–24, 2002. The AAA is a nationwide non-profit organization established in 1972, and headquartered in Washington, D.C. It provides public awareness of Armenian issues and democratic, humanitarian and development efforts. Also, it serves as a forum to provide a national framework for the promotion of communication within the Armenian-American community. In addition, it provides the means by which the Armenian community can speak effectively on issues of importance and concern.

We stayed at the L'Enfant Plaza Hotel. The first evening, we were introduced to the delegates from all walks of life from all parts of the USA and Armenia. This was a highly educational event.

Henry and Virginia going to dinner at L'Enfant Plaza Hotel.

Virginia and Henry had their respective assignments to meet with designated legislators.

For the duration of this conference, there were seminars, discussion groups and panel presentations. Indeed, it was very well-organized from beginning to end. The conference attendees with ARAMAC (Armenian-American Action Committee) badges were well-informed through the days of the conference as to what issues to bring to their elected officials. All the appointments were set and the time was wisely used to meet legislators and their aides.

311

After meeting with the Congress members and Senators, we all went to the Rayburn House Office Building's foyer with numerous Congress members and Senators and their aides. The reception area was warmly decorated with Armenian Genocide maps and pictures. A video was shown pertaining to the genocide. In addition, there was a long table of appetizing and inviting hors d'oeuvres and warm food for all to enjoy. Then, Peter Vosbigian, the 2002 Board of Directors chairman, greeted the guests and conference attendees with a heartfelt message, and Annie Totah, the vice chairman, introduced the renowned legislative speakers supporting Armenian issues through legislation. The main speakers in this category were Congressman Joseph Knollenberg of Michigan, Congresswoman Connie Morella of Maryland, and Congressman Frank Pallone, Jr. of New Jersey. These Congress members and others were great proponents on Armenian issues.

*Congresswoman Connie Morella and Virginia
Apelian at the reception.*

312

Congressman Frank Pallone and the author.

Being the representative of the New Jersey Ethnic Advisory Council, I brought a Proclamation from the N.J. Governor declaring April 24, 2002, as Armenian Martyrs' Day, which bore the State of New Jersey golden seal embossed on it. I read it to the audience at the Republic of Armenian Embassy Reception at 2225 R. Street NW, Washington, D.C. After reading this proclamation, I handed it over to the Armenian Ambassador, His Excellency Armen Kirakossian.

The delegates were given two important tours during this conference. One was at the Holocaust Museum, which was a very moving experience. Then we were guided by Ross Vartian on a tour to see the future Armenian Genocide Museum and Memorial (AGM&M) building. This old building was originally the National Bank of Washington at 619 14th Street NW, Washington, D.C. The building is very close to the White House; actually, from its windows one can see the White House. Constructed in 1925, it is a five-story structure consisting of about 34,000 sq. feet. A Genocide Museum and Memorial Planning and Development Committee had been formed. The committee is responsible for devising and executing a contribution and endowment program to fund completion of the redevelopment plan and the operation of the property: the Museum and the Memorial.

313

L–R: Virginia Apelian; His Excellency, Armenian Ambassador Armen Kirakossian; Mrs. Kirakossian, and Henry Apelian, at the Embassy.

In addition, this structure is a landmark listed in the Inventory of Historic Sites, and on the National Register of Historic Places. It is estimated that in the near future this will become a reality as the Armenian Genocide Museum and Memorial.

The newly acquired site of the future Armenian Genocide Museum and Memorial.

Some Other Meaningful Committees I Have Served On

1981: At the request of His Grace Bishop Mesrob Ashjian of the Prelacy of the Armenian Apostolic Church of America of New York City, I was invited to serve on the Executive Committee in planning the 66th Anniversary Commemoration of the Armenian Genocide. Our first meeting took place on February 19, 1981, at the Prelacy Headquarters, 138 E. 38th St., at 8:00 p.m. sharp. His Grace, the Prelate, opened the meeting by thanking everyone for their time, having come from the tri-state areas. There was much planning to be done for the preparation of this commemoration on April 24th.

The tasks of each committee member were assigned, and they were all important ones for the success of the day. We had eight special meetings at the Prelacy Headquarters from February 19 through April 22, 1981. Dr. Ara Caprielian was selected to be the chair of the Committee and Dr. Vahe Apelian as the Secretary and the Chair of the Finance Committee to act as the Treasurer of the event. I was on the public relations committee among other members to complete the day's commemorative booklet with all the necessary information. The day had arrived and it was a beautiful day. The Rally at Rockefeller Center was planned for two hours, and then there was a special dinner of the leaders at the Waldorf Astoria.

The speakers and committee members of the Commemoration at Waldorf Astoria. L–R: seated, Senator Paul T. Tsongas and Staten Island cardiologist Dr. Megerditch Panossian: standing, Mrs. Virginia Apelian, Exec. Bd. Member, Clark Twp. Council member, and N.J. Ethnic Advisory Council representing the Armenian community; Exec. Member Judge Sarkis Techoian of Mass.; Mr. Onnig Marashian, a committee member; and attorney Alexander Drapos of Mass.

Afterwards, we all marched with an entourage to St. Patrick Cathedral for the main commemorative program. Nearly 3,000 people were in the audience. The program opened with the Rev. Msgr. James F. Rigney, rector at the Cathedral. Proclamations were given by and read from Mayor Edward Koch of NYC and Governor Hugh L. Carey of New York. Virginia Apelian read the N.J. Senate resolution for the occasion, and a proclamation by Senator Paul Tsongas of Mass. who also was the main speaker of the commemoration ceremony.

1982: The grand ballroom of New York City's Prince George Hotel was transformed into a "Little Armenia" through a photographic exhibit and lecture series with its theme "Assault on a Culture." This commemoration of Armenian Martyrs' Day was sponsored by the Prelacy of the Armenian Apostolic Church of America, under the auspices of His Grace Bishop Mesrob Ashjian. This exhibit commemorated the 67th anniversary of the Armenian Genocide of April 24, 1915.

At the official opening ceremonies which began on April 23, I, as the Clark Township Council President and as a representative from New Jersey, presented the special proclamations. One was given to me by Gov. Thomas H. Kean and the other by State Senator Donald T. DiFrancesco who represented Clark. There were foreign dignitaries in attendance also.

Virginia Apelian reading Gov. Thomas Kean's Proclamation to the audience.

*His Grace Bishop Mesrob Ashjian introduces Virginia Apelian
to His Excellency Mr. Theophilos Theophilon of the Consul
General of Greece. (Part of exhibit is in the background)*

Probably the most popular expression of Armenian culture and artistic life are illuminated manuscripts. The most famous manuscript displayed was from the Holy Bible of Etchmiadzin, the headquarters for the Catholicos. The exhibit ended with Adolph Hitler's chilling words, "Who today remembers the Armenian Genocide?" The exhibit mainly depicted the Armenian people's resurrection. In the end stood the victorious monument of Dzidzernagapert (Citadel of Swallows) and the picture of an Armenian youth whose eyes hold the future of his nation and stamped on his chest were the words of the poem:

"We exist,
    We will persevere,
        And we will increase."

1986: The Clark Historical Society was holding programs at the Clark Library Hall on the topic of "My Heritage" by any given group. I was asked to do a special on Armenian History. I gladly accepted and planned a nice cultural program for the Clark public to enjoy. Thus, I made all the preparations for the May 28 meeting. First of all, I prepared with my art work booklets of the whole program, with a picture of Mt. Ararat on

317

the cover. Also, I invited New Jersey Assemblyman Chuck Haytaian, the majority Assembly leader of N.J., to speak about his own Armenian heritage. Then I invited the famous Armenian "Nayiri" dance group from New York, under the direction of Ms. Nevart Hamparian. They demonstrated a beautiful medley of Armenian dances, and the audience loved the dancers. They have performed at the New York World's Fair, at the Democratic National Convention in Atlantic City, at Carnegie Recital Hall, and Rutgers University. At the final dance, they threw fresh flowers to the audience's amazement. There was an added highlight to this evening's festivities: I had prepared during the whole week a buffet selection of Armenian delicacies for everyone to enjoy at the end of the program. Everyone left happy and content, having learned a little more about my Armenian heritage.

Nayiri Dance Group of New York.

I was involved in politics from local, county, and state to federal levels, and I enjoyed and learned a great deal from each of the sources. Learning and utilizing what you have in helping people is the greatest feeling one can attain. To make a difference is such a great honor to bestow upon another. I was also the coordinator for Reagan's Presidential campaign in Clark. I received a very kind certificate from President Reagan. He is one of my favorite U.S. presidents. I have a few others that I will talk about later. All I want to say at this time is, God bless this great country of ours, the USA, to be able to celebrate our identity with freedoms that no other country gives to its people. This freedom of free choice and enjoyment of opportunities should teach us all a lesson of humility and unity as being a strong country with so many different talents coming together.

PART NINE:

Travels

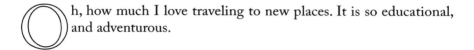

Moscow, Soviet Armenia, and Jerusalem

Oh, how much I love traveling to new places. It is so educational, and adventurous.

Moscow

It was very exciting, intriguing, and kind of apprehensive to get ready for traveling in Russia. Russia still had the hold on its fifteen republics including Armenia, with KGB watch. This trip was sponsored by the Armenian Prelacy of New York City, under the leadership of His Eminence Archbishop Mesrob Ashjian. The people of this group were from all over the U.S. It was a great opportunity to meet and get to know other patriotic Armenians toward their motherland, Armenia. We joyfully left the JFK Airport with the Sabena Airlines, flight SN548 on April 21, 1986. Our first stop was in Brussels for a flight connection on Aeroflot flight SU1232 to Moscow. This was called the Armenian Heritage Tour. Leaving New York City, April 21, and our trip would last until May 7, 1986, making our pilgrimage at the Holy Land at the end.

On April 22nd, when we got to Moscow, it was a gloomy day and quite cold. We went through security and we were interrogated, each one of us, quite a long time. The questions were such as, "Why you are visiting Russia as U.S. citizens, and how long you are planning to stay, and where else are you planning to visit?" Also, we had to declare how much American money we had in our possession, and they did actually count it. In addition, if we had any gold jewelry it had to be shown and declared on a written report. After each one did that, it took a long while to get through.

However, before a person was released from the interrogations, the person checking us very sternly would also ask, "What has been your job at home, and what languages can you speak?" Everyone had to answer those questions before being released. Now my turn came, going through all the routine things that I was asked, and when it came to the part, "How many languages can you speak?" I told this very grouchy man, and I added I knew a little Russian, too. He wanted to know what did I know in Russian, and he asked me to say something. So, I did, answer saying "*Paso vite doctora.*" (I need a doctor) Oh, my goodness, he started laughing so hard, and all my group friends were wondering "W*hat did I say to that grouch that spilled such a loud laugh from him?*" I then told them that I said, "I need a doctor." I had a Russian engineer friend who taught me quite a few sentences in Russian, just in case I needed them.

As this security man, signaled me to pass, still laughing, I said, "*Spacibo*" (Thank you) and moved on.

I am afraid to say that this was the only time we laughed when we were in Moscow. Soon after everyone went through the interrogation line, we saw the Archbishop Ashjian being taken away to a room and the door got closed. We, a group of thirty-three, were scattered all over the airport not knowing what happened to our leader.

The group scattered at the Moscow Airport, not knowing the fate of Archibishop Ashjian. Author has a hat, second person standing at the right.

After five hours of interrogation, the KGB decided to deport him to Frankfurt, Germany, thus he could not enter Armenia, which was our main journey, to be there to commemorate the April 24 at Dzidznagapert. That saddened all of us. The tourist representative then escorted us to our hotel, the Dwin.

What followed after we got to the beautiful old hotel was another revelation of being in a government-controlled situation. All our passports were taken at the front desk. After we were given our hotel room numbers, we proceeded to take the elevator and to reach our rooms. There was always an unknown person coming in the elevator, no matter when we took the elevator and listening intently to what was being said by anyone. Not only that, but also as we had one day to visit some areas in Moscow, taking a tour, we noticed strange things. First of all, they did not give us our passports, until we left Moscow the next day. Also, I am not kidding when I say this, we could not see even one person smiling in the streets or places that we visited; that was a fact. Another thing, the artist in me who loves to see color and smiles in people, did not find it. All the people, young and old, scurrying around headed to some destination, wore dark clothing, either black or dark brown. That just amazed me. There was no cheerfulness anywhere.

Virginia Apelian at the Red Square.

Then, we could not but notice as we passed a certain bakery that people were queued in a very long line to get a loaf of bread. The sad thing again was that, as we returned, the line was still there; only halfway through, they were turned back because the bakery had run out of bread. One has to see this to believe it. This was a small example of the way the Communists ruled their country. As we were getting the propaganda by the tour guide that there were no homeless people in Russia, I knew better that four-five families were jammed in one little apartment with all their children and one bathroom. You try to imagine that in the USA. You see this was an eye-opener. Not that I did not know about Soviet oppression, but it showed how its people were being treated by witnessing it, with complete control by their regime. Before leaving for Yerevan, we had to have our dinner at the hotel that was part of the tour deal.

By this time, I had taken under my care a nice elderly lady Mrs. Arminee Melikian from Arizona. She was such a sweet lady and I wanted to help her fill out her forms and simply to keep an eye on her. She was very fragile and I think she had a heart problem, because she would breathe very heavily. At the dinner, we were all sitting at a large table to be served. We had a very chubby waitress who lacked personal etiquette for serving us. First of all, I know this was 1986, the food in Russia was not appetizing at all, the meat served was like leather and the peas served with it looked green, but you could not chew them. They were hard as rocks. Don't ask how they processed their food, but, thank God, I had brought with me several jars of peanuts, chocolates, and crackers. That is how my husband and I made it through those few days in Moscow. Later on, we learned that they served horsemeat regularly. How little we knew, since we were not given menus to make a choice, but all got the same thing without questions asked.

Here was an interesting scene at dinner time. When dinner was finished, you could see most of the food was left on the dishes to no surprise of mine, including Mrs. Melikian's dish. When the waitress brought the dessert basket filled with bonbons, a kind of candy pastry with fondant with a cream filling, everybody hurriedly grasped one and ate it to satisfy their hunger, including me. Now, one lady from the other end of the table let the waitress know that she did not get one and that she wanted her dessert. Oh, my Lord, I noticed Mrs. Melikian was shivering; I surmised what had happened. Of course, I said nothing. However, the waitress with her chubby figure bouncing back and forth pointed her finger to the group, saying,

"I had counted that each one of you would have one." She looked at everyone suspiciously. "Who had two?" she inquired firmly.

No one answered. She repeated something in Russian and left the room. As that other person was still complaining not having had her share, Mrs. Melikian was very quiet and I know she felt guilty, the poor thing. But the waitress did not return with another bonbon. That was incredible for me to see. Would one more bonbon have broken the Soviet economy down? Don't ask; this was an education by itself.

Soviet Armenia

Now we were heading to Yerevan, Armenia, the next day, to be there for the Armenian Martyrs' Commemoration. The one thing that I was really overjoyed by was that the flight attendants in the Aeroflot airline were Armenian. Even the pilot spoke on the PA system in Armenian, as did the flight attendants. That was a novelty for me. But still we were very sad that our leader had to be detoured from this trip and only join us in the Holy Land, in Jerusalem, in a week. After all, he sponsored this whole trip and it did not seem fair and just. We discovered later that because he had religious books and Armenian Chants hymnals with him, they refused to give him passage. It was a threat to them, since it was such a closed society. We arrived in Yerevan, and we were brought to our Hotel Dvin.

Author at the Hotel Dvin balcony, from where one could see Mt. Ararat in the distance, now on the Turkey side.

327

Henry and Virginia Apelian at Sardarabad.

Our visit to Yerevan was much more pleasant and interesting. It had been a dream of mine since I was a little girl to see Yerevan and all the Armenian people. I had read about the city longingly in poetry and history. The first day, April 24, we first embarked on our tour buses, which took us to Dzidzernagapert, the famous monument for our martyrs of the 1915 genocide.

There was a long climb up from the bus stops. At this point, Mrs. Melikian was huffing and puffing until she got to the top. I was truly concerned about her. Several times she had to rest, and then continued with my arms around her. Thank God, she made it. After we laid our flowers at the Eternal Flame area, we took another walk to the area called Sardarabad where in 1918 Armenians fought with the Turks on that famous field and achieved short-lived independence. After all that, we went to an Armenian grill restaurant where they made superb shish-kebob and all the Armenian trimmings to go with it. That was a good meal. Then we had another tour in the afternoon. We went to our hotel rooms to dress more appropriately to meet the Supreme Patriarch of all Armenians, Catholicos Vazken I. Our trip to Etchmiadzin was very serene and educational, and it was a dream come true for all of us.

Virginia Apelian at Etchmiadzin Seminary.

Author receiving the autograph of the Catholicos Vazken I.

To my extraordinary surprise, in Armenia the word got around that Armenians, especially of Musa Dagh extraction, were visiting. People were coming to the hotels to see if any compatriots of theirs were visiting Armenia, and then obtain their itinerary from the hotel and make every effort to meet them.

We arrived at Etchmiadzin, visited the Catholicos, and then went to the Mass. It was so crowded, not even room for standing. As our group came out, my dear friend who had migrated to Armenia in 1946, was waiting for me at the entrance door with a big bouquet of flowers. I immediately recognized Lucine with her sweet face, which I had not seen for forty years. We recognized each other immediately. This was an amazing surprise for me; she was there with her husband and son, and her younger sister, whom I did not know. We hugged and smiled and cried at the same time. We had so much to talk about. They invited us to their home, but we could not go because our schedule was very tight. However, we planned for them to stop by our hotel before we left Yerevan. They did come, with gifts, which I still cherish with loving thoughts.

We had such a great time in Armenia; we could have stayed there for another week. I still want to go back to see Armenia in its independent state, since at that time, it was still a Soviet Republic. Yerevan had so many European and other continent tourists to see the birthplace of Christianity as a government. St. Etchmiadzin is a very special treasure for the Armenian nation. It is full of expensive relics which are unique in structure and beauty. They all are enclosed in glass cases. They were just breathtaking. In my opinion, there is much wealth in there, and they are highly supervised for safekeeping. His Holiness, Catholicos Vazken I, gave our group a special reception time to sign autographs and greet us all individually. That was, indeed, a great honor for us all.

The author in front of the Opera House.

The next day, we went to the Opera House. The Armenian people love music and the arts. The place was packed, not by tourists only, but by Armenians with their whole families. The prices were just right for people to be able to pay and enjoy the arts. The *Anoush* opera was presented in its glorious colors and with talented performers. That was a great treat to us.

The following day, we had the whole tour of Yerevan, and the famous old churches that still stand in their original glory. We visited Khor Virab (Deep Pit) where St. Gregory the Illuminator was left in a dungeon for thirteen years because he was preaching Christianity. In 301 A.D., the king became a Christian, too, and declared Armenia a Christian nation, the first in the world.

You can see the top of Khor Virab, which author is heading up to.

The author sitting on the wall of the church of Khor Virab.

Afterwards, a group of us went to Lake Sevan, and had its famous trout, made at the restaurant near the lake. Our taste buds were very satisfied with the delicacy of those famous fish. It was a fantastic day, all in all.

The next day was our last day, and we wanted to spend it with Henry's Uncle John Apelian, and his son Nishan and family and three sisters and their children, and Uncle John's grandchildren. I met them for the first time, but oh, my goodness, what a big party for Henry. Uncle John and his children had originally immigrated to Armenia in 1946 from Keorkune, Kessab, Syria. Henry had not seen them since then. And now, Uncle John had great grandchildren and they were a big family. I should say "a tribe."

Basically, Armenians are very hospitable people. No matter how little they had, they prepared a king and queen's feast for us. It was so heart-warming. I was interested to see the village of Musa Ler (Town of Moses), depicting the Musa Dagh people. Nishan was so nice he took us there in the afternoon, the road sign showing the name of the town in Armenian and Russian.

The road to Musa Ler, and the author.

Henry and Virginia near the Musa Dagh Monument.

Henry, Nishan and I went up to the Musa Dagh Monument and you can see the new village of Musa Dagh, now in Armenia. That was a very moving sight. The Turks had wanted to destroy us, but here we had built another Musa Dagh. Too bad, it was under Soviet rule, but not anymore, not since 1991.

That evening, April 28, was our last evening in Yerevan. We were to leave for Moscow the next morning, and then to Belgium. But what an evening that was! All the children dressed in their best attire entertained us with recitations and singing. The adults played their musical instruments, sang and danced. The food was plentiful, and the merriment went on until 2:00 a.m. We needed to have a restful sleep for the next day's trip.

However, I asked the matriarch and Nishan to come and see us before we left. I had an idea. I packed our biggest valise with all kinds of goodies: clothes and shoes, and gave it to them to share with all the families and their children. Things were so expensive for them to splurge spending money on fancy shoes and clothes. I was humbled having so much, and they had shown us such hospitality with all they had. So I felt to do something nice for them in appreciation. I left enough for a change of clothes, until we got to Jerusalem: the gray suit I had on with a red blouse, purse and shoes to match. I kept a blue silk long pants ensemble for dressy occasions and undergarments, another pair of shoes, a pair of white slacks and a top, and all the rest I gave to them. That gesture made me feel good. The matriarch of the family graciously accepted all, and thanked me profusely, saying they were going to have another party among themselves to divide everything fairly. We gave them both big hugs and thanked them for their hospitality and warmth. They left happily.

We still had about two hours' time, and now we did not have that much luggage anymore. We wanted to take a stroll. We went to the nearest souvenir shop as a last-minute excursion. To our amazement three interesting things happened in those last few hours. First, we were encountered by a well-dressed gentleman who approached us for American gum: Chiclets. I was so surprised to think that a nicely dressed gentleman would ask us for gum. I had some in my purse. I took a packet full of Chiclets and gave it to him. He was so happy and thanked us over and over. My curiosity was piqued; I wanted to see if they had Chiclets in their stores. They did, and it was being sold for four rubles. At that time, each ruble was four American dollars. You figure it, how much one little packet of Chiclets was selling for.

Then on the way to the Buryaska stores for souvenirs for only dollar exchange customers, and not for the Russian people, we met another man who seemed a bit of a questionable character, because as he approached us, he kept looking around and behind him. He wanted to see if we had any American jeans to sell to him; he kept saying in a low voice, anything you want for them. We politely said that we did not have any and walked away. We were originally warned about these types of requests, because that was a way of entrapment for us and then we would pay the consequences. As we entered Russia, we had to declare how much money we had and all the gold items we were wearing. Now here was the clincher: if we had more money when we were leaving, we would be in deep trouble. Also, if we had additional gold pieces, we would be stopped. They wanted to keep their wealth and they merely wanted our dollars.

Anyway, we arrived at the Buryaska. There were many nice things in there: statues, pictures, jewelry, etc. I love window shopping. I looked at everything, admiringly, and the young woman and the gentleman behind the counter smiled at us, saying, "*Drasti*" ("hello" in Russian). We returned the salutation, saying, "*Drasti.*" Then the young woman, with her broken English said, "I luv your ealrings." I smiled and said, "*Spaseba*" (Thank you).

"I relly relly luv it," she insisted.

I did not know what to make of it, so I kept looking around some more.

"Miss, you can pick anything here you want if I can have those ealrings," she begged on.

I looked at my husband perplexed as to what this is all about. Then I thought to myself, *what I have on is just costume jewelry—why not give it to her?* My clip-on earrings were a fine quality costume jewelry made in a shape of a hanging loop with a shiny gold finish. As I took them off, she was in her glory that this transaction could take place. Anyone could see how deliriously happy she was. I thought, so be it.

"Go see and take what you wont," she said happily.

Of course, I did not want to pick anything heavy like a statue or a big item. I finally saw something on the wall. It was a very artistic piece, which had a story behind it that I knew. It was a carved on copper of a young maiden called "Tamar" standing on a cliff, with her long tresses blowing in the wind and a lantern in her hand, looking desperately out, calling for her lover. It was such an enchanting piece; I could not resist picking it. It was 7 inches by 15 inches long, about a quarter inch thick. I thought this would be a marvelous exchange for my earrings, which of course, I can get another set when I return home. The piece that I picked fit perfectly on top of my valise with no difficulty.

I figured I would not get in trouble for it, and the young woman knew that, too. Besides, it made her very happy. And I was happy to own the piece I chose, which is on the wall of my family room now. Every time I look at it, it brings back that special incident in Armenia, and it brings a smile to my face.

In the evening of April 28, we departed from Yerevan for Moscow for an overnight stay, and then on April 29, from Moscow to Brussels for an overnight stay. There was something different in the air in Moscow when we departed for Brussels. It seemed the air was very heavy and foggy. Since we were leaving, we did not care nor did anyone make us aware of anything. However, when we got to Brussels that day, April 29, all the newspaper headlines were heralding a major catastrophe that had occurred in Russia, the Chernobyl nuclear disaster. This was a major health and economic threat to the Soviets, and even to the world.

My husband and I immediately thought of our children, who must be absolutely terrified to hear about Chernobyl since they knew we were in Russia at that time. Our daughter was married and our sons were in college. We called them all. They were so worried. Why did the Soviets keep the news from us all while we were there? I guess their secrecy was no surprise to anyone. The Chernobyl atomic power reactor was near Kiev, which was the third largest population center in the Soviet Union. The human toll of that tragedy had been kept secret from the world, even from their own residents in Soviet Russia. The *Washington Times Insight Magazine* reported in 1986 that several thousand persons had perished, and 50,000–100,000 people were exposed to doses of radiation that warranted long-term concern. However, all that was considered a state secret on their part, as has been a traditional response. In the Ukrainian Soviet Socialist Republic (Ukrainian S.S.R.) in 1932, a state-created famine killed an estimated 2–10 million people. The Russian government will never admit to creating this catastrophe and open the books to historians.

Jerusalem

Knowing all that, we left Russia. We were relieved to be heading to the Holy Land, to the city of Jerusalem. On Wednesday, April 29, 1986, we departed from Brussels, Belgium, and arrived at the Tel Aviv Airport. We had traveled with the El Al Airlines, I must say the most expertly organized airline we have ever traveled on. The security was absolutely thorough in every aspect. Once we got there, the checkpoints were just as secure and safe as one would imagine. At first, when we saw two army tanks lined at the dismissal of the passengers from the plane, it was a bit intimidating, but safe. As we were checked, I had a hat on with my long hair up in a French twist hairstyle. I was asked to take my hat off. I did, and then a security matron took my hair down—that did not bother me. There were so extremely cautious, which made us all feel safe. We were given pink and blue passes indicating we were an American citizen or having been born in Lebanon or Syria. They took us to two different rooms and released us to our destination of Hotel Intercontinental in Jerusalem. We arrived there on April 30th.

Hotel Intercontinental was a beautiful hotel, right above the Mount of Olives.

Hotel Intercontinental in Jerusalem.

My husband and I would get up real early to take a serene walk on the Mt. of Olives, which was so soothing every morning. The brisk fresh air gently touching our faces, to think of this holy place of our Lord centuries ago, and that these olive trees are still growing on cliffs and hilly areas. The panorama was just superb from the hotel window, and the rose garden. On the other side of the rose garden were rows and rows of hardy, fragrant rosemary bushes, trimmed neatly and professionally. It was a very enchanting environment to be in.

May 1st, we were scheduled to have the tour of Jerusalem, including the St. James Cathedral, which is owned by Armenian Christians. But before we took our tour, camel riders were outside on the hill to give a ride to whoever wanted one. This was my chance to have that challenging ride. Just another young man and another young woman of our group had tried it.

It felt so good and sort of scary. As the camel took a step each time, I thought I was going to fall down. It seemed that I was so high, on top of the world, and it was a great feeling. I could see the whole city of Jerusalem—what a sight!

The author on a camel. It looks easier than it feels.

Every good thing comes to an end; others were waiting for their turn. Gently, the guide made the camel sit, and I was helped to come off of that enormous animal. In the Middle East, they eat camel meat, just as I had learned in Russia that they eat horse meat. When one travels in different lands, one can learn so much.

The St. James Monastery and the Cathedral is a vast area of Armenian stores, boutiques, restaurants and jewelry stores, all run by Armenians. Here, there was no restriction of buying gold like there had been in Soviet Russia. I purchased beautiful souvenirs of Christian nature, such as a napkin holder made of metal, but with the *Last Supper* painted on them. I also bought plaques of the Armenian alphabet on china and on other materials. I could

339

not resist gold chains of Armenian crosses, which were more reasonable in price here than any place else I could purchase them. From the outside merchants, I bought a necklace, the beads made from olive wood from the Mt. Olive Garden.

The next day, our tour included the famous Dolarosa; Church of the Holy Sepulcher, and the afternoon of May 2nd at the special service at the Garden Tomb.

Then on May 3rd, our morning tour was to go to Bethlehem and Garden of Gethsemane. In the afternoon, we went to Bethany, Jericho and the Dead Sea. All these Biblical places were enchanting for us to be a part of. No amount of money could equal it. I was fascinated. The whole group was so delighted that our leader His Eminence Archbishop Mesrob Ashjian, was enjoying all these tours with us now, unlike the Armenia tours.

May 4th, the Sunday Service was beautiful at the St James Cathedral. We celebrated Easter this year twice, now with the Julian calendar in Jerusalem. Then, we moved on to tour Nazareth, Tiberias and Capernaum.

Virginia has a coke in Nazareth.

May 5th, Monday, was a free day to enjoy shopping. In the evening, we were given a party by the Jerusalem Armenians with recitations and music and food. This took place at the St. James courtyard. And on the morning of May 6th, Tuesday, we were all ready to depart to Brussels again for an overnight stay, then head home to United States on May 7th, to JFK via Sabena flight 541 at 3:00 p.m.

Between tours, the group is waiting for the bus. At the right, seated, Archbishop Mesrob Ashjian, and standing in the back, Virginia Apelian.

This trip to Jerusalem was most glorious. No words can express the feeling other than that I would like to go there again to savor all the Biblical places and the delicious food we enjoyed. Travel there was quite reasonable price-wise, too. Any Christian will enjoy this trip so enormously that is a must-see destination. In Armenian tradition, if you go to Jerusalem, you become a "pilgrim." Therefore, you must get a tattoo to remind you of that. I got mine on my right hand, right on back of my thumb, a cross and the date "86." Now, any Armenian can tell that I have been to Jerusalem on a special pilgrimage. And Praise be to our Lord's name.

27

France, Spain, Switzerland, Austria, and Scotland

France

It had always been a dream of mine to visit the most romantic city in the world, which I considered to be Paris. Its fascination for me was the world fashion being born there. I was granted my wish to visit France, and specifically Paris, at least three times in my lifetime so far.

The first time, we went to France in 1975 after I graduated from Rutgers University, Douglass College. Our daughter Arminee wanted to come, too. Our sons were watched by my parents. Arminee was fifteen and she was interested in fashion and wanted to join us. Very dear cousins of Henry, George and Aimee Bedirian, lived in Paris. They made our reservations for us at a hotel near their home. So, we were all set, and looked forward for our adventures.

As in New York City, Paris never sleeps; there is much going on. We went to the Eiffel Tower, parks, boat rides on the Seine, and visited art exhibits. Our daughter was fascinated by the Louvre and all its fanfare. Paris was very clean in those days, and the parks were a great place to read and to admire the flowers arranged in such an orderly manner and the shrubs manicured so proficiently.

We had fun with our relatives, who took us around to quaint restaurants outside of Paris, and to their country house in Biaritz. This was a beautiful house with many fruit trees on the property. George was the architect of their spacious garden. We had fun there and we were able to see many more of Henry's cousins near there, the Moscous.

There were other occasions, too, that Henry and I traveled to France: in 1989 after our daughter and our eldest son were both married.

Henry and Virginia at the Eiffel Tower.

The author goes shopping in Paris.

Again in 1994, we were on our way to Paris. The Bedirians had visited us in Clark, and insisted that we visit them next. That was no big ordeal for us, since we loved spending time with them, and it was always delightful to go to Paris. We enjoyed several visits to the nightclubs in Paris with Aimee and George, also their dear friends Dr. and Mrs. Michele Kazanjian. They were such lovely people and we had much fun with them.

*At Ani Kazanjian's house in Paris.
L–R: Virginia Apelian, cousin Aimee,
and Ani Kazanjian.*

Ani took the author to the new Louvre.

Author's last shopping spree at the Lafayette Department Store.

The last few days in Paris, shopping was a must. It was July 4, 1994, and I had my American flag scarf's red, white and blue colors on as we went to the bank to exchange some money, and then to the big Lafayette department store. The salespeople were so nice to me; they even gave me ten percent discount because they knew I was an American, as indicated by my flag scarf, and that it was our Independence Day. They seemed to know more than I thought they knew. I don't know why some people say that the Parisians are not very friendly. I found just the opposite to be true, but maybe because I was trying very hard to speak to them in French. They appreciated that. I noticed another thing in Paris: the French I learned in college was quite the same. I understood them and they understood me. However, I cannot say the same when we visited Montreal several times. They could not understand my French, nor did I understand theirs. I guess they use a different dialect.

The last time we were in Paris, the city was not as clean as it used to be. People walk their dogs, and the refuse is all over the parks. You cannot find

347

a place to sit without being extremely cautious not to step in dog refuse. That is a shame. I brought this to Aimee's attention, pointing out that they should have some laws against that. She said they did, but no one heeds the law. She also complained that the nature of the residents of Paris has changed enormously, and that is why she is now most of the time at her Laredo, Spain apartment.

All in all, we have had much fun in Paris. The last restaurant we visited with them was Restaurant Sannine, run by a Lebanese owner. Sannine is a beautiful mountain in Lebanon, and as a child I climbed it on school outings. This restaurant had fabulous Lebanese dishes, and was located at Rue Montmartre.

Spain

Spain is very interesting, too. We have been there twice. The first time was in 1975, and we visited again in 1994. I found it quite different in many ways. The attitude of the people is more non-attentive to tourists. That is the way I experienced it. Maybe because I could not speak the language, I had a communications barrier. When my husband and I travel anywhere, we like to go across country to get the true flavor of that country's culture. Madrid was very up-to-date for finding English-speaking people, but not the rest of the towns or villages that we traveled to. They don't speak any English and do not make an effort to see what you need. I don't know, maybe things are different now, we hope.

The first time we visited there, in 1975, we went to Santander to see a bullfight. We figured, we must see one when in Spain, at least once in our lifetimes. Our daughter Arminee was with us then; she thought it would be a different experience for her and that she could give a book report on it for school. This was quite a big celebration for the Spanish people. The arena in Santander was quickly filled to capacity. People came all dressed up as if they were going to ballroom dancing. That was surprising to us. Then the big show of an enormous fanfare at the beginning ceremonies started with beautifully dressed young women on carriages with Spanish regalia, and all the matadors lined up in a parade. This part of the show was very entertaining and quite long. The people cheering in the stands could deafen our ears, but that goes with the occasion. Soon the bullfights were to begin as shown by the anticipation of the people jumping up and down with their wine flasks in their hands and taking a sip on and off. This was allowed because many people were doing it, and there were many policemen around; no one seemed to mind.

348

The first bull and the matador were announced. They came out and the crowd went wild jumping and shouting and drinking. This was a new sight for us to experience. The bullfight started. Oh, my goodness, every time the matador pierced through the bull's body, the crowd went wild. It was beginning to get real bloody. I could see our daughter was closing her eyes with her hands, and I kept hugging her, telling her that soon it will be over. I kept saying to her "just don't look at it if you don't want to." The first bull was dead; the sword had pierced right through its heart, and blood was gushing out of the bull's mouth. It succumbed to its death and dropped down. Then, we had thought the crowd was excited before, we had seen nothing yet. The people stood up in their places, shouting things that we did not understand, and this kept going on and on, until the matador went and clipped the ears of the dead bull and threw them out to the people. More cheers and more shouting continued. We learned that if the matador in a short time pierces through the bull's heart and kills him, he is more revered. This matador got a standing ovation, and the people in a frenzy of adulation were nearly uncontrollable. This was such a new experience for us. As we were getting ready to leave, our cousins told us, this is only the beginning.

"What? The bull is dead, and they love the matador, what else is there?" I inquired.

"Oh, my dear, there is more," said our cousin Aimee with a cute French accent and a smile on her face.

At that point, I did not feel like smiling, and I was thinking about our daughter.

"I want to leave now, now," she demanded.

Just as we were getting ready to leave, another bull was released in the arena, and another matador appeared to fight him. It began quite swiftly; again the piercing and the blood flow had begun. At this point, our daughter started crying out loud, and wanted to leave. Everybody was looking at her as if she were crazy or something. In that culture, they could not understand our daughter's behavior. I turned around and spoke to my husband that perhaps we should leave now.

"Would you or I take her out of here now?" I asked my husband urgently.

"I will," he said quickly. He continued, "You stay with our host and hostess."

I had to, at that point, because they had paid for us and I thought it would be rude to leave them there and we all left. My husband and daughter left, she crying loudly, and people looking at her in amazement. I was so sorry she was having such a hard time, but I understood—here were animals being brutally killed right in front of our eyes. She definitely was not ready to get acclimated to the Spanish culture so suddenly.

Personally, I was not enjoying it either. One after one, each bull was being killed in front of our eyes. At one point, about the fourth bullfight, the matador was being booed. I did not understand why.

"Why is he being booed?" I asked curiously.

"Because he is taking too long to kill the bull, and he has not pierced his aorta yet." They both said in unison.

Oh, my goodness, here I was learning so much, but it was getting quite gory. Finally, the matador killed the bull, but it took the longest so far. He was booed out of the field quickly. This was an education by itself, hard to swallow. as they say, but just this one time I was witnessing a real Spanish bullfight. I promised to myself that this will be the only bullfight that I will ever attend.

"When is it going to be over?" I asked Aimee and George.

"Two more," they replied.

At this point I was cringing and wishing that I was on the outside of the arena with my husband and daughter. But I said nothing, and tried to be polite and stay until the end. I could not wait until it ended. Yes, two more triumphant matadors got their standing ovation, and soon we left. My husband was waiting patiently outside the arena having treated our daughter with the tallest cone of ice cream to soothe her. I needed more than a cone of ice cream to soothe my nerves after what I had seen. It is just amazing to me how each culture has its own way of entertaining themselves to have an exciting time. It reminded me how the Romans would have a grand time releasing lions and human beings and watching them be killed. Occasionally, I see a bull run on a news channel, an event that seems foolish and dangerous, but it does not come close to a Spanish bullfight. I understand that the Mexican bullfights are a lot tamer. Now, I kept thinking and asked our hosts why one bullfight would not be sufficient; why have seven of them at the same time?

"Because people pay the money and they want to see more of it," said our cousin George.

Then, we wanted to have a nice dinner. They suggested this special restaurant that always had fresh fish and it was the best ever. So, we went. As we were still having our dinner with their freshly baked bread, our daughter asked where the bathroom was. The owner of the restaurant said, they did not have one, but we could walk down a block. There was a soda place and they had one. Here, now I was biting my tongue, thinking how this little excursion will end up. While they were still finishing their dinner, I rushed out with my daughter to find this soda fountain where she can go to the bathroom. As we got there, I had to buy a coke so that we would be allowed to utilize their bathroom. Then, very quietly, I asked the person behind the counter where the bathroom was. This person pointed to a door and, as a woman was coming out of it, I said this must be it. My daughter opens the door and goes in and then I hear a scream "Oh, no, I can't do it here." I was embarrassed, but I walked in and to my complete surprise, there was no toilet there, but a hole in the floor. The stench was indescribable. I did not know what to do other than urge my child to relieve herself and then we could leave very quickly.

"Mom, I can't. I think I am going to puke," she cried, holding her nose.

Finally, she had to. Then I noticed a string hanging from the ceiling with a can attached to it. After she finished, I pulled the string and the can released water on the hole. We got out of there so fast; I don't ever want to remember that incident. Whereas, as we are walking back to the restaurant, she wanted to tell me that she did not ever want to leave America again, and that she will vacation in the U.S. only.

"That's a promise, mom, and I mean it," she said firmly.

"Fine, fine, honey, you may change your mind when you get older," I said lovingly.

"Never, never," she replied.

I told her when we returned to the restaurant to please keep herself calm, and we can tell them later about the situation. I said, "try to relax now," and then we will go to their nice apartment and have a restful evening—take a nice shower—and we will feel better.

The next day, George took us for a ride on his boat. It was very relaxing. My daughter took my picture on the boat with Uncle George's captain's hat on my head. This was at the Laredo shore, very calm and peaceful.

Here, I want to remind all the children of our beautiful country, the USA, that you all take simple things in life for granted until you are faced with things that are not so pleasant to get used to. I think, indirectly, this is a lesson to us all to appreciate what we have, and until you miss not having what you normally have, you'll never know the worth of it. I have heard and seen people chronically complaining about minor things or big things that this country does not offer them; my friends, all of you young or old ought to try to live in a foreign land, yes, even in civilized Europe, not even a third-world country, you will see the vast difference of standards of living. No comparison at all to our beloved country here in USA. Please do not think that I am preaching to you, dear reader. It is what it is, and I have lived on both sides of the world to know this.

Virginia on the boat at Laredo.

The last time, in 1989, when we went to Spain, we did not have our daughter with us. She was married then. But the memory of the first visit to Spain, I will never forget, nor will our daughter ever want to remember.

At this visit to Spain, we noticed other things that had changed; such as, the restaurants had security at their doors now, whereas they did not have that before. Also, the parks in Madrid were beautiful and very clean before with all their monuments, but at our last visit, there were homeless people scattered all over the park, and debris all over. What had happened, we did not know. It was very sad to see that.

Switzerland

Of the two most beautiful places that I have been to, Switzerland is one of them. My husband and I have been to Switzerland three times. First in 1975, and returning in 1989 and 1991 for pharmaceutical meetings, when my husband became the Director of Schering-Plough Labs. Our trip was after the children were all settled, two were married, and the twins were in graduate school.

I just love the Chapel Bridge of Lucerne. It is the oldest wooden bridge in Europe. In 1975, our first photo was taken right beside it.

Henry and Virginia at Chapel Bridge.

This Chapel Bridge is one of the most famous tourist attractions. It is 670 ft. long, crossing the Reuss River in the city of Lucerne. It was constructed in 1333. It was specifically designed to help protect the city from attacks. It is amazing to see all the paintings inside from the 17th century showing Lucerne's history. However, it is sad to say that what we saw inside, all these historical paintings, were destroyed in August of 1993 through a fire.

Adjoining the bridge is a tall water tower 140 ft. high. It is an octagonal tower built from brick, which is believed to have served as a prison, torture chamber of yesteryear, and a watchtower. This bridge with its famous water tower is Lucerne's most photographed monument in Switzerland.

During the fire on August 19, 1993, the bridge did not burn down completely; the pillars remained intact, but the roof was destroyed with the paintings inside. I heard from our Swiss friends that it has been restored. I am glad for that because I want to go and visit it again. I cannot remember with our three visits there, but I have crossed that bridge back and forth countless times. And when I came to America, I made a large painting of it which is on our living-room wall. I often look at it and think of the great visits we had there.

Another beautiful landmark of Lucerne is Mount Pilates. We went up there in 1975 with cable cars and lifts. Words cannot describe the beauty of this natural scenery.

The author on Mt. Pilates.

I have been on three beautiful mountains. One was when I was young. We went on our school outing to Mount Sannine near Bekaa Valley in Lebanon. This was a beautiful mountain with brooks running through it and fragrant violets, and bright red and pink cyclamen. Also, a very good herb, oregano, covered its slopes with its pungent taste and smell. This mountain has very beautiful memories for me as a child.

The second mountaintop I have been to was Mount Pilates in Lucerne, Switzerland in 1975. That was such a picturesque scene that it made your soul rejoice of God's magnificent creations and natural beauty of sheer joy.

The third climb up a mountain was Musa Dagh in 1991. This one was of a bittersweet nature. I did not climb it for its beauty, but for its history. This is where the Musa Dagh battle took place when my ancestors were being chased by the Turks. As you know from the previous chapters, I have described this battle fully; it is a very important part of me. I am glad that I was able to go there.

In 1991, my husband and I went to Switzerland again. We always stayed at the Palace Hotel. What a gorgeous hotel! Many celebrities have chosen this hotel for its beauty and first class service. Again, of course, we would walk across the Chapel Bridge to go to the other side for shopping and just looking around.

The Apelians went to a nearby Protestant church.

355

There was a very interesting scene I witnessed one evening when I went up to our room to get something, as my husband was sitting in the main lobby downstairs. It was very strange to see a man with a beard, not dressed well, sitting at the door right across from our room, eating a chicken leg from a small table in front of him. He was eating it as if he had not ever seen any food before. He showed no manners at all. I went into our room, got what I needed and came right out and went downstairs. I told my husband of this strange scene happening right across from our room. He laughed and thought I was joking.

"No, I am not joking!" I said firmly.

"Well, can you explain why a man would be sitting in the hallway and eating his dinner there?"

"Yes, it does sound stupid and weird, I know." I got up and went to the front desk.

"Sir, I know what I saw, there is a man across from our room [giving our room number], in the hallway, and having his dinner," I said to the desk clerk, and continued, "That is very strange in this type of a first class hotel."

"Let me explain," he said in a very low voice.

"Yes, please do," I said politely.

"You see we have the King of Jordan's son staying in that room, and that man is his body guard." He continued, "We don't normally have people sitting in the hallways having their dinner."

"I see," I said surprised. "Couldn't he have done it in a more discreet manner?"

"It was the King's order, and they paid us well; we cannot refuse an international request such as that."

"Thank you, sir." I left quietly.

"So, what did you discover?" my husband said in a joking manner.

"You know, you'll never find out anything if you don't ask," I said.

"So, tell me," he urged.

"No, I won't until you go up to our room and see for yourself," I said with a faint smile on my face.

"OK, I will." He left to go see what was up there. As he came back, he looked like he had seen a ghost.

"Oh, my God, who is that guy? He looks very suspicious. He looked me over from head to toe." And Henry added, "He looks like a slob."

"Now you know that I was not imagining things, right?"

"I am sorry, honey, that was too weird to hear that a strange man was sitting in the hallway and having his dinner. All these years that I have traveled here and to other countries with my work, I have never seen anything like that," he said apologetically. Then I explained everything that the man at the desk had told me.

The next morning, when we were having breakfast, sitting next to our table also having breakfast were that very man, the Prince of Jordan, and many of his entourage. Everyone was catering to the young Prince. He looked neat and dressed very well in a light blue suit, and was fair complexioned. He looked very young, about eleven or twelve years old. I assumed that he could be the son of Lisa Halaby, the new Queen Noor. Lisa Halaby was born in Washington, D.C. by an American family of Lebanese, Swedish and British descent. King Hussein had married Lisa Halaby in the summer of 1978, and she was his fourth wife. I remember clearly that she renounced her American citizenship marrying the King. Now this was an interesting story to tell our children when we got back. The intrigue of traveling overseas is just full of surprises. You see, hear, and learn something new every day.

On Sunday of our stay, Henry and I were dressed in our Sunday attire, and went to this Protestant church on the other side of the bridge. The sermon was all in German, and the only word that we understood was Jesus Christ, and we recognized the hymns. That was good enough for us. Also, there was a beautiful baby who got baptized, which was lovely to see. We prayed in the church, and that is all that mattered. The Lord understood that we had come to worship Him there, even though we did not understand the sermon in German.

Switzerland is such a beautiful country, clean and the people's pace is just like ours, just the opposite of Spain. Swiss people are very precise people and friendly. Almost everyone there spoke English very well. We bought some watches from there, which they are famous for, and embroidery items with their fine needlework. It is very expensive though to live there. Also, the hotels are very expensive. However, we found all of Europe very expensive, but I must say we got the best of service and everything in Switzerland.

The boat ride we took was very pleasant over the Lake Lucerne. It stopped at several villages, then we would embark, and it continued our ride and returned to Lucerne. When we stopped at different farm villages, we saw cows grazing on pastures with bells hanging around their necks, and the young maidens tending them. The girls looked so clean with their white caps and white aprons. Even the cows looked clean. This is silly to say, but truthfully, the whole scene was like a pretty picture in a book or a postcard. If possible, everyone should make an effort to go and see the beautiful country of Switzerland.

Taking a boat ride on Lake Lucerne to go to other villages.

Austria

Austria is another beautiful country, with its awesome cathedrals. We enjoyed it there, too, with amazing tours. We visited there in 1989, and in 1991 for a pharmaceutical convention. We loved Vienna, and we stayed both times at the Hotel Capricorno. This was a cozy small hotel with all the amenities, near the convention center. We enjoyed this old and outstanding city with all its unique places that we visited. In addition, seeing their horse show at the Spanish Riding School in the Hofburg Palace is a must. Joseph Fischer von Erlach completed what was then known as the "Winter Riding School" in 1735. This is where classical riding art exhibitions are held and continue to survive nowadays only in Vienna. Our Austrian friends told us that these horses are Lipizzaners, a noble and intelligent breed, developed at the Lipizza stud farm from 1580 onward. Today, Lipizza is in Yugoslavia. How these horses perform in their dancing and prancing steps is just amazing and mesmerizing. We enjoyed this unique show immensely with our Austrian friends, in this amazing, ornate baroque Grand Hall of the Winter Riding School with its Corinthian columns. What a show this was!

Another thing one cannot forget is the taste of their chocolates. So, so good!

The last day of our trip, my husband and I took a nice long stroll through the busy streets to savor the European atmosphere once more, when we came across an Armenian rug store. It was called Vartian Rug Company.

Henry and Virginia in Vienna, strolling.

Panos Feslian and the author.

"Let's stop and say hello to them," I said to my husband cheerfully.

"We don't know these people, c'mon."

"So what, we can say we are visiting from America and we just wanted to say hello, OK?"

"Fine, let's do it." He said it to please me, but really he did not want to. "Thank you."

So, we went in, and introduced ourselves, and they told us their names Vartian (Rose). We exchanged niceties, and then they offered us Armenian demitasse coffee and *paklava* (an Armenian layered pastry) from a backroom. Their daughter, a pretty young lady, a son, mother and father—all were in the family business. They were very sweet. We chatted a while, then they told us that there was a very nice young man working across from their store in that nice restaurant, as a concierge. They mentioned that he was from Ainjar, Lebanon. I perked my ears, and said,

"Did you say Ainjar, Lebanon?"

"Yes, he is a nice looking young man, and he is from Ainjar," said Mrs. Vartian, adding, "too bad he's married," looking at her daughter.

"We must go and meet him, honey," I turned around and told my husband.

My husband said nothing at this point, while he was enjoying his coffee and the *paklava*. After a while, we thanked these nice people and asked them to visit us in America some day, and left.

We headed straight to the restaurant across from the Vartians. We went in and met a nice young attendant at the doorway, and asked for the concierge. She told us to please wait, and she went into another room to get him. Here came this very nice, tall, dark and handsome young man. He said, "May I help you?"

"*Took Ainjaren ek esin mezi.*" (We are told that you are from Ainjar.)

"*Ayo,*" (Yes) he said surprised.

"Yes, *al Ainjaren em,*" (I am from Ainjar too) I said gleefully.

"*Inch e tzer anoone?*" (What is your name?)

"Verjine Matosian Apelian," and I continued, saying, "*ou ku announet?*" (and your name?)

"Yes, *Panos Fesliann em.*" (I am Panos Feslian.)

"*Ayt announe intzi shad modig ge tvi.*" (That name sounds very familiar to me.) Then I continued asking, "*Ov e ku mayrt, er announe arach vor amusnatzav?*" (What was your mother's maiden name?)

"Mari Atamian."

"Mari Atamian? *Ev ku kerinert Chahen, Setrak, Haik yev Hagop?*"

"*Ayo.*" (Yes)

"Oh, my God, you are my first cousin Mary's son!" I gave him a hug, and we exchanged addresses and telephone numbers as my husband kept taking photographs of us.

Now, what was the chance of me meeting my cousin in Vienna, not knowing that he had existed when he was born in the mid-1960s, when I already was out of Ainjar and he was not born yet. What an amazing and shocking surprise this was.

After we got home, I called his uncle Chahe in Canada and I told him that I met Mary's son Panos in Vienna. He did not believe it, and said, "Please don't kid me about something like that." I told him I would send him a picture. I then gave him Panos' telephone number. Then it started sinking in, and he asked me other questions.

That was an amazing stroll for me to have taken that last day of our stay in Vienna. Life can be full of surprises, from the least places we expect them from.

Scotland

I had never been to Scotland before. I was very excited to be visiting there at the 21st International Congress on Arts and Communications Conference as a delegate, and as International Woman of the Year. This special conference took place from July 3rd to July 10th, 1994. I took the British Airways Flight #4732 on July 2nd to London Heathrow Airport, en route to Edinburgh, Scotland, to reach our conference hotel. The conference delegation stayed at the Scandic Crown Hotel, Edinburgh.

This conference was sponsored by the American Biographical Institute (ABI) and International Biographical Center (IBC) of Cambridge, England.

Upon arrival, all the delegates had invitations in their assigned rooms for a special reception on July 3rd, by the special invitation of the general manager of the Scandic Crown. At 7:00 p.m., the reception was held to meet all the delegates from all parts of the world, called the "Who's Who at the Conference." At 8:00 p.m. we had dinner.

It was such a jolly reception and all the bagpipe players in their native kilts was a picture to see. That evening I met very interesting people from all over the world, among them was Russian scientist, Dr. Tangis V. Golashvili, head of the Scientific Data Center, Department of Atomic Energy in Russia. He told me that his father was Russian and his mother an Armenian. He spoke fluent Armenian with me. He was a very gregarious gentleman, and insisted that we get a photo taken with the Scottish bagpipe player.

Monday, July 4th was a very busy day. After a lavish breakfast, we met with the delegates to get our agendas for the week, and met all the new arrivals also. Then we were told that after lunch, the Queen of England was going to pass our hotel with her family: Prince Philip and Princes Charles and Edward; also, their guests, the King Harold and Queen Sophia of Norway. Oh, this was going to be an extraordinarily interesting day.

Right after lunch, I changed into my American attire, with a white hat, white pants suit and an American flag scarf around my neck and one tied on my hat. Among our own delegates, there were many others who had traveled from London to see their Queen. I was standing next to a nice English woman and her teenage son, who were waiting anxiously to see their Queen. I asked her, "Is this the first time you are going to see your Queen?"

"Yes, indeed", and she continued, saying, "I am so happy to see her." I thought to myself, *Wow, I am here only as a visitor, and I will be seeing the Queen of England.* What more could one ask for? The Scandic Crown Hotel on the Royal Mile was the focus of jubilant activity that day and two days after because of the Queen's route of travel for her visit.

The architecture of Edinburgh, capital of Scotland, is superb. The Royal Mile, where our Congress hotel was located, is one of the most famous streets in the world.

We witnessed the Queen's full entourage three days in a row, July 4, 5, and 6. We read in the papers that Queen Elizabeth was visiting Edinburgh to be with special friends for a child's baptism. This was an extra bonus for us all to see the royal family, three times in a row. The pomp and ceremonial march of the entourage was a sight to see, with all its colors and fanfare.

As the music was bellowing in the air that first day, July 4, we could hear the horses' hooves. The crowd was getting restless and, lo and behold, in the first carriage, a very royal looking Queen Elizabeth smiled and waved to the people. In pictures, most of the time, she looked matronly; however, in real life, she looked very exuberant and her skin seemed soft and silky. The reason I can describe this so lucidly is because I was on the front row of the people lining the street, no more than eight feet from her. She looked straight at me and waved and I got a big smile from her. I think I know she was trying to say "Happy July the 4th" to me. Even the English woman next to me said, "I think she knows you." When I heard that I laughed heartily.

That afternoon, our group had a bus tour around Edinburgh. Before I left for this trip, I asked a Scottish friend of mine in the U.S. at church what advice would she give me about Scotland. She said, "Virginia, take an umbrella and a raincoat for sure." I thought who wants to be carrying an umbrella and a raincoat on a trip to Scotland. But thinking it over, I said, she must know, after all she lived there. So, I listened to her, and I took my foldable umbrella and a light raincoat. Am I glad that I did! Not a day would pass without some rain. It did not last long, but if you did not have an umbrella or a raincoat handy, you would be drenched in five minutes. They were always very brief rain showers, but quite often.

That afternoon we had a special tour "In the Scottish Borders." We visited the Melrose Abbey and the Abbotsford House, where we had afternoon tea. We also visited the Cistercian Melrose Abbey, founded in 1136, which is notable for its traceried stonework. Abbotsford House was the last home of the famous Scottish novelist, Sir Walter Scott. The romantic mansion house in the heart of the Borders had been preserved as it was when he lived there, containing many of Scott's belongings and literary collections. After dinner that day, we had a full plenary session with seminars and a concert.

The next day, July 6, after seeing again the Queen's entourage for the third time, we had our luncheon, then a tour in the afternoon in Fife. We were driven by the picturesque fishing villages of Fife to the famous university town of St. Andrews. We had a brief tour here, which is considered one of the most beautiful locations in all of Britain.

Even before the founding of its university in 1410, St. Andrews occupied a key position in Scottish history. The 16th century castle perched on the cliff edge was first a palace, a fortress and a prison. The remains of the Cathedral still give a clear impression of the spectacular scale of what was once Scotland's largest church.

Virginia Apelian at the beach of St. Andrews where the movie
Chariots of Fire *was filmed, where it is raining again.*

The Holyrood Palace was walking distance from our hotel. My fellow delegate friend, Dr. Parsegh Tuglaji, from Turkey (his real name was Tuglajian, but working in Turkey, he had shortened it to Pars Tuglaji) knew of an Armenian architect in Edinburgh around the Holyrood Palace. He and I decided that we would walk down from our hotel and meet this Armenian former architect who had emigrated from Armenia when he was a young child, whose house was a famous Armenian restaurant.

However, now this gentleman, Bedros Vartanian, a very patriotic Armenian had transformed his brick house into an Armenian Museum calling it "Armenian Aghtamar/Lake Van." Dr. Tuglaji and I took a nice stroll down to Mr. Vartanian's museum house. He was delighted to see us, and was very hospitable offering us Armenian coffee and *paklava*. We had a very nice visit with him and you could see the Hollyrood Palace from his house, less than half a block away. So, all three of us walked to the Holyrood Palace and I had this photo taken by Dr. Tuglaji in front of the Palace gate.

The next day, aside from our tours and other activities, my two newly found friends, Dr. Tangis Golashvili and Dr. Pars Tuglaji, Ambassador for the Parliament for Safety and Peace in Turkey, had time to meet. He also had received the title of Count from the Swiss government, and Baron from the German government. I had been selected as the International Woman of the Year at that time. (I will explain in a future chapter how I attained that title.) We were all discussing our next seminar: issues of "World Peace" for 21st century.

In front of Holyrood Palace gate. This is the official residence of Her Majesty, Queen Elizabeth II in Scotland.

Falkland Palace and its gardens were enjoyed by Virginia.

I truly can go on and on about the renowned places we visited, such as the Prestonfield House, then a show of entertainment of singers and Scottish dancers, and the visit to the Edinburgh castle, which is one of the most famous castles in the world. It stands on a rock, which has been a fortress. I visited the house of famous Presbyterian theologian, John Knox, in Edinburgh, not far from our hotel, and his resting place. We visited art exhibits both in Edinburgh and the delegates' works brought with them to exhibit. There was a talk on Scottish literature by Professor Ian Campbell

Three delegates discuss the next seminar's agenda for "World Peace." L–R: Dr. Pars Tuglaji, Virginia Apelian, and Dr. Tangis Golashvili in Edinburgh Conference.

of the University of Edinburgh, poetry readings, and special greetings from the Lord Provost of Edinburgh.

And who can forget the "Roll Call of All the Nations" which included Argentina, Australia, Austria, Belgium, Brazil, Bulgaria, Canada, China, England, Ethiopia, France, Germany, Indonesia, Israel, Japan, Jordan, New Zealand, Philippines, Russia, Sweden, Switzerland, Turkey, Uganda, USA, and West Indies.

One of the attendees was Billie Wood of Arkansas, who is a direct descendant of John Napier, the Scottish mathematician. All of the attendees were high caliber people of their origin countries. The friendships made during that week would be a lasting, memorable page in each of our lives. We saw all these castles and palaces, met great people and had the privilege of seeing Her Royal Highness Queen Elizabeth II, her family and King and the Queen of Norway, too.

To end this fabulous week, we all dressed in formal attire, for a "Scottish Evening" with traditional cuisine, wine and entertainment, including singers, a fiddler, and highland dancers. During the evening, haggis was served with great ceremony as the bagpipes played while the Robert Burns poem "Address to the Haggis" was recited.

This was a heartwarming week I will never forget. I still get correspondence from friends I made there from all parts of the world. It was a learning process to hear, see and learn how other cultures live and survive. There was a special bond among all the delegates. We respected each other's differences with goodwill and exhilaration. We all must acknowledge our individual differences and respect those people who are different than we are, no matter what their skin color is or what backgrounds they come from. This is human dignity. Visiting other countries is a humbling experience, besides making us appreciate more what we have.

28

Middle East, 1991 and 1996

I had a long-cherished desire to travel back to where I had spent my early youth. It took me forty long years to have this wish fulfilled. Because of certain circumstances, I could not return until 1991. But I was very elated that finally the day had come; I would see my cousins, and the very places that I had fond memories of. Also, my husband wanted to see his mother, whom he had not seen for thirty-seven years.

The 1991 Visit to the Middle East

This was to be a two-week trip, August 4–18. We hoped to divide our stay in two parts: one week in Lebanon and one week in Syria. However, when we got to Damascus, we were supposed to have had my nephew and his wife from Ainjar, Lebanon meet us. They did not show up at the airport. We waited and waited, but they never got there. They were to meet us at 12:15 a.m., which meant after midnight. We learned later that they were there 12:15 p.m. on the arrival date, August 4th. They had their a.m. and p.m. all mixed up. Anyway, having arrived around 12:30 a.m., we waited until about 3:00 a.m. We were tired and wanted to get to a hotel, take a fresh shower and rest a bit, because the next day we had to get on the road with a taxi to leave for Latakia where we were to meet Henry's cousin, Steve Apelian.

We were getting frustrated to a point where there was a big commotion at the Damascus airport that no one seemed to want to process us to expedite our leaving from there. We suddenly heard an Englishman talking and we searched him out to ask some advice as to what was happening. He told us that as we hold out passports, we should have some American money showing at the edge; we would see how quickly we would be led to a line to leave the premises.

"We have to bribe them to get out of the airport?" I said surprisingly.

"Yes, and you will see fast action right away," said this tall Englishman.

"We would get in trouble for this kind of thing in America," I said to my husband, quietly.

"I know, but what can we do?" replied my husband.

We were exhausted from a very trying and long flight, which is another story that was very unusual. All the people from our Paris transfer flight were from Jordan and I had never seen a flight so unorganized and unruly ever. People were dancing in the aisles and the bathrooms were unapproachable, to say the least. And no one was listening to the flight attendant's pleas for people to take their seats. In other words, we needed a shower and some rest immediately.

In desperation, my husband put a $20 bill slightly showing at the edge of the passport. As the Englishman had suggested, immediately, someone came and escorted us to the departure desk. We looked at the Englishman; he winked at us as we waved good-bye to him in appreciation. At the desk, it was a routine procedure with them. The customs person took the passport, laid it down near a front drawer, very cleverly dropped the $20 bill in the drawer, stamped our passports and that was it.

"Oh, my God," I said, sighing, as we got out of the door. There were a line of porters ready to make some money by helping us. There was so much unemployment there. I noticed a skinny, young boy no more than eleven years old on the line, and he kept jumping and waving to us. I thought for sure that would be our little helper to get us a cab. My husband pointed to him, and he came running and picked up our two valises with joy and ease. It was amazing that he was so elated that we picked him. He got us to the end of the street and fetched a taxi—it was no more that two minutes. When we gave him $5, you should have seen his joy, jumping up and down and kissing my hand over and over. I think that morning we made that young child very happy to bring some money to his family. We were happy about that. During that year, the Syrian money had so inflated that one American dollar was equal to 1,500 Lebanese or Syrian pounds. Imagine how much money that was for them?

We asked the taxi driver to take us to a nice hotel since we did not have a reservation, thinking that my nephew and his wife were going to take us to Ainjar. We got there, we tipped him, too. As we came to the desk, the person behind the counter knew we were Americans. He immediately said that there was no available room. We knew that this was a tactic they used. The clerk we were talking with spoke a little English, but we insisted that we just needed to get in for several hours to bathe and rest, then have breakfast and leave afterwards. Listening to all that, he said fine; it will be $350. We were desperate, and we took the offer and paid the money, just for those few hours. We went to our room, took showers, and rested a bit.

We had a very nice breakfast in the main dining hall. We ate many fresh apricots, which were absolutely delicious. They ripen them on the trees before they are picked, so they have the essence of the taste of a real apricot. That was the only little pleasure we had before leaving Damascus. You could see many men, young and old, in the streets hanging around the street corners—no jobs.

Here, let me explain about Damascus a little bit. I have been there before, when I was a preteen. Once my father took us there to visit some cousins, and another time we went with a church group to see where the Apostle Paul was dropped down in a basket to flee Damascus when the Jews were seeking him. He had converted to Christianity with his amazing trip on the road to Damascus. He was blinded and later, he was able to see, and became the most ardent Jesus follower to spread the "Good News." Damascus is a very old city. It was flourishing a couple thousand years before Rome was founded in 753 B.C. That makes it the oldest continuously inhabited city in the world. It is a very interesting city and bustling with people everywhere.

My husband and I rented a taxi to take us to Latakia to meet Henry's cousin, Steve. We got started right after that excellent breakfast. It was going to be a long journey through the Syrian Desert. This trip reminded us of many former Armenian sad events when the Turks deported the Armenians from their native lands and persecuted them through the Syrian Desert.

Even though we were traveling in an air-conditioned car, it was very hot. We could feel the heat. All you could see was sand and more sand, and Assad's humongous statue right in the middle of the desert. This was an example followed from communist Russia. As we had visited Soviet Russia in 1986, we had seen enormous statues of Lenin in many quarters. This was part of their inflated glory for themselves.

We finally saw a building to stop and rest and have a soft drink. The building looked good, but what was in it is not worth mentioning. We each had a bottle of Coke, and then needed to visit the bathrooms. I am not going to describe the restroom, because it made me nearly sick. Soon, we left this building; we had more traveling to do. People ran toward the car in the middle of this dusty, sandy atmosphere to try to sell us American cigarettes on the black market, the brand: "Lucky Strike."

The driver asked us if we wanted him to stop, we said, "No".

Then we saw a bus traveling and passing us, filled with 150 percent capacity of people. One wonders about their rules and the laws. Not only did the bus have people sandwiched in like sardines, but also people were hanging out by the front door and on the roof of the bus. It was just incredible! Thank God, we finally got to our destination after six to seven hours. What a journey, but we knew it would be worth it because Henry was going to see his mom after thirty-seven years of separation. I was also looking forward to meeting her and all of Henry's cousins in Keorkune, Kessab, Syria.

It was delightful to meet Steve. After chatting and reminiscing, we started out for Henry's birthplace: Keorkune, Kessab. On the way, Steve asked Henry how much he paid at the Damascus hotel. When Henry told him, Steve said, "Oh, my God. You paid that guy a year's wages."

Here is a note of warning: if anyone goes shopping in the Middle East, always take someone who can negotiate in fluent Arabic. But when we were desperate to get in that hotel room, we had no one to negotiate for us. Anyway, we needed to freshen up and have a nice breakfast in the morning. It was a very costly breakfast, especially in those days. As they say, "Live and learn."

All the family members were waiting for us with a big feast. In the coming days, we enjoyed spending time with Henry's mom, especially, and the cousins too. My nephew and his wife in Lebanon came to greet us in Kessab. They were very sorry that they had mixed up the time—that they had confused a.m. and p.m. I promised them that in few years, I would make a special visit to them in Ainjar. I gave them all the gifts I had brought for them.

We had a great time in Kessab, because we also witnessed the wedding of Henry's nephew. It was interesting to see their traditional ways. It was very different.

Since we had a little extra time now that we did not stop in Lebanon, I wanted to see Musa Dagh where my people had fought the Turks in 1915. The Musa Dagh road was very close from Kessab, Syria. So, our dear cousin Steve again brought us to the Turkish border to get us a private taxi to take us to all of the Musa Dagh villages and back by dark. We gave him copies of our passports, and the telephone numbers of the American embassies both in Syria and Turkey, just in case we did not return by dark.

Many of Henry's relatives were trying to convince us not to go, because we would be on Turkish ground and we might be kidnapped or killed. I said that my passport said that I was born in Turkey, that I wanted to see my birthplace, and that I am an American citizen. Those three facts, I thought, should be good reasons for the Turks not to harm us. With that in mind and with lots of prayers, we started our journey to Musa Dagh.

We had a nice young Turkish driver who we thought knew English, since we had asked for an English-speaking driver. He told us that he spoke English "a little." I think basically those two words were the main ones he knew well. As we started, we said we wanted to go to Musa Dagh. He corrected us saying "No, no Musa Dagh—*Saman* Dagh" very slowly, and soon we came to the sign reading: "Saman Dagh." The Turks had changed the name from "Musa Dagh" to "Saman Dagh," meaning "Mountain of Hay." We were aware that this had been done because the Turks wanted to eradicate the history behind Musa Dagh battle.

Author stands beside the Saman Dagh sign.

He was very patient, listening to us to take us where we wanted to go. There were times when we would say "Stop here." He would stop and wait until we got into the car to continue. He understood that much and we were managing to communicate with gestures and intonations with our speech. He took us to several villages, and according to my parents' description, our house was very unique with a Spanish tile roof and the Yoghoun-Olouk fountain very near to it. Also, my parents had told me that we had circular balconies all around the house. None of the villages that we went to came close to that description. I kept saying "More, more," he understood and kept driving us to the next village.

Arriving at Yoghoun-Olouk in the center of Musa Dagh, I thought we had hit the jackpot. We saw the house with the round balconies, where men were sitting and playing cards and *tavli* (backgammon). There was the fountain very near it. My husband started taking photos of the house as our taxi had stopped in front of it.

Author locates the house where she was born in Yoghoun-Olouk, Turkey.

Henry continued taking photos of the house. Virginia was supposed to have been born with help from a midwife on the second floor.

Here is that Yoghoun–Olouk fountain.

375

The only addition there now was a minaret added on the other side of the fountain. I wanted to take a photo of the whole village, so we signaled our driver that we wanted to go higher, gesturing with our hands. He understood, we got in that lemon yellow car and continued our journey. We got the Yoghoun-Olouk picture.

The panorama of Yoghoun-Olouk. By the middle left is the minaret; the house on the right is the Matosian's former house, where author was born.

Now that it was getting late, we hurried to the top of the mountain without stopping at any other village. What a panorama! This is what my ancestors saw from the top. What a sight, scary, but awesome with its history. I looked for the monument that my father had talked about, which was built in 1935 in memory of our heroes, but it was not there. It was destroyed; we could see its remnants. Too bad, but I sat on a big rock at the very top, reviewing the whole history of that brave battle of my people in August of 1915. And we were there on August 15, 1991. Exactly 76 years ago to the month this visit of ours took place. What a historical place was this; the very rock I was sitting on probably could tell me such unimaginable incidents on that rough mountain. Then I stooped down from the rock and picked some thistle seeds, which I have kept in a jar in my breakfront at home.

Then we signaled the driver to take us down, all the way down to the shore area. He wanted to take us to his house, he said in his broken English. We said that we could not, because if it got dark, and we were not back yet, we would alarm Steve to call the American Embassy. The driver was not happy about that, and insisted still, but finally took us to the shore area.

There was a nice Turkish restaurant there; we figured, we had better eat first before we started our journey. We had skipped lunch, being so preoccupied. We were offered a very nice round table outside with a large umbrella over us. The sea breeze fluttering on our foreheads was a great feeling of restfulness and contentment after all we had seen. All three of us sat and we treated the driver, too, to a sumptuous shish-kebob dinner with good bread and a fabulous large plate of salad. We ate heartily and, to our amazement, listened to Armenian music on the PA system bellowing all over the near shore area. We thought to ourselves, how could this be—a Turkish restaurant playing Armenian melodies? That was a real surprise to us.

We left this shore area with our tummies full. This was the same shore from where my people were saved by the French battleship, *Le Guichen,* in September of 1915. I felt this was a trip well worth its time. I was happy to have done it.

My dream had come true, having been on top of Musa Dagh. What a feeling that was. We headed to the border of Turkey and Syria, from where we had taken the taxi. We paid the young driver and tipped him. He was very thankful and shook both of our hands in appreciation.

Our cousin Steve was waiting for us already. We thanked him and told him that we appreciated all his help while we were in Syria. He could speak Arabic very fluently and he was a prosperous businessman in Kessab. When we got back, everyone cheered and they were thrilled to see us, because some of them were truly afraid for our safety. They could not believe that we had heard Armenian music at the Turkish restaurant. They said maybe the owners were of Armenian blood.

Who knows? Maybe they were. During the massacres, many young Armenian maidens were forced to marry Turks—that was a possibility. Even our taxi driver looked quite like an Armenian, my husband kept repeating to me. Maybe that is why he was coaxing us to go to his home. That is still an enigma left in our minds, for him to insist that we go to his house.

Author sits on top of Musa Dagh, site of the 1915 battle.

Author stands near the shore where her people had come down from the top of Musa Dagh to board the ships to freedom.

The next day we went to church first, where the former schoolhouse used to be connected to it. Henry found the same school bench there as when he had gone to school as a little boy. This was in the Keorkune (a village near Kessab) church school. In the afternoon was the wedding of Henry's nephew. That was held at the Protestant Church of Kessab. After the church ceremony, there was a big party at the house of Henry's brother. Everybody comes to these weddings, invited or not; that is the tradition. The people come, dance and have a great time. Their motto is eat, drink and be merry.

In a few days, we got ready to leave Kessab. We were very happy to spend special time with Henry's mother. Steve again took us to Damascus, where we caught our flight home. Even though we had a marvelous time with family and were able to reach the top of Musa Dagh, it was great to get back home to USA. No place like it.

Our Visit to Ainjar, Lebanon in 1996

Now, this time, I was going to spend time where I grew up and until we came to America in November 1950. I had lived in Ainjar almost nine years, and I had such special memories and many friends. The first year of living in America, I had shed many tears, wanting to go back to Ainjar. But those tears had melted away long time ago, and I did not think about those tears anymore.

This time we landed in Beirut, Lebanon, and my nephew Albert, his wife Lucine and her cousins were all there to greet us. This arrival was a better flight, and we did not have to bribe anyone to get out of the airport. We were elated to see them all. We headed to Ainjar in their car. When we approached the town, there was this big sign welcoming us to enter in three languages: Arabic, English and Armenian.

Sign welcoming author back to Ainjar (Anjar).

379

As I earnestly looked around, I could see there were buildings added to both sides of the road, where there were none when I was growing up. As we got to their house, there were so many people awaiting our arrival with a big feast ready to be enjoyed. I was so tired that I felt like going to bed and having the festivities tomorrow. But I stayed up and endured it all. Again, this trip was in August, and it was for two weeks only, since both my husband and I were to get back to our jobs.

Each day was full of interesting activities. We visited my schoolhouse where I had gone to school.

The little schoolhouse where Virginia Apelian went to school.

Henry and Virginia Apelian sit in the Armenian Evangelical Protestant Church of Ainjar; Virginia had spent many hours there in church services, Sunday school, and youth groups.

Then the next day we visited the Omayyad Ruins, which is now found in Ainjar. I spoke about this in a previous chapter. This area has become a very big tourist attraction. I visited neighboring women grinding their wheat on rolling stones, which is a tedious job for the homemaker to do, yet is a necessary chore in preparing their dinners. I was surprised that they still did that.

However, now, they all had running water in their homes, the roads were paved and the houses had many additional rooms and electricity. Many, many changes had occurred, thank goodness. This was a pure Armenian town and the people were quite prosperous. They raised cattle and other farm products, and there were apple orchards and vineyards that brought in good incomes for the people. Also, the Armenian people are very education-minded. There were two successful high schools, and three major churches.

Actually, I attended our high school reunion. I was one of the first-year students there when I came to USA. I had skipped grades, and my classmates were much older than I. There were only my friend Zabelle

(Kerkezian) Kendrjian and I from that class. The rest had emigrated to Soviet Armenia.

Now Ainjar has beautiful restaurants and stores, and very nicely built additional houses. I was very happy to see all of the improvements.

Sister Hedwig and Sister Marie had done so much good for Ainjar. They had served there for twenty-five years. These two missionaries were angels sent from God. Both of them had passed away. How I would have liked to see Sister Hedwig again. She was one of my favorite mentors. Their good deeds will never be forgotten. I respected both of them. At the entrance to the school garden, stands the bust of Sister Hedwig. Halfway through our trip, my husband became very ill, throwing up and running to the bathroom every other minute. I felt so bad. The change in our diets and the local water were the culprits. And yet, I had absolutely nothing. That was amazing to me. In a few days, my husband's stomach settled down.

So, before we left for the USA, I wanted to go once more to visit Baalbeck. This is a famous, ancient city in Lebanon from way back, with Greco-Roman ruins.

The Apelians at Baalbeck ruins. On the upper left side, part of the Jupiter Temple columns can be seen.

*Virgnia Apelian midway in the center, below the
Temple of Jupiter.*

*Author sits at the massive foundation of stones beneath
the Roman Temple of Jupiter with finely crafted pieces.*

Here is a little background history about Baalbeck. As a young student in
Ainjar, I had visited Baalbeck several times with my class and teachers. We
had studied about its history and wanted to know more about it. Baalbeck is
located on top of a high point in Bekaa Valley in the eastern part of Lebanon,
about 85–86 kilometers from Beirut. This is a neighboring town to Ainjar,
which is also located in the Bekaa Valley. The Romans had conquered the
site and had built a Temple of Jupiter there.

Virginia watches the women grinding wheat for their dinner, still the old-fashioned way.

After the time of King Solomon, the Phoenicians were masters of Syria, and they had chosen the site of Baalbeck for a temple to their sun-god, Baal-Hadad. It is believed that the golden age of Roman building at Baalbeck-Heliopolis started in 15 B.C. when Julius Caesar settled a legion there and began constructing the great Temple of Jupiter. Centuries later, Baalbeck was controlled by various Islamic dynasties, including the Omayyads as in the ruins at Ainjar and others, as well as Seljuks and the Ottoman Turks. The history of Baalbeck is quite long and intricate; it can be a study by itself. But it is a must-see place when visiting.

My nephew called upon the Ainjar town's *zurna* and *tumboog* group (drum and fife group) to have the last evening of our stay a jovial one. They played on as we enjoyed delicacies prepared by Lucine, and danced all night on their front patio. Relatives and neighbors joined us to bid us "Good-bye."

*Last evening in Ainjar, the Apelians dance away most of the
evening with friends and relatives.*

During this night there was much barbecuing of lamb for shish-kebob,
and the scent was roaming all over the neighborhood. The dancing and the
merriment continued. However, the next morning when we were about to
leave, I did not feel so great. My stomach was warning me that I was going
to get sick like Henry had been. I had a delayed reaction to the new menus
I had ingested. You see, the animals are slaughtered and hung on spears
outside in front of the butcher's shop. No refrigeration at all. One wonders
how they can survive that kind of handling of the meat.

Anyway, when we boarded the plane in Beirut, I was very sick on the
plane. I was so embarrassed to be offered everyone's paper bags for my
throwing up. After we were home, I went to my physician, and he gave me
three different kinds of medication, and things subsided after that. I asked
him why I had become sick when my trip was almost over, whereas my
husband had gotten sick almost immediately. He said I had taken a little
longer to be effected by it. Then I asked, "How come in Lebanon they don't
get sick eating the same thing, meat sold that is not in refrigeration?"

"Because they are used to it, and if you had stayed there another month or so, you would have also gotten used to it," he replied.

That was not a pleasant ending, but I try not to think about it, since I had so many more happy incidents during that trip; I wanted to concentrate on them.

Lebanon

I grew up in Lebanon in my formative years as an American citizen. I loved this country. It is a beautiful country with its famous "Cedars of Lebanon." I have been told that the "Cedars of Lebanon" and the country "Lebanon" are used seventy-five times in the Bible. The cedars of Lebanon were very important to various civilizations. The trees were used by ancient Phoenicians for building trade and military ships. They also built houses and temples with the wood. The cedar of Lebanon has always been the national sign of Lebanon. It is proudly placed on the Lebanese flag in the center on a horizontal white stripe, edged by two horizontal red stripes, one on top and one on the bottom.

Lebanon has more than forty universities. A famous one is the American University of Beirut (AUB), where my husband studied in a pre-med curriculum. Most universities are located in Beirut, which is the capital of Lebanon.

Nearly half of the Lebanese people are Christians, which is the highest percent in all of the Arab countries. There are about four million people living in Lebanon. It is also believed that Jesus Christ had his first miracle in Lebanon, in Sidon, turning water into wine at a wedding.

Lebanon is located at the eastern end of the Mediterranean Sea, north of Israel and west of Syria. I could go on and on about Lebanon. There is much more to tell, but I wanted to give you a little sample of its identity.

The Middle East has always been an important part of the world history. It has been the crossroads of commerce and civilization among three continents. The Middle East was the cradle of Judaism, Christianity, and Islam.

At this time, I would like to speak of some of the Musa Dagh people who were very dear to me, both in Ainjar and the USA, and who have contributed a great deal to their people and society in general, whether they had remained in Lebanon or emigrated to the USA or elsewhere. I am going to start with the people with whom I went to school in Ainjar.

Mary (Janbazian) Sarmazian and I had so much in common. After high school, she studied in Germany and went to seminary there to become a missionary. In addition to that, she went to England afterwards and studied to be a registered nurse. She was a very warm person and helped her people in Ainjar in counseling and social work. She, too, was a pupil of the Sister Hedwig I described as influencing me, Mary and many others. Upon a special trip to the USA, Mary visited me and my family in September 1985 in Clark, N.J. with her brother, Rev. Dr. Movses Janbazian, and family. Our families had a great picnic in our backyard. We had so much to talk about.

September 8, 1985, Mary was visiting her brother's family and came over to the Apelians' home with them.

She returned to Ainjar, but then we saw each other more often when Rev. Sarmazian, her husband, had a call from Cambridge, Ontario, to be the pastor of the Armenian Evangelical Church. They moved to Canada in 1990. After that, she attended many of the Armenian Missionary Association of America (AMAA) meetings, and we saw each other often.

Mary and I always had this desire of helping people, no matter what kind of situations we were in. We often saw each other at the AMAA annual meetings and special conferences and dinners.

She passed away on November 5, 2002, with an unexpected heart attack. Mary is sorely missed by many and by me. I lost a great, irreplaceable friend.

Her brother, Movses Janbazian, also went to the same schools as I did in Ainjar, Lebanon. He was younger than Mary and me, but also a faithful Christian. We grew up in a Christian school and were geared to helping humanity in any way we could, under the guidance of Sister Hedwig. Movses became a minister. He served in South America first and later came to the USA. He became the field director of AMAA, and soon after, he became the executive director of AMAA. This organization has helped people in many countries to build churches, schools, and to feed the poor, the helpless, and the elderly.

My husband and I were invited to his ordination ceremony on Sunday, October 21, 1984. We had another commitment that we cancelled; we wanted to be there for Movses. So, at the Armenian Evangelical Church of New York, at 152 E. 34th St. in New York City, Movses Boghos Janbazian was sworn in "to the Christian ministry." He was such a great organizer

L–R: Virginia Apelian; Louisa and Rev. Movses Janbazian; his mom, Agnes Janbazian; and my niece Margo Habeshian; sitting with Vahak and Ani, Rev. Janbazian's children is his father Boghos.

and unifier that he would fly to Armenia and other countries for the sake of helping people in times of great need. Rev. Dr. Movses Janbazian was a great help to the human race. When the Armenian earthquake happened in 1988, he organized groups and ways to help those poor people. I participated in that big task of having quite a few Presbyterian churches in Union County involved in raising funds. As busy as Rev. Janbazian was, he would never forget to write a thank-you letter appreciating everyone's effort. He, his wife Louisa and his family have been to our house, and we, to theirs. When his parents were visiting in the USA, he made sure he let us know, since I knew them when I was a little girl.

At this point, Rev. Dr. Movses Janbazian was a major contributor in faith and action to bringing this major project of the AMAA headquarters to fruition on October 17, 1998.

Occasionally, he gave a sermon at the Armenian Presbyterian Church of Paramus. The great spirituality that he passed on to the listeners was

At the opening of the AMAA headquarters in Paramus, L–R: Rev. Hovhannes and Mrs. Sarmazian, Rev. Dr. Movses Janbazian, and Virginia and Henry Apelian.

evident. He was tireless, always on the go to help the human race in all corners of the world. Too bad his life ended too in a sudden heart attack in 2000, sitting at his desk, at the age of 55. His philanthropic legacy will live on. With the kindness of his wife, Louisa, we were gifted with Movses' book, *Man of Vision with a Mission,* with wonderful sermons of his and portraying his life from beginning to end. In Yerevan, there is a school named in honor of Rev. Janbazian; also, a street is named after him in Ainjar, Lebanon. And just recently, the July-September 2010 issue the *AMAA News* informed us that there is a special hall named after Rev. Janbazian in Ainjar. This is the celebration of the 70th birthday of Ainjar. Therefore, this special multi-purpose hall includes a sound system and LCD projection, and will be utilized for workshops, lectures, meetings, and a chapel for students.

Here, I would like to say a few things about the work of the AMAA. It was founded and incorporated in 1918 as a non-profit charitable organization in 1920. Its purpose is to serve the physical and spiritual needs of people everywhere, both at home and overseas. The AMAA is a worldwide outreach, charitable organization. The countries it covers include Argentina, Armenia, Australia, Belgium, Brazil, Bulgaria, Canada, Cyprus, Egypt, France, Georgia (former Soviet republic), Germany, Greece, Holland, Iran, Iraq, Russia, Syria, Turkey, United States, and Uruguay.

The Armenian Missionary Association of America's headquarters is in Paramus, N.J., which helps all the mentioned countries with churches, college and seminary scholarships, and Christian literature. It has aided many countries mentioned with relief aid, both money and food, and has provided emergency relief aid to victims of natural disasters. It has also sponsored an orphanage in Mozambique.

On several occasions, I have visited my early childhood classmates and dear friends in California who had emigrated from Soviet Armenia. They were happy now, but originally were sent to Siberia by Stalin, the cruel Soviet leader. Stalin had discovered that both of my friends' fathers, in youth, had belonged to the Tashnag political party. Whoever was found to be sympathetic to Tashnags ended up in Siberia, my friends told me. Lucine's father became ill in the frigid climate there, and died. Both Iskuhi's and Lucine's families had a very bad time, and nearly starved in that frozen forest of Siberia. When they told me the story, they cried, would tell a bit more, cried, and continue the horrific story. These were the two friends that I had missed when they left Ainjar for Armenia in 1946. At that time, I cried my eyes out wanting to go to Armenia, too. God works in mysterious ways. Those Russo-Armenians did not accept my father when he told them that he had been in America.

*Childhood friends seen again with such glee in California in
1994, L–R: Iskuhi Hovsepian, Virginia, and Lucine Igarian.*

*Virginia visited her cousins in Glendale, Houry Dorian and
Jirayr Der Kaloustian, and was very happy to see them.
They had moved there from Lebanon.*

392

I spent such happy times with Iskuhi and Lucine and their families and cousins. Lucine made her famous *kufte* Armenian dish, which was very good. Sorry to say, I lost Lucine as one of my friends to her heavenly rest a few years back. She had suffered too much in Siberia, and it caught up with her. Iskuhi lost her husband last year. We talk often on the telephone. It is so amazing that I saw them again after so many years since we were so little. Thanks be to God.

Houry Dorian is a favorite cousin of mine. We talk often on the telephone, and visit as much as we can. Her brother Jirayr lives nearby. I used to tutor him in Lebanon, even though I was in grade school at the time.

I also visited other Musa Dagh folks and I interviewed them about the Musa Dagh Battle of 1915.

In 1994, Hovhannes Hajian talks about his experience on Musa Dagh to the author and her father's first cousin, Mrs. Victoria Gambourian.

Both of these people were so sweet and remembered a great deal about the Battle of Musa Dagh. Again, I am sorry to say that both of them have gone to their heavenly rest also.

Haroutune P. Boyadjian—I met this distinguished gentleman in Trenton at a celebration that we were invited to by the Speaker of the State Assembly Chuck Haytaian, on behalf of our Governor Thomas Kean of New Jersey. That was in April of 1982, when we were at a special luncheon commemorating the Armenian Genocide. Mr. Boyadjian learned that I was a Musa Dagh descendant, came over to our table, and had a very long and interesting conversation with me. He had written a very nice inscription in his book, *Musa Dagh and My Personal Memoirs,* to present to me. I was quite surprised and elated for this gift. I thanked him graciously, and he said we could meet again to continue our conversation about our people. He was of Musa Dagh extraction and was from the village of Hadji-Habli. A very well-educated person, he had lived most of his life in Jerusalem, after the deportation from Turkey. I heard he lectured again regarding the genocide in celebrating the Armenian heroic battle of Musa Dagh in Philadelphia.

I did not see Mr. Boyadjian after that first meeting, but he had left a good impression on me. One day I was at the Armenian Presbyterian Church in Paramus for a special program, and there I met his daughter. I knew of Lucy Jangigian, but I did not know that she was the daughter of Mr. Boyadjian. We started talking, and she revealed to me that she was of Musa Dagh descent. I became interested to know her maiden name. Then we put the pieces together, and talked about her father.

Now, let me tell you about Lucy who is a magnificent artist. She has been published in many periodicals and has traveled all over the world with her art exhibits. She is unique in her field of graphic and expressive art which depicts the Armenian massacres and other compassionate issues. She has a series of paintings called "The Uprooted."

Dr. Vazken Der Kaloustian—is a fine gentleman and a friend. He is a medical doctor, and was a teaching medical professor in Canada's McGill University. He is retired now, but would travel miles to see and be with his compatriots to celebrate our heritage. I had met him in Ainjar when he was a young boy, and then again in 1965 when I had organized the Musa Dagh Educational Association of America (MEAA), he made a long journey to enjoy the festivities with us. And later on, he joined our executive meetings for planning future programs that took place at my house in Clark, N.J. He has stayed at our house as a guest. When my husband and I traveled to Canada, he graciously invited us to dinner. He comes from very good stock. His father, Movses Der Kaloustian, was one of the major leaders of the Musa Dagh battle in Turkey in 1915 and was loved by all. He had also served in the Lebanese Parliament for a long time and was very respected by all of his constituents, whether they were Armenian or not.

Here, I must mention about his writing talent. Movses Der Kaloustian, as a young man after the Musa Dagh battle, had written a beautiful and impressive piece of prose called *"Ardasvogh Abarajé"* (The Weeping Rock). This exceptionally well-known piece was written under his pen name, "Anoushavan Leylanie." It depicted this rock as a place where the pilgrimage of the Musa Dagh people went to fight for their freedom with many tears, and candles having been burnt on it with fervent prayers. And the writing ends with a proclamation of peace and harmony.

When I was eleven years old and in the first year of high school in Ainjar, Lebanon, I was asked by my teachers to recite this piece verbatim at our year-end pageant.

Years later in the U.S., after I was married and had children, I recited this classic piece of Anoushavan Leylanie in one of the ARS conventions that I attended. Thus far, it has not been translated into English or any other language, as far as I am aware. Maybe one day, I will and hope I will do justice to it, because sometimes in translating an important writing, some of the sense of the original essence may get lost.

Also, Dr. Vazken's grandfather, Father Apraham Der Kaloustian, was another brave leader of the resistance of the Musa Dagh people in 1915. They were from the village of Yoghoun-Olouk, where I was born.

On April of 1982, when I served on the executive committee of the Armenian Genocide Commemoration, tri-state level, there was another Musa Dagh member, Miss Baydsar Keoshaian. The New Jersey newspapers had headlined three young men of 14 and 15 years old, who had, or would be,

At the Armenian Prelacy in NYC, R-L: Virginia Apelian, Rev. Dr. Janbazian, Miss Keoshaian, Louisa Janbazian, Miss Baydsar Keoshaian, and friend.

395

graduating from Rutgers University at that tender age. They were Sehrope Sarkuni, who graduated from Rutgers on May 19, 1999 at 15; his brother Hannes, who had graduated at 14; and their cousin, Shant Sarkuni, 14, who was going to graduate in 2000. Those are the children of the Keoshaian brothers of Baydsar. The boys' father has a master's degree from Columbia University, and runs his own software business.

I knew of John Vartan from Dr. Vazken Ghougassian of the Prelacy. I had never met Mr. Vartan, but heard a great deal about him. He was another Musa Dagh gentleman, the uncle of the young Rutgers graduates. Mr. Vartan had made an outstanding name for himself by donating $4.5 million to the Prelacy Endowment Fund. He was born in Ainjar, Lebanon on February 8, 1945, six years after the Musa Dagh villages were refugees in 1939 in the Bekaa Valley and had grown up in Ainjar.

He came to the USA and became a devoted American citizen. He became a real estate developer, banker, restaurateur, building contractor, and a noted philanthropist in the Harrisburg, Penn. area where he lived.

He obtained an engineering degree from the Michigan Technological University, and a master's degree from the Pennsylvania State University. Then, beginning in the early 1970s, and subsequently, he started his own firms. He succumbed to throat cancer and died on December 14, 2004, having done much philanthropic work for colleges and other schools in Pennsylvania.

Also, working at the Armenian Prelacy as the executive director is Dr. Vazken Ghougassian, another Musa Dagh talent who executes all the activities of the Prelacy under His Eminence of Archbishop Oshagan Choloyan. Dr. Ghougassian is also a native of Ainjar, and lives in New York with his wife and son.

I am also glad to say that the first Armenian president was of Musa Dagh extraction. That is when Armenia gained its independence in September of 1991 from USSR rule. My husband and I met the first President of Armenia, Dr. Levon Der Bedrossian, on September 25, 1994. This was the third anniversary event of the independence of the Republic of Armenia held at the Broadway Ballroom of Marriott Marquis Hotel in New York City, near Times Square. He gave an ovation-deserved speech. The audience could hear his command of language and understand the essence of his speech.

In 1994, the director of public relations of the Diocese of the Armenian Church of America, Christopher H. Zakian, upon my request had supplied a beautiful biographical sketch of the first president of the Independent Republic of Armenia. Thus, Levon Der Bedrossian was the first non-communist president of Armenia. He was born on January 9, 1945 in Aleppo, Syria, of a Musa Dagh family that had immigrated to Armenia in 1946.

June 9, 2002, at the Requiem of Catholicos Karekin I at the St. Vartan Cathedral in NYC. L–R: Dr. Vazken Ghougassian, Virginia Apelian, and Henry Apelian.

In 1968 he graduated from Oriental Studies in the Philology Department at Yerevan State University. Then he continued his studies at the Leningrad Institute of Oriental Studies and completed his master's degree in 1971, specializing in Armenian and Syriac philology. In 1972, he became a doctoral candidate; thus, from 1972–1978 he was a junior scholar at the Institute of Literature of the Armenian Academy of Sciences. Also, from 1978–1985, he worked at the Madenataran in Yerevan. As a mater of fact, in 1985 he was appointed as a senior scholar at the same institution, at the Mesrob Mashdots Manuscript Repository Madenataran. While doing this important job, he taught at the Patriarchal Seminary of Holy Etchmiadzin. In 1982, he was awarded a Ph.D. in philology.

397

Der Bedrossian started his political activities in the 1960s. He participated in student movements, and ran a campaign for the recognition of the Armenian Genocide of 1915, and he was jailed in 1966 for ten days. At that time, the Soviets had constricted all the historical freedoms of Armenians. He got recognized as a member of the Armenian National Movement, and became a member of the Karabagh Committee. Right after the December 1988 earthquake in Armenia, he was imprisoned again in Moscow with the other leaders of the Movement. However, three months later, he was elected as a deputy to the Supreme Soviet of Armenia and as its president in the February 1990. Then in September 1991, the people of Soviet Republic of Armenia voted in a special referendum to have a free independent state. Of all the votes cast, 99 percent voted for independence. Der Bedrossian was elected by a landslide receiving 80 percent of the votes cast.

When my husband and I met Dr. Levon Der Bedrossian on September 25, 1994, it was a great celebration for the tri-state Armenians who were present. He was addressed as His Excellency in celebration of the third anniversary of the Independent Armenia. The program was from 7:00–10:00 p.m. The master of ceremonies for the evening was Benon Sevan, who was the Assistant Secretary General of the United Nations.

Although I have not met him, I have spoken to another renowned Musa Dagh scholar: Dr. Vahram Shemmassian, Assistant Professor of Armenian and Director of Armenian Studies, California State University at Northridge. His specialty is Musa Dagh history.

I am sure there are many more deserving Musa Dagh famous people that I have not met, but I know that they are out there in the Diaspora. Kudos to all of them for the great faith they have kept to excel in opportunities given to them in serving people of all backgrounds, in making a difference in society. If each one of us adheres to hard work, dedication, sacrifice, and patience, we will succeed in reaching our goals. And having faith in our Almighty God, we will not be derailed from our goals.

29

Hawaii and Three Cruises

Hawaii

What can one say; all four times I have been in Hawaii, I have found it a sheer paradise. This is one of the two most beautiful places I have ever been to. I am glad now that it is our newest state as of August 21, 1959. It is very beautiful, and the only state of ours made up of islands. Its capital is Honolulu on the island of O'ahu. We stayed in Honolulu the first time we visited Hawaii in 1987. This newest state of ours encompasses almost the whole volcanic Hawaiian island chain, which is spread over 1,500 miles.

Honolulu has become much too crowded, even the beaches are extraordinarily busy. So, the rest of the visits that we went to Hawaii, we preferred to go to the Island of Maui. Its beaches are clear and vast, and the white sand in contrast to the blue Pacific Ocean is an artist's dream. We stayed at the Westin. All the hotels are beautiful, each one is better than the other, with magnificent flowers, flamingoes, and luaus. We visited many historical places, and attended quite a few luaus. While in Honolulu, my husband and I visited the Presbyterian Church on Sundays. The people were mostly tourists, and the minister was originally from New Jersey, so he made it a point to go through all the states, and called on people to rise and be greeted. He was thrilled that we were from his home state. Another thing that caught my eye was that people attended with leis around their necks and flower crowns on their heads. That was so novel for us.

In 1987, at a luau with Don Ho, Henry and Virginia are toasting the occasion.

The Apelians meet Don Ho.

Don Ho performed so well, and his friendliness was apparent. He was willing to take photos with us.

In 1989, we went to Hawaii again, to a pharmaceutical convention. There were many special programs prepared for our entertainment.

We just could not stay away from Hawaii. We, again visited Hawaii, and this time we stayed on the Island of Maui, at the Westin. After a major pig roast, came the dancers. The women had a class to teach us how to make orchid lei. It was very interesting and fun to do. We were allowed to keep them.

After the pig roast and making an orchid lei, the author sits and relaxes in the lush environment.

One more time, 1995, we visited Hawaii, this heavenly place. This time we had a two-prong plan. The first week, we would spend in Hawaii in December, and celebrate Christmas there, which would be very unusual and exciting. Imagine going to the beach in swimming gear, singing Christmas carols, and having beautiful Christmas trees erected everywhere with the brightest of red poinsettias. This was a very unusual sight to see. In the back of our minds, we were imagining snow shoveling and frigid weather in New Jersey. But we were glad we were experiencing this tropical Christmas at this time.

The Apelians stroll down by the oceanfront, dressed as the natives.

The author is saying "Good-bye" to this heavenly place by the hotel oceanfront.

Yes, it was sheer heaven to be in such beautiful surroundings. To visit Hawaii at least one time, creates such beautiful memories for a person for a lifetime. The second week, we spent with Henry's sister, brother and family in California. I also visited my cousins and my dear friends from Armenia.

Our First Cruise, Celebrating Our 25th Anniversary

We took a Carnival Cruise Line "Fun Ship" to the *Mardi Gras* in 1985, the month of June to celebrate our 25th Wedding Anniversary. This was our very first cruise. Now that we had raised our children, our daughter was married, and our three sons were in college, we were ready to travel leisurely. The programs of the shows, the recreation, and the food, all were super. One can stay on a ship like that for a month, but thank goodness they have good exercise rooms, too. If one does not exercise daily, with all that great food, one will return home thirty pounds heavier. No one wants that.

The sad thing was that our best friends, Mr. and Mrs. Donald Turner, were going to celebrate with us and their 27th anniversary, but could not. Don, a successful architect, became ill and developed a brain tumor. It is a sad story. He had made all the arrangements for the cruise. He passed away after a few years. One never knows what is ahead of us. It is good to be content with what we have and enjoy life as we can when we can. They were sorely missed by us on the cruise.

Our first stop was Mexico. We found the country very poor. Our next stop was Grand Cayman Islands. The scuba divers had fun for a few hours. My husband and I are not divers, so we went strolling in the market places and shopped. There was a big fair with a craft show sponsored by the local school parents' organization. It was lovely by the waterfront. I bought some souvenirs there, and then we went back to our ship. We headed to Jamaica.

The author in Jamaica by the ship.

Strolling Jamaican streets with friendly Jamaican children.

Jamaica was a happier atmosphere than Mexico, and a busier place than the Grand Caymans, perhaps because we did not do any scuba diving. The people were especially very cheerful and friendly in Jamaica. I purchased some very beautiful ivory bracelets with real gold weave through each piece. Also, I purchased a family of carved wooden birds from a young craftsman. They are very appreciative when you buy their handmade crafts. Soon, we embarked our ship happily, and there was much waiting for us in the ship, with special shows and anticipation for Captain's Ball.

They sang "Happy Anniversary" to Virginia and Henry.

At our table, we were sung to, "Happy Anniversary," by the ship personnel. Then before we dined, the captain of the ship met each couple with a photo shooting opportunity. Formal attire was requested for this special occasion.

Mr. and Mrs. Apelian meet the captain. (Courtesy of *Mardi Gras.*)

Next was the big show, the "Passenger Talent Show." We were there for fun, so I joined the talent show to sing. After all, the very first time that my husband saw me in 1955 was when I sang a solo at the commemoration of the Armenian heroes of Musa Dagh.

The Passenger Talent Show on the Mardi Gras.

It was a fantastic cruise, and we had much fun and met new people and made new friends. For major relaxation, this is the tonic for it. When we came home, we had another major celebration for our 25th Wedding Anniversary. Our children had worked very hard to get everything arranged, having called all our friends, and arranged for catered food. This took place a week later, when our daughter had purposely taken us on an outing, while everything was being arranged and prepared at our house. When we returned, we were utterly surprised. Our house was buzzing with friends all over the place and we were really amazed how much work they had done in about three hours. The furniture was rearranged, balloons and silver decorative bells were hung over the railings, and all kinds of appetizers were plentiful at the tables. Some of the people there we had not seen since our wedding. Our daughter had discreetly kept our wedding party list and worked from that. That was really good planning on her part. What can I say? God has blessed us with wonderful children. Thanks be to God.

Our Second Cruise—to Alaska

Our second cruise took place in August of 1998. This was a two-week journey. The first week was to Alaska, and the second week we took a bus tour to see major historical sights in USA. This time, we took the Holland America Line, the *Maasdam*. It was a beautiful ship and extremely clean. Holland America is known for that. All the rooms and hallways were immaculately clean. They also did not demand any tipping, just as you wished to do so. Since they were so organized and helpful in every way, people felt obligated on their own to tip generously. We did. Every night before bedtime, our room would have a big bowl of fresh fruit besides all of the festive foods served already on board.

Alaska is the largest state in the USA by area. It is in the northwest edge of the North American continent, with Canada on the east, the Arctic Ocean in the north, and the Pacific Ocean to the west and south. Russia is in very close proximity. Alaska was bought from Russia in 1867. It became the 49th state of the USA on January 3, 1959, right before Hawaii, which became the 50th state on August 21, 1959. Alaska is the least densely populated state in the U.S., and most people are in the proximity of Anchorage.

I guess it is the least populated state because, in my opinion, it is farther than the mainland for many conveniences, plus it is quite frigid there. When we got there in August, many states were hot and sizzling, whereas, we were lucky if we reached 65–70 degrees. The ship provided blankets to wrap around us in order to go out on the deck and enjoy the scenery of the icebergs.

Henry and Virginia on the deck to watch the icebergs.

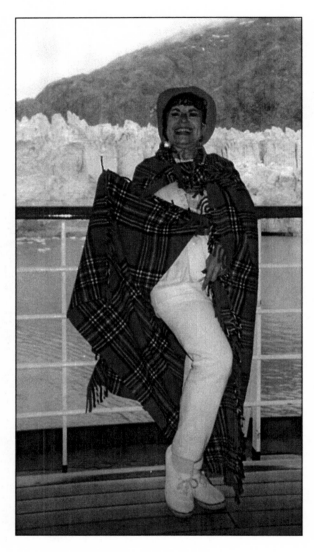

Posing on the deck with the icebergs behind.

The fresh air was quite welcome by us all, and some of us took special walking tours on ice. Others took helicopter rides within close proximity to see all, and perhaps some roaming animals.

Once we reached the Alaskan soil, we visited Juneau's salmon farm, which was very educational. Also, we were taken to Skagway to the shops that sold gold jewelry quite easily because of their marked-down prices. My husband bought me a gold ring and a bracelet of the native flowers of Alaska, forget-me-nots designed into a pretty bracelet. I enjoyed the shopping, too; I always enjoy the shopping part of a trip. Then we went back on the ship, and dressed for dinner.

The Apelians go to dinner.

This was a wonderful cruise, and it was a dream of my husband to take it. We were glad to do it. Then the ship brought us to Vancouver, Canada. From there, we boarded a bus tour to many states and much fun. The only thing I did not like was that we were continuously packing and unpacking. At the end of the complete trip, having seen Hoover Dam, Yellowstone Park, Mt. St. Helens, and many other sights, we caught a plane from Los Angeles and headed home. We were thrilled with the whole cruise and land vacation, but we were in need of a quiet restful vacation already.

Our Third Cruise—Nova Scotia

In June of 2006 after our first grandchild's graduation from high school, we decided on a cruise to Nova Scotia. Christee Angela Curran, our first grandchild, had graduated with high honors in June, and we wanted to gift her with a cruise, which she had never had before. She is our daughter's child, and at the present time, she has a year to complete her studies at the Pratt Institute of New York. She has been our pride and joy, having been picked as the first Miss Colonia in 2008. She received a $3,000 scholarship from her township for exemplary records of her schoolwork, volunteerism, and the way she portrayed herself at the competition.

When I was about to send our check for the cruise, Christee called me excited. She was so happy that we were taking her on this cruise. She added, saying sweetly,

"Can my friends come, too?"

"You really want that?" I asked her.

"Grandma, I was telling my two best friends about it, and they said they wished they could come, too." Then she begged, "Please, please."

"OK, I guess it will be fine. Of course, they have to pay their way."

"Yes, yes, they said that they would." And she raised her voice, adding, "Thank you, thank you, grandma."

At that point, I had to inform the Carnival Cruise reservation center in Florida about an extra cabin, and that I wanted that cabin to be right next to ours. We had balcony cabins, and we were granted the cabin next ours for them, which made me very happy. Then talking to my friends, they expressed wanting to join us, too. I said fine, and made reservations for them; the more, the merrier.

Soon I was sent an affidavit from the cruise line making me completely responsible for three beautiful 17-year-old young ladies. There were numerous questions for me to answer, and I had to be sure that I would not have any problems with these young ladies. I called my granddaughter.

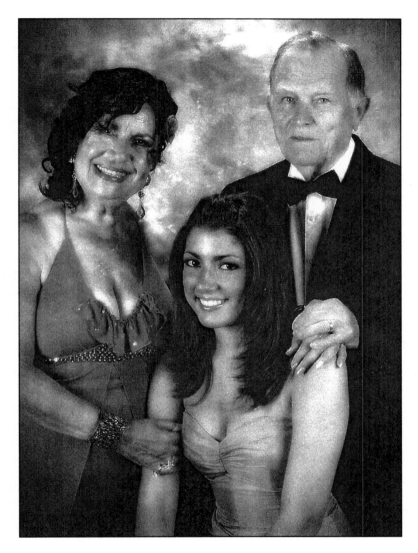

Grandparents and Christee, their first grandchild.

"I know I can trust you 100 percent. May I ask if these friends of yours are nice young ladies and have not been in any kind of trouble. I have to know that."

"Of course, grandma, I would not be friends with losers." She sounded a bit flustered.

"I am sorry, sweetie, but I have to ask that to be sure."

"Yes, yes, grandma, I understand," she said politely.

"I will be getting special applications for them, and they have to fully complete it with their parents' consent and signatures, and then we are in business."

"OK, OK, that is great," she exclaimed cheerfully.

My two grown-up friends did not need any supervision, but I had to be extra careful about those three young ladies. I knew I could handle the situation well, since I had been a teacher and had dealt with young people often. I was very happy that our granddaughter was going to have a super fun time on her first cruise with her best friends, Dasha and Rosie.

The Carnival Cruise Line ship *Victory* started from New York City to sail to Nova Scotia, Canada. It was a lovely cruise and many special programs for young people of all ages. It was a great family cruise. Many families took it with their teenage children. There were special programs, shows, and dances for the youth. Having the responsibility on my shoulders, I did not want the girls to be served alcohol. The cruise was good in checking their birthdates to keep an eye on things. I had given them a curfew of 12 midnight. I had told my granddaughter that if they were even five minutes late, I would ground them the next night. She understood and explained it to her friends. Everything went smoothly. Not even once were they late getting in their cabin. I was very pleased and commended them for their good behavior.

Our balcony touched the girls' balcony; we would sit there and watch the cruise ship speed away to its destination. There were shows and extravagant dinners with entertainment. On the last evening, all of the serving workers put on an excellent show. The night before, there was a talent show that I participated again by singing a medley of songs in three languages: Armenian, English, and French. I received another gold statue for my talent, and I had many Armenian and French people later thanking me for doing a good job. I had a good audience of my husband, granddaughter, and her two friends rooting for me. It was a fun evening.

As a whole, it was a great cruise. I was happy to have those young girls enjoy it so much, plus my friends Kathy and Grace were thankful to have joined us. We had dinner and lunch together every day. It was such a great friendship; I had known Kathy for forty years.

Another amazing thing that happened during that cruise was that I had met a young Armenian Relief Society (ARS) member who had been at one of our conferences in Atlantic City in 1968. Her name was Anahid Bashian. As we sat down to eat at our assigned dinner table, she called out my name. My back was at their table, so I turned around and saw her. I had not seen her for thirty-eight years, and here she was sitting with her family,

Standing: Dasha, Rosie, and the author; sitting: Grace, Christee, and Kathy.

son and wife, and other cousins at our next table. We greeted each other with hugs and caught up with our lives in a quick summary. We had hit it off very nicely at that 1968 convention in Atlantic City, but then we met many nice people and had lost contact with them. I was so elated to see her again after almost forty years.

This amazing cruise came to an end. It made beautiful memories of friendship and fun for everyone. Time marches on, and I do not know when my next cruise will be. Maybe there will be another one and maybe not. Traveling to different lands is an education by itself—to see different people, different cultures, other ways of living gives a perspective on life to appreciate what we have. Even on cruises where people were from the USA, each person had a different background and a unique story to share. All in all, those precious days and moments were gifts from God as we were able to share and savor that fun and friendship in a happy atmosphere. We all returned to our routine jobs and situations rejuvenated with a new joy and hope for a better outlook in life.

PART TEN:

Awards and Honors

Awards

I have received many awards and honors in my lifetime. We all enjoy receiving them. If someone says, "I don't," he or she is not telling the truth. When anyone does something for others, it is nice to be appreciated.

However, in my whole life, whatever I have done and am writing about is not because I had to do them, but because I wanted to do them. When someone does something lovingly, it comes from within, and that is where the satisfaction comes in. There may be times when you are not appreciated, but you don't stop in doing what you love to do, making people or even just one person happy. If a person does not have that underlying desire to make a difference by doing well, no one can force that person to do so. This is an innate gift from God Almighty. And those of us who have it must cherish it as long as we live. It is a precious gift.

I am going to enumerate some of these awards because I want to show young and old that we are all capable doing good, helping someone or many because we desire to do so. In telling these, it may give young people the example to do the best they can to reach that beautiful rainbow that they are aiming for. It is possible. But, you first have to have faith in God and faith in yourself for the best possible, sincere way to work very hard to attain your goals. Nothing is handed to anyone on a silver platter. There are some people who get inheritances of much wealth. That still does not give them the spirit of compassion and doing good for others. However, some may do that, but the premise of them being ultra-rich does not guarantee a productive life to make a difference for humanity.

If someone has been taught by loving parents or has seen loving adults, good moral principles will be ingrained in them as a child growing up. They will have more fruitful results in life than someone who did not have those beneficial experiences of compassion. However, that is not always 100 percent possible, because there are other factors contributing to our whole being. There are individual biological differences. These comments suffice for now; however, this topic is very dear to me and one which I have covered for twenty-six years in my "Assertiveness" teaching courses.

Here are some awards I have received:

1954—Art Contest Winner while in high school, won a gold trophy.

1955—National Honor Society gold pin; and the highest Service Award from Central High School for that time and date

1977—Frank K. Hehnly School Certificate of Commendation from the Parents and Teachers Organization

1980—Armenian Relief Society (ARS) golden pin for 25 years of Active Service for Humanity

1982—Kean Univ., Professional Women's Organization, sponsored a program, "A Tribute to Women of the Garden State." I was one recipient, among others: Jane Burgio, Secretary of the State of New Jersey; and Assemblywoman Maureen Ogden

1983—received the Union County College Outstanding Alumna Award. Also, State Senator Anthony Russo presented a resolution to me

Assemblyman and Mrs. Chuck Haytaian congratulating Virginia and Henry.

Chief of Police of Clark, Anthony Smar is congratulating Virginia.

Friends coming to celebrate with Virginia.

421

Judge Bercik giving the oath to the author for JCC office.

1983—I was honored to be installed as a member of the Juvenile Conference Committee (JCC), a highly essential service to the community. Judge Steven J. Bercik conducted the oath of office in his office. The purpose of this board is to assist young people, who have evidenced early signs of antisocial behavior, in their formal court processing.

1984—installed to the Elizabeth Presbytery Board's Resources Leadership. The installation took place at the Connecticut Farms Presbyterian Church by the Rev. Sidney Pinch.

1984—I was honored by the New Jersey General Assembly with a resolution for outstanding professional accomplishments, civic leadership, and service to community. This resolution was signed by the Speaker of the Assembly Alan Karcher, and presented to me by Assemblyman Chuck Haytaian.

Assemblyman Haytaian presents author the resolution.

1985—The Supreme Court, Family Division of Union County Judges Edward W. Beglin, Jr., William J. McCloud, John J. Callahan, and James J. Walsh gave a Certificate of Recognition to me for community services to the youth and their families.

1987—upon its 10th anniversary, Kean University's Professional Women's Association honored women for their leadership abilities on the local, state, and national level. I was one of the honored people that day, on May 8.

1990—organized Christian Mission Work for the AMAA to get funds for the Armenian earthquake victims. I was able to encourage five Presbyterian Churches to join in this program. The program was a fantastic fashion show of authentic biblical costumes, presented by Farah and Hanan Munayyer free of charge. The contributing churches were: Cranford Presbyterian Church; Garwood Presbyterian Church; Linden Presbyterian Church (where the fashion show took place); First Presbyterian Church of Metuchen; and the Osceola Presbyterian Church of Clark. A good sum of money was gathered and donated to the AMAA. They were very appreciative of this good deed.

1994—received a Certificate of Appreciation from Congressman Bob Franks of District 7, in recognition of long service to the community of Clark, and for efforts to promote food and clothing for needy children around the world.

Congressman Bob Franks presents the author
with a Certificate of Appreciation.

1994—was presented to me by Dr. Thomas Brown, president of Union County College, Service Award for serving as president of Alumni Association, member of the Board of Governors, and as a UCC alumna lecturer on "Stress Management," plus serving as mistress of ceremonies at the awards presentations, and for multifaceted duties at the college.

1994—the Alumna Honoree and N.J. Council of County Colleges' Excellence Award. The awards were presented by Richard W. Roper, Director of the Office of Economic and Policy Analysis of the Port Authority of N.Y. and N.J. Dr. Thomas Brown was on hand and came up to the stage and congratulated me. This was, indeed, a big honor for me and for the college. The plaque was on black stone etched with gold lettering.

Virginia receives the Excellence Award by Mr. Roper at the podium, and is congratulated by Dr. Thomas Brown of Union County College.

Well-wishers with author: L–R: A trustee member, Mr. Milteer of UCC, author's son Dr. Christopher Apelian, the author, a dear friend, Nadine Brechner, the Executive Director of Development, and author's husband Henry.

425

1995—admitted to the Douglass Society. This is the highest honor that Douglass bestows upon its graduates. Part of the content of the resolution indicated that: "she has contributed significantly to the betterment of contemporary society through her continued affiliation with organizations that work with handicapped children, address human rights and health issues, and fight drug abuse.

"For her distinguished civic leadership and her commitment to serving others, Douglass College and the Associate Alumnae are proud to name Virginia Matosian Apelian to the Douglass Society."

I also received an inch-thick Lucite, 14-inch round, medallion with the gold inscription of Douglass College, a Douglas fir in the middle, and the year, 1995, and my full name.

Martha A. Cotter (left), Acting Dean of Douglass College, congratulating Virginia Apelian.

1995—Union County College Certificate of Appreciation for providing scholarship support to UCC students

1996—attended the 23rd International Congress on Arts and Communications in San Francisco received "A Certificate of Honor" for my lecture on "Ethnic Harmony." Here is a part of it:

"We must eradicate prejudice to make a better society for all especially for our new generations. Each one of us can make a difference in order to propagate harmony and goodwill toward all human beings. We must have the vision to see beyond the obvious in order to make a difference towards betterment of our society, not just standing by while wrong is done, but to keep constant vigil against discrimination. We must teach these things to our children at a very early age. The most effective teaching tool is by being good models."

1996—my husband and I have sponsored children overseas for paying their education through the channels of AMAA. I also, had appealed to the Presbyterian Women (PW) of the Fanwood Presbyterian Church and, in return, they, too, sponsored a child's needs, which cost $250 for each child. Rev. Dr. Movses Janbazian of AMAA very kindly had submitted a special citation for this purpose for helping needy children, to us, and to the PW of Fanwod Presbyterian Church.

1997—received a Master Teacher Award from the Presbytery of Elizabeth for teaching Sunday school forty years, from K-adult classes.

2000—received Service Award certificate from Judge Edward Beglin, Jr., Union County Superior Court, for being chair of the Council for helping troubled youth.

Judge Beglin presenting the Service Award to Virginia.

2001—Victor Richel of Union County College, Board of Trustees Chairman, presented a "Citation of Thanks" to me, a gold-sealed, framed resolution emphasizing my many contributions to the College and the community, as well as activities (for instance, the first-ever Armenian historical and cultural event I presented at the College in February 2001). It was a great portrayal of the Armenian case.

Victor Richel presenting the "Citation of Thanks".

In addition, Dr. Brown, then President of UCC, presented a Union County College sweatshirt to me that would make me a lifetime emeritus member of the Board of Governors of the college. This year, we moved to Manchester, N.J. in Ocean County. This was a special program for my honor.

Dr. Brown presents the UCC sweatshirt to author, who is already sporting a UCC cap given with plaque.

Encyclopedia Listings

- *Who's Who in New Jersey*
- *Who's Who in American Women*
- *Who's Who in America*
- *Who's Who in American Education*
- *Who's Who Among Human Services Professionals*
- *Who's Who in the World International*
- *Who's Who of Professional and Business Women*
- *Who's Who in the East*
- *Who's Who of International Intellectuals*
- *Asian/American Who's Who*

Professional and other affiliations

- National Honor Society
- New Jersey Council for the Humanities
- Union County College Alumni Association
- Armenian Missionary Association of America (AMAA)
- The Pride of Rutgers Network
- Douglass Alumnae Association
- New Jersey Ethnic Advisory Council
- First Presbyterian Church of Boonton
- Armenian Relief Society (ARS)
- Armenian Literary Society of New York

Thanks be to God for all of his blessings, for having gifted me with my health, perseverance, dedication, and the time to be able do these things. I humbly end this chapter, hoping it has given future generations respect and love for human dignity.

31

Honors

I am often asked, "How did you attain the title of International Woman of the Year?" It was not wishful thinking on my part, but it came by having done "random acts of love." Let me explain how I think I became the recipient of that title.

Aside from being active with the ARS, with the "plate of food" project for needy poor people overseas, and the AMAA's work for paid tuition for needy students and the aid to the earthquake victims—there was more.

1981: I had a call from a friend of mine and, would you believe, this friend was a Turkish person, born and raised in Iran? We were the best of friends, and she had married an Italian architect, Jim Scampato; they had met in college here in the U.S. Nina was a sweet and very gregarious person with whom I have had much fun. I have had Nina and Jim at my house as guests and vice versa. God works in mysterious ways. Since they were both Presbyterians, we had much in common, in spite of Nina's brutal Turkish ancestry of the Ottomans. Nina was a very kind person. She called and asked me to please help a Jewish couple who were going to be married in a little over a week. They wanted to have their grandmother from Tel Aviv be at their wedding. She said they had tried everything to no avail. Now that was a great idea, but I was only a local councilwoman and had no jurisdictional rights to demand an international request. So, I called to find out more about the situation before I could even think about it. I visited Nina who also lived in Clark.

"Dearest friend, Nina, tell me more about this situation of the Jewish couple getting married," I said very intently.

"Of course, of course," she replied.

"Please give me more details so I can pursue this more efficiently," I said gently.

Nina gave me their name and address and told me where the groom's family lived, plus their telephone number if I needed it for more information.

"I will see what I can do, but I want to talk to the groom-to-be, Abraham Neissani, and the family first."

"I know you can do it, my dear friend," she said cheerily.

"I will try my best," I said hopefully, and left Nina's house.

This was the end of March 1981. I decided that the only person who may be able to help me would be Congressman Matthew Rinaldo. I explained to his staff the situation that was presented to me, and asked if he could help Mrs. Malekijan Zaraby come to the USA to see her first grandchild, Abraham Neissani, get married on April 9. I was told by the Neissani family that they had tried unsuccessfully to get a visa for Mrs. Zaraby. This is when the situation had come to my attention. I asked Congressman Rinaldo's staff if they could send a telegram to the American Embassy in Tel Aviv that might speed things up. But they told me it would take at least six weeks, because of procedural methods.

"Oh, no," I said anxiously, "Mr. Neissani is getting married on April 9th."

They were sorry, but that was it. I told them that I knew Congressman Rinaldo would like this very happy reunion and the wish of Mrs. Zaraby be fulfilled. I asked again if they would send an urgent telegram immediately and it could be worked out.

"That would cost extra money. If Mr. Abraham Neissani would like to pay for the urgent telegram, your plan may be possible."

"Thank you, thank you," I said cheerfully, and continued, "I will call them to make sure they can pay, and will get right back to you."

"Thank you," said the office administrator, "the sooner the better."

"Please give me an hour," I said, hurriedly and thankfully, and then I hung up.

I called the Neissani residence, but the line was busy. I said, "Good, they are home." I got in my car and drove to their house in Clark, which was about five minutes from my house. I gave them the news that if they paid for an urgent telegram to be sent to the American Embassy, there was a possibility that their grandmother may make it to the April 9th wedding. They were willing to pay, and I immediately called the Congressman's office to verify that the cost was fine with the Neissanis. The Congressman's office was very thankful for the speedy answer I gave them. They told me that they would let me know as soon as they could.

Soon, I received a special delivery letter from Congressman Rinaldo that all was well and that Mrs. Zaraby will get her visa the beginning of April. This was fantastic news for the Neissanis, and I was thrilled that this nice lady would be able to witness her first grandchild's wedding in America.

The happy day arrived; she came to America for a visit on April 5, 1981, to be present at this special wedding. I am delighted to say that I was invited to this big wedding that took place on the evening of April 9 at Temple Torah in Little Neck, N.Y. A joyful reception followed with songs and music in many languages. Mrs. Zaraby, along with the bride and groom, gave me a very cordial welcome and a hug and thanked me profusely. It was lovely to see the Neissanis' reunion with their grandmother, and the happiness she was experiencing. That sight was worth more than a million dollars.

Neissani wedding photo, L–R: Mr. and Mrs. Abraham Neissani; Mrs. Zaraby, the grandmother; and Councilwoman Apelian.

In a day or two, the local papers covered the story as "Councilwoman Helps Unite Two Families."

In 1992, I had a call from Mr. Garo Ketsemanian with an urgent request for me to help five young Armenian men who were about to be hanged or beheaded in Azerbeijan by the Azeri Government without any due process as we know it in this country. I was called by the Armenian Revolutionary Federation (ARF) Dro Committee's desperation because they wanted to seek help from America, and I was the member of the New Jersey Governor's Ethnic Advisory Council, who could help them. This was an international matter again of intense nature. Again, I called and spoke to Congressman Matthew Rinaldo about this in person. Since this was such an urgent matter, he wanted to know more information as to who the five young men were. I got the list from Mr. Ketsemanian immediately and submitted it to the Congressman. The five men to be hanged were as follows: Grachig Petrossian; Arno Mgerditchian; Gagig Harutunian; Arvid Mangassarian; and Karnig Aroustanian.

MATTHEW J. RINALDO
7TH DISTRICT, NEW JERSEY

WASHINGTON OFFICE:
2469 RAYBURN HOUSE OFFICE BUILDING
WASHINGTON, DC 20515-3007
(202) 225-5361

DISTRICT OFFICE:
1961 MORRIS AVENUE
UNION, NJ 07083
(908) 687-4235

COMMITTEES:
ENERGY AND COMMERCE

SUBCOMMITTEES:
TELECOMMUNICATIONS AND FINAN
(RANKING MINORITY MEMBER)
TRANSPORTATION AND
HAZARDOUS MATERIALS

SELECT COMMITTEE
ON AGING
(RANKING MINORITY MEMBER)

Congress of the United States
House of Representatives
Washington, DC 20515-3007

April 2, 1992

Mrs. Virginia Apelian
85 Rutgers Road
Clark, NJ 07066

Dear Virginia:

Thank you for contacting my district office about Azerbaijan's
threat to execute five Armenians. I appreciated hearing from you
again.

I share your distress about this situation, and I have urged the
State Department to actively intervene on behalf of the
prisoners. This afternoon, I was informed that the executions
have been stayed pending negotiations with Armenia over hostages
held by both countries. I am hopeful that this is the first step
towards the release of these people. They were tried during an
intensely emotional period, when the leaders of Azerbaijan were
seeking to prove how nationalistic and anti-Armenian they were.
Under no circumstances could this be called a fair trial.

Again, thank you for sharing your views with me. I hope that you
will continue to correspond on other issues of concern to you.

Sincerely yours,

MATTHEW J. RINALDO
Member of Congress

MJR/dcj

P.A. Best personal regards.

*Letter from Congressman Rinaldo to author pertaining to the
planned execution of the five young men.*

Thus, Congressman Rinaldo sent an urgent message through the State
Department to Azerbaijan's acting president, Yacoub Mahmetov, making his
plea very strong to not kill those five young men. They were saved. Thanks
be to God, and thank God for the likes of Congressman Matthew Rinaldo,
a true public servant.

1993: I received a call from a Russian Jewish lady that she had a friend from Odessa, Ukraine who is visiting her in the U.S., and who wants to find refuge here. She gave me her friend's name and described her as an educated person, and that she was a dentist in Odessa. I asked her why she called me. She said that she had seen my picture and that I was the representative for the Armenian community of New Jersey on the N.J. Governor's Ethnic Council. I told her that it was true, and I would see what I could do for her friend, but I needed more information. I invited them to my home for afternoon tea. This way I could meet both of them, and I could ask questions of this friend of hers who was supposed to be Armenian.

Anyway, the day arrived. They were very nice ladies, who arrived at my house promptly. The woman who wanted to stay in America was Dr. Marina Oganessian. She told me that she had an abusive husband in Ukraine and a little boy who was not supposed to be with his father—the law had given him to her. She expressed in Armenian that she was willing to work and stay in America rightfully, and not go back to Ukraine. She had a visitation visa for staying with her Jewish friend in Union, N.J., but soon that visitation was to end, and she was seeking help.

In this type of situation, I knew that I had to find her a sponsor for a job. However, she did not speak any English, and that was a minus for trying to find a job for her. I thought and thought and it came to me. First, I tried the Armenian Diocese and the Armenian Prelacy of New York to see if they could possibly have a position for her. Neither party did have an opening.

Then it came to me as a 'flashing light' that she could be helpful at the Armenian Home for the Aged in Emerson, N.J. I called my husband's cousin, Dr. Vahe Apelian, who was on the Board of Directors at the time. I explained the situation to him and asked if they could give Marina a job; she could be quite instrumental in keeping the elderly in good dental health. Also, I asked if she could have her own quarters there with her son. Of course, I knew that their attorney would need to apply and document her position with the Immigration Office. Vahe, being the good person he is, was happy to get things started, and asked me if the Board of Directors could meet Marina immediately. Joyfully, I said that could be arranged. After my talk with Vahe, I called Marina and told her about it. She got very excited and thanked me. I gave her my very best wishes. She thanked me over and over.

The Armenian Home Board of Directors met and spoke with Marina. They were very pleased to see this young woman of forty-two years old, who could really be an asset for their institution. Their attorney started the work immediately. This process was done quite efficiently and Marina Oganessian was soon a full-time employee of the Home. She was given a room in the facility with all its amenities for her and her son to live there. Her nickname was "Nazig." She called me and thanked me profusely. I said to her just thank God for this opportunity for you and your son.

Father's Day at the Armenian Home for the Aged in Emerson, N.J. L–R: Marina Oganessian and Virginia Apelian.

On June 19, 1994, at the main fundraiser for the Home, usually on Father's Day, an enormous picnic was held on the grounds. People came from many states to be there since the residents come from all over the U.S. At this big gathering, at which the food and good music were always plentiful, I was invited by the Board of Directors to be their bilingual keynote speaker. I enjoyed doing that, and I was delighted to see Marina (Nazig) again. She sought me out in the big crowd, after I delivered my speech, and I was glad to see her. We chatted for a long time, and she expressed her joy at working there and thankfulness to me again and again. She was also happy for her nine-year-old son, who was doing great in school, and that she was learning English, too. I commended her, and said to keep the good work going. It gave me so much joy to see her so happy in a safe place.

These accomplishments are why I think I was selected to be "International Woman of the Year" for the term 1992–1993.

436

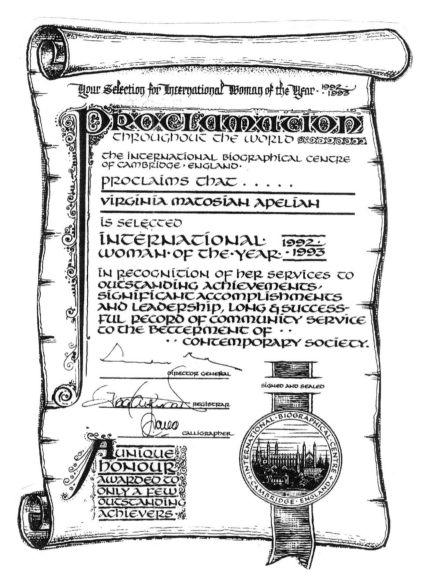

A copy of the Proclamation the author received from the International Biographical Centre of Cambridge, England.

Nominations for International Woman of the Year are made by the Editorial and Advisory Boards of the International Biographical Centre. Tens of thousands of biographies are reviewed each year by the Boards and from these only a handful is selected for this unique honor. This information is received through many of the encyclopedic data that I am listed in.

The very next year, for the year of 1993-1994, I was selected again for "Woman of the Year" by the American Biographical Institute.

Three years later, on May 30, 1997, I was honored by my Lord and Savior by granting me my life. A commercial garbage truck ran a red light, hitting my car with a great force. I was heading to my daughter's house in Colonia. That was my *third* near-death experience in my life, which the Good Lord granted me the biggest honor of all—saving my life again. Thanks be to His glorious name, so I am able to write this book of mine. The things that I have done for others do not come close to what our Almighty God gives us on a daily basis. If we recognize all that, we will do anything possible for humanity, because we learn to value life through it all. I thank God for my life being saved again, and what little things I do here and there, do not even come close to what I get back. But we must be cognizant of it all, because when I saw my car a complete wreck after the accident, and I came out of it one piece, what a glorious miracle that was.

My minister, Rev. Stephanie Miller, from the Fanwood Presbyterian Church visited me when I was recuperating from a whiplash and much pain at home.

"Was it a big car that hit you?" she said curiously.

"Oh, yes," I replied.

"A station wagon?" she inquired.

I said, "No, come again."

"What then?"

"It was a 60-ton, commercial garbage truck."

"Oh, my Lord," she sighed and continued saying, "Virginia, the Good Lord is not finished with you yet." Then we both chuckled over that statement.

"For of him, and through him, and to him, are all things; to whom be glory for ever. Amen." (Romans 11:36)

All that which I have received, all the glory be to the Lord.

PART ELEVEN:

Patriotism

32

What Is Our Obligation?

"Patriotism" is not a dirty word as many liberals would like to make it. Let us define it.

The *American College Dictionary* puts it this way: "patriotism—love of or devotion to one's country."

The *American Heritage Dictionary of the English Language* defines patriot this way: "patriot—one who loves, supports, and defends one's country."

So, why cannot we all do that for this country, which is the most freedom-loving country in the world? We are not talking about a dictatorship, or a state of anarchy, or a communist country, or anything like it. We are talking about the USA, which was founded by true patriots. We should follow in their footsteps, because they worked long and hard to attain a very unique constitution to form the Union. Our Founding Fathers were intelligent, God-fearing men who sacrificed a great deal to form this constitutional republic. We are not merely a democracy. Having completed such a valuable job, these Founding Fathers went through many persecutions after the work was done. They all knew the consequences, but their courage and dedication was so exemplary as great Godly men who had no fear for their actions and beliefs. That was, indeed, a great accomplishment.

What is our individual obligation to be considered as a patriot? It is to keep our country safe from any enemy activity that may harm it or anything in it, including human beings. We honor our country by revering its flag and its war heroes who have defended our rights and freedoms. What more can a nation ask for? This great nation of ours has survived since 1776, and most people who are patriotic would like to keep it that way. So, what seems to be the trouble? One does not have to be a NASA scientist to know what is happening in our country today. In plain English, the administration is gearing towards socialism and Marxism. This is not hearsay. Look what has happened in a very short time, from 2009 on, in this beloved country of ours.

Dr. Charles Krauthammer, who is a great patriot and whom I admire very much, wrote the following in *The Washington Post* on September 4, 2009.

"Obama gave his most deeply felt vision of America, delivering the boldest social democratic manifesto ever issued by a U.S. president. In

American politics, you can't get more left than that speech and still be on the playing field."

And Dr. Krauthammer continues, "Accordingly, Obama unveiled his plans for a grand makeover of the American system, animating that vision by enacting measure after measure that greatly enlarged state power, government spending and national debt. Not surprisingly, these measures engendered powerful popular skepticism that burst into tea-party town-hall resistance."

When people's intelligence is attacked, and no heed is paid to them, this is what happens. The Tea Party is a very orderly group; however, leftist groups are applying negative names to it. People are wiser and they have the proof of what is happening to our businesses, economy, and the morale of this country—it is way down to the bottom of the scale. That is not acceptable to the hardworking citizens of this country who are patriotic and love this country. This is not fair to this generation, to the next one, or to the one after. Thus far, our country and our future generations are buried in extraordinary debt, the kind that has never been seen before, in this short time.

I always admired Margaret Thatcher, who said and believed the following: "The trouble with Socialism is that you eventually run out of other people's money."

How very true that is. Don't they think when Obama and Biden keep repeating to "share the wealth," they are trying to change our form of government? It is so obvious. That was not in our Founding Fathers' agenda. It has been said that:

- "You cannot help the poor by destroying the rich."
- "You cannot strengthen the weak by weakening the strong."
- "You cannot bring about prosperity by discouraging thrift."
- "You cannot further the brotherhood of man by inciting class hatred."
- "You cannot build character and courage by taking away people's initiative and independence."
- "You cannot help people permanently by doing for them, what they could and should do for themselves."

Does the President mention some great presidents' names to be like them, visit places like the Lincoln Memorial, or give a speech at the Brandenburg Gate for effect? Mr. Obama's words have not always been sincere, genuine, or accurate. His actions show otherwise. That is a sad commentary.

Also, many of the voting legislators who do not read the proposed legislation they impose on us have become a farce. House Speaker Pelosi openly said on television—I heard with my own ears—(I am paraphrasing) that they would pass the bill, and then "we can see what's in it." Does Rep. Pelosi think we are all imbeciles? Why don't they take their jobs seriously? I want to know, and a multitude of other people does, too.

The November 2, 2010, congressional and governorship elections were definitely a referendum on the Obama Administration. And, thank God, I can say this because of my freedom of speech in this constitutional republic of ours. Another point, this Congress has tried to impose the so-called "Fairness Doctrine" on us, granting them the power to silence opposing points of view and conservative opinions. The liberal media has become so lax in reporting what really is happening to this country it is sickening. But patriotic people of this country are not asleep; we are aware of everything.

Also, isn't it absolutely and ferociously wrong to have a terrorist in our civilian court? On November 17, 2010, Guantanamo detainee Khalid Ghaliani was convicted on one count of conspiracy to destroy government buildings and property, being acquitted of 284 other charges for alleged terrorist acts. And yet, our president calls those who inflict pain, terror and death upon our citizens, mere common criminals. President George W. Bush did not mince words; he called them "terrorists" and "enemy combatants," which they are. What is this all about? Is it to be politically correct and ruin the safety of this country? This is beyond comprehension.

Since I am a history buff, I am very much interested to know what is happening to this country on a daily basis. It is obvious what some influential liberal lawmakers are doing. They like to keep all the minorities under their control, so that minorities are subjected to their liberal agenda and will vote for them, and further keeping the poor enslaved to their authority. That is not freedom. But a worse thing is that social service programs tie the hands of those people who should be able to make it on their own. That is, there is no incentive to proceed with their lives by seeking opportunities for and succeeding in jobs. Initiative is to be encouraged. People should not be subjugated to a government welfare state. That form of government neither generates enthusiasm nor causes citizens to be willing to become successful on their own right and merits. That socialistic idea has not worked for other nations. Why put that malaise in our midst? Aren't good leaders supposed to study and follow history to see what has happened to other nations and how they have failed; thus, not to follow them? One does not have to be a genius to figure this out.

A good example is the Obama Health Plan. This type of plan has failed in many countries, including UK, Canada and others. Why then force that same principle upon our system? Our system is more workable, without putting enormous tax burdens on all of us. Why should people who do not pay for it, for example, illegal immigrants, and others who do not work, be eligible to get the same services as we do? This is not justifiable any way you look at it—period.

Speaking of the illegal immigrants, PolitiFact.com informs us that three of our former presidents were able to control this issue somewhat. They were Presidents Hoover, Truman and Eisenhower.

Back during The Great Depression, President Herbert Hoover ordered the deportation of illegal aliens to make jobs possible for the American citizens that needed work.

Then in 1954, President Dwight Eisenhower deported Mexican nationals, under a program called "Operation Wetback." However, the rumored number of 13-15 million total illegal immigrants deported is questioned by historians such as Scott Wong of Williams College. He states that there is "some truth in this post—that the government deported illegal immigrants in the past—but it was never 12 million over two years." Also, Mark Krikorian, the executive director of the Center for Immigration Studies, a group critical of illegal immigration, said the following: "the idea of the e-mail is correct; the numbers are way too high."

What PolitiFact.com had received were accumulated e-mails saying that those three presidents had deported 15 million illegal immigrants. The official total from 1930 to 1960 was 477,000 formal removals of illegal immigrants and 5.4 million people left voluntarily. That 30-year period included Roosevelt's terms, and not just the three presidents mentioned in the e-mail. So, added all together, the number is less than 6 million, which is less than half of what the e-mail had previously claimed. And 90 percent left voluntarily.

However, here is the crux of the issue. If the laws were enforced to deter illegal immigration, that would be a start. Why should states such as Arizona, Texas and others be under siege from criminals who cross the border and kill our law-abiding citizens? Here, I would like to emphasize that this problem did not start with the Obama Administration, to be fair. But since things have gotten worse, no big effort is being made to curtail the situation, once and for all. The illegal people crossing the borders and killing our own citizens has to stop, no matter which administration is in power.

The Tea Party movement is a focus group that is saying "enough is enough." They are the ordinary people and law-abiding citizens; they are you and me, the next door neighbor, your physician and the grocery shop owner, and all of the people who are working diligently to save their country from socialistic ways. The price is too big to pay; we do not want higher taxes and we do not want to lose our homes. We all want jobs to support our families. We do not want any handouts; we want opportunities to make it on our own. The change Mr. Obama promised us is not acceptable: more debt, higher taxes, more welfare, more regulations, more wasteful spending, more corruption, more company failures, and more of our individual identities to be gone forever. What happened to our personal motto to be individually the best that we can be?

I believe there are present-day patriots in the public eye who warn us continuously about the status of our present government and its faltering effects on people. I truly respect men such as Sean Hannity, Mark Levin, Rush Limbaugh, and Thomas Sowell. I like that they are well-informed and are fearless to say what they have to tell us. That requires a lot of guts. I truly like that in people. They do their homework, and say it as it is. I have read all of their books and it is a delight to see that we have such people defending our country's rights and our Constitution; they are people who educate the public.

I also admire patriotic women who are outstanding examples of our society at present and who set the pace of our country on the right track. They are Sarah Palin, Michelle Malkin, Ann Coulter, Laura Ingraham, and Monica Crowley. In addition, they are endowed with God-given inner and outer beauty to put their ideas across. These are well-educated and experienced women who know what they are talking about. Kudos goes to all the men and women who love this country, and who communicate those thoughts, expressions, and facts to us continuously. That is an obligation well-deserved and respected by us.

Here is a quote from Thomas Carlyle, which I think is pertinent as to with whom our leaders, specifically our president, have made connections, associations, and friendships:

"Show me the man you honor, and I will know what kind of man you are...." The only word I would change in that thought would be instead of "man," I would substitute "person."

On October 21, 2010, I heard Rush Limbaugh say on his radio program that the liberals are always insisting on "political correctness." What they are doing really is "political censorship." I agree with this. Most liberals, when they are in fear of facing the truth, always label what they do not like with a derogatory name or phrase. That is being immature, like a spoiled child having a tantrum. They keep continuing this type of rhetoric, but people see right through them as to what their intent is. What a shame that is. It has become so farcical.

Let us recall and savor President Ronald Reagan's philosophies and actions that prospered this country and the world. I was so happy when I met him in Union County in 1980 when he made a speech at the Lincoln Day Dinner in February. He was gifted with great diction and showed command of his convictions as he spoke. That year I became Reagan's Presidential Campaign coordinator for Clark Township. I was proud and happy to do it.

It does not matter if we are a Republican, Democrat, or an independent. For those of you who did not know, Reagan was a Democrat years ago. But when he discovered certain weaknesses in the government's role, he made a complete U-turn with his conservative and healthy philosophy. President Reagan was a master communicator—we all know that, even though some people called him just an actor and a cowboy. He paid no heed to that, but exemplified his deep love and conviction for this country by being a fearless leader, not just for America, but to the world. In 1983, in his speech, he called the Soviet Union the "evil empire." Some people thought that was a very strong comment; in today's lingo, it was "politically incorrect." But it was true. Reagan changed history and caused the Communist world to shrink. How and why did that happen? President Reagan shifted the U.S. from the long-failing policy of containment. The Cold War did not have a chance to survive any longer.

I have this opinion, you do not have to agree with me, but it certainly makes sense to me that if President Jimmy Carter had been reelected in 1980, the Soviet Union would still be around today. And my beloved ancestors would still be under Soviet rule, but thank God, Armenia became an Independent Republic in September 1991, as many other Soviet republics, too, became independent.

The magnificent speech that President Reagan gave at the Brandenburg Gate on June 12, 1987, made it very clear to the Soviets by saying, "Mr. Gorbachev, tear down this wall!" This was a historical moment, and it will never be forgotten in our memory, and in history books. That was, indeed, very gutsy of him, and it could have had risks involved. But, he did not care, and was fearless to say so, and the Soviets got the message. I hope like many other important historical events, this will not be forgotten, but will be taught to our future generations. Only two years later, in

November 9, 1989, East Germany issued a decree to open the Brandenburg Gate and allow the people travel to West Berlin. Also, the wall got torn down by the end of 1990. Thereafter, all the Soviet Republics gained their independence.

Why am I going back to history? First of all, we can learn from it. Also, it matters a great deal not to be weakened. A strong leader like President Reagan changed the course of history. Yes, it took about ten years, but it was a success not to be taken over and ruled by Communism. We are an example to the free world, and we want to stay that way. We, the people, have spoken; there will be no dangerous and radical philosophies to be dabbled with, changing our constitutional republic under God. There should be no hesitation about this issue among the elected members of the House of Representatives, all 435 of them; 100 senators; 9 Supreme Court justices and one commander-in-chief. According to the 2010 census, 308.7 million people are dependent on this, in order to flourish and sustain what our Founding Fathers had worked for.

The period of 1980–1990 was an amazing decade that changed the world. Thank you, President Reagan, who also believed very strongly in God Almighty, saying, "If we ever forget that we're one nation under God, then we will be a nation gone under." I am proud to say that I have been a member of Ronald Reagan Presidential Library Foundation since 1987.

As I mentioned before, I have several favorite presidents; one of them is George W. Bush, and I will tell you why. The liberals, including Mr. Obama, still blame Bush for everything under the sky. How childish. Look at the record. First of all, I will say this that President G.W. Bush made some mistakes; no president is 100 percent perfect all of the time. However, let us look at fundamental issues to be the judge. Bush was a compassionate human being; it showed in all of his actions: in dealing with the public, the veterans and their families, in his faith, and his attitude as a whole. Compassion is not bought, and it is a quality that cannot be attained by just saying it; compassion has to be modeled. George W. Bush came from a very gracious family. He also believed in prayer, and was not ashamed of it.

PRESIDENT
GEORGE W. BUSH

Dec. 21, 2004

Dear Virginia,

Thank you for your great help on my campaign in New Jersey.

With your help, we achieved an historic nationwide victory, winning a record total of over 61 million votes.

I am honored by the trust of my fellow citizens, confident in our purpose, and looking forward to continuing to lead this Nation for four more years.

Laura joins me in thanking you for your steadfast support and in wishing you and your family a wonderful Holiday.

Sincerely,

Gw Bush

Handwritten letter from President G.W. Bush to the author.

I have received several letters from him, but I was most touched by this handwritten letter that arrived. He was so busy, taking care of this country and the world affairs, with the war in Iraq, yet he found time to thank me and write to me in person. How many people can say that they got a handwritten letter from the President of the United States of America? I was so humbled to receive it.

He always fought for freedom, not just for our country, but for other nations, too. He had nothing to gain by attacking Iraq, except to get rid of that horrible dictator, Saddam Hussein, and his two butcher sons, Uday and Qusay, who had murdered thousands and thousands of their own people. Iraqis are happy that we got rid of Saddam and his sons, and their country is flourishing better than they ever have. Of course, there is still work to be done, but the country is on the right track now. There is continuous reconstruction going on. Of course, we see some sporadic incidents of terrorism here and there, instigated by Iran and other groups, but Iraq is not under siege as it was before. But we do not hear of any improvements that have occurred in Iraq since Saddam's fall from power from the liberal media.

Also, some time ago when the politicians were asked, "Who do you admire in this world?" G.W. Bush answered "Jesus Christ," and they made fun of him. This was all over the news as I recall. Was that the beginning of the liberals' efforts to take God out of the public arena?

Today, people are intimidated if they declare any Christian words or mottos. When and why did this all happen? Since, perhaps Mr. Obama declared to other nations that we are not a Christian nation? Some people may argue that Mr. Obama had more to say on that issue—that other religions are free to worship in this country, too. That is fine, except the essence of our country's Founding Fathers' faith, which built such a strong nation. This faith should not be lost in the rest of the President's statement. We know that this country has freedom of religion of all people to choose what they believe. Mr. Obama's statement lacked the emphasis expressed by the Founding Fathers' principles. Also, he ceased having a National Day of Prayer at the White House.

This country was built and founded on Judeo-Christian principles, there is no question about it in my mind and many other people's minds, whether some people like it or not. We have freedom of religion since all other religions are able to practice their beliefs. But why is there this emphasis to eradicate the name of God, or saying "Merry Christmas" around December 25th? We are told and encouraged to say "Happy Holidays." When I was growing up, this did not exist in America. Where are we heading with this now?

When the Iraq war began in 2003, all the Democratic leaders stated succinctly that Saddam had weapons of mass destruction. The UN proposed to have Iraq checked, but Saddam refused time after time, and resolution after resolution. Eventually, Congress authorized the use of armed forces in Iraq. Then the Democrats and the liberal media and Mr. Obama demonized Bush on every account without any justification.

President Bush and his family had class and endurance with the help of Almighty God. He was humble, yet forged through all criticism to challenge Saddam and his awful regime. Saddam had to fall, and Bush accomplished that. Former Prime Minister Tony Blair of England supported Bush 100 percent. Blair was asked by his parliament, in criticizing his job as prime minister, why he sided with Bush. Blair replied, "I would do it again."

Bush is loved by the majority of the Iraqi people. There was news that some of the baby boys are named after Bush. Also, so many other nations joined us on that war, not wanting to risk their freedoms. President Bush's courage was admirable, and I know he will go down in history as one of the great presidents. Laugh if you must, but mark my word for it to happen in 20–25 years from now. I do not know if I will be around to know that, but the younger generation will.

I also was the Bush Campaign Manager in Manchester, N.J. in 2004. And when he won, my husband and I had a special invitation to go to his Inauguration. On that frigid day, January 20, 2005, we headed to Washington, D.C. very early, not to miss the inaugural address and the ceremony. After an arduous Amtrak train ride, and bad weather conditions, we made it on time.

*Henry and Virginia are all bundled up within
the railed area at the Inauguration of President
George W. Bush.*

We met other folks and made friends with the Jenkins from Pottsville, Penn.

L–R: Mrs. Jenkins and the author in Washington, D.C. at President G.W. Bush's inaugural ceremony on January 20, 2005.

This was my first attendance at a presidential inaugural ceremony. It was exciting and patriotic to hear the President's Second Inaugural Address in person. Here is a brief part of his speech, which rang out clearly in the chilly air, but warmed our hearts with joy:

"On this day, prescribed by law and marked by ceremony, we celebrate the durable wisdom of our Constitution, and recall the deep commitments that unite our country. I am grateful for the honor of this hour, mindful of the consequential times in which we live, and determined to fulfill the oath that I have sworn and you have witnessed....

"We are led, by events and common sense, to one conclusion: The survival of liberty in our land increasingly depends on the success of liberty in other lands. The best hope for peace in our world is the expansion of freedom to all the world....

"In America's ideal of freedom, citizens find the dignity and security of economic independence, instead of laboring on the edge of subsistence. This is the broader definition of liberty that motivated the Homestead Act, the Social Security Act, and the GI Bill of Rights. And now we will extend this vision by reforming great institutions to serve the needs of our time. To give every American a stake in the promise and future of our country, we will bring the highest standards to our schools and build an ownership society. We will widen the ownership of homes and businesses, retirement savings and health insurance—preparing our people for the challenges of life in a free society. By making every citizen an agent of his or her own destiny, we will give our fellow Americans greater freedom from want and fear, and make our society more prosperous and just and equal....

"When the Declaration of Independence was first read in public and the Liberty Bell was sounded in celebration, a witness said, 'It rang as if it meant something.' In our time it means something still. America, in this young century, proclaims liberty throughout the world, and to all the inhabitants thereof. Renewed in our strength—tested, but not weary—we are ready for the greatest achievements in the history of freedom....

"May God bless you, and may He watch over the United States of America."

It is so obvious to those who study our government that Reagan got rid of the Cold War and broke the barriers of the USSR. He had the courage to do that. In following that challenging task, George W. Bush was driven to make freedom possible for other countries who were suffering under tyranny. He so sincerely believed this and pursued it to make our freedoms shared by others. At the same time, he believed strongly for a unified and strong America with free enterprise and opportunities for all. Let us be honest and remember that the unemployment rate during Bush's administration was only about 5.3 percent, unlike what we have now, about 10 percent, and in some states it is 12–16 percent. The last year of Bush's administration in 2008, things became a bit shaky. Little did he know, and the rest of us, too.

In our American history, we have never been in such a big hole as we are right now in debt with over $14.1 trillion—thanks to the excessive spending of the people's money by the Administration. There is absolutely no excuse for this, except the radical and inept agenda of spending, which is burying this country in debt; thus, our children and grandchildren are left to suffer the consequences.

On a happier note, my friends and I went to a big rally when President George Bush came and spoke to us all. This was on May 30, 2007, in Edison, at the New Jersey Convention and Exposition Center. My friends, the N.J. State Senator Leanna Brown, JoAnn Petrizzo of Ocean County, Priscilla

Anderson of Burlington County and I were there to greet our President, among many other admirers. It was a great rally and we had much fun and the crowd was most enthusiastic to see their Commander-in-Chief in great, patriotic mood. And there were others outside at the parking lot with placards calling the President, "a thief," "a liar," "killer" and other despicable names. (Of course, none of that was true, but they were merely practicing their freedom of speech.)

At the Bush Rally in Edison, N.J. on May 30, 2007.
L- R: Virginia Apelian, N.J. State Senator Leanna Brown,
JoAnn Petrizzo, and Priscilla Anderson.

So, what is our obligation as citizens? It is somewhat simple, yet intricate to follow. First of all, having said all that I have in this chapter, great lessons are not to be forgotten. We, who are of voting age, must be vigilant to vote for those who run for office with certain criteria in mind. We should ask ourselves the following questions:
- Is he/she an honorable person?
- Has he/she had experience in good standing?
- Check their backgrounds. Are there any connections with questionable people or organizations that do not generate good, wholesome ideas in comparison to our government?
- Would they obey the Constitution?
- What are their philosophies? Put them on a spot and pursue their actions.

The action test is critical. If candidates deviate from what they promised and get elected, the task is very simple. They do not get elected again. It is simple and easy to vote out someone. The electorate should not be lazy in finding out the facts. Because those of us who believe in equal rights, equal justice, and equal opportunity, regardless of race, creed, age, sex and disability, will succeed in the task of choosing the right people. Also, because we believe in free enterprise, which encourages individual initiative, this country has so far thrived in economic growth and prosperity.

But, sad to say, this is not what we are all experiencing right now. It is so obvious, since 2008, our Founding Fathers' mottos and works are being cast out. Our government must practice fiscal responsibility. Government should not interfere with people who are trying to keep their hard-earned money for their future dreams and needs. These criteria represent the moral clarity we should all seek in choosing our candidates, no matter what level of position they are seeking. To be a public servant is an honorable job, but one must be worthy of it. And that is up to us, to be educated and be cognizant of all the facts.

How Do We Pass It On?

This is, indeed, a very good and healthy question, "How do we pass on patriotism?" It is very simple, through *education*. Those of us who are adults and have children can guide our children and grandchildren in our daily lives, to show what our Constitution tells us. Also, with our own moral compass, we can show them the way. And the advice for the young people is if you do not have family guidance, through school and analyzing the news, ask questions. Ask those adults that you can trust who are well-informed and trustworthy.

Don't just follow the crowd for the sake of not making waves if you disagree with a certain philosophy. I hope schools are not completely ignoring our country's history since our Independence in 1776. Whether you want to be an artist, a teacher, a jeweler, a banker, a scientist, a farmer or whatever line of work you would like to do, you ought to know what your government is doing and who are running for office to make the laws. Because the laws they pass will affect you, for better or for worse. If anyone, old or young, does not care to know, then they deserve what they get. It is as simple as that.

We all at one point had to be taught to know "right from wrong." If not, that is sad. Our lives are governed by the Ten Commandments for good and sound judgment. Even though nowadays to be politically correct that is not accepted in our courtrooms, whereas it was before.

First of all, it is a privilege to serve our country in any way we can, but it is a bigger privilege to live in a country like ours. Why?—because we believe in freedom and liberties for individuals. This is a constitutional republic, and the rules apply to all of its citizens, elected officials, and private citizens.

Education

This avenue is of utmost importance. Education for a happier and a safer life is imperative. However, education cannot be one-sided. It is what we teach our children in the school system and what you establish with them at home, gearing them with a good moral compass and modeling patriotic acts. The Spanish-born American philosopher, George Santayana (1863–1952), put it well when he said, "A child educated only at school is an uneducated child." And we know for a fact that not all teachers are parents, but all parents are teachers. So, parents always have had the first and the most responsibility for educating their children. If adults do not have the incentive of bringing up children with good moral fiber, then they should not have children. Having said that brings up the issue of sound judgment. Thus, having good judgment and making decisions wisely bring purpose and meaning to human lives. Almighty God has created us with a purpose. Each one of us is very special and should recognize our identity in society. Who am I? Who are you? Do we have a solid unique idea about each one of us; if not, why not? And what is our responsibility towards other human beings? All these questions help us find a system of true values.

Also, the Greek philosopher Aristotle (384–322 B.C.) wrote: "The fate of empires depends on the education of youth." The fate or the aim of all education, whether at home, school, work, or play, ought to be the teaching of what we call "values," not merely passing on information through blank minds, or just about technical matters, but the education of living life fully.

Paul Kroll wrote in *The Plain Truth*, October 1987 issue, the following: "True education is the most important commodity we receive in life. Lack of true knowledge, or false education, can destroy individuals or nations." Those are awesome words and thoughts. False education, which is tampered by untruths and omissions of true facts, can be highly detrimental to our future and our country as a whole. We must be alerted to those radical professors who are teaching our youth to get them on the wrong track; it is tragic. Something very soon must be done about it. Even President John F. Kennedy was aware of it when he said, "A child miseducated is a child lost." Then, of course, in the long term, it will affect society as a whole.

Many of the students today, both in high school and college, are confused because of the way that society is putting things forth. Why is that? The answer is because our government has become lax and is avoiding principles set forth with our Founding Fathers. Our whole court system is based on the principles of the Ten Commandments, and yet it is not allowed to be visible in public. The word "God" is fought to take out from our Pledge of Allegiance and other places. Has a small minority of atheists the power to curtail our religious freedoms? This is a country where all religions are allowed, one can worship as she/he wishes. There are mosques, churches, temples and synagogues in our land, no one denies their existence. But, why must we forget the Founding Fathers' beliefs and expressions if we want to retell our history? That is our country's history. Let no one distort that. I emphasized in the beginning of this book, the present Turkish government is very vehemently trying to distort history regarding the Armenian Genocide.

That act is not acceptable by any means or reasoning. The same rule applies to our American history: our Founding Fathers were highly moral individuals and believed in Almighty God. There are numerous documentation and monuments to prove all this. Who are we, or those who try, to deny all that? There is not a single legitimate reason that could apply to it. Any lucid, thinking person is cognizant of that 100 percent.

However, the schools cannot be the only educating instrument of society. Beyond the home and the schools is the society at large, today's entertainment, media, religious upbringing and leadership, and the political and the business communities. They all are affecting the overall education. If our formal education is not teaching what we need for our students, it is partially the effect and fault of all these other contributors mentioned above.

In the religious community, I had admired Dr. Norman Vincent Peale for his positive thinking with Christian spirit. He is gone now, but he served us well. I also admire the work and dedication of Billy Graham, the Evangelist. People of this caliber give life the "oomph" that it deserves. Also, I have been to Washington D.C. with our children when they were growing up to show and tell them about our American heritage. Our children enjoyed those trips tremendously, and learned from them. Our American Capital is full of religious inscriptions everywhere. "*Laus Deo*" is on top of the Washington Monument, which means "Praise Be To God." And there are numerous other religious murals, monuments and inscriptions on many other areas. We should not need to make excuses for them or change them. And how could our president declare to other nations that we are not just a Christian nation. What is the purpose of that? Is he purposefully deviating from true facts with a different agenda?

Why have the Federal Courts and the Supreme Court misinterpreted the U.S. Constitution? Fifty states could not be wrong by having the preambles to their constitutions mention a strong belief in God. Every one of them glorifies God Almighty very lucidly. I recommend to the young and old to go and read all of the fifty states' preambles, which show their strong feelings about the Creator. I will just give you my own state of New Jersey's preamble as an example.

New Jersey 1844 Preamble

"We, the people of the State of New Jersey, grateful to Almighty God for civil and religious liberty which He hath so long permitted us to enjoy, and looking to Him for a blessing on our endeavors to secure and transmit the same unimpaired to succeeding generations, do ordain and establish this Constitution."

459

All the other forty-nine states have gloriously praised God's name also. Please look it up, whatever state you live in. As one studies all these pre-ambles to the fifty states' constitutions, you start thinking that how could they all have been wrong, passing them at different dates, of their own free will? And how can the ACLU and out-of-control courts be justified and considered right?

"Those people who will not be governed by God will be ruled by tyrants."
William Penn

And why are tax-funded universities' officials censoring the freedom of speech rights of Christian young people wanting to share their faith and stand up for what they believe? Why change history? The historical record is very clear. . . .America is built on Christian principles! Let me put forth some statements by some of our founders:

"Our laws and our instructions must necessarily be based upon the teachings of the Redeemer of Mankind. It is impossible that it should be otherwise; and in this sense and to this extent, our civilization and our institutions are emphatically Christian."
— **U.S. Supreme Court**, 1892,
Church of the Holy Trinity v. United States

"It is the duty of all nations to acknowledge the Providence of Almighty God, to obey His will, to be grateful for His benefits, and to humbly implore His protection and favor."
— **George Washington**, proclaiming
"A Day of Publick Thanksgiving and Prayer,"
October 3, 1789

"I have a tender reliance on the mercy of the Almighty; through the merits of the Lord Jesus Christ. I am a sinner. I look to Him for mercy; pray for me."
— **Alexander Hamilton**, dying words, July 12, 1804

"We have been assured, Sir, in the Sacred Writings, that 'except the Lord build the House, they labor in vain that build it.' I firmly believe this; and I also believe that without His concurring aid we shall succeed in this political building no better than the builders of Babel."

—**Benjamin Franklin**, statement before the Constitutional Convention, June 28, 1787

"God who gave us life gave us liberty. And can the liberties of a nation be thought secure when we have removed their only firm basis, a conviction in the minds of the people that these liberties are a gift of God? That they are not to be violated but with His wrath? Indeed, I tremble for my country when I reflect that God is just; that His justice cannot sleep forever."

— **Thomas Jefferson**, 1781

"We hold these truths to be self-evident, that all men are created equal. That they are endowed by their Creator with certain unalienable rights, that among these are Life, Liberty and the Pursuit of Happiness."

— **Declaration of Independence**, 1776

There are many more similar statements by our former patriots. They cannot be discarded, but we can learn from them. If anyone, that means anyone in leadership positions at this time, is trying to reinvent the existence of this constitutional republic, he/she is a fool and not worthy of being a part of it. These may be strong words, but otherwise those who try to destroy what this country has stood for since 1776 are committing blasphemy of first degree, which is not acceptable.

July 8, 2004, Freedom Concert at Jackson, N.J. with Sean Hannity.

461

Sean Hannity waving to the Apelians.

Our people, especially the young people, should take the good example of Sean Hannity who has done "Freedom Concert" tours for many years to encourage patriotism and raise money for the Freedom Alliance. He appreciates our military men and women who fight for our freedom, and is working with the Alliance to fund college educations for children of killed or 100 percent disabled military personnel. That is such an exemplary act for any citizen. Our military take the risk of dying for us every day. Sean Hannity is a great American and a patriot!

This type of enthusiasm, which is clean-cut, and non-violent, energizes people to be proud of their country. I was there on July 8, 2004, in Jackson, N.J. one of Sean's Freedom Concerts. I cannot remember when I had as much fun as that day. The music, the people's cheers and exuberance, and the U.S. flags everywhere made an American proud to be a part of this country. There were young people and people of all ages celebrating their freedom boldly. It was a great memory and a fantastic picture to carve in one's mind, never to be forgotten. Young people, and all age people, should look up to genuine citizens like Sean to exemplify what one can do for their country.

As also one of our former Presidents had said, "The cost of freedom is always high, but Americans have always paid it. And one path we shall never choose, and that is the path of surrender or submission."

— **John F. Kennedy,**
Cuban missile crisis address to the nation, October 22, 1962

So, my dear reader, as they say, "Freedom is not free." When we liberated France, no one in those villages was looking for the French-American, the Irish-American, or the German-American. French people only saw American soldiers carrying the American flag representing our country. We should honor and display our flag proudly, not only on Flag Day, June 14, but every day of the year.

Another important point I want to bring up is that we must keep educating ourselves and our youth by the kind of books that generate true knowledge and wisdom about our country. That is the book by Mark R. Levin, *Liberty and Tyranny*. Mr. Levin knows his Constitutional Law and talks about it in plain English I had Constitutional Law classes in college, and I found this book to be an example of a perfect guidebook on the subject. He explains what may happen (It may already have started happening) to a people when their freedoms are taken away and the government tries to control everything. It creates chaos, and people will be yearning of the days of yesteryear. This is an instructional book, and should be read by all citizens in order not to fall in the same trap of other countries who did not survive.

Mr. Levin explains the liberal agenda very clearly so that everyone will understand it very easily. He calls the liberals "statists" who worship government and work in government to expand its power. He also quotes President Reagan having said, "Freedom is never more than one generation away from extinction." Ronald Reagan was correct in many of his statements, and this one is a scary one for us, because of the direction our government is now moving. This is very risky and dangerous. I enjoyed reading this book, and I am sure you will too, good reader.

Freedom

Our most precious possession is freedom. In America, freedom starts with the following "self-evident truths" in the Declaration of Independence, July 4, 1776: "...That all men are created equal, that they are endowed by their Creator with certain unalienable rights, that among these are life, liberty and the pursuit of happiness...."

Here are the sixteen freedoms built into the Constitution and laws of the U.S.

1) *Freedom of Religion*—the colonies had escaped to America to have religious freedom. One may belong to any church she/he wishes or no church at all. Bill of Rights, Amendment I

2) *Freedom of Speech*—our Constitution guarantees citizens the right to express their opinions, even if they are against the government. (No dictatorship allows this.) Bill of Rights, Amendment I

3) *Freedom of Press*—this right includes newspapers, books, TV, radio, and motion pictures. (I do not see burning of American flags in this freedom. That is merely an interpretation of the court, which I do not agree with. Our flag should be honored.) Bill of Rights, Amendment II

4) *Freedom of Assembly*—peaceful picketing and sit-downs are guaranteed, as long as they do not result in rioting or disturbing the peace. Freedom of assembly is linked to freedom of speech. Bill of Rights, Amendment I

5) *Freedom of Keeping and Bearing Arms*—with this freedom, the federal government cannot prohibit gun ownership, but may regulate the purchase, possession and use of firearms. Bill of Rights, Amendment II

6) *Freedom of Search and Seizures*—protects privacy of person, home, papers, and personal effects against unreasonable search and seizure by making the police obtain a search warrant. Police must cite probable cause before searching private places. Bill of Rights, Amendment IV

7) *Freedom from Double Jeopardy*—a person cannot be tried twice for an offense that would put life or limb in jeopardy. Once tried and found not guilty or sentenced, a person cannot be tried again for the same crime. Bill of Rights, Amendment V

8) *Freedom from Testifying Against Self*—prevents a person from being forced into confessions or incriminating testimony

464

that might convict themselves. There should be evidence and witnesses by the prosecution. Bill of Rights, Amendment V

9) *Freedom of Deprivation of Due Process*— protects a person from being deprived of life, liberty, or property without due process of law. Bill of Rights, Amendment V

10) *Freedom from Discrimination in Seeking Citizenship or the Right to Vote*—because of race, color, or sex. Constitution, Amendments XIV, XV and XIX

11) *Freedom of Work in Localities of Your Choice*—this is indirectly guaranteed by the Constitution; Bill of Rights, Amendment I; and Amendments XIII and XIV, plus by Common Law

12) *Freedom to Go into Business to Compete and Make a Profit*—This free enterprise provision allows competition and improves the economy of our country. Constitution, Article I, Section 8; Bill of Rights, Amendments IX and X

13) *Freedom from Cruel or Unusual Punishment.* Protection against an unjust court desiring cruel punishment, which may violate human dignity. Bill of Rights, Amendment VIII

14) *Freedom from Religious Tests for Public Office.* This guarantees separation of church and state by prohibiting any religious test for civil office. Constitution, Article VI, Clause 3

15) *Freedom from Suspension of Writ of Habeas Corpus*—a court order forcing the jailor to bring an arrested person before a judge in order to decide whether there is a good reason for being held. Writ may only be suspended in times of rebellion or threats to public safety. Constitution, Article I, Section 9, Clause 2

16) *Freedom from Ex Post Facto Laws*—a person cannot be convicted for a crime committed before the law was enacted that made the act a crime. Constitution, Article I, Section 9, Clause 3.

Our Founding Fathers were geniuses thinking about all these freedoms; however, these are the basic list, and each day new laws, and new court decisions are made.

Knowing all this, young and old, it is up to us to do our part to pass the wisdoms of our freedoms on to all people and especially to our future generations in order to protect all these rights. It has been said: "Freedom is not free." This is not just a jingle. How much are our freedoms worth to each one of us? I guarantee you, it is a great deal.

In recent years, and days, we are always hearing of terrorist acts all over the world. What is our guarantee to be free of that fear? There is no 100 percent guarantee, except trusting God, and seeking help from knowledgeable people to learn and defend our country against terrorist acts upon us or any other human being in the world.

I recently heard Dr. Walid Phares, a gentleman who is very knowledgeable about Middle Eastern politics and the jihad terror activities. He is a man of integrity, who was born in Beirut, Lebanon, and is highly intelligent in knowing the ways of jihad activities globally. This is a person that our government should listen to in order to protect us from terrorists who want to wipe us off this earth. This is not sheer fear, but reality. Dr. Phares is well-spoken and well-educated and is an American. He emigrated to the U.S. in 1990. And from the author's website (see "Endnotes"), we can learn a great deal about this genuine, knowledgeable man's background. He has practiced law in Beirut after having completed studies and attained degrees in law, political science, sociology, International Law and strategic studies. In 2008, Phares taught Global Strategies at the National Defense University in Washington, D.C. He is a Senior Fellow and the Director of the Future Terrorism Project at the Foundation for Defense of Democracies in Washington, D.C. We can learn so much from him about the ideology of jihad in a short time; he is like a walking encyclopedia. He was on Neil Cavuto's Fox News show on October 29, 2010.

Why am I talking about this? Because we need to defend our country; we should know about enemies who want to annihilate us from the face of the earth. In the last week of October 2010, mail bombs were being shipped to this country to cause much damage. These originated from Yemen. Due to the jihadists, as part of al-Qaeda, we have to be extra vigilant to protect our country. We need to educate ourselves and our next generation in every possible way that we can. Knowledge is power. Once we do not sit idly, but keep watch over any type of aggressors by being vigilant, we are performing our major task to uphold all those freedoms that I talked about. We must defend life, liberty, property, citizenship, and pursuit of happiness for all. Our leaders should stop finding fault with their predecessors and, thereby, losing precious time. They should find solutions to ensure our human dignity and prosperity. Blaming others always and not take responsibility is the cowardly way.

Living life to the fullest is one of my mottos; let us pass this thought to our next generations and beyond. We should feel obliged to perform that task in order to have a better educated society that will govern the people as our Founding Fathers had intended.

PART TWELVE:

Happiness

34

Happiness Is...

Happiness is the state of being content—being happy with what you have and what you do with it. You cannot have happiness by just wishing to have it, but it comes from within. A happy person always exudes cheer and joy around her/him on a daily basis, whether things are going perfectly or not. So, you may ask, what is the secret of being happy? Let us look at some of the things that have made me the happy person I am.

1)   *Happiness is ... faith*

Knowing "For God so loved the world that He gave his only begotten Son, that whosoever believeth in Him should not perish, but have everlasting life." (John 3:16)

That thought alone gives me joy to think of God's tremendous love for us all. How could we not be elated extraordinarily about that?

Also, "And thou shalt love the Lord thy God with all thine heart, and with all thy soul, and with all thy might." (Deuteronomy 6:5)

Knowing this, I feel enormous strength and hope to carry me through life.

David in Psalm 118:24 tells us: "This is the day which the Lord hath made; we will rejoice and be glad in it." As I get up each day, I look forward to it to praise God, and do the best I can during each day. No matter what I face during the day, it does not get me down. I am always able to reason with myself not to feel helpless.

Apostle Paul is such a great example when he says in Philippians 4:4, "Rejoice in the Lord always; and again I say, Rejoice." He can say that because he had the joy of the Lord, no matter how badly he was persecuted. That is the greatest example we can follow. Paul suffered much, and yet the joy, the happiness, was in his heart.

Even Jesus said to his disciples, "... I am with you always, even unto the end of the world." (Matthew 28:20) If we have faith, what more can we ask for? That, in itself, is a joy to have that knowledge.

So, I think our first source of happiness comes from our faith and it becomes a part of us. If we have happiness, it comes from the Lord, and not by worldly things, such as wealth and the things we own. Because those things are perishable and do not have an everlasting effect on people. Those things do not make a person happy within their whole being, they are temporary things and do not give you peace within.

Another Biblical passage that is very dear to me is Psalm 23. When I am sad about something or disappointed in something, I always repeat this Psalm, which is a Psalm of David, "The Lord is my shepherd; I shall not want. ..." I repeat the whole Psalm, and then I have solace and joy, and nothing can take that away from me.

2)   Happiness is . . . family

The bond of family is a very strong part of a person's happiness. Family portrays belonging and safety. "To belong" is a very big part of someone's self-image. Parents, siblings, cousins, aunts and uncles, grandparents, grand-children, husbands and wives—they are all part of that bond and links of life. The interrelationships add to the zest of being happy and alive in life. The connection of family ties is strongly associated to the elation of a human being's psyche. The extension of family to all the members is a gratifying feeling, emotionally, for each person in that family tree. You might say everyone in every family is not the same and not all are happy. That is true; however, that first link is important, and then comes the individual choices of a person to be an independent and a giving person. When I say, a "giving person," I mean that person who will attain happiness by giving of himself/herself, becoming a contributor by helping others.

That impetus to give could be done a number of ways. But the dedication and the desire have to be there. So, in other words, there is a choice to make on the individual's part to forge ahead, to be that person who does not just think about herself/himself. The giver has joy to share with others—family members or outside people—and is a special human being.

3)   Happiness is . . . your heritage

What do you know about your heritage? Are you aware of it at all, or do you not care? Where have your ancestors come from? To have a distinct profile of a group of people that either you are proud of or not, will make an impact on your behavior. A good and solid background on your ancestry will strengthen your values in life and the examples of their good deeds will have a great impact on you. Thus, you will choose to propagate certain philanthropic ideas and goodwill toward human beings. In doing so, that satisfaction will give you the joy within to share goodwill with others.

Here, I would like to mention that the original Armenian Church, which was the very first church to be declared by a Christian nation in 301 A.D., has been a significant teaching tool for Armenian history. The church's motto has been church (faith) first, then family, and then devotion to country (heritage). If a person takes these three points seriously, a great foundation is laid for being a happy person. That is, if the individual is serious about each of these three levels. If not, no one can force the issue for someone to be happy if they choose not to. It is very important for a person to know her/his roots. This will give them their identity, which is a major factor for a person to feel self-assured, and deal with life's journey, with all its sadness and anxiety.

Author's Armenian heritage attire.

*Henry M. Apelian,
Virginia's husband.*

4) Happiness is . . . having a loving husband

A loving husband or wife is crucial to creating a wholesome family. Both parents are committed to each other and to their children, if they have children. This commitment is not just sexual, but one of respect and honor. And how the couple behaves will have a great impact in raising their family. They must be good models to the children.

5) Happiness in . . . taking my granddaughter Christee to Sunday school

Since I taught Sunday school for many years, I felt obliged to bring our grandchildren to Sunday school from very early on—that is the grandchildren who lived close by. Their being nurtured in church was very important to me and to our daughter, Christee's mother. All three of our grandchildren: Christee, Holly and T.J., are outstanding students and citizens, and they enjoy going to church.

Christee and author going to Sunday school; Virginia was her teacher.

6) *Happiness is . . . celebrating New Year's with grandkids*

It is such a joy to do things with my three grandchildren—celebrating holidays and making them a part of our lives. And this teaches them to be thankful for many blessings that the Lord has bestowed upon them. This is how they learn sweet occasions, by celebrating with the family, and knowing that they are loved.

Celebrating New Year's with my grandchildren Christee, Holly and Tim J., Jr.

7) *Happiness is . . . picking blueberries with Grandpa*

To do routine, happy things with our children or grandchildren, makes them appreciate both being involved in doing the task and teaches them about the benefits of nature.

Christee, Holly and Tianna picking blueberries at author's Clark, N.J. house's backyard.

8) *Happiness is . . . picking apples from my own tree that my Dad had planted*

To some people, this may not be such a big deal, but to me it was a great joy. First of all, because I like nature and fruits, but most importantly, this tree was planted by my father. My dear father was no longer with us, but his deed of having planted that little seedling brought so much joy to me and my family, made me very happy.

Author picking an abundance of apples from her tree.

9) *Happiness is ... being at a Yule log burning at the Voorhees Chapel on the Douglass campus*

I have always enjoyed this ceremony of burning a Yule log at Christmastime. The Yule Log Ceremony at the Voorhees Chapel fireplace is very beautifully done, and so relaxing to witness! This is a really beautiful tradition! The theme was, "One Night of Light, Where All Unite." The Douglass young women all dressed in white, with lit candles in their hands, lined up on a specially designed movable staircase and the balcony is a sight to see. This is a very beautiful event as the music and the fireplace all add to its glorious presentation. Every time I think of it, it brings back tender feelings in me and warms my heart again.

10) *Happiness is ... greeting the new millennium at Lambert Castle*

This was such a happy occasion to greet the year 2000 with dear friends at such a historical place so dear to me since my teens. This big New Year's Gala was sponsored by The Passaic County Historical Society, and it was very well-organized.

The Lambert Castle, built in the late 19th century by a local silk tycoon in Paterson, N.J.

Henry and Virginia celebrate New Year's Eve 2000 at Lambert Castle on Garret Mountain, Paterson, N.J.

11) *Happiness is . . . going to a real luau in Hawaii*

Such a refreshing time we had at our first luau in Hawaii—to savor the food, the customs and the culture of the islands. We also celebrated Christmas at the same time. The novelty of celebrating Christmas with balmy palm trees and the sweet ocean air was quite a different experience.

Going to a real luau in Hawaii.

12)   Happiness is . . . painting murals

How I enjoy painting and creating pictures and sceneries of places that I have been to.

"The Hawaiian Sunset" mural Virginia painted in their Clark house on the kitchen wall.

Mt. Ararat, Khor Virab, and Lake Sevan, all at one scene, painted on foyer wall in the Manchester, N.J. house.

These places were very meaningful to me and enjoyed visits there tremendously. Every time I think of them, they put a smile on my face.

13) *Happiness is . . . listening to Sipan Armenian School children of Armenian Presbyterian Church in Paramus, N.J. singing "Yerevan Erepooni"*

This is such a beautiful song about Armenia. When I hear it, and I love it with such joy that I get tears in my eyes. It is such a melodious song and the words are so meaningful too. I would travel miles and miles to hear this song sung. The lyrics are written by Harooyr Sevak and the music is by Edgar Hovhannessian. Such geniuses they were to give so much pleasure to people with their unique talent.

14) *Happiness is . . . loving thy neighbors as thyself*

This saying is from the Bible and it is certainly a great way to be happy. If you treat your neighbors as yourself, in turn you will make them happy and respectful of you. That is the humane thing to do.

The Apelians' neighbors often had block parties to enjoy each other's company. Pictured are the Manchester Gascony Circle neighbors, which are considered friends.

15)   *Happiness is . . . having friends from all walks of life*

We are all creations of God, and to respect each other and have relationships dear to us with friends, is the nurturance of our lives.

With friends at the Philadelphia Flower Show. L–R: Virginia, Pat Frydendahl, Rita Kemptner, Carolyn Baumann, and K-Hee Yang.

George and Aimee Bedirian visiting from Paris. George, a WWII hero, passed away recently. Aimee is one of author's best friends and considered a sister.

Virginia's Turkish friend, Nina Scampato.

Distance does not matter; I speak to Aimee in Paris and in Spain often. We enjoy our friendship. If she is not in Paris, she usually is at her Laredo, Spain home, which we have been to several times.

To be friends with people, one has to have some common ground of philosophy and understanding. However, you do not hold a grudge or an indifference towards somebody because of their ethnic background. So, after having said that, I have friends of many different religious and ethnic backgrounds. Nina was Turkish, but she was a Christian, and I did not hold a grudge against her for being Turkish. She was the sweetest and the kindest person I ever knew. She passed away of a heart attack in 2009, and I miss her dearly. I had known Nina for thirty-nine years. Gilberta is a Jewish lady I met at the Armenian Assembly Conference in Washington, D.C. in 2002. We have been friends since then. She loves Armenian people, food, customs and all. She has been to Armenia at least twenty-five times as of this writing.

To have good friends of all backgrounds is the spice of life. They are gifts from God. "There is neither Jew nor Greek, there is neither bond nor free, there is neither male nor female; for ye are all one in Christ Jesus." (Galatians 3:28)

What more can we ask for? The answer is not to be prejudiced at all. I love the following quote, "Don't walk in front of me, I may not follow. Don't walk behind me, I may not lead. Just walk beside me and be my friend." — *Albert Camus*

I have this quote framed and hung on my wall at home for everyone to see, including my family members.

16)   *Happiness is . . . compassion, to feel for others.*

The following is not a posed picture. Most of the time, I carry a camera with me. Photography is one of my hobbies. When I noticed this family moment, my granddaughter giving comfort to her little brother, the scene touched me. Capturing that moment was worth a million dollars to me: Little Holly, consoling her little brother T.J. He was scared seeing a strange animal in the vegetable patch. I adore this picture, because it tells such a beautiful story. By the way, compassion is not verbally taught, but learned by modeling. I give credit to my daughter for having shown compassion to her youngsters.

We can all show compassion in our daily lives with people in need of it. It does not cost us anything, but goodwill, and that someone receiving it will be so thankful and accepted.

Holly comforting her little brother T.J.

17) *Happiness is . . . bringing my niece and nephew to the U.S. from the Middle East*

Both my nephew Mardo and niece Margo were very happy to join us here in the U.S. They were very hardworking people, and my parents were so happy to see them. They were orphans when they came to America; they were my parents' first child's children. My sister Rosemary was born and brought up in America until she was in her teens.

I did all the paperwork for my nephew and niece through the Immigration Department and found jobs for them, too. That made my parents extremely happy. In 1992, Margo married her boss, James Burns, and I was her matron-of-honor.

L–R: The author, and her nephew and niece, Mardo and Margo.

Virginia is matron-of-honor for Margo.

18) *Happiness is . . . helping others*

This is the most rewarding thing one can do, to give special time for a good cause.

Clark Township Council and Mayor. Serving 27,000 citizens was most rewarding.

Even though I had to go through numerous obstacles to win my council seat and being the only woman on the Council was not easy at times, I still found helping people rewarding and a real joy for me.

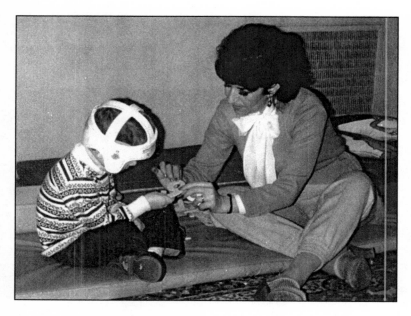

Helping handicapped children is worth more than $1 million.

Assisting handicapped children on their Kindergarten graduation day.

490

To have been part of the Mountainside Children's Hospital volunteer team, the Westlake School Branch at Mildred Terrace School, Clark, is one of my most cherished memories. To help these beautiful children, who had multiple problems, was rewarding and made life worthwhile.

While in Manchester, Ocean County, the Town Hall had a great program to make Christmas a happy occasion for families who could not afford gifts for their children. They bought dolls without any clothing, and volunteers signed up, made clothing for them and brought the dolls back on a certain date.

Virginia delivers the dolls she dressed to Town Hall.

491

This was one of the more fun things that I had ever done. I made different outfits for the dolls and I enjoyed it tremendously. I had some white satin, with which I made a bride with a gown and headpiece. Then I fashioned a Girl Scout with her attire, and other dolls with party clothes to make some little girls happy.

Author's Sunday school class at Fanwood Presbyterian Church.

I always enjoyed teaching God's word to innocent, beautiful minds, which were so eager to listen and learn. All these things gave me tremendous inner peace that no money on earth can buy. Praise be to Almighty God.

19)   Happiness is . . . snoozing with your grandchild

That was such a cozy and peaceful feeling that one cannot put to words. But time goes by and the good Lord blesses the children and the grandparents manifold.

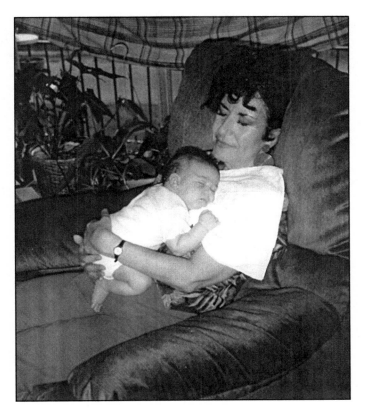

Snoozing comfortably with granddaughter Christianna when she was 2 months old.

Our eldest son's children, L–R: Henry M., Sarah V., and Christianna Apelian.

God's gifts to us in so many ways are so abundant. We should always be cognizant of that fact.

20)   *Happiness is . . . freedom*

We have a right to freedom from fear, anxiety, subjugation by anyone, and, in plain English, to do things that we like such as freedoms of speech, press and religion. And the happiness comes in liking what you do, not just merely doing something.

21) *Happiness is . . . having family gatherings*

It is so nurturing to come together and have family picnics and dinners and be joyful for having each other.

Apelian family picnic with children and grandchildren.

Family dinners are opportunities to share good food and conversation.

Family gatherings are freedoms and blessings that should not be taken for granted. As we look around, things happen without our control. Life is too short sometimes. We have to live each moment in the very best way we can to savor life fully.

22)　*Happiness is . . . just resting*

Yes, just doing nothing but resting comfortably is joyful, enjoying the blue sky, a soft breeze touching your face, smelling beautiful fragrances of flowers in the garden, and counting your blessings.

This is one of those moments of resting: Grandson Henry Michael and Virginia under the apple tree.

Can anything match sitting with your adorable grandchild with his chubby toes dancing on your lap, and a contented feeling that nothing else matters going through your mind? We all should savor such times because somehow those moments never come back, but the mere impression is imprinted in our memory pages. As shown in the above photo, the sun's rays flickering through the apple tree branches warmed our hearts.

23) Happiness is . . . growing things

Have you ever grown anything? If not, you are missing a great joy in life. The experience is inexplicable because of its nature of pleasure. I always found comfort and beauty in my rose gardens.

Author at one of her rose gardens.

Of course, it is strenuous and continuous work, but who thinks of the weariness as you look at the magnificence of a rose and its beauty. The work of pruning, feeding, weeding, cultivating and continuously checking for bugs that love to eat rosebuds and petals is worthwhile when looking at and enjoying the rose garden if even for a few moments. At least, that is how I feel about the whole thing. Who can make such a beautiful thing, but God?

Author enjoying her iris garden. This flower is the queen of May flowers.

I love all kinds of flowers, but irises are very unique in my book. The iris is the queen of flowers in the month of May. I have every color one can imagine. Irises are so beautiful in their statuesque way with their glistening beards shining like diamonds through the sunlight.

I was told that a Virginian or a Southern Magnolia does not grow in New Jersey. I did not want to believe that; since I had seen those magnolia trees grow in Washington, D.C. I figured they have snow, too. Thus, I wanted to buy a little seedling and try to have one in my garden. I had to order it from a nursery in Trenton. And for a two-foot little tree I had to pay about $250. Well, it was a miracle. This little tree grew so beautifully and tall, and gave me the most gorgeous large flowers, the size of a paper plate. It was amazing. And that was not all, its fragrance was heavenly!

A sample of Southern Magnolia blossoms.

Since we moved from the house in Manchester where I had planted this tree, I gathered seeds from it, and now I have a Southern Magnolia tree growing at my present front yard. It is such a wonder and joy to grow things and enjoy them in their beauty. A second one I grew from a seed, I gave as a gift to my daughter-in-law Heidi, who also loves growing things.

499

24) *Happiness is . . . to sleep over at Grandma and Grandpa's house*

This is one of the most fun activities that the grandchildren can have. Also, the parents enjoy a little break to have some private time and peace and quiet.

Grandma Virginia greeting the crew arriving for sleepover.

We had them over Friday afternoons until Sunday nights. They came with much anticipation for fun, cheer, and learning. Christee, Holly, and T.J. lived about five minutes away from us. That made it easy for us to have them over often. Our daughter and family lived in Colonia, N.J.

I figured if I am around, they can have some extra fun of having pillow fights after they awakened on Saturday morning. That was something novel for them. At first, they were cautious and they said they never had pillow fights at home. I assured them that they could have pillow fights here, but don't do it at home if mom does not allow you to have one. They were delighted to their hearts content and enjoyed the whole thing. Our grandson had a front row seat to watch his sisters go at it. He just watched the girls having the fun of their lifetime.

The girls and their brother T.J. watching.

501

*And here we had a winner, the big sister, and
T.J. is still enthralled.*

This whole pillow fight thing was very exhilarating for them and they could not wait to tell their parents about it. Then on Saturday, we made hard jello so we can cut up shapes and eat them. They also took their bubble baths, and watched some appropriate television. Saturday, they went to bed at a reasonable time to go to church with us the next morning. However, Grandpa treated them with his famous blueberry pancakes, while they watched and helped him make the pancakes.

Jello time.

Grandpa making pancakes and the little ones helping.

All was enjoyed by our three little angels, and they went home refreshed and happy and asking us when will be the next sleepover. We all had so much fun; this was a part of their growing up that we will cherish always.

25)   *Happiness is . . . having sheer, clean fun*

We moved to Renaissance in Manchester in June of 2001. This was a gated community with many facilities for swimming, tennis, drama, chorus, golfing and a lot more. It was a 55+ community with many interesting people of all professions. I had belonged to Aquababes, which was a swimming exercise class with a lively healthy group.

One day, they asked me to be the Queen Mother of a Red Hat Society. I had heard about the group, but never thought that I would be the Queen Mother. To make a long story short, I accepted. Then I had to plan a meeting to set some rules so that the group would be manageable. The Renaissance population was 1,900 homes. I put an ad in our newsletter to start a group. I said first come, first served; I had only 25 members in mind. However, we settled on 35, and at that point, I wanted to stop the registration.

We had our first meeting and this was the first group being formed in Renaissance. I filed with the Director in 2003, and called our group the Renaissance Red Hat Romantics (the RRR). Soon, the neighboring towns' newspapers took photos of our group, and I began getting calls from outside of our community from women who wanted to join us. I went as far as 50 members, and then decided to train some ladies to have their own groups, so that the numbers would be manageable.

The aim of the Red Hats was to have fun: trips, high teas, Broadway shows, etc. We would wear purple clothing and red hats. If it was a member's birthday, they would reverse the colors, with a purple hat and a red outfit.

This whole thing had started as a joke in California, and caught on like wildfire. After my group started in our Renaissance community, eleven other chapters formed and soon we had our convention. It was loads of fun.

The Renaissance Red Hat Romantics: Virginia is the fifth on the left of the front row. This was the original group, and then it grew further. (A few women were absent.)

Shirley Zarrilli, the Lifestyles Director at Renaissance, joined us at our meeting congratulating us upon our initial meeting, and being the first group to start it. I had arranged many fun trips for my group, such as the Italian Fiesta at the Poconos, a *River Lady* paddle wheel cruise, and many more outings.

I had too many other obligations that I had to attend to, such as being the president for three other groups, I handed my title to Adele Hamilton who graciously took the job. It was very important to have fun and relaxation with friends. It was very satisfying.

After two years, I left the group and they gave me a big party. One of the red hatters, Lucille Rabinowitz, was very talented, and had written a special poem for me, which they all sang in the tune of "Sound of Music." It was delightful, and was called, "To Virginia, with Love and Appreciation." I was not aware of this until I walked in the room. They all started singing the song enthusiastically. They gave me a bouquet of long-stem red roses, and the song in an 11"x14" golden frame.

26) Happiness is . . . having great children who made great parents

This is every parent's wish to have decent children. We thank the good Lord for His love and blessings. My husband and I are proud of our three sons and daughter.

Husband Henry and our three sons, L–R:
Christopher, Henry, David and Gregory, the eldest.

All three of our sons made great fathers.

Eldest son Greg, and his son Henry.

Twin sons: Chris with Ellie, and David with Kate.

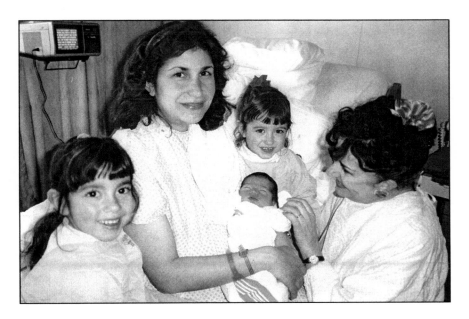

Daughter Arminee and her family on Easter Sunday when she delivered her son T.J. Jr. in 1995.

We are grateful to Almighty God, for our four children and eight grandchildren.

Our eldest son Greg turned an old theater into a church, where he helped the needy with food banks and clothing for the homeless in Glassboro, N.J. Upon the culmination of this work, he gave the homily on Thanksgiving at the First Presbyterian Church in Glassboro, N.J. He is a writer and a poet and loves to do social work.

Christopher is Professor and Chair of the Mathematics and Computer Science Department at the Drew University in Madison, N.J. He received his Ph.D. from NYU.

David is a medical doctor who lives in Boonton Township, N.J.

Arminee, our daughter, is a special education teacher and lives in Colonia.

509

27)   Happiness is . . . bonding with and teaching your grandchildren

Bonding with your grandchildren is such a nurturing process, which is worth every second of it. The long-lasting effect is just amazing upon their lives. I will show you some photos which tell a story of their own.

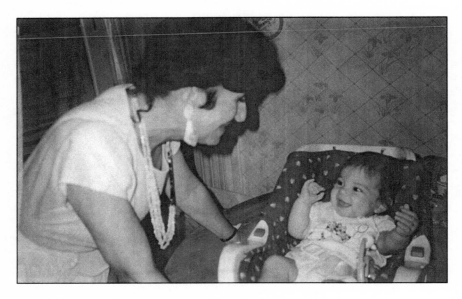

Author talks with her first grandchild, Christee. She is so animated, her eyes are glowing with joy.

To see that child's face lit up with such a glow, and listening to every word uttered, is fascinating. The learning process had begun, and I enjoyed every second of it.

On a hot summer day, I am giving my granddaughter, Christianna Apelian a bath in the kitchen sink in a laundry basket. She was so happy and she was making gurgling sounds of joy as I was bathing her.

Virginia bathes Christianna in the sink.

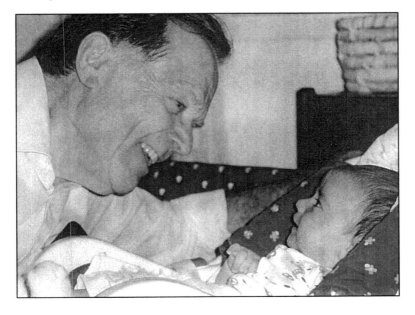

Henry is having a big conversation with T.J.

When it is my turn to have a long chat with T.J., he is chatting a mile a minute. I would ask him, "How big is T.J.?" He would extend his arms out and show me. What precious moments.

T.J. gestures to Grandma that he is "so big."

Teaching moments: Those are so essential too. Even though they cannot express themselves fully in a verbal manner initially, children may comprehend more than we think.

Here grandpa is reading to little Henry.

Christee and Holly want to learn how to knit.

At one point, the granddaughters were so eager to learn to knit, and I was glad to take that opportunity to teach them. Young minds are amazing; they retain a great deal.

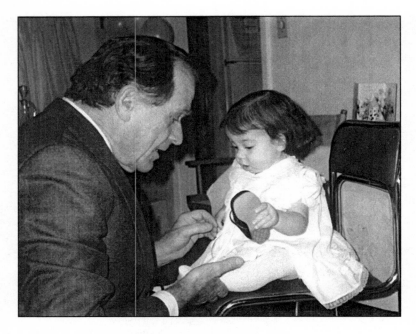

Grandpa showing Christee how to put on her shoes.

Christee is totally immersed in the story that Grandma is telling her.

And to build a snow family was most interesting and exhilarating. It was a bit cold, but the fun they had warmed all of our hearts.

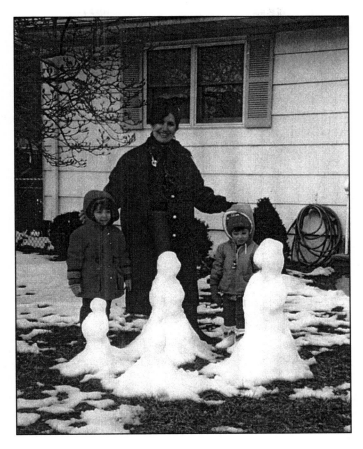

Making a snow family with Christee and Holly.

When children are kept busy constructively, their minds develop in that direction to learn more about their surroundings and things in general. Who can forget those precious moments—nothing can replace that fun of bonding and in teaching process.

515

28) *Happiness is . . . being satisfied with what you have*

This is a simple and a realistic fact. People who are always yearning what other people have will never be happy. Be satisfied with whatever you have and make the best of it. Continual thoughts of not being satisfied are very harmful. Constant dissatisfaction always demeans what one has or what one wants to be. It shows immaturity and selfishness. This person who is always searching for happiness will look for faults in those around them or herself/himself. We can be content with what we have and make the best of it. No matter how much money we have, it cannot buy permanent happiness. Happiness comes from peace within.

29) *Happiness is . . . a smile*

A smile seems such a simple thing, but it goes a long way to make a person happy, both the giver and the receiver. It may seem so trivial, but it warms the souls of others. Thus, smiling makes you happy, too. You can even tell a smile in your voice when you speak on the telephone with someone. They do not see your face, but they will recognize your smiling voice, which has a very distinct intonation from that of a normal or a flat tone.

I used to teach special role-playing in my college assertiveness classes; you may use the same words, but the connotation is quite different depending on "how you say it." Let's take the simple phrase, saying "Thank you" to someone. Now you may say that is a polite expression and quite innocuous. How could you spoil saying, "Thank you" to anyone? Well, repeat this to yourself, saying "Thank you" with a smile, and then raise your voice, and shout it out with a little anger attached to it. You would be shocked by the reactions of people.

So, when you say something with a smile, you have to live it as you mean it. That way, the sincerity will be well-sensed by the receiver. Just a plain nice smile goes a long way to make the person receiving it very happy and accepted, and paid attention to. In return it makes you happy even more so. Here are some beautiful samples of smiles that I cherish.

Christee, our oldest grandchild, now 21.

Ellie, our youngest grandchild, now 5.

Kate, our grandchild,
now 6.

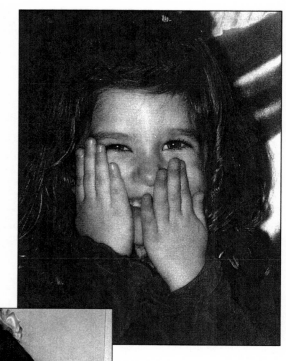

Smiles and hugs, Christee
and Holly, when they were
younger.

30)   *Happiness is . . . sharing*

Why are some rich people so unhappy? Because it is not money that makes a person happy, but helping people in need, willingly and lovingly. America is known to be very charitable to all other nations, more than any other nation in the world. That is a great gift we can possess, to make someone else happy, who may be less fortunate than us. However, it is not just money we use in sharing a kindness; there are other ways to give. One way is to share our time with a shut-in, give them a call to see how they are doing, and ask if they need any kind of help. Or call a lonely person on a regular basis, as a routine, to make that person feel important, and give some of our time to talk to them. I used to call several elderly people to chat with them and make them feel good within our conversation. That really used to perk them up, and they felt important that someone had thought about them and called them. What an easy thing to do, and yet the impact of it was so great in making someone happy. These acts of kindness make you happier by having given someone that special kindness.

31)   *Happiness is . . . celebrating your 50th wedding anniversary*

Henry and I have celebrated many happy wedding anniversaries, praise be to God.

Our 40th Wedding Anniversary with our six grandchildren.

520

We had only six grandchildren on our 40th anniversary, but by our 50th, we had eight! Our son David gifted us with a vacation to Florida to celebrate our Golden Anniversary last year.

In Florida, our 50th Wedding Anniversary.

We had a marvelous week with our grandchildren, too, in Florida. It was restful and very meaningful to all of us.

All of the above are very important factors in my happiness. You can have yours too. It is a choice that we make and work towards consciously and positively.

I have some other memorable moments and meaningful incidents that I would like to make a note of. All of them made me happy.

Our second granddaughter, Christianna, is marveling at those round balls on the ground having fallen from the apple tree.

She soon learned that those were apples not balls; it is a marvel to watch little ones as they grow up. Their innocence is so pure.

Here is another marvel with our Christee, who is looking at this beautiful candy house that my nephew Mardo had made for us. Mardo is very creative to have made this gingerbread house and others for public display in store fronts. However, besides being thankful for his kind gesture, Mardo being so generous and creative, little Christee is looking at the glorious house with such happy thoughts, but is restrained not to break a piece off of it. We can see the joy on her face. What an interesting moment to watch.

Christee and the gingerbread house.

The joy of seeing our grandchild Holly on stage performing so elegantly is always a delight. She has been in numerous plays on stage in school and "Plays in the Park," receiving many accolades for her performances. She has had leads in plays such as Maria in *West Side Story*; Cinderella; Julia in *The Wedding Singer*, and Belle in *Beauty and the Beast*.

Holly as Belle in Beauty and the Beast. (Courtesy of Rich Kowalski, 2008)

There have been precious moments such as dressing up with hats and gloves with my daughter to go to church. These unforgettable moments are printed on my memory pages to last and make me happy the rest of my life.

Mother Virginia and daughter Arminee going to church.

Also, it was delightful to go to my 50th Central High School Reunion in 2005. I had graduated in 1955, and had kept in touch with some of my classmates. But to see most of them at the reunion was absolutely fantastic. I was saddened to learn that we had lost about 20 of my classmates. Since our reunion, Doris Rofino Ververs and I have become close friends. We had lost contact for a while after we got married. Doris had organized and along with another classmate, Marjorie, had done most of the work for the reunion. They did a superb job. It was wonderful to renew our friendships from such a long time ago.

The Apelians' table at the 50th Anniversary Reunion of Virginia's Central High School graduation class.

Next morning, having breakfast after the gala of our reunion. L–R: back row: Husband Henry Apelian; Doris Rofino, the organizer; seated: classmates Lorraine, Virginia, Mickie and Charlotte.

526

Then, the classmates wanted another reunion, for which I sponsored a river boat cruise on the Toms River. We had great fun dancing the night away that evening of August 12, 2006.

The classmates have a great fun night on the river. L–R: Rosemarie, Phyllis, and Virginia.

I had the joy of knitting an Easter coat for my granddaughter, Christianna.

Christianna's happy smile while wearing that Easter coat is a marvelous gift to me.

Oh, how about that warm hug from my grandchild, Sarah; it is priceless, indeed.

The nicest hug ever, from Sarah.

Meeting the famous actor, John Gavin, was such a novelty. I met him at one of President Reagan's rallies in Union County in 1980. He was a gentleman, and a great friend of President Reagan. On February 26, 1981, the *Dallas Times Herald* had reported that President Reagan had settled on John Gavin for the U.S. Ambassador to Mexico. Both Reagan and Gavin had served on the board of directors of the Screen Actors Guild.

The *Star Ledger* reported in its issue of February 27, 1981, that Gavin had appeared in many famous films such as, *A Time to Love and a Time to Die*, *Psycho*, *Thoroughly Modern Millie*, *Midnight Lace*, and *Spartacus*. Gavin is half Mexican (his mother was a member of a powerful family in Sonora), and he is fluent in both Spanish and Portuguese. He graduated from Stanford University with a major in Latin American economic history. He served in the U.S. Navy and the Naval Reserve, and retired with the rank lieutenant colonel. It was a pleasure to meet such an outstanding actor and U.S. citizen.

I have many more miraculously happy moments that I cherish, but I am going to conclude my happy moments with this last one.

Christee had such zest and determination from early on, and later on in 2008, she entered the Miss Colonia contest. She had to write an essay to tell of her future plans for herself and the community. Among many contestants, she won the title of the first Miss Colonia, and received a $3,000 scholarship to apply to her college. She is now at Pratt Institute in New York City.

The happy picture with her mom and dad when Christee was chosen Miss Colonia to represent her town.

531

It was a happy day for all—the township, Christee, her parents and, of course, grandma and grandpa.

Whatever I have written about so far and a lot more, I thank my Lord and Savior for all His blessings. None of these happy events would have been possible merely by our efforts; the driving force has been continuous faith in God.

So, the recipe for happiness in life is connected to the many factors I have written about. Those are my important reasons to be happy in life. My advice to anyone is to enjoy every moment as if it was your last day in life. I do not want to be morose about it, but life is not always smooth sailing. I have experienced that, too, having had three major near-death experiences in my life.

As recounted earlier, the first one was when I was little, having had a vaccination that had killed many children. The second time was when I contracted the measles virus from one of my Sunday school pupils in 1966. Again, many adults who had gotten the virus died that year. The last brush with death was when a commercial garbage truck crashed into my car, after the driver crossed on a red light in 1997.

So, I think to appreciate our happy, rosy days, we all go through some, or many, obstacles in life. Somehow, we can still have the capacity to love life and continue being a happy person. One of my greatest philosophies is "Enjoy life to its fullest." Our friends make us the owner of much happiness. I always try to remember that passion for life is the essence of it all. No one is in charge of my happiness, except me, and you, for yours. We cannot blame anyone else for us not being happy. The inner peace in us will exude joy and happiness.

Finally, summing all this up, happiness is personal growth. To attain it is finding yourself and not trying to find it in someone else. We make our happiness, but we must be cautious not to form expectations beyond our control.

"The LORD hath done great things for us, whereof we are glad."
(Psalm 126:3)

Epilogue

No matter what kinds of tribulations we have to get through in our lives, may they be of historical magnitude or simply personal, trusting Almighty God will bring us divine guidance and will direct us throughout our lives. I truly believe this.

I think everything that happens to us is a learning tool if we heed all the consequences and learn from them. Here are some wise words by Dr. Leo Buscaglia:

"Joy is a great teacher, but so is despair. Hope is a great teacher, but so is disillusionment.... to deny yourself any of these is not experiencing life totally."

The legacy that my parents and my Armenian ancestors left me is my uplifting attitude toward life: live it fully. All the horrible situations they were forced into made them strong and resilient, because of their strong faith. God fought their battles, more of them than one can count. God never forsakes us.

To have knowledge of historical facts is highly important to guide us through our future years. To distort historical facts is cowardly. We should learn from history not to repeat genocides and atrocities of the past against humanity. By having learned these fundamental facts, the human race should be guided to a more desirable and safer world.

Having gone through extreme, difficult times and then being victorious in the end, gives a person or a nation enduring strength and resilience to last for a long, long time. Endurance produces character and character, in turn, produces hope. And let us not measure our character by money, but by faith in Jesus Christ, our Lord and Savior.

Once we establish our faith in God, we will respect all his creations, of which we are a major part. Therefore, as Dr. Leo Buscaglia says,

"I don't believe in luck, and I don't believe in fate. I believe in you, and I believe in me, and it's never too late."

Those are important words. Once you and I establish that strong feeling and the assurance of faith and hope in our Lord, we will respect the gift of life that has been bestowed upon us all. And we will feel the strength and assurance of our precious lives—to live them fully and intelligently. This, my friends and readers, I call the "The Blueprint of Life": to enjoy life fully, thankfully, wisely, and knowledgeably.

No matter what kind of business we may be in, as long as it is benefiting society as a whole, life given to us should and could be a beautiful choice among many other temporary choices. Thus, having said all this, life lived fully will give us the assured happiness that we all are seeking.

I would like to end with his quote by Stephen Grellet (a French-born aristocrat, Etienne de Grellet du Mabillier, who became a Quaker in New Jersey):

"I shall pass through this world but once. Any good that I can do or any kindness that I can show to any human being, let me do it now. Let me not defer it for I shall not pass this way again."

I hope this book gave you a lucid explanation of what life may offer us. No matter what kind of obstacles come in our way, we should not deaden our spirit for a fruitful life. Life is not all fun all the time; there are many ups and downs to survive through. But not giving up is the essence of victory. If we depend only on our own strength, we will not succeed. If we have faith in God, we will have the hope and encouragement that no one can stand in our way. These are all gifts from God that we savor with confidence to face any kind of challenge. I hope this book has inspired you, whether you are young or old. It is the quality of life we choose that enables us to live happily ever after.

Endnotes

Akcam, Taner, *A Shameful Act: The Armenian Genocide and the Question of Responsibility*. New York: Henry Holt and Company, LLC, 2006.

Antreassian, Rev. Dikran, *Escape to Musa Dagh or The Banishment of Zeitoun and Suedia's Revolt*, tr. Knarik Meneshian. Paramus, N.J.: Armenian Missionary Association of America, 1993.

Auron, Yair, *The Banality of Denial: Israel and the Armenian Genocide*. Piscataway, N.J.: Transaction Publishers, 2003.

Avakian, Dr. Ara S., *The Armenians in America*. Minneapolis: Lerner Publications Co., 1977.

Barton, James L. "A Cry From Armenia," *The New Armenia*, 1916;8(2):339-340.

Charney, Israel W. editor-in-chief, *Encyclopedia of Genocide, Vols. I & II*. Institute of the Holocaust and Genocide, Jerusalem, 1999.

CIA, "World Factbook, Armenia." December 10, 2010. Accessed December 27, 2010. <https://www.cia.gov/library/publications/the-world-factbook/geos/am.html>

Douglas, John M., *The Armenians*, New York: J.J. Winthrop Corp. Publisher, 1992.

Downing, Charles, (tr.) *Armenian Folk-Tales and Fables*. London: Oxford University Press, 1972, pp. 207-211.

Hassassian, Manuel S., *Armenia's Struggle for Self Determination*, Jerusalem: Hai Tad Press, 1983.

Hovannisian, Richard G., *Republic of Armenia, Vol. IV: Between Crescent and Sickle, Partition and Sovietization*. Berkeley: University of California Press, 1996.

Lang, David Marshall, *Armenia: Cradle of Civilization*, London: George Allen and Unwin, 1970. (First published in 1970 under the Berne Convention.)

——, *The Armenians: A People in Exile*. London: Unwin Hyman, 1988.

Lifton, Robert Jay, *The Nazi Doctors: Medical Killing and the Psychology of Genocide*, New York: Basic Books, 1986.

Mead, Margaret, *Culture and Commitment: The New Relationships Between Generations in the 1970s*. New York: Columbia University Press, 1970.

Morgan, Jacques de, *The History of the Armenian People* (tr. Ernest F. Barry). Boston: Hairenik Assoc., Inc., 1965.

...hau, Henry, *The Murder of a Nation*, New York: Armenian General Benevolent Union of America, Inc., 1974.

Papajian, Rev. Sarkis, *A Brief History of Armenia*. Fresno, Calif.: Mid-Cal Publishers, 1974 (Third Printing 1985).

Phares, Walid. "Phares to Fox News Neil Cavuto: "We are facing Political Jihadism." Oct. 29, 2010. Accessed Dec. 29, 2010. <http://www.walidphares.com>

Reagan, Ronald, "Tear Down This Wall," delivered June 12, 1987. The History Place, Great Speeches Collection. Accessed Dec. 27, 2010. <http://www.historyplace.com/speeches/reagan-tear-down.htm>

Takoosian, Harold, "Armenian Americans," accessed February 20, 2010. <http://www.everyculture.com/multi/A-Br/Armenian-Americans.html>

Terjimanian, Hagop, *Who Are the Armenians?* (*Armenian History in a Nutshell.*) Los Angeles: Abril Publishing Co., 1996.

Toynbee, Arnold J., *Armenian Atrocities: The Murder of a Nation*, London: Hodder and Staughton, 1917; New York: reprinted by Tankian Publishing Corp., 1975.

Vartanian, Serkek, *Armenian Capitals*, Yerevan, Armenia: 1985, p. 167.

Acknowledgments

The origins of this book go back to my parents who instilled the good sense and the honorable history of the Musa Dagh Armenians in me. My special gratitude goes to my dad Hagop (James) and mom Christina for having kept the spirit of faith in me to write this book. I want also to thank them for the many important photos that they had left me, which I have used in this book. Most importantly, my sincere thanks go to them for the many sacrifices they made for me and my siblings.

Also, I must thank so many other people who made it possible for me to write this book with pertinent conversations from Dr. Vazken Der Kaloustian, son of one of the heroes of Musa Dagh battle and Dr. Vazken Ghougassian the Executive Director of the Armenian Prelacy of NYC. In addition, helpful conversations took place with Professor Vahram Shemmassian of Northridge College of California. My special thanks go to Mary (Vartanessian) Dabagian who provided the Port Said photos, which were given to her by the Archbishop Mampre Calfayan. The sister of the Archbishop had personally taken those pictures in Port Said when she served in the Red Cross.

I must not forget to thank Dr. Rouben Adalian of the Armenian National Institute (ANI) of Washington, D.C., who had helped me during my Armenian Genocide lectures in schools, churches, colleges, and the public arena with his videotapes on the Armenian Genocide, and the "American Case."

Also, I had personal interviews with Musa Dagh people, such as Mr Hovhannes Hajian and Mrs. Victoria Kambourian, who recounted their personal experiences on the Battle of Musa Dagh. I truly appreciated their precious time in 1994 in California, when I visited. Special thanks go to the Musa Ler Association in California for obtaining the Musa Dagh villages map, and the photo of the Musa Dagh people embarking the French battleship, *Le Guichen*, when rescued from the Turks.

I am grateful to Leanna Brown and Dr. Thomas Brown (not related) for their example and advice all those years I worked with them and for their kind words on behalf of this memoir.

My very loving thanks go to my son, Dr. Christopher Apelian, who patiently worked with me to set up my computer so that I could write this book. He also did all my graphic work for me. Many thanks go to Kathleen Pizar, my friend and proofreader, who also edited my book with professionalism. Brett Nickel and Bryan Culleny of Nickel Artistic Services created a striking book cover. In addition to all the people I have mentioned, I would like to thank Matthew Barron for the expertise to make my manuscript ready for publishing.

Finally, Henry M. Apelian, my husband, deserves many thanks for encouraging me to write this book. Henry and my understanding family—Arminee, Gregory, Chris and David and our grandchildren—have generously shared me with time spent on this memoir.

Kudos to all these wonderful people for having me complete this task that is so dear to me. This work is truly a dream come true.

Breinigsville, PA USA
30 March 2011
258717BV00001BA/2/P